Approaches to Teaching Gaines's
The Autobiography of Miss Jane Pittman and Other Works

For Wendell:

Whom I am sure Miss
Jane would want to
meet!

Peace,

Herman
27 Sept 19

Approaches to Teaching Gaines's
The Autobiography of Miss Jane Pittman and Other Works

Edited by

John Wharton Lowe

and

Herman Beavers

Modern Language Association of America
New York   2019

MLA and the MODERN LANGUAGE ASSOCIATION are trademarks owned by
the Modern Language Association of America. For information about obtaining
permission to reprint material from MLA book publications, send your request
by mail (see address below) or e-mail (permissions@mla.org).

Library of Congress Cataloging-in-Publication Data

Names: Lowe, John Wharton, editor. | Beavers, Herman, 1959- editor.
Title: Approaches to teaching Gaines's The Autobiography of Miss Jane
Pittman and other works / edited by John Wharton Lowe and Herman Beavers.
Description: New York : Modern Language Association of America, [2019]
Series: Approaches to teaching world literature, ISSN 1059-1133 ; 161
Includes bibliographical references and index.
Identifiers: LCCN 2019012812 (print) | LCCN 2019013860 (ebook)
ISBN 9781603294225 (EPUB) | ISBN 9781603294232 (Kindle)
ISBN 9781603294607 (cloth) | ISBN 9781603294218 (pbk. : alk. paper)
Subjects: LCSH: Gaines, Ernest J., 1933- Autobiography of Miss Jane Pittman.
Gaines, Ernest J., 1933—Study and teaching (Higher)
Classification: LCC PS3557.A3553 (ebook) | LCC PS3557.A3553 A85 2019 (print)
DDC 813/.54—dc23
LC record available at https://lccn.loc.gov/2019013860

Approaches to Teaching World Literature 161
ISSN 1059-1133

Cover illustration of the paperback and electronic editions:
William H. Johnson, *Woman Beside Yellow Chair*. Smithsonian American Art Museum,
Gift of the Harmon Foundation.

Published by The Modern Language Association of America
85 Broad Street, suite 500, New York, New York 10004-2434
www.mla.org

CONTENTS

Other Novels

Short Stories

ACKNOWLEDGMENTS

It has been a great pleasure editing this volume. The process reconnected us with old friends and created new ones. The MLA survey produced essays on subjects we had not imagined and demonstrated, yet again, the myriad aspects of this great writer's oeuvre. In addition to the scholars who contributed to this final version, we want to thank colleagues who provided advice and encouragement along the way: Keith Cartwright, Thadious Davis, Susan Donaldson, James Dormon, Mary Ellen Doyle, Marcia Gaudet, Fred Hobson, Barbara McCaskill, Derek Mosley, Brenda Marie Osbey, Matthew Teutsch, Mary Anne Wilson, Cheylon Woods, and Rafia Zafar. We are also indebted to colleagues we lost over the years this book took shape: Rudolph Byrd, Huel Perkins, Jack May, Milton and Patricia Rickels, and Joseph T. Skerrett, Jr.

Our understanding of Gaines and his work has been facilitated by our conversations with him and his wife, Dianne; their insights have been enriching and illuminating. We also thank the Gaineses' friends and family members who have spoken with us over the past few years.

The publication staff members at the Modern Language Association have supported this project at every step; their patience and advice have been invaluable. We thank James C. Hatch, Sonia Kane, Katherine Kim, Margit Longbrake, and Sara Pastel. Finally, we salute our wives, June Conaway Lowe and Lisa James-Beavers; their warmth, wit, and wisdom have strengthened our resolve and enriched every aspect of our lives.

PREFACE

Students today—even African Americans—often have scant concept of the specifics of slavery, Jim Crow culture, sharecropping, or the civil rights movement. One of the reasons we concentrate on *The Autobiography of Miss Jane Pittman* here is the novel's ability to provide a healthy antidote to this problem by providing an "alternative history," one told dramatically within black culture by a black woman to a black teacher. *Miss Jane* remains the best known of all Ernest Gaines's works; the novel, his personal favorite, has enjoyed a lasting readership, partly as a result of the Emmy Award–winning television adaptation of 1974. Teachers who wish to explore Gaines's sense of history naturally gravitate to *Miss Jane*, a palimpsest of the memories of a 110-year-old woman. She renders a chronicle that spans her enslaved childhood, the Civil War, emancipation, Reconstruction, sharecropping, modernization, the Great Flood of 1927, Huey Long's effect on the South, black baseball players, and the civil rights movement. It is instructive to remind today's students that the teacher will undoubtedly disseminate her story in the classroom, just as Gaines, our teacher, does for us. In all his works—and not just in *A Lesson Before Dying*—Gaines takes on a pedagogical role, correcting stereotypes, providing alternative histories, and teaching not by preaching but by dramatizing. Indeed, he has stated that if he had migrated to New York City rather than to San Francisco, his chosen genre might well have been drama, for his narratives are studded with tension-filled scenes, dramatic confrontations, and vexed family and personal relationships.

The first part of the novel comprises one of the earliest examples of the neo–slave narrative, and it can profitably be compared and contrasted with many other examples of the genre; two recent examples are Edward P. Jones's *The Known World* and Colson Whitehead's *The Underground Railroad*, both of which won the Pulitzer Prize for Fiction. On the other hand, the last section of Gaines's novel, dealing with the civil rights movement, offers a compelling portrait based on real events to set beside memoirs of leading activists of the time, such as Anne Moody and Martin Luther King, Jr., and his lieutenants, but also fictional works like *Meridian*, written by Gaines's friend and fellow southerner Alice Walker.

We hope that this volume will also encourage teachers to consider Gaines's powerful drama of interracial love, *Of Love and Dust*, which coincidentally appeared in 1967, the same year that the Supreme Court decision *Loving v. Virginia* struck down state laws prohibiting interracial marriage. The release of the film *Loving* (2016), which tells the story of the couple who were the subject of the Virginia case, underlined this issue anew for viewers, at a time when interracial love affairs and marriages have experienced a sharp increase. Our students need to understand the history of these issues, and Gaines's novel provides a point of interrogation and opportunities for reflection.

Although Gaines often sets his works in the past, they are keenly relevant to the situations we face in this new century, an era some have described as the "New Jim Crow," a time when voting rights, access to education and health care, and equal employment opportunities have all been threatened. His emphasis on "the importance of standing" is seen in his depictions of both male and female figures, but it has special relevance in an age when young black men are too often viewed with suspicion or, worse, as targets. Gaines initially intended to set *A Lesson Before Dying* in the 1980s but decided to use 1948, partly because he wanted to employ the notorious portable electric chair that was in use then but also because he knew that the much more open practice of racism and juridical and carceral strategies employed against African Americans then could speak to issues in our own time, when more black men are in prison than in college. This powerful novel should be read in context with the works of such academics as H. Bruce Franklin, Angela Davis, and others who have laid bare the inequities of our carceral system and its disastrous effect on the poor and people of color. This has been borne home by Gaines's perceptive observation that young black men of our time are demanding to be recognized as men in a society that devalues and stereotypes them; his writings can function as a powerful incentive for the Black Lives Matter movement and the many organizations seeking to provide support systems for young black men, who urgently need ways to realize "the importance of standing."

We hope the essays we have selected on his other works—which extend the thoughts we present here—will also help readers from all communities draw lines of connection between our troubled past and the issues we face today, which are sadly familiar.

Ernest J. Gaines (b. 1933) grew up poor in rural Louisiana and had to navigate the repressive racial codes of that time. His early education, which took place in a one-room church on the plantation where he lived, was irregular, as students had to work in the fields during growing season. The inner life of the quarters, however, where plantation workers clustered, was rich with tall tales, supper parties, church festivals, baptisms, weddings, funerals, and all kinds of folk games and pastimes. Louisiana's great "pantry" of seafood, domesticated swine and fowl, easily grown crops, and game hunted in the woods was put to good use in the quarters' kitchens. African Americans, however, had to kowtow to the white plantation owners and to superior clerks in nearby New Roads. There was no high school available for black children, and all public facilities were segregated, so Gaines was fortunate that his mother and stepfather, who had relocated to Vallejo, California, sent for him in 1948. Gaines now lived in a multicultural neighborhood and was able to read freely in the integrated libraries near him. He determined to become a writer and never looked back. His courses at Vallejo Junior College got him writing in earnest, and he subsequently pressed on during off-hours as a soldier in the Pacific. Released from duty, he attended San Francisco State College and began to publish short stories. After acquiring the services of a fine editor, he was accepted in Wallace Stegner's famous writing seminar at Stanford University. The works listed in this volume began to appear in the 1960s, but with scant readers until the sensational publication of *The Autobiography of Miss Jane Pittman* in 1974. Its transformation into a celebrated TV movie was the great turning point of his career and presented him with many new opportunities for lectures and short-term teaching appointments and, best of all, more time away from the temporary jobs he had been forced to take to sustain himself.

There is much more to say about his life: his many successes and awards after *Miss Jane* trace the trajectory of a dedicated and inspiring career, a life story in keeping with key tenets of our democracy. His constantly expanding following grew further in 1997, when Oprah Winfrey selected *A Lesson Before Dying* for her book club. The novel catapulted to number one on *The New York Times* bestseller list and won the National Book Critics Circle Award for Fiction. Gaines was awarded the prestigious MacArthur grant in 1993, the year he married Dianne Saulney. The recipient of more than fourteen honorary degrees from colleges and universities, he was presented the National Humanities Medal by President Bill Clinton in 2000, and he accepted the National Medal of Arts from President Barack Obama in 2012. Four films have been made from his works, and his short stories have been widely anthologized. Despite these honors, Gaines has remained somewhat on the periphery of American letters, perhaps because he has set almost all of his works in rural Louisiana, rather than in urban settings. Attentive readers, however, soon understand that his characters have a wisdom and a cultural heritage that speak on a wide human frequency. The issues these figures confront illuminate not only our past but also our present and our future. We hope the essays in this volume and the teaching aids that accompany them will lead to a new generation of readers at all levels who will find inspiration, challenge, and pleasure in the works of an American master.

Part One

MATERIALS

Editions and Anthologies

Novels

Catherine Carmier. Published by Atheneum in 1964; reissued by North Point Press in 1981.

Of Love and Dust. Published by Dial in 1967; reissued by Norton in 1979.

The Autobiography of Miss Jane Pittman. Published in 1971 by Dial and reissued by Bantam in 1972, it has never been out of print.

In My Father's House. Published by Knopf in 1978; reissued by Norton in 1983.

A Gathering of Old Men. Published by Knopf in 1983 and as a Vintage book in 1984.

A Lesson Before Dying. Published by Knopf 1993; reprinted by Vintage in 1994.

The Tragedy of Brady Sims. Published by Vintage in 2017.

Short Fiction

"The Turtles." *Transfer,* vol. 1, 1956, pp. 1–9. Reprinted in *Mozart and Leadbelly: Stories and Essays,* edited by Marcia Gaudet and Reggie Young, Knopf, 2005, pp. 77–86.

"Boy in the Double-Breasted Suit." *Transfer,* vol. 3, 1957, pp. 2–9. Reprinted in *Mozart and Leadbelly,* pp. 87–96.

"Mary Louise." *Stanford Short Stories,* edited by Wallace Stegner and Richard Scowcroft, Stanford UP, 1960, pp. 27–42. Reprinted in *Mozart and Leadbelly,* pp. 96–113.

"The Sky Is Gray." *Negro Digest,* vol. 12, Aug. 1963, pp. 72–96. Reprinted in *Bloodline,* pp. 83–120.

"Just Like a Tree." *Sewanee Review,* vol. 71, 1963, pp. 542–68. Reprinted in *Bloodline,* pp. 221–50.

"A Long Day in November." *Texas Quarterly,* vol. 7, 1964, pp. 190–224. Reprinted in *Bloodline,* pp. 3–82. Revised as a children's book published by Dial in 1971.

"My Grandpa and the Haint." *New Mexico Quarterly,* vol. 36, 1966, pp. 149–60. Reprinted in *Mozart and Leadbelly,* pp. 114–30.

Bloodline. Dial, 1968. Reissued by Norton in 1976 and by Vintage in 1997.

"Chapter One of *The House and the Field,* a Novel." *Iowa Review,* vol. 3, 1972, pp. 121–25.

"In My Father's House." *Massachusetts Review,* vol. 18, 1977, pp. 650–59. Reprinted in *Chant of Saints,* edited by Michael S. Harper and Robert B. Stepto, U of Illinois P, 1979, pp. 339–48.

"The Revenge of Old Men." *Callaloo*, vol. 1, May 1978, pp. 5–21.

"Robert Louis Stevenson Banks, aka Chimley." *Georgia Review*, vol. 37, 1983, pp. 385–89.

"From *The Man Who Whipped Children*: Chapter 3." *Callaloo*, vol. 24, Fall 2001, pp. 1015–20.

"Christ Walked Down Market Street." *Callaloo*, vol. 28, Fall 2005, pp. 907–13.

"My Uncle and the Fat Lady." *Callaloo*, vol. 30, Summer 2007, pp. 684–95.

Essays Included in Mozart and Leadbelly

"Miss Jane and I"

"Mozart and Leadbelly"

"A Very Big Order: Reconstructing Identity"

"Bloodline in Ink"

"Aunty and the Black Experience in Louisiana"

"Writing *A Lesson Before Dying*"

Additional Essay

"Old Jack." *Callaloo*, vol. 24, Winter 2001, pp. 69–70.

Courses and Contexts

A survey of instructors revealed that Ernest Gaines's *The Autobiography of Miss Jane Pittman* is taught in high schools, junior colleges, and colleges and universities across the United States. It has had wide popularity in other countries as well, particularly France and Japan. While it is used most frequently in African American literature classes, it also appears on syllabi for courses in southern studies, American history, ethnic literature, and literature and film. *A Lesson Before Dying* has been taught in an even greater variety of courses, including the fields just mentioned, but also in law schools and in legal studies courses. Romulus Linney's play, adapted from *A Lesson Before Dying* and bearing the same title, is often paired with the novel in theater department offerings. Religious studies and literature and religion courses have been attracted by the interplay between two central characters, Grant Wiggins and Reverend Ambrose. The third most popular work by Gaines, *A Gathering of Old Men*, has also been featured in film and literature courses and occasionally in sports and literature classes. Gaines's short stories have frequently been anthologized, especially "The Sky Is Gray," which has been featured in virtually every kind of short story collection. Also popular are "Just Like a Tree" and "A Long Day in November." More recently, Gaines's prison tale, "Three Men," has been selected for classes on masculinity and has been adopted by teachers in gender and queer studies courses.

The Instructor's Library

The reference and background works for teaching Gaines that survey respondents mentioned most frequently are Gaines's essays "Miss Jane and I" and "Writing *A Lesson Before Dying*." A number of teachers made use of book reviews of Gaines's novels and, sometimes, of the films made of his works. Others recommended the thirtieth anniversary DVD of the film made from *Miss Jane*, which has a second documentary disc featuring interviews with Gaines, comments from scholars, and footage of Gaines's home, family cemetery, and childhood church/ school that inspired one of the main locations of *A Lesson Before Dying*.

Reference Works

There are no entire reference books devoted to Gaines; however, there are two useful collections of interviews: *Conversations with Ernest Gaines*, edited by John Lowe, and *Porch Talk with Ernest Gaines: Conversations on the Writer's Craft*, edited by Marcia Gaudet and Carl Wooton. Marcia Gaudet is currently editing a second volume of interviews.

Background Studies

Karen Carmean's *Ernest J. Gaines: A Critical Companion* presents biographical and reception facts and offers basic readings of the six novels and of *Bloodline*, a collection of five stories. Brian J. Costello's *A History of Pointe Coupée Parish, Louisiana* provides rich context for the fiction.

Classic Journal Articles on The Autobiography of Miss Jane Pittman

William L. Andrews's "'We Ain't Going Back There': The Idea of Progress in *The Autobiography of Miss Jane Pittman*" usefully considers Gaines's argument against flight from the South. Lorna Fitzsimmons's "*The Autobiography of Miss Jane Pittman*: Film, Intertext, and Ideology" offers a telling critique of the omissions of the film adaptation of the novel. Blyden Jackson's "Jane Pittman through the Years: A People's Tale" gives a magisterial view of the intersection of Gaines's fiction with lived African American history. Michel Fabre's "Bayonne or the Yoknapatawpha of Ernest Gaines" compares Gaines's creation of his fictional realm with Faulkner's Yoknapatawpha County and maps the confining features of this rural domain. Robert J. Patterson's "Rethinking Definitions and Expectations: Civil Rights and Civil Rights Leadership in Ernest Gaines's *The Autobiography of Miss Jane Pittman*" discusses the novel's theme of racial leadership—and martyrdom—and situates it against the history of the civil rights movement.

Biographical Studies

John Lowe is currently writing the authorized biography of Gaines. Anne K. Simpson's *A Gathering of Gaines: The Man and the Writer* includes a one-hundred-page general biography up to 1991; it contains valuable quotations from Gaines's unpublished papers but has numerous errors of fact and should therefore be used with caution. The aforementioned collections of interviews contain much biographical material. There are wonderful photographs of Gaines, his family, and the land that sustained them in *"This Louisiana Thing That Drives Me": The Legacy of Ernest J. Gaines*, by Reggie Scott Young, Marcia Gaudet, and Wiley Cash (with an introduction by Gaines).

Critical Studies

Simpson's *A Gathering of Gaines* covers all the fiction up to 1991. Another early, but still valuable, work is Valerie Babb's *Ernest Gaines*. David Estes's anthology *Critical Reflections on the Fiction of Ernest J. Gaines* contains fourteen essays by leading Gaines scholars, including several who taught with him for years in Louisiana. The most exhaustive study of Gaines's fiction is Mary Ellen Doyle's *Voices from the Quarters: The Fiction of Ernest J. Gaines*, which includes a lengthy discussion of *A Lesson Before Dying*. Key chapters on Gaines have appeared in the following studies: Philip Auger, *Native Sons in No Man's Land: Rewriting Afro-American Manhood in the Novels of Baldwin, Walker, Wideman, and Gaines*; Herman Beavers, *Wrestling Angels into Song: The Fictions of Ernest J. Gaines and James Alan McPherson*; Keith Byerman, *Fingering the Jagged Grain: Tradition and Form in Recent Black Fiction* and, especially, *Remembering the Past in Contemporary African American Fiction*; John Callahan, *In the African-American Grain: The Pursuit of Voice in Twentieth-Century Black Fiction*; Keith Clark, *Black Manhood in James Baldwin, Ernest J. Gaines, and August Wilson*; Brannon Costello, *Plantation Airs: Racial Paternalism and the Transformations of Class in Southern Fiction, 1945–1971*; Trudier Harris, *Saints, Sinners, Saviors: Strong Black Women in African American Literature*; Jack Hicks, *In the Singer's Temple: Prose Fictions of Barthelme, Gaines, Brautigan, Piercy, Kesey, and Kosinski*; Jeff Karem, *The Romance of Authenticity:*

The Cultural Politics of Regional and Ethnic Literatures; and Thadious Davis's searching use of Gaines's sense of place and space in *Southscapes: Geographies of Race, Region, and Literature*. Other critical articles and book chapters on Gaines's novels and short stories are referred to in the essays in the "Approaches" section.

Multimedia, Internet, and Other Resources

Ruth Laney wrote and coproduced a documentary, *Ernest J. Gaines: Louisiana Stories*. A short film documentary created by PBS and featuring the journalist Bob Faw concentrates on Gaines's sense of religion and includes an intriguing conversation between Gaines and Faw (Faw).

Gaines's works, most often *A Lesson Before Dying*, have been adopted by many cities across the country in the popular Big Read program. The program's video that introduces Gaines to readers is available online ("NEA Big Read").

The Web site of the Ernest J. Gaines Center at the University of Louisiana at Lafayette contains many resources for Gaines's readers (ernestgaines.louisiana .edu/center).

Part Two

APPROACHES

Introduction

John Wharton Lowe and Herman Beavers

We intend for this collection of essays to assist teachers at every level, ranging from secondary to graduate study, as they present Gaines's masterpiece, *The Autobiography of Miss Jane Pittman*, in the classroom, along with other works by Gaines that deserve greater attention and increased course consideration. Our approaches consider, among other things, southern and racial history, criminal law and prison narrative, conversion stories, the gothic, gender, Cajun culture, humor and folklore, symbolism, the pastoral, the epic, tragedy, blues motifs, sports references, the black power and black arts movements, the civil rights movement, and international approaches to Gaines's works. This volume also suggests how the films based on Gaines's work can be integrated successfully in a literature or history course.

Prior to publishing *Miss Jane*, Gaines had already produced an impressive body of work. But he achieved much wider acclaim after its publication and the subsequent use of the novel as the basis for an award-winning television movie. Because the narrative achieves such temporal scope, running as it does from the Civil War to the civil rights movement of the 1960s, the novel is a key component in African American and southern literature courses, in large part because of the increased attention paid to neo–slave narratives like Sherley Anne Williams's *Dessa Rose* (1986), Charles Johnson's *Oxherding Tale* (1982) and *Middle Passage* (1990), Toni Morrison's *Beloved* (1987), David Bradley's *The Chaneysville Incident* (1981), and Edward P. Jones's *The Known World* (2003).

Gaines's work, like that of Zora Neale Hurston, profits from his deep immersion in the folk culture of Louisiana, where he was born and raised. As Hurston also did, Gaines goes beyond scenes of black-white conflict to investigate the "black space" of the quarters community, limning its creativity, buoyant humor, and rich folklore. Foodways, agricultural practices, and religious traditions all receive detailed portrayals. Gaines's fiction is also distinguished by his depictions of the various classes of white Louisianans, from poor whites to plantation owners, and including Cajuns and Creoles of color. He also highlights the troubling elements of southern juridical and carceral practices, the strictly observed racial codes, and the complications that ensue for those individuals who dare to challenge institutional and social practices. His alternative history in these texts has a crucial role to play today as America struggles anew with police brutality, restrictions on voter rights, and a legal system that has sent an inordinate number of black citizens to prison.

Gaines sets most of his fiction in mythical St. Raphael Parish and its largest town, Bayonne. These locales are mirrors of his home parish, Pointe Coupee, and its largest city, New Roads. Here Gaines follows William Faulkner, who made Mississippi's Lafayette County and the town of Oxford into the mythical Yoknapatawpha County and the city of Jefferson. Again like Faulkner, Gaines seeks to penetrate the affective surfaces of the Jim Crow South. Reading Gaines, we come to understand how a large portion of the challenge facing blacks who wanted to mount resistance against the racism circumscribing their lives was moving beyond the racial skirmishing that occurred between individual blacks unwilling to accept second-class citizenship and the whites who saw it as their duty to punish such thinking. In such circumstances, punishment was often meted out at the hands of poor whites, who failed to recognize the common plight they shared with blacks seeking to wrest their livelihood from the land, just like them. It was the land-owning whites, like Marshall Hebert in *Of Love and Dust*, who used them as pawns by emphasizing white supremacy as an advantage that must be maintained at all costs. In works like *Of Love and Dust*, Gaines demonstrates how the fear of reprisals against all black inhabitants often served as the brake on efforts to mobilize collective resistance. Gaines's approach to his native culture eschews the sentimentality and parochialism of literary regionalism in favor of a robust, multifaceted literary realism. Choosing to dramatize rather than merely describe, Gaines often employs narratives mainly consisting of dialogue, spiced up with the local vernacular peculiar to south Louisiana, where French, Spanish, and Native American cultures have created a unique polyglot of dialects and inflections. The lives of his characters often revolve around agricultural and climatic calendars, but they are repeatedly intersected by the events of their time, such as Reconstruction, catastrophic floods, the Great Depression, emigration, Louisiana's particular brand of southern politics (as demonstrated by figures like Huey Long), sporting events (which muse on the extraordinary effect of black athletes such as Joe Louis, Jackie Robinson, and Willie Mays), and racial revolt. Hence, acts of remembering prove to be essential elements of Gaines's narratives. This is especially so in *Miss Jane*, which involves not only the memories of Miss Jane but also those of a large group of individuals whose amendments, corrections, and alternative narratives join hers, thereby creating the dynamism of the oral communal construction of history. One finds Gaines's characters using the aforementioned calamities and milestones as anchor points in wide-ranging acts of narration that situate both them and the reader in the flow of time around their peculiar space.

Gaines was able to create distance between his passionate love for this culture and the harsh facts that needed exposure through the lens of his years in California, where he lived in a multicultural, liberal setting, complemented by the excellent education he acquired in the San Francisco public schools, at San Francisco State College, and at Stanford University. His experiences in Guam and the Far East, which he visited while in the army, widened his perspective as well. While this volume does not consider his unpublished novels, stories, and essays, we find that they also demonstrate the range of interests Gaines cultivated during his time in California and the Pacific. He certainly learned about protests of all kinds (indeed, two of his brothers were members of the Black Panthers) and began to measure West Coast militancy against that of the South's civil rights movement. It was only in 1963, however, when he returned to Louisiana, that he was able to see his culture anew, equipped by both his experiences elsewhere and the literary apprenticeship he set for himself in California.

It is equally important to note that contrary to common assumptions, Gaines did not read widely in African American literature until he began to write *Miss Jane*, which required substantial research in archives containing documents on slavery and Reconstruction. The classic slave narratives he read (including Solomon Northup's Louisiana classic *Twelve Years a Slave*) helped him to create a voice for the early chapters of *Miss Jane*, while his archival research at Louisiana State University and elsewhere in the state enabled him to participate in the grand tradition of the historical novel. At the same time, his myriad trips back to the quarters refreshed his memories of old tales and vernacular conversation.

Fortuitously, the fictions that stirred him most during his writing apprenticeship were by the Russian giants Leo Tolstoy, Anton Chekhov, and especially Ivan Turgenev. Reading the works of these authors, Gaines found that the presentation of serfs, the great Russian estates (which shared many of the characteristics of feudal plantations in Louisiana), and the landed aristocracy offered him a template for generating a facsimile of his own culture and history. Later, he would recognize similar elements in the work of Faulkner, and he was profoundly moved by both the style of Ernest Hemingway and his concept of grace under pressure, which corresponds so well to Gaines's own belief in what he called, in the dedication of *Miss Jane*, "the importance of standing."

His pared-down style and reliance on dialogue resembles that of the latter, while his close examination of race and sexuality builds on Faulkner's masterworks, such as *The Sound and the Fury, As I Lay Dying, Absalom, Absalom!*, and *Go Down, Moses*. He has also employed the method of distinct narrators that Faulkner practiced in *As I Lay Dying* in "Just Like a Tree" and *A Gathering of Old Men*. At the same time, he has gone beyond Faulkner in his depictions of the inner life of African American characters: as he has stated, "Faulkner gets Dilsey talking her story from his kitchen; the young school-teacher in my book gets Miss Jane's story from Miss Jane's kitchen. And it makes a difference" (Lowe, "Interview" 313).

We believe this collection of essays offers compelling evidence that Gaines is an essential stop in any consideration of post–World War II southern and American literature. By creating works whose use of first-person African American narration emphasizes the importance of finding and asserting voice, he has carved out a particularized niche in contemporary literature. Further, though he has been consistent in his declaration that his work is not political, it is difficult to read Gaines's fiction and overlook the many ways in which it evinces a key element of the black liberation struggle, namely that one cannot shrink from the necessity of fighting to retain a sense of human dignity. What this means is that despite southern racism and the rigid social hierarchies it creates, his characters suggest that heroic temper is on constant display in ways great and small. Further, Gaines's unwillingness to turn away from depictions of transracial relations that belie the impenetrability of racial boundaries offers strong evidence that his strongest commitment as a writer is to insist that love transcends the triviality of racial difference. The characters residing in the Louisiana portrayed in his fiction revise Faulkner's sense that blacks' most endearing trait is their endurance, arguing instead that the effort to create a just and equitable community—both local and national—is so relentless that it spans generations.

The Novels

The Autobiography of Miss Jane Pittman (1971), an excellent early example of the modern neo–slave narrative, was built on several sturdy foundations, chiefly Gaines's profound knowledge of the black folk culture of Louisiana, which produced and continues to inspire him. No one in the state's rich literary tradition has given us more fully observed portraits of the fertile fields, the shifting weather, the troubled racial situations, and, above all, the buoyant, creative folk culture, which was somehow fashioned out of the darkest days of enslavement. Miss Jane, like Huckleberry Finn, speaks in a rich and expressive vernacular, but her observations are anything but simple. The wisdom she has acquired over her hundred-plus years informs and animates every page of the novel. Gaines was determined, however, that she would not perform a monologue, so he created a fascinating cast of supporting figures who help her tell not just her story but the entire community's to the teacher who has come to document her life.

The novel never strays too far from Miss Jane, but it actually follows a second track that brings in the heroic but also tragic lives of four men—three African American, one white. A very young Miss Jane joins emancipated people on the road, hoping to journey to the North; defeated in this plan, she stays in Louisiana, where she adopts a young boy whose mother has been killed by white marauders. This child, Ned, proves to be "the one" (someone destined to become a community leader), as his dedication to literacy leads him to activism and, ultimately, to leave the South for a better life in Kansas. He returns, however, married and with children, to teach his native state's people and to urge them to stand up to injustice. A corrupt Cajun hit man, a sometime friend of Miss Jane's, kills Ned; the latter's legacy lives on, however, through a great sermon he had delivered by the river that continues to reverberate with the people. Miss Jane's subsequent marriage to Joe Pittman presents readers with an independent, courageous man who breaks horses for a living. He moves Jane to the Texas border, where they have more opportunity, but he is killed by a black stallion that challenges his manhood. Miss Jane then works on the plantation, where she and the white Creole Jules Raynard observe the growing love of Tee Bob, the young white heir, for the plantation schoolteacher, Mary Agnes, a Creole of color. His doomed passion leads to his suicide, an ironic inversion of the usual tale of the tragic mulatto. The final section of the novel concerns the upbringing of Jimmy, also designated as "the one." Like Ned before him, he leaves to acquire the education he needs in order to revitalize the community he loves. After he becomes involved with civil rights workers and leads demonstrations, he too is shot down. At the novel's end, the ancient Miss Jane defies orders by the white plantation owner and joins the people of the quarters as they march to town to demonstrate. Despite the tragic events that punctuate the narrative, other parts of the novel limn the vibrant folk culture of the quarters, including religious practices, hoodoo, folktales, folkways, and foodways; the characters speak in a creative vernacular and often engage in comic repartee.

This masterwork was preceded by other works that deserve to be better known. As a student at San Francisco State College and later at Stanford University, Gaines began by writing short stories, but, as he told John Lowe in a personal conversation, a publisher told him he needed to produce a novel if he wanted to become well known. Accordingly, with the encouragement of his agent, Dorothea Oppenheimer, he returned to an early work he had written and then burned, a novel that became *Catherine Carmier* (1964). Gaines labored over this work for years and created at least four versions. The story relates the tragic love affair of the dark Jackson and the near-white Catherine, whose Creole father, Raoul, disdains contact with black folk. A subsidiary cast of characters helps fill in the complexities of Louisiana's color codes and the rural sharecropping system, which was changing with the invasion of Cajuns with tractors. The beautifully written and meditative novel provides gripping scenes and builds to a shattering climax.

Of Love and Dust (1967) begins by focusing on the corrupt prison system that enabled plantation owners to take charge of convicts for field labor. Jim Kelly, the narrator, describes how Marcus, a dangerous dandy from town who has killed a man in a brawl, is leased to the plantation where they both work. Persecuted by the Cajun overseer, Bonbon, Marcus attempts to seduce the man's black mistress, who rebuffs him. Subsequently, however, he meets and falls mutually in love with the overseer's neglected wife, Louise. The narrative employs a chorus of quarters folk, who supplement Jim's observations. This daring presentation of two interracial romances contains some of Gaines's most accomplished writing.

After the triumph of *Miss Jane*, Gaines had a great deal of difficulty in writing his next novel, *In My Father's House* (1978). The central story concerns a troubled relationship between Reverend Phillip Martin and the son he abandoned years earlier, along with his first family, a pattern present in Gaines's own life. Now married and a leader in the community, Martin has to make some hard choices as he confronts his past. The story takes place in the midst of the civil rights movement and has much to say about looming racial conflicts.

Gaines scored another popular success with *A Gathering of Old Men* (1983), which was made into a well-received television film, starring Louis Gossett, Jr., Woody Strode, Holly Hunter, and Richard Widmark. The novel, constructed like Faulkner's *As I Lay Dying*, consists of twenty first-person narrations. The story opens with the mysterious murder of a white Cajun, Beau Boutan, presumably by one of the black men in the quarters. The victim's large family plots revenge, much to the dismay of a younger son who is the quarterback on the Louisiana

State University football team and has a pioneering and successful partnership with a black receiver; they are known as "Salt and Pepper." The evidence points to old Mathu, who raised the young white missy of the plantation, Candy. She and her journalist boyfriend, Lou, try to shield him, and the other old men on the place bring their guns to the quarters, each claiming to have killed Beau. Sheriff Mapes interrogates the old men one by one, but we learn much more about them through their moving and detailed individual monologues. At the end, the old men stand together heroically, as the mystery of the murder is untangled.

Many readers and critics feel Gaines's penultimate novel, *A Lesson Before Dying* (1993), is his best. Most of this tale takes place in the Bayonne jail, where a young black man is waiting to be executed for a crime he did not commit. His godmother and her best friend enlist the aid of the local schoolteacher, Grant Wiggins, as they try to ensure that Jefferson, the prisoner, dies with dignity. The supporting cast includes the white plantation family that owns Grant's school, the local sheriff and his deputies, Grant's lovely Creole girlfriend, Vivian, and numerous schoolchildren, who stand to gain the most from learning Jefferson's heroic final message, which is immortalized in the jailhouse diary he keeps until the day he dies.

Gaines's latest novel, *The Tragedy of Brady Sims* (2017), follows reporter Louis Guerin as he attempts to discover why Brady Sims shot and killed his son upon the latter's conviction for robbery and murder. This assignment leads Guerin to the local barbershop, in which the majority of the novel takes place; the men in the shop recount Sims's life and the events that led to his son's murder.

The Short Stories and the Essays

Gaines's early work was mostly in the short story genre; he published some keenly observed Louisiana tales while in graduate school. His first major publication was the story "The Sky Is Gray" (1963), a deeply affecting tale about a little boy going to the dentist with his mother on a cold winter day. This has become Gaines's most anthologized story and was made into a memorable short film. "A Long Day in November" (1964), an often comic yet poignant tale, is cleverly narrated by a little boy who is troubled by the impasse between his parents; they are at odds about the husband's obsession with his new car. Eventually the story was transformed into both a children's book and a short film. Another fine tale, "Just Like a Tree" (1963), concerns the efforts of a divided family to get their matriarch to move to the city. Told by ten successive narrators, the story pays tributes to the elders' heroic struggles, which have laid the foundation for a new day or racial opportunity. Gaines gathered these three stories together with two new ones to create the collection *Bloodline* (1968). The new tales were "Three Men," a gripping prison encounter of the title figures, who must make hard choices in their quest to achieve a dignified manhood in a carceral setting, and

"Bloodline," which involves the return to the South of an alienated black man, who seeks recognition from the white family that sired him. This title tale is narrated by an old man, Felix, and ponders intergenerational and racial divisions against the backdrop of the civil rights movement.

Gaines didn't publish many of his short stories, and in 2005, Marcia Gaudet and Reggie Young edited a collection that includes some of these, along with Gaines's earlier student publications and a few of his essays. The volume, *Mozart and Leadbelly: Stories and Essays*, takes its title from the author's catholic taste in music, a symptom of both his cosmopolitanism and his investment in the folk culture he has immortalized. Readers of this volume will be particularly interested in the essay "Miss Jane and I," which has much to say about the composition of that masterwork. The volume also includes Gaines's only non-Louisiana tale, "Christ Walked Down Market Street," which, he has stated, is his personal favorite among his tales (*Mozart* vii). The editors, for lagniappe, included an interview that they and Darrell Bourque did with Gaines, which often discusses the contents of the volume.

"On His Own Two Feet": Teaching Gaines's *The Autobiography of Miss Jane Pittman* through Racial History

Simone A. James Alexander

Ernest Gaines's 1971 novel, *The Autobiography of Miss Jane Pittman*, can be challenging to teach because of the breadth of time, history, and stories it spans. The setting of the novel during several wars—the Civil War, World Wars I and II, the Vietnam War (additionally, the titular protagonist, Jane Pittman, references the Spanish-American War)—and the plethora of fictional characters and nonfictional (historical) figures that populate Jane's narrative, which chronicles 110 years of recollection, present a challenge to students. Most students appreciate the storytelling tradition employed in Jane's narrative, the "authenticity" of her voice. They also tend to appreciate the way the text talks (back) to African American icons such as Booker T. Washington, Marcus Garvey, Frederick Douglass, Rosa Parks, and Jackie Robinson and to value Jane's wit and humor and the personal, humane relationships she has with the community at large as well as with her husband, Joe Pittman. Capitalizing on the students' enthusiasm, I seize the opportunity to discuss the black vernacular tradition, particularly the speaking voice and its importance in the African American community. This approach further allows me to focus discussion of *Miss Jane* on its exploration of race, gender, female sexuality, and racial history. Through the interplay between race and reproduction, we examine the various forms of female resistance employed by slave women to thwart the control of their reproductive rights.

Black expressive culture is at the foundation of African American literature and culture. To underscore its importance, we trace how the black vernacular tradition manifests textually and rhetorically. Henry Louis Gates, Jr., calls attention to the powerful vernacular tradition that black slaves brought to the New World. He stresses that the relationship between the African and African American vernacular traditions and black literature fosters the articulation of the black voice that speaks for itself. Jane's recollection, her oral testimony, authenticates her narrative (voice) and accords credibility to African American oral and cultural history. In other words, Gaines creates a "speaking voice" for his female heroine, rendering her a speaking subject (Gates, *Signifying* 131). Gates duly reminds us: "Black people had to represent themselves as 'speaking subjects' before they could even begin to destroy their status as objects, as commodities, within Western culture" (129). This embrace of her subjectivity-cum-humanity is crucial to Jane's transformation from an object to a subject, from slave to freedwoman (157). Through his analysis of the trope of the talking book, Gates illustrates that having control or command of the narrative is pivotal in reclaiming the text and the black body.[1] To this end, Gaines, via the schoolteacher who asks Jane her story, is invested in having Jane control the voice in the text: "What I have tried to do here was not to write everything, but in essence everything that was said. I have tried my best to retain Miss Jane's language. Her selection of words; the rhythm of her speech" (*Miss Jane* vii).[2] Gaines/the schoolteacher confesses that the catalyst for documenting this history was Jane's blatant omission in the master text. Questioned by Jane's caretaker, Mary Hodges, about his interest in documenting Jane's story—"What's wrong with them books you already got?"—Gaines/the schoolteacher rebuts, "Miss Jane is not in them" (v). Thus, Gaines is quite cognizant "that black people could become speaking subjects only by inscribing their voices in the written word" (Gates, *Signifying* 130).

The retention of Jane's language, her choice of words and the rhythm of her speech, epitomizes the figurative language of the black vernacular tradition. Gates surmises that through the analysis of the trope of the talking book we witness the expansive influence of intertextuality in Afro-American literary history. Focusing on eighteenth-century authors of works about slavery, Gates depicts how their narratives defy the traditional autobiographical genre.[3] Along similar lines, Gaines's novel defies strict categorization, prompting many to have doubts whether it is fiction or nonfiction. *Miss Jane* comprises a tale within a tale or, more accurately, several tales within tales, as it appropriates a vast range of other texts about the abolitionist movement, the American Civil War, World Wars I and II, and the civil rights movement, even as it challenges the writerly (Western) text. This literary cannibalization of different genres and texts renders effective vernacular storytelling.[4] Moreover, what remains undebatable is that *Miss Jane* is a passionate call to action for the abolition of slavery. Drawing upon Gates's definition, *Miss Jane* is a "speakerly text" in that it imitates the black voice—the "black rhetorical rituals and modes of storytelling"—in African American vernacular literature (*Signifying* 194).[5] As discussed earlier, the tone and inflection of Jane's speech is captured in her oral narration. In essence,

Gaines unearths "the voice of the black oral tradition," allowing his characters, Jane and the community, to speak for themselves (Gates, *Signifying* 181).

The trope of the talking book authorizes a doublespeak or double-voicedness that Gaines captures in the following pronouncement: "Much of what . . . Miss Jane and the others said . . . was too repetitious and did not follow a single direction. When she spoke she used as few words as possible to make her point. Yet there were times when she would repeat a word or phrase over and over when she thought it might add humor or drama to the situation" (*Miss Jane* vii). Jane's economy of words does not take place at the expense of her narrative. Rather it legitimizes and privileges the oral language that comprises jests, gestures; in other words, it is performative by nature. In his brilliant analysis of the black Caribbean vernacular also known as nation language, the Caribbean poet and scholar Kamau Brathwaite establishes that the economy of words is part and parcel of the black vernacular tradition. Providing an apt definition of this ancestral language, Brathwaite writes, "It may be English, but often it is an English which is like a howl or a shout, or a machine-gun, or the wind, or a wave. It is also like the blues. And sometimes it is English and African at the same time" (266). In bolstering Brathwaite's argument, Gates, in his analysis of the role of the double-voicedness in Ishmael Reed's *Mumbo Jumbo*, opines that the black vernacular poses a formidable challenge to the so-called standard (text), the canon: "The double-voiced text emerges as the text of ultimate critique and revision of the rhetorical strategies at work in the canonical texts of the tradition" (*Signifying* 131). Evidently, Jane engages the trope of signifying via repetition, role-playing, and humor. The double-voicedness in Jane's narrative further manifests in the plurality of voices: "This is not only Miss Jane's autobiography, it is theirs (the residents of the community) as well. This is what both Mary and Miss Jane meant when they said you could not tie all the ends together in one neat direction. Miss Jane's story is all of their stories, and their stories are Miss Jane's" (Gaines, *Miss Jane* viii).

The African American vernacular tradition additionally manifests in the practices of sermons, including those performed at marriages and wakes and by the personas of the midwife and the obeah woman. The audience is pivotal, indispensable in African American oral cultures and performances; therefore "because of the multiple cultural functions of the spoken word, African Americans have tended to value oral performances much more highly than do cultures that are closer to the literate end of the literacy-orality continuum" (Wharry 204). We witness an alert, approving, and engaged audience at Ned's sermon by the river. Participation of the audience engenders what Cheryl Wharry defines as a "spontaneous sermon," a combined effort of preacher and congregation (205). Like nation language that "largely ignores the pentameter" (Brathwaite 265), black sermons that appear to have uniform meter vary widely in length. The irregularity of sermon lines is engendered by emphatic repetitions and dramatic pauses (Wharry 206). In short, "[t]heme (with irregularity and/or contrasts), not meter, is what primarily provides cohesion in African American sermons" (206). Ned's sermon, as does Jane's narrative, exemplifies these vernacular traits.

Ned's spellbinding sermon by the river about self-love and -determination and communal affirmation resonates powerfully with Baby Suggs's phenomenal sermon delivered in the Clearing in Toni Morrison's *Beloved.* For ease of analysis, the two sermons, Ned's followed by Baby Suggs's, are quoted at length and juxtaposed below. Both ordained, Ned is dubbed "the chosen one," and Baby Suggs is the consummate woman preacher.[6]

> This earth is yours and don't let that man out there take it from you. . . . It's yours because your people's bones lays in it; it's yours because their sweat and their blood done drenched this earth. The white man will use every trick in the trade to take it from you. He will use every way he know how to get you 'wool-gathered. He'll turn you 'gainst each other. But remember this. . . . Your people's bones and their dust make this place yours more than anything else.   (112–13)

> Here . . . in this here place, we flesh; flesh that weeps, laughs; flesh that dances on bare feet in grass. Love it. Love it hard. Yonder they do not love your flesh. They despise it. They don't love your eyes; they'd just as soon pick em out. No more do they love the skin on your back. Yonder they flay it. And O my people they do not love your hands. Those they only use, tie, bind, chop off and leave empty. Love your hands! Raise them up and kiss them. Touch others with them. . . . *You* got to love it, *you*! This is flesh I'm talking about here. Flesh that needs to be loved.   (88)[7]

The rhythmic cadence in the sermonic performance, the repetition, and the call-and-response format are all characteristic of the African oral tradition, but more specifically attuned to the black church.[8] While Ned names the slavers directly and denotatively as "the white man," Baby Suggs refers to them connotatively with "They, Yonder," effectively engaging the ritual of signifying. This strategy of revision and reversal is exemplary of a chiasmus that effectuates "a black textual grounding through revision" (Gates, *Signifying* 171).[9] Both sermons are exemplified by pauses and further provide readers with a fascinating insight into the conflation of land (earth) and body (flesh), engendering the trope "where the land meets the body": "your people's bones lays in [the earth]; it's yours because their sweat and their blood done drenched this earth. . . . Your people's bones and their dust make this place."[10] At the close of his sermon, Ned literally actualizes the land/body trope: "When Ned got through talking his shirt was soaking wet. He came back where we was and laid down side his wife (117–18). The conflation of Ned's male body with the land revises and reverses the trope that conceptually imagines the woman's body/land within the framework of masculine desire.

Sermons, as Wharry opines, "can be viewed as a structured stretch of discourse with room for individuality or relative creativity" (206). Shedding light on how orality lends itself to improvisation, Gaines / the schoolteacher writes, "I should mention here that even though I have used Miss Jane's voice throughout the narrative, there were times when others carried the story for her. When she was tired, or when she just did not feel like talking anymore, or when she had forgotten certain things, someone else would always pick up the narration" (vi–vii). We experience a parallel moment of improvisation, communal narration, and continuity in the following scene in *Beloved*: "Saying no more [Baby Suggs] stood up then and danced with her twisted hip the rest of what her heart had to say while the others opened their mouths and gave her the music. Long notes held until the four-part harmony was perfect enough for their deeply loved flesh" (89). Here we witness what Marcellus Blount refers to as "the perfect continuity between artist and audience" (584). Upholding this line of reasoning, Wharry articulates that a "good traditional African American sermon" is motivated by both the preacher and the congregation displaying "oral-tradition features" (223). Blount adds, "Early black sermonic performance was one of the rituals that defined for slaves and free African Americans their participation in a unique religious fellowship" (584). Skillfully incorporating in their sermons both "textual and discourse community knowledge," Ned's and Baby Suggs's sermons cross "the boundaries of conversation and lecture" (Wharry 223). Ned's sermon moves his congregation toward freedom, as does Baby Suggs's. Like an old experienced black preacher, Baby Suggs "talk wid [her] heart" (qtd. in Blount 854).

In the furtherance of African American expressive culture, Ned, in his sermon by the river, accomplishes a sermonic performance of "I've Been to the Mountaintop," the last speech of Martin Luther King, Jr. Ned's text reads: "*I might not be with you*—and *I hope it never comes to happen*. But if it come to happen. . . . Let us pray, warriors, this day never come. . . . If it do, it'll be the worst day of your life" (117). King's text is as follows: "Well, *I don't know what will happen* now. We've got some difficult days ahead. . . . *I may not get there with you*. But I want you to know tonight, that we, as a people, will get to the promised land!" (emphasis added). In this refracted speech (the ingenious use of intertextuality presents a formidable challenge to originality, to deciphering the original text), not only are we privy to the conspicuous patterns of repetition, but also there are a few instances of chiasmus as the following examples show: "I might not be with you" versus "I may not get there with you," "I hope it never comes to happen" versus "Well, I don't know what will happen," "Let us pray . . . this day never come" versus "We've got some difficult days ahead." This act of signifying, of repetition and revision, eerily prevails in the assassination of both Ned and King. King was assassinated a day after he delivered his "Mountaintop" sermon, while Ned is murdered a little over a month after his sermon by the river.

In equal measure, Ned's wife, Vivian, appropriates Coretta Scott King's political and community activism, working side by side with her husband. Cautioned by Jane to return to Kansas with her children to avoid a possible assassination of Ned, Vivian expresses her fervent devotion and commitment to her husband and the movement: "He told me when he was coming here he could get killed. . . .

But I came with him anyhow. I have to stay now" (111). Ned is subsequently replaced by his double, Jimmy, also dubbed "the one." Being preordained the one after "get[ting] religion . . . the year he made twelve years old," Jimmy's story has strong biblical resonance, for "*The Master* started when He was twelve, if you will remember" (223; emphasis added).[11] Jimmy's narrative voice is inscribed in the written text as the "word" takes on biblical proportions: "He was the One, and the One had to lead in everything" (224). Like Jesus, Jimmy is chosen to lead his people and save them from their sins: "He won't let us down" (224). The master's (read: biblical and colonial) voice is subverted as the text is refigured and revised within the black vernacular tradition.

Ned's sermon is not only exemplary of a preacherly moment, but also it serves as a teacherly moment. Referencing iconic African American figures such as Booker T. Washington, W. E. B. Du Bois, Marcus Garvey, Claude McKay, and King (for the most part, Ned signifies on these individuals via indirection), Ned engenders the teacherly moment as he arms his "students" with invaluable historical knowledge. Ned's audience at his sermon by the river is comprised primarily of children. Symbolically, he assumes the title "Professor Douglass," effectively espousing the value of education and self-determination promoted by the abolitionist Frederick Douglass. This teacherly moment extends to his impending plan to build a school, a plan that embodies revisionary impulses as it is undoubtedly imitative of Washington, who founded Tuskegee Institute.

One of the features of the black sermon, Blount argues, is to incorporate "disparate texts together to intensify [one's] own" (588). This argument holds true in Ned's fusion of the preacherly with the teacherly. Ned signifies upon Jamaica-born Garvey's back-to-Africa movement of the 1920s that called for the mass exodus of African Americans to Africa. Even while adopting Garvey's mantra of self-reliance and black pride, Ned rejects the idea of African Americans repatriating to Africa, dispelling any doubt regarding their status as American citizens: "You got black people here saying go back to Africa, some saying go to Canada, some saying go to France. Now, who munks y'all sitting here right now want be a Frenchman and talk like they do. . . . Be Americans" (115).[12] By the same token, he is punctuating the systematic and systemic denial of their rights. Adopting a strategic stance, Ned uses fellow Jamaican McKay's poetry of protest and resistance as counterargument to Garvey's line of reasoning. He sermonizes, "[M]any . . . have been killed because *they stood up on their two feet.* But if you must die, let me ask you this: wouldn't you rather die saying I'm a man than to die saying I'm a contented slave?" (117; emphasis added). The comparison between Ned's call to action and McKay's militant poem "If We Must Die" is compelling:

> If we must die—let it not be like hogs
> Hunted and penned in an inglorious spot
> . . . .
> Like men we'll face the murderous, cowardly pack
> Pressed to the wall, dying, but fighting back! (834)

The trope of standing "on his own two feet" has a central place as well in *A Lesson Before Dying*, Gaines's eighth novel. After being convicted and sentenced to death for a murder he did not commit, Jefferson's "Nannan" is adamant about him regaining his humanity: "I don't want them to kill no hog. . . . I want a man to go to that chair, on his own two feet" (13). Jefferson ultimately "walks to his freedom." Casting him as a Christ figure—in other words, having him assume the identity of the biblical character—has symbolic importance to his community, which depends on him for its own salvation.

Ned also indirectly rejects the accommodationist stance intimated in Washington's Cotton States and International Exposition address in Atlanta, Georgia,[13] demystifying the belief that if you adopt a nonantagonistic stance toward the white man you will be delivered from his wrath: "Now, that other thing—don't mess with the white man and he won't slaughter you. Well, let me tell you a little story. My own mother was killed by white men, not because she was messing in their business, she was trying to leave the South after she heard of her freedom" (116). Subsequently, he explicitly disapproves of Washington's political ideology: "I agree with Mr. Washington on trade. . . . But trade is not all. I want to see some of my children become lawyers. I want to see some of my children become ministers of the Bible; some write books; some to represent their people in law. So trade is not all. Working with your hands while the white man write all the rules and laws will not better your lot" (116). Here, Ned signifies upon the tension—the differing perspective between Washington and Du Bois. Denotatively, Du Bois's concept of the Talented Tenth is realized whereby Ned exemplifies the college-educated individual who provides leadership for African Americans after Reconstruction.

Ned's lament of the displacement and dispossession of Native Americans and African Americans—"America is for red, white, and black men. The red man roamed all over this land long before we got here. The black man cultivated this land from ocean to ocean with his back. The white man brought tools and guns. America is for all of us" (115)—revises and repeats Langston Hughes's poem "Lament for Dark Peoples":

> I was a red man one time,
> But the white man came.
> I was a black man, too,
> But the white man came.
> They drove me out of the forests.
> They took me away from the jungles. (39)

Another sustaining form of black cultural expression is the trope of jumping the broom, the custom that necessitates a couple stepping over a broom to legitimize their union. Dorothy Roberts articulates that out of necessity "[t]hese partnerships were consecrated by slaves' own ceremonies and customs" (28). Since slave marriages were not recognized by law, the tradition of jumping the broom, a signifying ritual, serves as counterculture to Western traditional marriages.[14] Furthering this signification, Jane reveals how slaves were able to survive their oppression by practicing and sustaining such cultural expressions as a means to affirm their cultural heritage. Chronicling her relationship with her husband, Joe, she expresses, "We didn't get married. I didn't believe in the church then, and Joe never did. We just agreed to live together, like people did in the slavery time. Slaves didn't get married in churches, they jumped over the broom handle" (81). In validating and celebrating her newfound freedom, Jane enacts a double revision of this tradition: "Me and Joe Pittman didn't think we needed the broom, we wasn't slaves no more. We would just live together long as we wanted each other. That was all" (81). Thus, enslaved African American women circumvented their denial of marriage and citizenship and even humanity.

Other forms of black rhetorical rituals are imbued in wakes, a social gathering after someone's death at which that person's life is remembered and celebrated, and in the midwife, a powerful female healer also known as a witch. As the term suggests, at a wake one keeps vigil by staying awake through the night. At African wakes, even while paying respect to the departed and giving comfort to the bereaved family, the attendees engage in merrymaking, celebrating the deceased's life. Illuminating the relative ease with which African Americans have adopted this funeral tradition, Karla Holloway explains that the rite "serve[s] to reconvene the family and its community to rehearse the situations and events of black death." She further establishes that the "particular kinds of racial conversation and memorializing that recurred with African America on these occasions imbued them with some cultural particularity" (*Passed On* 165). These cultural particularities are a focal point of Jane's remembrance at her husband's wake: "They waked Joe Pittman that night and buried him that Sunday, and the rodeo went on that Saturday. Before it started they toned the bell one minute for Pittman. Every man took off his hat. The ladies bowed their heads" (102). While the tribute to Joe captures the reverence and rhetorical ritual of the practice, "the community recollections . . . illustrate the community narratives that surround these individual moments" (Holloway, *Passed On* 165). Cultural continuity is a common feature of African American rituals, a point that Holloway reiterates as she reminds us that

> African American funerals during the twentieth century depended on the spectacle of the moment to involve the community of mourners as fully as possible in the emotions and the ceremony of the event. Community involvement in the African American funeral ceremony took its significance (if not its actual practices) from West African cultures that attended to death and burial as an important, public, elaborate, and lengthy social event.   (173–74)

The tradition of tolling the bell to announce a death in the community is an age-old African tradition.

A paragon of female agency and autonomy, midwives have control over pregnancy, childbirth, and women's sexual and reproductive health. Madame Gauthier, the hoodoo or the witchwoman, revises a Western doctor's misdiagnosis or under-diagnosis of Jane as barren, ascertaining that "[s]lavery has made [Jane] barren" (97). Jane's reliance on this female healer is unmistakable, as she feigns illness to Joe in order to pay her a visit: "I told him I wanted to go by myself. Because it wasn't the doctor, it was the hoo-doo woman in town I wanted to see" (96). The prescriptive phrase "the doctor" speaks volumes as it sheds light on this male-dominated profession. Nevertheless, this male-centric profession is usurped by the all-powerful female healer: Madame Gauthier, who poses a threat to Western medicine and practitioners. Whereas Madame Gauthier has access to the Western world of medicine, Western practitioners cannot gain access to her world, grounded in vernacular culture, with equal ease. A case in point: Madame Gauthier interprets Jane's recurring dreams about Joe as impending doom; ultimately Joe is killed by one of the very wild horses he attempts to break. Jane is eventually bestowed this gift of clairvoyance; this transferal of female power draws attention to the continuance, a repetition of sorts, of female agency. This repetition-cum–female continuity is rendered most palpable in the persona of Marie Laveau and her namesake, her daughter, who is her double and a fellow female practitioner.[15] Fittingly, the mystical aura surrounding the mother-daughter duo is given special attention: "Some people said the two Maries was the same one, but, of course, that was people talk. Said the first Marie never died, she just turned younger in her later years" (96). The power of Marie Laveau, Sr., and Marie Laveau, Jr. (i.e., their dismantling of patriarchal order) is self-evident. Not only does their craft usurp male primacy and supremacy, but also their names reappropriate and unsettle the customary patrilineal inheritance of naming.

Female empowerment occupies center stage as women are given their due accordingly. Even as King is hailed as a hero, the sexism of the movement is laid bare as Rosa Parks is authenticated as a key player in the movement and women in general are credited for their activism. Espousing a feminist critique, Jane champions female activism, fiercely challenging the masculinist history through revision while simultaneously punctuating female participation and resistance: "King couldn't do a thing before Miss Rosa Parks refused to give that white man her seat" (241). Thus, Parks's action serves as a catalyst for King's activism. By writing Parks into being, Jane simultaneously writes silenced black women into existence.

Moreover, women's bodies become the locus of female agency. In declaring that Jane's inability to reproduce is a direct result of slavery, Madame Gautier focuses our attention on race and reproduction, specifically on black female reproductive capabilities. "Slave women's procreative ability gave them a unique mode of rebellion" (D. Roberts 46), and Jane's assumed (read: orchestrated) barrenness engenders resistance as well, for it unhinges the master's efforts "to harness Black women's sexuality and fertility to a dominant system of capitalist exploitation" (Collins 50). Madame Gautier's resolute pronouncement—"Slavery has made you barren. But that is it" (97)—is compelling for it suggests that Jane willed herself not to reproduce. This self-imposed barrenness that bears resemblance to slave women's "self-imposed sterility and self-induced miscarriages" (D. White 85) thwarts the "efforts of enslavers to control female reproduction" (S. Alexander 87). After all, "some Southern whites were certain that slave women knew how to avoid pregnancy as well as how to deliberately abort a pregnancy" through manipulations (D. White 84). To echo Deborah Gray White, these suspicions were not unsubstantiated, as many slave women adopted manipulative strategies in the form of herbal abortifacients. Jane's ambiguous introduction of Unc Isom is not accidental: "Unc Isom was *a kind of advisor* to us there in the quarters. Some people said he had been a witch doctor sometime back. I know he knowed a lot about roots and herbs, and the people was always going to him for something to cure colic or the bots or whatever they had" (13; emphasis added). "Slaveowners controlled Black women's labor and commodified Black women's bodies as units of capital"; contrarily, Jane's infertility potentially interrupts the "increase of her owner's property and labor force" (Collins 51). Rejecting childbearing as an anchor for maintaining locational stability and enduring relationships, Jane establishes that her rootedness lies not in her ability to bear children but in her exercising control over her reproductive life. Moreover, by marrying/valuing Jane, Joe Pittman challenges the pervasive belief that the black woman's worth was determined by her ability to reproduce, for it was an established fact that "infertile women could expect to be treated like barren sows and be passed from one unsuspecting buyer to the next" (D. White 101). Treating Jane with utmost respect, Joe remains steadfast in his commitment to her, wherein he rejects her explanation that she "never looked at a man [because she] was barren" (80). Echoing Madame Gautier, he identifies the oppressive system of slavery that bound them in their victimization: "Ain't we all been hurt by slavery?" (81). Furthermore, by refusing to place a preponderance of weight on Jane's inability to reproduce, Joe, in an interesting instance of role reversal, ranks his marriage above motherhood.[16] By the same accord, Joe's manhood is not dependent on or determined by the number of children he has sired. Rather his relationship with Jane is based on mutual love and respect, substantiating White's assertion that "love and affection played a large part in male-female relations" (145). Whereas "slave men were solicitous . . . toward their women," slave women responded in kind (147). Consequently, Jane expresses unwavering respect and adoration for Joe, her life partner: "When Joe Pittman was killed a part of me went with him to his grave. No man would ever take his place, and that's why I carry his name to this day. I have knowed two or three other men, but none took the place of Joe Pittman. I let them know that from the start" (102–03).

Joe's persuasive response to Jane after she shares that she is unable to procreate validates othermothering as a viable substitution for biological mothering: "If you just say you'll help raise my two girls, I'll be satisfied." Jane in turn expresses respect and appreciation for Joe: "He was a real man, Joe Pittman was"

(81). Calling attention to the fluidity and viability of biological (blood) mothers and othermothers (surrogate), Patricia Hill Collins surmises that othermothers "traditionally have been central to the institution of Black motherhood" (178). One of the effective ways that African Americans resisted "the dehumanizing effects of slavery was by re-creating African notions of family as extended kin units" (49). Modeling a very different value system based on community organization, othermothers, in effect, are the backbone of the community, the ones who uphold the family infrastructure by virtue of their ethics of caring and community responsibility (192). Furthering this line of reasoning, Stanlie James ascertains that an othermother must have a sense of the community's culture and tradition before she can effectively administer care to the community (47). To this end, the practice of "othermothering remains central to African American tradition of motherhood and is regarded as essential for the survival of black people" (O'Reilly 6). A quintessential othermother, Jane is not only the culture bearer and the designated "church mother" but also the community's historian and storyteller (226). Accentuating the powerful position the "church mother" occupies in the community, Collins relates an incident in which a church mother in rural Alabama exerted control by insisting on speaking at a church service despite the fact that she was not on the program (193). The officiating minister acquiesced. Jane's power manifests not only in the persona of the church mother but also as a midwife who delivers Jimmy, preordained as "the one," or the Messiah. Giving birth/life to Jimmy, Jane's othermothering takes on spiritual characteristics (212).[17]

Community othermothers belong to a group of women who feel accountable for one another's children. In essence, they "work on behalf of the Black community by expressing ethics of caring and personal accountability" (Collins 192), which guarantee "that all children, regardless of whether the biological mother was present or available, would receive the mothering that delivers psychological and physical well-being and makes empowerment possible" (O'Reilly 6). As a result of Big Laura's unexpected and untimely brutal murder by the Secesh soldiers, Jane is prematurely forced to assume the role of othermothering to Big Laura's surviving child, Ned: "I sat there looking at Ned, wondering what I was go'n do next. I got this child to take care . . . I said to myself" (25). After witnessing Big Laura's murder, Jane resignedly (although not defeatedly) articulates: "I hardly knowed how to cry. I went back to Ned and asked him if he wanted to go to Ohio with me. He nodded" (24).

Jane's personal account of life on a Louisiana plantation offers students an insight into the daily restrictive lives of slaves. At the same time her personal, embodied account of the oppressive systems bolsters White's theory that "black males and females did not experience slavery the same . . . male and female slavery was different from the very beginning" (62–63). Expanding on White's argument, Roberts theorizes that women received harsher treatment than men did during slavery because of the physical violence and rape to which they were routinely subjected. Black women, unlike their white female counterparts, were constructed outside the realm of humanity; they were denied "Black humanity

in order to rationalize white supremacy" (D. Roberts 8). This denial of personhood is rendered most palpable in the scene in which a group of Secesh soldiers,
after its brutal murder of Big Laura and her infant daughter, further engages in
her demonization and dehumanization: "Goddam, she was mean. Did you see
her? Did you see her? Goddam, she could fight. They ain't human. Gorilla, I say"
(23). Unequivocally, the patriarchal, masculinist language that constructs Big
Laura as monstrous, as subhuman, is an attempt to harness her sexuality even
as it calls attention to her bestiality. The delineation of Big Laura's supposed ani-
malistic traits resonates strongly with the scene in Morrison's *Beloved* in which
Sethe is subject to intense scrutiny by her enslaver, a schoolteacher, who coaches
his nephews/pupils on the "proper measuring requirements in assessing Sethe's
humanity or lack thereof": "No, no. That's not the way. I told you to put her human
characteristics on the left; her animal ones on the right. And don't forget to line
them up" (qtd. in S. Alexander 27). Further, Big Laura's demonization evidences
the intertwining of motherhood and racism. Consequently, Big Laura's death signals her simultaneous denial of motherhood and citizenship.

Big Laura's vilification, which exemplifies a simultaneous condemnation of the
whole black race, is unsurprising ("They ain't human. Gorilla. . . ."), for Roberts
reminds us that "[w]hites invented the hereditary trait of race and endowed it
with the concept of racial superiority and inferiority to resolve the contradiction between slavery and liberty. Scientific racism explained domination by one
group over another as the natural order of things: Blacks were biologically destined to be slaves, and whites were destined to be their masters" (9). Thus, Big
Laura's supposed inhuman attributes are just cause for her subjugation and subsequent slaughter.

Big Laura's vilification resides within the framework of sexism; furthermore,
it solidifies the argument that black women "did not experience sexism the same
way white women did. Owing to their color white men saw black women differently and exploited them differently. Race changed the experience of black womanhood" (D. White 5). We witness the vicious beating of Jane at the hands of
her master, because she refuses to answer to the slave name Ticey and instead
demands to be called by her new (rightful) name, Miss Jane Brown.[18] Jane's beating simulates her being raped: "My master told two of the other slaves to hold
me down. One took my arms, the other one took my legs. My master jecked up
my dress and gived my mistress the whip and told her to teach me a lesson" (9).
Moreover, this sexualized scene of her being tied up and whipped conjures up
images of pornographic exposure. As Deborah McDowell succinctly articulates:
women who "are tied up . . . and unable to resist" personify "the classic stance
of women in pornography" (52). This reading of female sexual exploitation further lends itself to the exploration of the sexualization of the black woman and
of the vilification of black female sexuality in general. Black female exploitation
was deemed just and justifiable, because first and foremost, black women were
denied personhood, and second, they were considered deviants and therefore
they did not fit the American ideal of "true womanhood." We witness this

construction of black female deviance yet again in relation to the Creole schoolteacher Mary Agnes LeFabre, with whom Robert "Tee Bob" Samson, the son of the plantation owner, Robert Samson, Sr., is helplessly in love. Finding it difficult to fathom his son's romantic interest in Mary Agnes, Robert summarily arrives at the foregone conclusion that Mary Agnes is "leading him" on (179). After clearly delineating Mary Agnes's "animal characteristics," Tee Bob's friend Jimmy Caya reinforces the prevailing assumption that black women are propertied possession of white men—"Don't you know *who* you are? Don't you know *what* she is? That woman is a nigger, Robert. A nigger. She just look white. But Africa is in her veins, and that make her nigger, Robert" (emphasis added)—and duly reminds Tee Bob that she "know her duty, and all she expect from you is ride the horse down there. But that's far as she expect you to go. The rest is her duty, Robert. She knows that" (182). Later he adds emphatically, "If you want her you go to that house and take her. If you want her at that school, make them children go out in the yard and wait. Take her in that ditch if you can't wait to get her home. But she's there for that and nothing else" (183).

Despite her own subjugated position in the patriarchal system,[19] we bear witness to Miss Amma Dean's (the wife of Robert, Sr.) complicity with white patriarchy as she scolds Jane for thinking the unthinkable, that "Tee Bob could love a woman *like that* [despite knowing] all the time he was marrying Judy Major in the spring" (180; emphasis added). Noticeably, Miss Amma Dean uses the same language of patriarchy used by Jimmy Caya: "a woman *like that*" versus "Don't you know *what* she is?" The phrase "like that," similar to the word "what," performs the same function of negation and debasement and supports Miss Amma Dean's complicity in the oppression of black women. White's observation rings true: "The white woman's sense of herself as a woman—her self-esteem and perceived superiority—depended on the racism that debased black women" (6). Mary Agnes's fate, her inferiority, is predestined as she is constructed as a bearer of "incurable immorality," a clear validation that "Black bodies, intellect, character, and culture are all inherently vulgar" (D. Roberts 8, 9). In contrast, Tee Bob's fiancée, Judy Major, is configured within the framework of white femininity and, accordingly, inhabits the pure, chaste white body, perfectly fitting the description of "the beautiful and cultured Judy Major of Bayonne, Luzana" (203). Further, Big Laura's physical features, her unladylike attributes, engender her defeminization even as her bestiality starkly opposes Judy Major's respectability and her vulgar body stands at odds with Judy Major's delicate and chaste body. Judy Major's silence and submissiveness (although referenced several times in the novel, she never actually speaks; she dutifully makes scheduled appearances with her parents always in tow) become a marker of her complicity and are mandatory to fulfill effectively this preordained role.[20] Moreover, her womanhood "rested on a notion of femininity that made piety, delicacy, morality, weakness, and dependency the reserve of white women alone" (D. White 6).

Jimmy Caya's outburst exposes systemic racism: "He told Tee Bob what everybody had always told him. From his daddy to his teacher had told him" (183).

During the interrogation of Tee Bob's suicide, he remains steadfast in the popularly held white male belief: "I didn't tell him no more than what my daddy told me. What my daddy's daddy told him. What Mr. Paul told Mr. Robert. What Mr. Paul's daddy told him. What your daddy told you. No more than the rules we been living by ever since we been here" (201).[21] Maintaining racist thinking and racial hierarchy is designed to undercut the disruption and destabilization of the neat white masculinist narrative. Accordingly, the commodification of the black female subject/body is obligatory: her deviant sexuality must be exposed, tamed, and contained within the masculinist discourse to maintain interlocking systems of oppression.

Black motherhood is a tenuous subject, shrouded in suspicion, and "has borne the weight of centuries of disgrace manufactured in both popular culture and academic circles" (D. Roberts 21). The slaughter of Big Laura's infant child lends validity to the claim that "Black women bore children who belonged to the slave-owner from the time of their conception" (23). Robert, Sr., insists that he will be relocating his illegitimate son, Timmy, to the great house despite Verda's objection, punctuating that black mothers did not have control over their own lives, let alone their children's lives. Both Big Laura and Verda are denied the ability to mother; in essence, this deprivation renders their children motherless.[22] Furthermore, as propertied possessions, their bodies were not their own and, therefore, they were routinely subjected to sexual assaults. In equal measure, the murder of Big Laura's daughter signals the devaluation of the black body. As McDowell eloquently puts it: "Black women's children, like black women themselves, are not bodies that matter" (314). Big Laura's and her daughter's deaths arguably profess the need to suffocate the presumed inherent deviance of black subjects, for they engender the belief that "Black mothers are seen to corrupt the reproduction process at every stage. Black mothers, it is believed, transmit inferior physical traits to the product of conception through their genes. They impart a deviant lifestyle to their children through their example" (D. Roberts 9).

Redeeming Big Laura from obscurity, Jane renders her a respectable subject by illuminating her invaluable importance in and to the slave community:

> That was Big Laura. She was big just like her name say, and she was rough as any man I ever seen. She could plow, chop wood, cut and load much cane as any man on the place. She had two children. One in her arms, a little girl; and she was leading Ned by the hand. But even with them two children she had the biggest bundle out there balanced on her head. (17)

Emphasizing Big Laura's role as a community mother and a leader challenges her dehumanization. Big Laura's community involvement signifies on the abolitionist, the humanitarian, and the "conductor" of the Underground Railroad Harriet Tubman. Similar to Tubman, whose rescue missions freed numerous enslaved African Americans, Big Laura is engaged in a rescue mission of sorts. Embodying the nurturing, protective role of mother, she saves Jane from an

attempted rape by a man labeled a "slow-wit" (20). The "mother of all," Big
Laura uses this rescue mission as a teachable moment in which she not only issues a severe warning to the perpetrator—"You got just one more time to try
your studding round me. . . . Just one more time, and I'll kill you. . . ."—but also
chastises the men for perpetuating male patriarchal violence on their own
(woman)kind: "That go for the rest of y'all. You free, then you go'n act like free
men. If you want act like you did on that plantation, turn around now and go on
back to that plantation." Big Laura's reverence finds resonance in the childlike
obedience and silence that follows: "Nobody said a thing. Most of them looked
down at the ground" (20).

Furthermore, Jane's "speech" signifies upon Sojourner Truth's "Ain't I a
Woman" speech, delivered in 1851 at the Women's Convention in Akron, Ohio.
Jane's emphasis on Laura mothering two biological children and temporarily serving as her othermother calls attention to Truth being questioned by several white
men about her womanhood. This questioning of black womanhood was pervasive
because "Black women were unprotected by men or by law, and they had their
womanhood totally denied" (D. White 12). Truth's rebuttal is useful to better analyze the signifying motif, particularly repetitions and the use of chiasmus:

> Nobody ever helps me into carriages, or over mud-puddles, or gives me
> any best place! And ain't I a woman? Look at me! Look at my arm! I have
> ploughed and planted, and gathered into barns, and no man could head
> me! And ain't I a woman? I have borne thirteen children, and seen most
> all sold off to slavery, and when I cried out with my mother's grief, none
> but Jesus heard me. And ain't I a woman?

Like Truth who "ploughed and planted, and gathered into barns, and no man
could head," Laura "could plow, chop wood, cut and load much cane as any man
on the place." Whereas Truth inverts the white male gaze, pronouncing, "Look at
me! Look at my arm!," Jane delivers an equally empowering vision of Big Laura:
"She was big just like her name say, and she was rough as any man I ever seen."

Confronting the racist and sexist domination of black women and black womanhood, Truth brings attention to the contradiction between "the ideological
myths of womanhood and the reality of Black women's experience" (Crenshaw
220). Likewise, Jane rejects the portrayal of women as frail, delicate, and inadequate, "the claim that women were categorically weaker than men" (Crenshaw
220). Lending her voice in reclaiming Truth's womanhood, Angela Davis opines
that Truth "was no less a woman than any of her white sisters at the convention.
That her race and her economic condition were different from theirs did not annul her womanhood. And as a Black woman, her claim to equal rights was no
less legitimate than that of white middle-class women" (63–64). Evidently, Jane
shares the same conviction of Big Laura.

Miss Jane works well to spark discussion about black female sexuality, black
womanhood, mothering, and the black vernacular tradition. Despite the initial

trepidation of the pervasive use of the black vernacular, students eventually gain a deeply felt appreciation for the narrative structure and content, becoming very engaged, which leads to very rewarding class discussions. Suffice it to say that like the characters in the novel, students are able to stand on their two feet by the end of the semester.

NOTES

[1] Articulating that the "black use of figurative language" renders the trope effective, Gates establishes that the trope of the talking book first occurred in a 1770 slave narrative and was revised in successive slave narratives (*Signifying Monkey* 143).

[2] This essay quotes from the 1972 Bantam edition of *Miss Jane*.

[3] Gates concludes that respective works of authors about slavery revised the trope of the talking book, displacing it with "tropes of freedom and literacy" (*Signifying Monkey* 170).

[4] In upholding the theme of this essay, I often signify on the traditional definition of *intertextuality*. The term is revised to include the intermixing and literary cannibalization of genres and historical events.

[5] Gates acknowledges that the phrase "speakerly text" is derived from Roland Barthes's opposition between "readerly" and "writerly" texts and the trope of the talking book, the fundamental trope of the African American tradition (198).

[6] These designations lend themselves to the concept of slaves as chosen people. For further detail, see Blount.

[7] This essay quotes from the 1988 Penguin edition of *Beloved*.

[8] Wharry surmises that it is a moot point to discuss the black church without mentioning orality.

[9] Other examples of chiasmi that Morrison incorporates in Baby Suggs's sermon are: "In this here place" and "They don't love," succeeded by "No more do they love." Both sermons are grounded by repetitions.

[10] For a more detailed analysis of this trope, see S. Alexander, pp. 105–13. Moira Ferguson elaborates on this trope in her book entitled *Jamaica Kincaid: Where the Land Meets the Body*.

[11] The earliest hint we have of Jesus being self-aware is found in Luke 2.41–52, where he and his parents go to Jerusalem to attend the Feast of the Passover. He is twelve years old at the time.

[12] The decree "Be Americans" signifies, through repetition and revision, upon the line "I, too, am America" in Langston Hughes's poem "I, Too" (46).

[13] Washington's speech became the impetus for the Atlanta Compromise, an agreement made in 1895 between African American leaders and southern white leaders that assured the maintenance of white political rule in return for blacks receiving basic education and due process in law. For the speech, see Washington.

[14] The tradition of jumping the broom dates back to the 1600s and is derived from Africa. While it is not associated with slavery as it is practiced in parts of West Africa, enslaved Africans adopted the tradition. It originated in the nineteenth century in the United States and was practiced in antebellum slavery.

[15] Madame Gautier is forced to leave New Orleans because she had become a rival of Marie Laveau, the reigning queen, and it was public knowledge that "nobody dare rival Marie Laveau" (96).

[16] D. White argues that because slaveholders encouraged the primacy of the mother-child relationship, slave women ranked motherhood above marriage.

[17] It can be argued that Jane gives life to Ned as well when he is left in her care after the brutal murder of his mother, Big Laura.

[18] Jane's name changes from Ticey to Jane Brown to Jane Pittman, when she assumes her husband Joe Pittman's name. Other name changes that register resistance include Ned, formerly known as Ned Brown, becoming Ned Douglass, then Ned Stephen Douglass, and finally Edward Stephen Douglass. Influenced by Ned, the young men who followed and subsequently adopted his teaching take on such names as Brown (after John Brown) and Turner (after Nat Turner). The motif of naming oneself testifies to the importance of the act for the ex-slaves, as it demonstrates their newfound freedom, calling attention to self-ownership. For the same reason, having a proper name is a marker of legitimacy. Tee Bob promises to "legitimize" Mary Agnes by giving her the Samson name (185).

[19] Robert, Sr., has fathered an illegitimate son, Timmy Henderson, with his slave Verda; he is also known for having his way with other women on his plantation.

[20] The only moment in which Judy Major "re-acts" is in response to Robert, Sr., breaking down the door to Tee Bob's room to recover his lifeless body after his suicide. In this scene, she is depicted as emotional and infantile: "That gal, Judy Major, almost knocked her daddy over getting in his arms" (195).

[21] Tee Bob's major downfall was not following in the footsteps of his father, Robert, Sr., by having sexual relations with Mary Agnes, mirroring the relationship his father had with Verda.

[22] While othermothering is employed as an effective substitute for biological mothering, unsuspecting children are nonetheless deprived of their blood mothers.

An Interdisciplinary Approach to the Gothic Heart of Gaines's *The Autobiography of Miss Jane Pittman*

Ineke Bockting

When I teach Ernest Gaines's *The Autobiography of Miss Jane Pittman*, after having introduced the novel as a whole, I like to go to the heart of it: the scene where its protagonist, Miss Jane Pittman—after having lost her husband through an "uncanny" accident and her adopted son to racial violence—receives a sudden vision of Christ himself, showing her the way to lighten her burden by taking it "'cross yon river" (143).[1] While she uses the event to explain why she finally, after much hesitation, joins the church, it seems significant that just at this point the narrative comes to a halt, and the following chapter, "Two Brothers of the South," turns away from the autobiographical toward certain aspects of the southern gothic.

There are, to be sure, quite a number of other gothic elements in the tale, including the "Chariot of Hell" that comes to torment the Cajun assassin Albert Cluveau and the mysterious and terrifying aspect of both the black stallion that kills Joe Pittman and the old hoodoo woman who predicts the tragedy. The most sustained use of the gothic, however, comes in this third section set on the plantation.

The first question to discuss with my students becomes: is there actually such a thing as a specifically "southern" form of the gothic? Although certain experts on the gothic or on the South tend to respond in the negative, Elizabeth Fortson Arroyo, herself an author from the region, seems to imply that there is, when she writes in her article "The Asterisk Southerner" in the *Oxford American*, published in Oxford, Mississippi, "Yankee mythology does not have a counterpart to moonlight and magnolias; there is no Northern Gothic" (27). What is more, the same journal immediately afterward published a whole issue devoted to the subject, entitled *Is the South Still Gothic?*, thus suggesting that once, at least, it was. In his article "The History of the Southern Gothic Sensibility" in this same issue, the southern historian Fred Hobson argues, "Gothic is still alive in Dixie, but not only in Dixie," and he concludes, "The point is that the South doesn't have all the crazies, and it never did. It's just that the Southern writer has often seemed to possess a greater capacity for seeing beneath surfaces, for imagining and depicting evil, not to mention a capacity for capturing the ridiculous, the absurd" (18–19).

If it is true that the South has, indeed, this "greater capacity," then it is perhaps no accident that in Elizabeth MacAndrew's discussion of twentieth-century gothic as a literary genre, all the American examples are from the South: Flannery O'Connor's "You Can't Be Any Poorer Than Dead" and "Good Country People," Carson McCullers's *The Ballad of the Sad Café*, Truman Capote's *Other*

Voices, Other Rooms, and Eudora Welty's *The Robber Bridegroom*. So, in order to discuss the gothic heart of Gaines's fictional autobiography, it is important, first, to discuss with the students what seems essential to the gothic and, second, to investigate what might be a specific southern type. We can then, finally, ask what function it has at the heart of *Miss Jane*.

MacAndrew defines the gothic as "a literature of nightmare," which uses "the stuff of myth, folklore, fairy tale, and romance" to give shape to universal human fears (3). These universal fears can be recognized as existential ones, in that they are connected with threats to our human existence. If originally, in the earlier gothic, they seemed to come from the outside, in the form of different sorts of monsters and monstrous forces, over the years they have moved more and more to the inside, as threats to our human existence in a psychological sense—that is, to our sense of self. Perhaps this is especially so in the United States, the land of immigration, with the threat to a secure sense of selfhood, or identity, that this may entail. MacAndrew argues, "Settings were changed from medieval to contemporary, a man's house turned out still to be his Gothic castle[,] and his soul, already reflected in paintings and statues, began to look back at him from mirrors and, still worse, from his double, a living breathing copy of himself" (5).

It seems, then, that the *vehicle* of the gothic must be found in the field of various local characteristics, including sensory ones, whether visual, auditory, tactile, olfactory, or gustatory—my students easily identify elements like the ruins of old plantation houses, the rustle of palmetto trees, the eerie squeak of tree frogs, the roar of alligators, the mist over the bayou, or the touch of Spanish moss on your face in the dark—while the *tenor* consists of the universal fears, often hidden in the subconscious: Freud's *unheimliche* (the "uncanny"), which is thus given form (see Freud, "Das Unheimlich" and *The Uncanny*). Teresa Goddu insists that the American gothic is "most recognizable as a regional form. Identified with gothic doom and gloom, the American South serves as the nation's 'other,' becoming the repository of everything from which the nation wants to disassociate itself" (4).

The ruined mansions of the South are perhaps nowhere better portrayed than in the work of William Faulkner; certainly, students of southern literature remember the description of the house where Temple Drake and Gowan Stevens are forced to spend the night after they wreck their car on a nearby road in the novel *Sanctuary*: "The house was a gutted ruin rising gaunt and stark out of a grove of unpruned cedar trees. It was a landmark, known as the Old Frenchman place, built before the Civil War; a plantation house set in the middle of a tract of land; of cotton fields and gardens and lawns long since gone back to jungle . . ." (8). These ruins, so obviously pointing back to an earlier—and better—time, form only one of the many ways in which in southern texts "the past is never dead . . . isn't even past," as one of Faulkner's characters puts it (*Requiem for a Nun* 80). Even an outsider such as V. S. Naipaul was influenced by it when he took his "turn in the South" and saw the southern past "as a wound": "the past of which the dead or alienated plantations spoke, many of them still with physi-

cal mementoes of the old days, the houses, the dependencies, the oak avenues"
(99). Gaines has often spoken of the myriad ways in which Faulkner influenced
his work, and this extends to his use of the gothic.[2] Students may at this point
be introduced to the social critic Lillian Smith, who in the chapter "Distance
and Darkness" of her memoirs, *Killers of the Dream*, describes her childhood in
northern Georgia:

> When the sun set, the night began. There were no lights; only a kerosene
> lamp or a pine knot burning. And always the swamp back of you or the
> dark hills, or empty fields stretching on, on. . . . Far off, the Negroes sing-
> ing in dim lantern-lit churches, moaning their misery and shouting their
> joy. Sudden sharp laughter from nowhere. . . . Darkness comes. Sounds
> creep out: whippoorwill, tree-frogs, roar of alligator back in the pond,
> rustle of palmetto, restless, never-ending, as if an unseen hand brushes
> over it and it cannot let go . . . the scream of a cat in the swamp. Sounds
> like these weave in and out of lonely fantasies, pulling in hearsay tales,
> making a tight mat of facts and feelings and fancies and fears until one
> no longer knows the real from the unreal, and sometimes one no longer
> cares.   (159–60)

Smith explicitly presents this sense of the gothic within the southern character,
seeing it as an inclination toward "lonely fantasies" and "hearsay tales" that, as
she puts it, make a "tight mat of facts and feelings and fancies and fears until
one no longer knows the real from the unreal, and sometimes one no longer
cares." Many other writers approach the issue in a similar way. The journalist
W. J. Cash, in his highly influential work *The Mind of the South*, for instance,
detects in the southerner a "tendency towards unreality, towards romanticism,"
and he explains,

> He . . . lacks the complexity of mind, the knowledge, and, above all,
> the habit of skepticism essential to any generally realistic attitude. It is
> to say that he is inevitably driven back upon imagination, that his
> world-construction is bound to be mainly a product of fantasy, and that
> his credulity is limited only by his capacity for conjuring up the unbe-
> lievable.   (46–47)

Cash speaks of a "pattern of Southern unreality" (124). The students will notice
that, interestingly enough, these southern writers, Smith and Cash, both use the
unconventional term "unreality" or "the unreal"—also one of Faulkner's favor-
ites. For my students who have read Faulkner's short stories, Miss Minnie's "furious unreality" (175) and her "furious repudiation of truth" (174) in "Dry
September" may come to mind.

I tell students, then, that liminality—by which I mean here the limit to our
categorizing capacities—has traditionally been explored and exploited in the

gothic as a genre, presenting, for instance, characters that can be categorized neither as dead nor as alive, neither as absent nor as present (as in ghost stories),
neither as man nor as animal (as in werewolf stories), or neither as man nor as
machine (such as Frankenstein's monster). We can see that liminality in Vladimir
Nabokov's *Lolita*: it is the border between childhood and adulthood—Victor
Turner's original liminality—that is involved, turning toward the gothic when its
transgression is about to be committed (Bockting). I use a good example students
are all familiar with, the figure of the dead (or undead?) Madeline in Edgar Allan
Poe's "The Fall of the House of Usher." Interestingly, Freud used as the starting
point for his "gothic" 1919 essay "Das Unheimliche" ("The Uncanny") the work of
Ernst Jentsch, who presents as a good example of the uncanny a "doubt as to
whether an apparently animate object really is alive and, conversely, whether a
lifeless object might not perhaps be animate" (qtd. in Freud, *Uncanny* 135).[3]

Students can easily be made to think of other liminalities, such as there are
between good and evil, virtue and vice, innocence and guilt, madness and san-
ity, fear and fascination, and, in particular in the South, black and white, as we
find at the heart of Gaines's work. Indeed, most important here are the gothic
elements of the "southern situation." I ask the students to consider this long passage with which Smith begins *Killers of the Dream*:

> Even its children knew that the South was in trouble. No one had to tell
> them; no words said aloud. To them it was a vague thing weaving in and
> out of their play, like a ghost haunting an old graveyard or whispers after
> the household sleeps—fleeting mystery, vague menace to which each re-
> sponded in his own way. Some learned to screen out all except the soft and
> the soothing; others denied even as they saw plainly, and heard. But all
> knew that under quiet words and warmth and laughter, under the slow ease
> and tender concern about small matters, there was a heavy burden on
> all of us and as heavy a refusal to confess it. . . . This haunted childhood
> belongs to every southerner of my age. We ran away from it but we came
> back like a hurt animal to its wounds, or a murderer to the scene of his
> sin. The human heart dares not stay away too long from that which hurts
> it most. There is a return journey to anguish that few of us are released
> from making.   (25–26)

It is this brooding sense of guilt, and the inability to release it through confes-
sion, I believe, that creates the relentless "return of the repressed" that gives
many texts of the early-twentieth-century South their gothic character, including *Miss Jane*.

After this introduction on the gothic and its links with the issue of liminality, we
are now ready to turn to the gothic heart of *Miss Jane*. Students will easily see
that, indeed, what interrupts the flow of Miss Jane's narrative—even if she remains a witness—is the transgressive borderline story of two half brothers, one

white and one black; the latter, Timmy, resembles his father both in appearance and in aptitude, to a degree that is truly "uncanny" and that goes far beyond what the former, Tee Bob, ever could aspire to. It seems that Timmy is, in fact, quite openly acknowledged by his father, which is rather exceptional, as southern white fathers were not likely to recognize the children they produced with women of the "other race." James C. Cobb, for instance, writes about a child who resembled his white father so much that he was forbidden by city officials to pass his father's house on the way to school. In another case, a black woman who insisted on naming her child after the white man who had fathered him was forced to leave town (158). It is indeed not for nothing that Smith refers to these children as "little ghosts playing and laughing and weeping on the edge of southern memory" (125), and her contemporary, William Alexander Percy, in a sustained horticultural analogy, talks of hybrid flowers with root rot that would be better off dead (333). But here, despite the inequality in the situation of the boys—Timmy serving as "butler" to the six or seven years younger Tee Bob—the relationship is to all purposes one between brothers, such as the one Faulkner created between Henry Beauchamp and Carothers "Roth" Edmonds in the story "The Fire and the Hearth," a story that may fruitfully be presented in parallel to this chapter of Gaines's novel.

If the basic situation already described—that of Timmy as "butler" to Tee Bob—is the relative equilibrium that the drama starts out with, its complication begins one day when Miss Jane, already an elderly woman, rides out into the field with the two brothers, and Timmy makes her horse take off with dangerous speed, asking the utmost of her not to be thrown off. Miss Amma Dean, Tee Bob's mother, immediately guesses that the foolhearted joke was of Timmy's doing. As Miss Jane puts it, "She knowed it was Timmy, because Timmy was Robert's son, and Robert would 'a' done the same thing. No, not would 'a', did it" (150). I ask students to look very closely at Miss Jane's sentence—the white woman's mental representation of the situation the way it is attributed to her by Miss Jane in the latter's southern dialect—as it is quite interesting from a syntactical point of view.

Here I need to introduce the students to the various types of clauses with which a narrator (in this case, Miss Jane) can attribute mental activity to a matrix subject (Miss Amma Dean). In fact, four types of attributive clauses can be distinguished: the *small clause*, the *infinitive* clause, the *how clause*, and the *that clause*, which is used here. In the order given, these four forms convey an increasing epistemic awareness on the part of the subject, going all the way from pure, or raw, sensory perception without truth judgment to a conclusion that is based on prior knowledge.[4] I discuss with the students some simple examples like "He saw the monster emerge" (raw sensory input with no intellectual mediation, as in a dream or a hallucination); "He saw the monster to be emerging" (a certain awareness of a process); "He saw how the monster was emerging" (a certain awareness of manner); "He saw that the monster was emerging" (a conclusion based on prior knowledge with or without direct sensory input). In these phrases we see the mental activity verb *see* change from a pure sensation verb into an epistemic one.

In addition, the choice of the attributive verb may add the narrator's judgment with regard to the truth of the matrix clause. The verb *know* used here, a so-called factive, conveys the narrator's agreement with the assertion made in the matrix clause: Miss Jane agrees with Miss Amma Dean that it must have been Timmy. Miss Jane might, however, have used a different mental activity verb, for instance the verb *imagine* ("She *imagined* it was Timmy"), which would have conveyed her disagreement with Miss Amma Dean, or *believe* ("She *believed* it was Timmy"), which would have been neutral with regard to truth judgment. The students should thus be able to see how interesting this sentence is from a social point of view, as the internal focalization on Miss Amma Dean's conviction by a character-narrator, who cannot normally look inside the mind of a fellow character, emphasizes the degree of intimacy that, as many critics have argued, tended to exist between house slave—or servant—and her mistress.

Indeed, Miss Jane knows her mistress well, confidently reporting the emotions and the thoughts of the white woman and, if she wants to, not in her own dialect but in Miss Amma Dean's white woman's language: "at first she was mad enough to hit him with the spy glasses, but the longer she looked at him the more she saw of Robert. Robert would have done the same thing; no, he had done it." And she concludes, still narrating the thoughts of the white woman: "But Timmy wasn't Robert, even if he was Robert's son. He had to remember he was still a nigger" (151). Students can now see clearly how Miss Jane occupies the liminal position that servants often do. As Natalie Hess puts it in her article on the linguistic markers of transgression of class distinctions: "servant figures are perhaps the ultimate markers of liminality, . . . as they move between the domains of parlour and kitchen, between the preparation of food and the removal of filth, between upper-class decorum and kitchen earthiness, they are literature's natural code-switchers" (8–9). In fact, only after Miss Amma Dean finally speaks out with a forceful "Mr. Robert will hear about this" does the perspective return to Miss Jane herself, who gives her vision of Timmy's nonverbal behavior: "He was looking 'cross the yard at the big house. From the way he was sitting in that saddle, not slumped over like a nigger ought to be, but with them shoulders up, with that straw hat cocked a little over his eyes, he was telling us Robert wasn't go'n do him a thing" (151).

The transgression of the southern codes is all too obvious here; Timmy's behavior closely resembles that of Lucas Beauchamp, in Faulkner's *Intruder in the Dust*, who, being related by blood to the plantation owner, refuses *"to mean mister to anybody even when he says it"* (58) and thus puts his life in serious peril. In any case, it is clear that this kind of "uppity" behavior is not going to be accepted. Indeed, the next incident, Tee Bob breaking his arm on a ride together with his brother, causes Timmy to be attacked by the white foreman, who allows himself this violence because, as Miss Jane presents it, "he knowed no white man in his right mind would 'a' said he had done the wrong thing" (152). I ask students to recognize the same syntactic particularity that we saw before; indeed, it is again the attributive *that clause,* "he knowed [that]," which reveals not only that the subject of the matrix clause—the foreman—bases this conclusion on prior, cultural knowledge, but also that the narrator—Miss Jane—agrees with this conclusion, which presents, in a nutshell, the whole of the southern racial context. Afterward there is, indeed, nothing else to do for his father, Robert, but to give Timmy "some money and send him away" (153), to the extreme distress of Tee Bob, a distress that can only wait for the gothic dissolving of the borders between present and past: the Freudian "return of the repressed."

The real interest of this chapter, and the source of its rising action, is the fact that at the age of about twelve, Tee Bob has not understood some of the things that every southern white child must eventually learn. With respect to this issue, I introduce students to Melton McLaurin's article "Rituals of Initiation and Rebellion: Adolescent Responses to Segregation in Southern Autobiography," which makes a distinction between, on the one hand, "acquiring an awareness of race" and, on the other, "acquiring an understanding of the significance of race." According to McLaurin, the former takes place "at an early age, usually between four and six" for both black and white children, while the latter goes from "an almost immediate understanding for blacks to a much more delayed one for whites, often not until early adolescence" (7). In Tee Bob's case, his mother, Miss Amma Dean; his uncle Clarence; his godfather, Jules Raynard; as well as Miss Jane herself had all tried to explain it to him—all except his father, who thought "these things" needed no explanation, them being "part of life, like the sun and the rain was part of life," and his son would learn in due time (154).

To understand what the expression "these things" entails, I suggest to the students to look at what Smith at the same age—twelve—had already learned about the prescribed relation of the southerner with "the other":

> I knew by the time I was twelve . . . that my old nurse who had cared for me through long months of illness, who had given me refuge when a little sister took my place as the baby of the family, who soothed, fed me, delighted me with her stories and games, let me fall asleep on her deep warm breast, was not worthy of the passionate love I felt for her but must be given instead a half-smiled-at affection similar to that which one feels for one's dog. *I knew but I never believed it.*   (28–29; emphasis added)

Again, through the use of the attributive construction "knew that," in the sentence "I knew . . . that my old nurse . . . was not worthy of the passionate love I felt for her," we can see how the matrix subject—the young Lillian this time—has come to a rational conclusion on the status of black people, based on preexisting cultural knowledge, and that the narrator—the older Smith—still agrees with the conclusion reached by her younger self.

Now that students have become sensitive to this syntactic construction, it should be shocking that the rational consent with the ways of the southern world, which the attributive *that clause* expresses, is paired with an emotional distancing from this same world, as signaled by the attributive construction in the last sentence, "I knew but I never believed it," showing the origin of what Smith would later call a "cultural schizophrenia" that bears "a curious resemblance to the schizophrenia of individual personality" (Gladney 86). We can see it as a liminal position, a gothic in-between of true and false, a painful "un-reality." Tee Bob, it seems, was never able to confront this "cultural schizophrenia," and his suicide some years later is directly linked to the sudden disappearance of Timmy.

When Tee Bob, now called Robert, Jr., by those around him—if never by Miss Jane—sees the young schoolteacher Mary Agnes LeFabre for the first time and his face gets so red that Miss Jane is afraid he might "faint right there in the kitchen" (172), we are thus led to think that this extreme reaction finds its roots in his subconscious comparison between her very light, yet "colored," complexion and that of his beloved redheaded, but "black," older half brother. Not only that, soon Mary Agnes's self-confident manner seems to strengthen the comparison: like Timmy—and like Faulkner's Lucas Beauchamp—Mary Agnes does not adapt her behavior to the expectations of white people, addressing Tee Bob, in Miss Jane's words, as "'Mister' the way white people say 'Mister' when a nigger was there. Not like she felt she ought to call somebody like Tee Bob Mister, but you always said Mister or Miss in front of somebody like her" (174).

I ask the students now to closely follow the couple. As they readily notice, when young Tee Bob is seen in the company of Mary Agnes more and more often, this does not really cause suspicion because it is understood that he obviously "ain't sowed all his wild oats yet" (177); it is normal, to be expected, and even preferred for a young southerner to do so with a black woman, before, or even while, settling down with a woman of his own color and class. Here, again, some contextualization is necessary. This transgression of the border between black and white, according to the southern historian Bertram Wyatt-Brown, created almost no moral or ethical problems in the South if only it followed certain rules. The most important one was that the male was white and the female was black, but there also had to be an obvious disparity of rank between the partners, the woman had to be of great beauty in the eyes of whites (the lighter the better), the affair had to seem casual, no matter how long it lasted, and it had to be conducted with the greatest discretion. Indeed, it could be whispered about between men, but it should never be discussed in mixed company, and its offspring should be meticulously kept out of sight (308–09).

Although the first three of these requirements would certainly have been satisfied, the students will notice that the last one—discretion—is impossible, not in the least because Tee Bob seems to have been totally unaware of the need for it from the beginning. When asked to go further with this observation, they will see that what makes the situation more complex is that those more or less in-

volved all take a different position, using a different form of defensive justifica-
tion: Tee Bob's mother is afraid that he is taking advantage of the young woman,
while his father believes that she is leading him on but that he should be left
alone to figure things out, and Mary Agnes herself, when questioned by Miss
Jane, denies the problem, saying he is "nothing but a child. . . . A lonely boy" and
believing she can handle him (177). Still, it is Miss Amma Dean who makes ex-
plicit the link with the past, when she tells her husband that she wants "no more
Timmy Hendersons" (179).

Only Miss Jane, in the black servant's role of witness to the white man's tragedy, sees what is really going on: "He watched her till she had gone in that house,
and he didn't look at her the way you think a white man look at a nigger woman,
either. He looked at her with love, and I mean the kind that's way deep inside
you" (180). And she concludes, "I have not seen too many men, of any color, look
at women that way. . . . His face scared me. I saw in his face he was ready to go
against his family, this whole world, for Mary Agnes" (180–81). Miss Jane decides to tell Miss Amma Dean, who immediately sets out to organize a party that
would link him publicly to an eligible white girl.

We discuss how this would have normalized the situation immediately, if only
Tee Bob had understood the issue. Instead, it is at this party that things come to
a head. Not knowing where to turn, Tee Bob confides in his best friend, Jimmy,
and, in Miss Jane's words, tells him "right there in front of him, in his own car,
and that rain falling outside," that he "loved a nigger woman more than he loved
his own life" (181). Jimmy naturally reacts by trying to teach Tee Bob the "truth"
that he himself had always been told and that Tee Bob ought to have learned
years before: "If you want her you go to that house and take her. If you want her
at that school, make them children go out in the yard and wait. Take her in that
ditch if you can't wait to get her home. But she's there for that and nothing else"
(183). What one encounters here, then, is a new, more profound return to the
interracial relationship as a gothic subject.

I now ask the students to identify the gothic elements that have been accu-
mulating. Some elements that they readily find are the following: to begin with,
the story of Mary Agnes and Tee Bob starts in a gothic borderland between life
and death, as he sees her for the first time at the wake of his uncle. The consequence is that, because she is wearing a black veil at that time, Tee Bob is unable to see her face, so the question of race does not pose itself except in the
mind of Miss Jane. When Tee Bob does see Mary Agnes's face a few days later,
this is the occasion that Miss Jane mentioned, where he almost faints, bringing
to mind another gothic borderland, that between consciousness and unconscious-
ness. By this time a student at Louisiana State University, Tee Bob obviously
has acquired at least some racial awareness. In any case, the discourse between
him and Miss Jane places itself clearly within the danger zone when he asks,
"That girl almost white, ain't she?" and she answers, "Almost, but not quite" (172).

The students will notice that the drama begins to approach a climax when Tee
Bob openly starts transgressing social borders, showing up at the black school

where Mary Agnes is a teacher and where a white man has never been seen. The young female student who happens to be present there gives a description of Tee Bob that makes the story dive still deeper into liminality, which Miss Jane, again with an attributive sentence with the verb *know*, summarizes as follows:

> If he was a man she would 'a' knowed this was no place for her and she would 'a' begged Miss LeFabre to let her be excused. But Tee Bob was not a man. His mouth was too red and soft, his eyes was too big and sorrowful. His skin wasn't rough enough. He didn't have a moustache. He had never shaved in his life, and he never would shave.   (174–75)

The last sentence, which leaves the point of view of the young student, is somewhat ambiguous, as it hovers between the possibility of Tee Bob bound to remain a sort of eunuch for the rest of his life, never turning into a man, and the possibility of his impending death, before he reaches his manhood. In either case, the story continues in the gothic vein, creating the additional borderlands between adolescence and adulthood and between man and woman, as well as deepening the one between life and death: a triple gothic liminality.

Mary Agnes may well try to conflate the categories, saying that Tee Bob is "more human being than he is white man" (178), and Miss Jane may well qualify his looking at her as not "the way you think a white man look at a nigger woman, either" (180), but the students will recognize that society's need for a clear distinction between categories is too deeply ingrained to allow for these liminalities to stand. Mary Agnes knows it and she knows that Tee Bob subconsciously knows it too; why else would he never have asked her to mount his horse or climb into his car? In any case, it is obvious to her that she cannot do so now, nor can she run away to New Orleans with him and live together as a white couple, no matter if he tells her that without her, he has "no place to go," he has nothing (186–87).

Some attention to symbolism is warranted here. Indeed, the crisis of the drama of Tee Bob and Mary Agnes sets in with a torrential rainstorm, punctuating the different movements of the plot, drawing a gothic veil of unreality across the events and drowning the history in celestial tears. When Mary Agnes is found on the floor of her room and Tee Bob is seen running away from the house, it seems obvious to the black people on the plantation that she has been "ravished," while one of the white workers reacts by saying that "if he [Tee Bob] hadn't done it, somebody else had to do it. Playing like she Miss high-class" (189). A discussion of the different stereotypes concerning black women—the mammy, the tragic mulatto, the jezebel—can be useful here so as to see clearly how the southern myth, especially that of the black jezebel, is alive and thriving. Miss Jane, as we have already seen, clearly occupies a border position here, being able to register both the black and the white reaction to the drama. Not only that, her narrative presents a series of images of liminality, with open doors, closed doors, halls between rooms, and thresholds abounding and with its climax the locked door to the library in which Tee Bob eventually both hides and imprisons himself.

I ask the students now to fully concentrate on this climactic scene, the chopping down of the library door with an ax. Its sound, compared with that of the thunderstorm going through the old house, seems like the ending of an era and its sad reflections. Indeed, pictures of ancestors shake "on every wall" and a looking glass falls, breaks, and scatters all "over the floor" (195). And the fact that Tee Bob, surrounded by the cultural products of his era—too many books about slavery; too many books about history—finally feels forced to kill himself with the letter opener that was once used by his lawyer grandfather at the capital in Baton Rouge, can be seen as an accusation against law and learning in the South. It is not surprising, then, that this shaking up of history and its representations forms the first announcement of an impending epiphany, the lifting of a veil, a peripatetic emerging of a new awareness concerning white as well as black. Here too we have another parallel to Poe's gothic story of the house of Usher, as the narrator and Roderick Usher contemplate the ghostly Madeline, who has somehow broken the bonds of the tomb and her burial chamber to confront the living. Tee Bob, by contrast, has encased himself in the tomb of the library, whose books, Gaines tells us, speak of history and slavery and of horrific legal codes used to enslave other human beings; this gothic chamber of horrors and its legacy have led to Tee Bob's realization of the curse that now demands his life.

This epiphany is finally voiced by Tee Bob's godfather, Jules Raynard, who believes that in the moment when the black girl was lying on the floor—after Tee Bob had swung her against the wall in anger—the borders between past and present had dissolved instantly, leaving the proud and self-sufficient girl as the ghost of her own grandmother, "looking helpless and waiting" and—maybe only for a second—inviting him to lie "down there on the floor" with her, because that was what was expected of her, to serve the white man's lust in the basest of ways (205). Thus, by making herself into a victim, in a borderland between past and present, the girl had, in Raynard's perception, tried subconsciously to avoid the gothic transgression that the love of Tee Bob asked of her, thus becoming an embodiment of Faulkner's idea that "the past is never dead."

In the same brief moment, when he saw the timeless glance in his beloved's eyes, Tee Bob, according to Raynard, suddenly understood the lesson that Timmy's fate should have taught him long ago. In that earlier instant, he had, indeed, felt "the old curse of his fathers" (113) descend to him, as Faulkner expresses it so beautifully with regard to his character Roth Edmonds in "The Fire and the Hearth." But instead of entering "his heritage" like Faulkner's character had done (113), accepting the white man's superiority and thus losing his black brother, Henry, forever, Tee Bob had refused, locking himself into the gothic confines of the double bind, from now until forever unable either to leave Mary Agnes, as this would deny his love for her, or to approach her, because it would be as a white man, making her into a whore and thus distancing himself from her as his beloved. In the words of Raynard, it was the sudden awareness of the godly power that southern society deals out to the white man that made Tee Bob flee and finally take his own life. It is this understanding upon which his epiphany rests:

> We all killed him. We tried to make him follow a set of rules our people gived us long ago. But these rules just ain't old enough, Jane. . . . Way, way back, men like Robert could love women like Mary Agnes. But somewhere along the way somebody wrote a new set of rules condemning all that. I had to live by them. . . . But Tee Bob couldn't obey. That's why we got rid of him. All us. Me, you, the girl—all us.   (204)

Students may see that in his godfather's words, Tee Bob becomes a Christ figure who had to die for the sins of everyone. We see, then, how the circle is closed, as the vision of Christ—taking over the burdens of Miss Jane and of everybody caught up in the aftermath of slavery—is given flesh in the interracial love story at the heart of the novel. As in the famous sermon in Dilsey's section of Faulkner's *The Sound and the Fury*, redemption is brought about in the physical presence and death of Christ himself.

But as students come to see, the gothic intrudes in the interracial love story because of the traditional "blackness" of the genre. As Goddu has shown, this element has historical connections to slavery, employing elements of "possession, the iconography of entrapment and imprisonment, and the familial transgressions"—all present in both the gothic and the slave system (73). Mary Agnes, though almost white, nevertheless raises horrific specters for Tee Bob's family, and the denouement of the two fated figures' relationship rehearses the myriad aspects of blackness as infection and horror, which an awareness of gothic conventions in literature can vitally underline for students.

NOTES

[1] This essay quotes from the 1972 Bantam edition of *Miss Jane*.

[2] For a full discussion of Faulkner's influence on Gaines, see Lowe, "From Yoknapa-tawpha."

[3] Even though Freud tries to discredit Jentsch's idea of this type of "intellectual uncertainty" at the heart of the uncanny, as Hugh Haughten writes in his introduction to the essay, Freud keeps returning to this issue all through his essay (Freud, *Uncanny* xliii).

[4] For a discussion of these various attributive clauses, see van der Leek.

Miss Jane's South:
Southern Literature, Intertextuality, and
The Autobiography of Miss Jane Pittman

Terrence Tucker

Ernest Gaines's *The Autobiography of Miss Jane Pittman* depicts a South that encompasses the richest period in the southern literary imagination. Gaines famously noted the influence of William Faulkner on his work and, as a result, our critical examination of Gaines has followed the typical intertextual path in considering how Gaines's work "speaks" to Faulkner's. We never consider, however, how Faulkner's work speaks to the world that Gaines has created. Additionally, the treatment of Gaines is emblematic of the larger relationship between southern and African American literature. The expansion of southern literature to include minority voices maintains the cultural capital of whiteness that privileges white southern narratives and conventions. While many critics, in expanding traditional southern literature to include African American authors, have noted the ways in which the South has influenced African American culture, I would ask that we begin to consider more seriously, when we talk about southern literature and culture, the deep influence of African American culture and tradition. Gaines is an important figure in considering this question, because Gaines casts African American voices as principal subjects in the formation of a distinct southern identity, instead of a subculture of the South, which is often seen as a subculture of America. I argue that teaching southern literature through Gaines's *Miss Jane* not only disrupts the traditional discourse of intertextuality, but it forces us to recognize the more central role African American cultural traditions play in the landscape out of which white southern writers construct their narratives. As we move to consider the relationship between southern and African American literature, I pose a simple question as part of teaching Gaines's novel: how does southern literature build off of and speak to Miss Jane Pittman's South?

What is often underappreciated about *Miss Jane* is its audacity. The novel shrewdly takes aim at the crucial one hundred years between the Civil War and the civil rights movement. They are the most explosive, influential, and transformative years in the racial, geographical, and mythological identity of the South. Miss Jane's life fits snugly within this period and circumvents our traditional understanding of these moments and their often nostalgic, often demonized status. She situates herself and her community at the center of her telling. Our concept of the Civil War still remains, in some respects, about what the war was fought about instead of whom the war was fought over. We often see it as a war about slavery as an ethical, philosophical, or political concept, as opposed to a war about the humanity or equality of African Americans. In Frederick Douglass's *My Bondage and My Freedom* (1855), we are informed that Douglass is continually introduced at antislavery lectures as "a *'chattel'*—a *'thing'*—a piece of southern 'property'—the chairman assuring the audience that *it* could speak" (265). We witness the sacrifice of the rights of African Americans as the price for the desired reunification of the nation after Reconstruction. Yet Gaines's novel establishes a clear subjectivity from the beginning that becomes impossible to deny. The reason for Miss Jane's consistent refusal to tell her story to the history teacher who interviews her becomes clearer after she finally agrees to tell her story, for Miss Jane's story is not merely about her, nor can it be told only in her voice. As the teacher notes, "The only thing that saved me was that there were other people at the house every day that I interviewed her," who "carried the story for her. When [Miss Jane] was tired, or when she just did not feel like talking any more, or when she had forgotten certain things, someone else would always pick up the narration" (vi–vii).[1] The novel becomes a collective history, which fundamentally disrupts traditional constructions of history and myth. The teacher initially pursues Miss Jane's story because he rightly recognizes that "she is not in [history books]," but this is too narrow. What becomes clear is that *the community* to which Miss Jane is intimately tied has gone unheard.

Trudier Harris is correct in suggesting, in *The Scary Mason-Dixon Line*, that most, if not all, African American works must wrestle with the South in their fiction, but Gaines has been consistently willing to confront the South on its own soil and through its own myths, because he feels a sense of ownership. His African Americans lay claim to the land and the culture surrounding it, even as whites attempt to exclude them. For example, in an interview with William Ferris, Gaines points out, "When a lot of black writers and white writers leave the South, they want to totally wipe it out of their minds. They don't want to remember it. Or if they remember it, they remember it as a place that was not a happy place in their lives. When Richard Wright left this country and got involved in something else, the writing that he did about this place just did not come through as truly as when he was there" (Gaines, "I Heard the Voices" 11). So while other works to which his is often, if wrongly, compared deal with the South as a traumatic space (Wright's *Uncle Tom's Children* and *Native Son*, for instance), Gaines has always been willing to claim the South as his own and to highlight the myths and traditions his characters forged in the wake of, and sometimes alongside, the historical events on which traditional narratives focus.

In teaching *Miss Jane* as a central text in southern literature, a natural intersection with Faulkner emerges, particularly *The Sound and the Fury*. The story of the Compson family focuses primarily on the impact of the four Compson children, especially the impact of the sister Caddy on her brothers. On a much larger scale, Faulkner's novel traces the changing dynamics of the South from the end of Reconstruction through the first three decades of the twentieth century. Like *Miss Jane*, *The Sound and the Fury* casts the changes to the postwar South through its racial volatility, existential crisis, and economic transformation. Faulkner's stream of consciousness captures the chaos, anxiety, and rage of the white South through the alienated voices of the brothers. The novel draws a portrait of the Compson family unable to deal with the changing South, embodied in their discomfort with Caddy's willingness to defy their preconceived notions of southern white womanhood. Their responses to the absent Caddy, then, become a lens through which we view their concerns about the changing South.

Gaines's primary method in making his claim for the land and for the South itself comes, as we know, through the invocation of black oral tradition and storytelling, through his attempt to capture how the members of his community "speak." Mary Ellen Doyle points out, "Among rural black folk, conversation and storytelling have long been the basic ways of gathering news, entertaining, and remembering history" (*"Autobiography"* 92). While we see a similar transition at work in southern culture and tradition, the rugged individualism that stands as a central tenet of America identity often produced a more contentious relationship between the individual and the community. Doyle posits in *"The Autobiography of Miss Jane Pittman* as a Fictional Edited Autobiography" that Gaines "wanted to cover a century of Miss Jane's life and that of her people, to make her a distinct individual with her own thoughts and feelings who could yet embody their common experience" (91). Here Gaines balances Western privileging of individualism that we see in *The Sound and the Fury* with the intimate and, more important, symbiotic relationship we often see in African American literary tradition. Gaines seizes upon the use of call-and-response that we find in African American oral tradition that encourages participatory experiences and extends it to the relationship between the text and the reader. Although Gaines has argued in favor of American authors' superior use of first-person perspective, his willingness to include multiple perspectives moves toward omniscience and resists the dependence on a single, often alienated voice. Gaines's multiple voices speak directly to the other narratives, revising, updating, or affirming one another as part of the collective move toward the "truth" Gaines captures. The novel—what Gaines has referred to as a "folk autobiography" (Rowell 94)—becomes one of a community, one in which Miss Jane has served as anchor, observer, teacher, and activist throughout her 110 years.

We frequently, and sensibly, compare Gaines with Faulkner, and it is clear from Gaines's own comments that Faulkner is an important influence on his own work. Yet I would suggest that Gaines's works are often more interested in a larger text—an extraliterary text—that, while encompassing Faulkner's canon, is rarely bound by it. Gaines's work most comfortably and directly speaks to and signifies on the South's mythic past and complex present. The South he sees is a contested site, one rooted in deep pride, tradition, and defiance. Even as the United States increasingly comes to see itself as a cohesive whole, the South maintains its distinctiveness, indeed an autonomy that nonetheless impacts the cultural atmosphere and discourse. While the South's protection of its sovereignty has produced a significant amount of cultural and economic capital, it remains based on a perspective that not only ignores but marginalizes African American influence. *Miss Jane* centralizes a collective perspective and, perhaps more important, uses its narrative authority and autonomy to interrogate southern myth and history in a language that is distinctly black. Its source material, then, becomes that of the griot and the bluesman instead of the plantation owner or the poor whites in Faulkner. The mourning that we hear in Gaines's novel is not for the erosion of the land or antebellum southern culture as we see in white southern texts but for the reconstituting of slavery through segregation and sharecropping.

Let me suggest, for instance, that instead of the traditional intertextual reading that finds Gaines responding or speaking to the world that Faulkner creates in *The Sound and the Fury*, and eventually *Absalom, Absalom!*, that those novels speak to the landscape to which Miss Jane has laid claim. The presence of Miss Jane as a central, active subject and storyteller produces the anxiety that permeates *The Sound and the Fury*. Caddy's assertion of her subjectivity is similarly viewed with a fear, dread, and anger on which her brothers fixate and link to notions of blackness as part of the material political reality of African American subjectivity postslavery. Gaines's novel exposes the crisis that the brothers experience through their fixation on Caddy. Their imposition of their own anxieties and desires is part of their concerns with legacy and gender. So, Quentin's lament, *"Caddy? Why must you do like nigger women do in the pasture the ditches the dark woods hot hidden furious in the dark woods"* (92), reveals his assumptions about black sexuality, just as Jason's anger toward Caddy's daughter, which plays itself out in attempts to restrict her, reveals the misogyny behind the proclamations of protecting white womanhood. Reducing white female behavior as either befitting the suffocating, unrealistic pedestal of white womanhood or the "nigger wench" Jason casts his niece as speaks to the deep intimacy between notions of blacks and the white South. Thus, attempts to cast the Civil War, Reconstruction, states' rights, labor, and femininity apart from race fall apart in *The Sound and the Fury*.

Richard Godden's "Quentin Compson: Tyrrhenian Vase or Crucible of Race?" suggests, "By the mid 1880s the problem appeared to have worsened in that a generation of young blacks was coming to manhood without the 'civilizing' effects of slavery" (105). Miss Jane's adopted son, Ned Douglass, clearly becomes the embodiment of white fears of blacks who "don't know their place" with the absence of slavery. The decision to kill Ned acts as part of what Godden calls "the weaponry of Jim Crowism (disenfranchisement, segregation, lynching)" (106) that whites used against African Americans after Reconstruction; he points out, "White self-revision turned on the image of the black male. The plot runs as follows: during the antebellum period, Southern white males of the owning class idealized womanhood, by raising the female gentry on pedestals above the reality of interracial sex between slave women and slave owners" (106). For example, the imposition of blackness onto Caddy's body also occurs in *Light in August*, when Joe Christmas is accused of murder—an act that attempts to rein in the chaos that surrounds the community stemming from Christmas's uncertain racial heritage. It mirrors the attempts by the Klan and other lynch mobs to reestablish clear racial distinctions and hierarchies at a moment when modernism (or at least the Depression) threatened to reorganize fundamental concepts of

American identity. In Miss Jane's South, of course, this means the inclusion of Cajuns, who often serve as chief foils in Gaines's fiction. In *Miss Jane*, the Cajun assassin Albert Cluveau becomes a central figure. Hired by whites to kill Miss Jane's surrogate son, Ned Douglass, Cluveau is also Miss Jane's fishing companion. Yet for a man who, as Miss Jane says, "had killed so many people he couldn't talk about nothing else but that" (108), he shows telling ambivalence before killing Ned. He informs Miss Jane when complaints about Ned begin, and when he is asked to kill Ned, he tells Miss Jane that he responded by saying, "If [Ned] must stop, let [the other assassin] Maurios stop him. Not Albert. Albert and Jane, side by side, fish there in the St. Charles River" (110). What the novel reveals here is the intimacy between African Americans and whites in the South, one that has often resulted in the sharing of cultural traditions and rituals. Cluveau's eventual murder of Ned, committed because, as Cluveau confesses to Miss Jane, "I must do what they tell me," suggests that he remains bound to the authority of the whites of the area. His status as a white man, clearly impacted by the lens of America's racial dichotomy, remains tenuous and demands a strict adherence to a racial code that speaks to the more complex universe that Miss Jane details by reinscribing racial hierarchies that exclude African Americans and privilege whites in the formation and maintenance of southern identity and narrative.

We see a similar process at work in *The Sound and the Fury* as the Compson brothers attempt to reinscribe patriarchal control over the Compson legacy, either through their memory of Caddy or through her daughter. Caddy's consistent defiance of patriarchal norms upends the lives of each brother and, as with the whites in *Miss Jane*, the Compson brothers react violently in an attempt to restore their sense of normalcy. Frederick Hoffman rightly points out that Benjy lives "in a fixed world outside of time and change. Benjy does not want change; it upsets him," and his section presents us with "a simple world, from which all decline and decay and breakdown are to begin" (53–54). Quentin longs for a world as fixed as Benjy's, even as the mourning we experience in Benjy's chapter emerges from our realization of Benjy's disability. Quentin's ability to articulate his position reveals the larger implications for the world he seeks to preserve. The novel exposes Benjy's desire for Caddy's nurturing as connected to the larger misogynist expectation of southern womanhood to which Quentin and Jason expect her to submit. Her relationship with her lover Dalton Ames challenges their expectation of sexual purity, and the absence of any economic benefit in her intended marriage to Herbert Head informs us of how deeply connected the South remains to Victorian notions of both (white) womanhood generally and the female body specifically. Quentin and Jason cast her behavior as consistent with that of a "nigger wench" as a way to uphold their preconceived gendered and racial expectations. They simultaneously bind white women to the role of object upon which the moral and economic culture of the South rests, while relegating black women to sexual objects whose bodies exist for either white pleasure or labor.

Godden calls *The Sound and the Fury* "difficult, unfinishable, and torn apart by contradiction" (133), in large part because of its inability to reconcile questions about the Compson brothers' history, their legacy, and their sister. The interior monologues exacerbate the novel's modernist sense of alienation and make the resolution of the Compson men's various perceptions impossible. Without the creation of a space where their perceptions, anxieties, and memories can be explored, the contradictions from their incomplete one-dimensional portraits collapse in their minds, leading to an increasing dread and estrangement expressed in their chapters. The mourning in *The Sound and the Fury* emerges from the anxiety caused by the Reconstruction period when African Americans began to collectively move toward agency; the Compsons' fixation on Caddy represents a desire to return to an "innocence" that allows them to reimagine a romanticized past. A significant part of teaching *Miss Jane* is examining the novel's production of a space where Miss Jane and other members of the black community piece together Miss Jane's life and the lives of the black community at large. Instead of disconnection or alienation, we see a collection of voices working in concert, contesting existing perspectives and filling in gaps to create a fuller portrait of the narrative.

Not surprisingly, much of southern literature's lionizing of Faulkner resulted in works where characters (or the authors) devoted themselves to the romanticizing and maintenance of white privilege, an act that has frequently downplayed the intimate cultural relationships between African Americans and whites in the South. If not consciously done, then it has been necessitated by the tones at work in southern literature. So the rage and mourning that we see in Faulkner's *The Sound and the Fury* and William Styron's *The Confessions of Nat Turner* are inseparable from the vision of African American perspective and power as a disruptive, destructive force. In Styron's controversial novel, the decline of the land coincides with Turner's rebellion, a moment that is teeming—at least in Styron's narration—with uncontrolled rage and sexual desire and dysfunction. With Turner's voice as the central and lone black voice in the novel, the voices of other members of the African American community are often excluded or marginalized. Readers are led to ignore those voices and fear the insatiable sexual desire and the uncontrolled, pathological violence of Turner's rebels. In Gaines's novel we hear those voices and perspectives that reinforce alongside others that challenge. The multitude of voices provides a context that moves beyond the depiction of African Americans as either passive spectators or hated participants in the downfall of a beloved antebellum South.

Faulkner's African American characters frequently bear witness to the fall of his white aristocratic families and, in some cases, are the only heirs to the flawed, disintegrating legacy of the South. In *Absalom, Absalom!*, African Americans are frequently objects of anxiety and fascination for white characters, objects whose attempts to assert their subjectivity usually lead to violence, sexual confusion, and destruction for the white characters. Thomas Sutpen is unable to separate his narrative of the self-made man from the racial violence of his past or the grand vision of his legacy from the reality that his interracial son, Charles

Bon, has as much claim on that legacy as his younger children, Henry and Judith Sutpen. The murder of Charles at the hands of Henry is not simply about denying him Judith's hand in marriage, a marriage that Henry had consistently supported; it is about the fear of his blackness, whether it is Charles's legal claims to the plantation Sutpen's Hundred, anger over the possibility of interracial sex with his sister, or the anxiety of his own erotic feelings toward Charles. Charles and eventually his half sister Clytie become the chief witnesses and agents of the destruction of Sutpen's Hundred, Charles in terms of what he represents and Clytie in literally burning down the main house. More important here, however, is that Charles and Clytie become the chief targets of blame for the fate of the Sutpen legacy. They have no story outside the presence or the imagination of the Sutpens' narrative. It is here where reading Faulkner through the lens of *Miss Jane*, as opposed to the other way around, provides us with a fuller, deeper portrait of African American life in the South. In particular, the agency of Gaines's African American characters—Ned or Jane's husband, Joe Pittman, for example—exists outside the perspective of the white characters in the novel and exposes an emergent and complex culture that Faulkner does not provide through his isolated and often tormented black characters.

Perhaps the clearest difference lies between Faulkner's depiction of the Compsons' maid, Dilsey, and Miss Jane herself. Dilsey's presence in *The Sound and the Fury* may be a dominant one in the final section of the novel, but it comes at the expense of the other African Americans on the land. Her focus and her concern center around the state of the Compson legacy, of which she claims to have seen the beginning and the end and to which she believes she is bearing witness. She defends Benjy against the blacks and whites who object to her taking him to church, and she is single-minded in her approach to bringing order to a house filled with the chaos of Mrs. Compson's paralysis, Jason's rage, and Benjy's mind. It is here that Faulkner's portrait of Dilsey becomes instructive, for he reveals the ways in which the chaos of white southern identity and myth centers on intimate relationships with Africans Americans. However, this portrait is inseparable from a narrow viewing of the relationship, one that reinscribes the racial hierarchy and a specific concept of blackness. That concept relies on an unyielding black loyalty to whites that supersedes their own community and finds, as in *The Sound and the Fury*, African Americans more interested in upholding the mythic southern narrative instead of considering the ways in which their voice and perspective inherently problematize and reject it.

By contrast, in discussing *Miss Jane*, Gaines has said, "the difference between Dilsey and Miss Jane Pittman is that Faulkner gets Dilsey talking her story from his kitchen; the young school teacher in my book gets Miss Jane's story from Miss Jane's kitchen. And it makes a difference" (Lowe, "Interview" 313). The space of the kitchen becomes significant because it allows stories that are told from a site of authority and eventually leads to a collective call-and-response approach that fundamentally rejects the singular, exclusive perspective that is traditionally used. In the Compsons' (Faulkner's) kitchen, it is the mere presence of black people that transforms them into objects upon which the white characters project their anxieties and rage or through which the end of the antebellum South can be passively observed. From Miss Jane's kitchen, African Americans are active participants in claiming their humanity. In *The Sound and the Fury*, Dilsey becomes the stabilizing force as the Compsons transition from their aristocratic glory to the working-class brutality that Jason represents. She is tasked with protecting and preserving the Compson legacy, without any sense of her life outside the needs of Benjy, Mrs. Compson, and Jason. Miss Jane, by contrast, leaves the main house on the plantation in order to have her own house in the quarters with the rest of the black community. Her desire to build a life outside the world of the Samson family, who owns the plantation, allows Gaines to deepen his portrait of the African American community—as opposed to Dilsey's relative isolation—and forge an identity that is based on African American oral culture's desire to embrace the full range of African American humanity. We see this especially at the end of the novel, when Miss Jane decides to protest segregation in Bayonne during the civil rights movement. When Jimmy Aaron, a young man born in the quarters of the Samson plantation where Miss Jane lives, attempts to recruit the community to protest the segregated bathrooms and drinking fountains in the town, Miss Jane is supportive. Although many of the other blacks have invested in Jimmy in the hopes that he will be the community's savior, they are afraid that if they join the protests, they will be kicked off the plantation, despite having lived there for decades. Here, Gaines characterizes Miss Jane's decision to continue with the protest as less about the end of the white South and more about her desire to honor Jimmy's sacrifice and to take responsibility for achieving her humanity. The scope of Gaines's novel—not just the years it covers but the full depiction of the lives of African Americans, Cajuns and working-class whites, and white plantation owners—makes it a foundational text in southern literature and an ideal lens through which we can read other, earlier writers. The novel destabilizes the master narrative often presented by white writers of the southern literary renaissance by allowing readers to more fully conceive of the African American characters in works that relegate African Americans to passive objects or as isolated, self-hating observers.

In *Miss Jane*, Ned Douglass proclaims,

> This earth is yours and don't let that man out there take it from you. . . . It's yours because your people's bones lay in it; it's yours because their sweat and their blood done drenched this earth. . . . No, your people plowed this earth, your people chopped down the trees, your people built the roads and built the levees. These same people is now buried in this earth, and their bones's fertilizing this earth.   (112–13)

Ned's contention invokes the labor and struggle during and after slavery as a primary reason for African Americans to lay claim to their world. His link of that labor and struggle to the land, to the earth in which countless anonymous African Americans had sweat, bled, and died, is characteristic of southern literature's intimate relationship to the land. Instead of viewing the southern landscape as a site from which to escape to the urban North, Gaines's work lays claim to it and, in the process, challenges the larger southern myths and traditions that have excluded or marginalized an African American community and culture from which much of what we describe as southern emanates.

As many African Americans return from the North to a post–civil rights, twenty-first-century South, we must embrace a more inclusive and fluid method of conceiving and maintaining southern identity, history, and myth. However, we risk replicating our tendency to treat minority perspectives as additions to a master narrative of the South. Instead, the presence of African American migrants in the South and African American authors in the southern literary tradition should realign fundamental assumptions of voice, narrative, and authority as we begin to consider the modern African American community and its impact on the South and America at large. *Miss Jane* begins this work by reimagining the crucial century between the Civil War and the civil rights movement. More specifically, it is not just the presence of African Americans but the recognition of the ways in which African American cultural tradition has acted as a primary element in the formation of southern culture. In much the same way jazz was primarily driven by black cultural tradition, we must begin to consider how southern literature has been driven not merely by race and racism but by the voices and rituals of African Americans. John Callahan states, "Gaines keeps faith with the oral tradition—a tradition of responsibility and change, and, despite violent opposition, a tradition of citizenship. In turn, his novel's spirit of call-and-response invites readers to pick up the loose ends, join in the storytelling, and, like Miss Jane Pittman, come home" (*In the African-American Grain: Call and Response* 214). Gaines has suggested that if there is to be an audience for which he writes, it would be the black and white youth of the South, with the clear implication that the next generation of the South has the opportunity to create a more inclusive southern identity that is based on the equality of perspectives and a relationship that finds the voices of black and white youth speaking to each other as a way of building a new and distinct southern myth and tradition. Instead of relying on a single perspective or master narratives that limit form, concept, and experience, we will see texts and stories speaking to each other and creating a dynamic, complex, and collective narrative that can be consistently revised and updated and that builds on the cultural capital that has emerged and has served as the backbone for America's racial and national identity.

NOTE

[1] This essay quotes from the 1972 Bantam edition of *Miss Jane*.

Humor and Folk Culture in
The Autobiography of Miss Jane Pittman

John Wharton Lowe

Ernest Gaines's enduring masterwork *The Autobiography of Miss Jane Pittman* has often been admired as a meticulously crafted work of fiction that mimics the nonfictional form of autobiography and as one of the best examples of the neo–slave narrative. It has just as often been praised, however, as a valuable reflection, albeit fictional, of actual history, as it views a turbulent hundred years of our nation's past through the eyes of a black woman. The novel's signal strength is the degree in which both these modes and several others are enhanced and, indeed, made magnetic through the use of humor and folk culture. Characters engage in conversation with Miss Jane and one another in a dazzling mix of Louisiana voices and cultures, from the inhabitants of the big house to the field hands; from the decorous Creole schoolmarm to the raucous Cajun roustabout. All of these voices summon up pungent, local forms of address and expression, and the common people depicted provide, through their richly figured speech, indelible portraits of folk culture and a shrewd awareness of the uses of comic expression. To Gaines's credit, his narrative demonstrates that comic uses of vernacular and folklore are dynamic, anything but static, and are reflective of changing times, both in the region and the nation.

As I tell my students, any discussion of Gaines's oeuvre must take into account his reiteration that he is writing about peasant culture and its folk traditions, a perception that led him to rely on Russian writers for models:

> I wanted to read about my people in the South. . . . When I did not find my people in the Southern writers, I started reading books about the peasantry in other places. I read the John Steinbeck people of the Salinas Valley, the Chicanos as well as the poor whites. . . . I went into the Russians and I liked what they were doing with their stories on the peasantry; the peasants were real human beings, whereas in the fiction of American writers . . . they were caricatures.　　(O'Brien, "Ernest J. Gaines" 28)

On another occasion, he complained, "Northern liberals and radical whites were the only people who bought the works of Black writers, and they didn't care for tales about Black peasantry. I think they were much more concerned with the Black problem than with the Black Character" (Carter 83).

The comic and folk aspects of *Miss Jane* can and should be stressed in the classroom, for several reasons. I have students focus on particular scenes where Gaines's characters engage in vibrant dialogue and verbal dueling, activities that indicate the instructive and corrective aspects of comic conventions, which might be read merely as folk forms of entertainment. We also examine Gaines's "speakerly" participation in the community through his vernacular descriptions of daily rural life, usually—but not always—through the perceptions of Miss Jane.

Students see that Miss Jane offers examples of folk humor and wisdom repeatedly. On the first page, when she ignores her friend Mary's advice to say nothing to the eager young history teacher who wants to transcribe her story, she says, "If I don't he go'n just worry me to death" (v).[1] This teacher, we remember, wants her story because he thinks it will help him explain things to his students. In this respect the "lesson" Miss Jane teaches is similar in utility to the one taught by the example of the condemned prisoner Jefferson in Gaines's later masterwork *A Lesson Before Dying*; there the story is meant for the teacher Grant Wiggins's students, the rising generation, who need to know in their turn the concept Gaines cites in his dedication to *Miss Jane*, the "importance of standing." Miss Jane's lessons, however, are made lively and entertaining by her shrewd wit, sense of irony, and pungent insertion of folk sayings.

She also speaks in dialect, which has been used by whites in literary depictions to demean blacks. Gaines, however, like Zora Neale Hurston before him, understands the creative and subversive potential of black language and uses it to show us Miss Jane's mockery of her white masters. She takes license to reconstruct the parting words of her master as he leaves for war: "Don't put my food up . . . don't give it away. I'm go'n kill me up a few Yankees and I'm coming right on back home. Who they think they is trying to destruck us way of living? We the nobels, not them. God put us here to live the way we want live, that's in the Bible," to which Miss Jane adds, "I have asked people to find that in the Bible for me, but no one's found it yet" (4).

Students always appreciate the ways in which this elderly narrator makes the dry subject of history palatable through her modes of narration. Reconstruction politics, for instance, is handled humorously, through the comedy of metamorphosis (which of course traditionally involves animal forms). The turncoat black Democrats are said to have white mouths and a tail. Miss Jane hears one speak in Alexandria: "When a nigger Democrat got up on the platform, somebody hollered, 'Pull his pants down, let's see his tail. We already seen he got a white mouth.' The nigger Democrat said, 'I rather be a Democrat with a tail than be a Republican that ain't had no brains.' The people on the Democrat side laughed and clapped . . ." (67). But the humor, as so often is the case in this book, leads to violence, and Miss Jane and Ned have to take shelter under the platform as the men fight.

Later in the book, animal signification is used for another purpose. Miss Jane's favorite, Jimmy, who will grow up to be "the one" and a leader in the civil rights movement, leaves the quarters to visit New Orleans. His usual duty of writing letters for illiterate elders falls on a substitute: "we got that ugly boy there of Coon to read and write for us. That boy was ugly as a monkey and had ways twice as bad. He had a little ugly brown dog that used to follow him everywhere, and the children here in the quarters used to call the dog Monkey Boy Dog. The dog's name was Dirt, but the children . . . called him Monkey Boy Dog" (205). This

boy's discourtesy to his elders is underlined beforehand by this comic signification, but the passage also underlines Jimmy's very serious function in the community, which has much invested in his future.

Miss Jane's folk idiom boils things down to their essence, an invaluable tool in
Gaines's economical rendition of history, and we all know the old saw that "brev-
ity is the soul of wit." Her summaries of remembered times and events are often
colorful but concise: "He [Ned] stayed there [Kansas] till that war started in Cuba,
then he joined the army. After the war he came back here. He wanted to teach at
home now" (80). In two sentences students learn about black participation in the
Spanish-American War and find a way to date the events of the book, the war
having taken place in 1898. Here and elsewhere, Miss Jane's oral tradition is notably lacking in actual time markers. I encourage students to talk about the ways in
which supposedly uneducated people can understand and interpret history quite
well, and I ask them to provide examples from their own families and experiences.

As I point out to students, Gaines also uses humor to animate conversations
of his white characters, even when they are speaking of serious matters. When
the white Tee Bob's parents are concerned about his attention toward the Creole of color Mary Agnes, the unsaid thing (which we readers know) is that Tee
Bob's father, Robert, sired a black son himself. When Robert tells his wife, Amma
Dean, that he understands the situation, she says, with heavy irony, "You ought
to know. . . . No more Timmy Hendersons," referring to the name of her husband's bastard. Robert replies, "Whoa, Eve, don't touch that apple" (170), a comic
rejoinder to a serious charge, enabling the couple to dance around the issue.

When Jane and Joe Pittman live on the Louisiana-Texas border, where he has
a good job breaking horses, Jane starts to have dreams about his violent death.
Joe deals with it humorously: "Now, little mama, man come here to die, didn't
he? That's the contract he signed when he was born—'I hereby degree that one
of these days I'm go'n lay down these old bones.' . . . When the time come for
them to lay you down in that long black hole, they can say one thing: 'He did it
good as he could'" (89–90). Through folk humor, we perceive Joe's courage and
determination, as he thumbs his nose at racially determined fate. And when Jane
sees the black stallion Joe has to break one week and recognizes it as the horse
in her dreams, Joe laughs; when he tells the folks around, they laugh too: "'Well,
if Joe don't ride him, reckoned I'll have to do it,' Clyde said. When he said that
the rest of the men laughed even harder. Joe laughed so much he cried. He was
Chief" (90). Here again, Gaines shows the role of humor in black male bravado,
as the men face the dangerous jobs they must accept to make a good living. Students can easily relate to these exchanges, particularly the male students.

By contrast, Albert Cluveau, the Cajun assassin who kills Ned, crosses over
into black culture; for years he is Miss Jane's fishing companion on the river. Her
description of him proves comically blunt and telling: "A short bowlegged
Cajun. Face looked like somebody had been jobbing in it with an ice pick. Had
that big patch of hair out the left side of his head, his head white where the hair

had been. Sitting there telling me about the people he had killed" (102). This passage is in keeping with the traditional stereotyping of Cajuns by blacks. As Gaines has stated, "[M]y people were sharecroppers. . . . Their competitors were the Cajuns, the white people there. The people you make fun of more are the people who are closer to you. So when my people had to make fun of something, when they had to laugh, they made fun of the whites. You always make fun of your competitors" (Fitzgerald and Marchant 9).

An important part of the book comes from its rendition of rural labor. Gaines himself was sent to work in the fields as a child, and he clearly desires the reader to become acquainted with the humorous rituals of the field. Toby is the best field hand and often engages in working duels with others, which are paralleled with comic verbal dueling. These lighthearted contests, however, have a tragic counterpart. Harriet Black is called Black Harriet because, Miss Jane explains, via comic (and negative) significations, "She was so black (she was one of them Singalee people). . . . She didn't have all her faculties, but still she was queen of the field . . . tall, straight, tough, and blue-black." Harriet is challenged by Katie Nelson,

> a little tight-butt woman from Bayonne. No kin at all to the Nelsons on the St. Charles River. They wouldn't own her. What sent Katie to Samson with that little red nigger she called a husband, only God knows. He looked about much a husband as one of them fence posts. Soon as she got in the field she started running off at the mouth. "I'm go'n beat her. Queen, huh? Well, she ain't go'n be no queen for long. You wait, I'm go'n queen her." . . . One morning she came out there and said: "This the morning. That man I got gived me so much loving last night I'm just rarrying to go. . . . Watch out there, queen of spade, here I come." (131)

This passage affords an opportunity to explain the convention of comic signifying to students. This comically promising duel, Miss Jane tells us, has them "all for it. . . . That's how it was in the field. You wanted that race. That made the day go. Work, work, you had to do something to make the day go. . . . We all knowed Katie couldn't beat Harriet, but we thought the race would be fun" (131). I explain to students how work songs, impromptu games, and verbal dueling involving signification helped relieve the tedium and exhaustion that backbreaking field work generated.

And there is more: in a startling flash-forward, Miss Jane tells us that trying to catch Harriet was "like me trying to fight Liston." Katie's taunts to Harriet are cruelly based on color: "Queen of spade . . . I'm go'n run all that black off you. When I get through with you you go'n be white as snowman" (132). Here, Gaines is rehearsing the many jokes in black culture told by lighter-skinned citizens about their darker kin. I usually bring in some examples from Zora Neale Hurston's folklore collections to illustrate this point further.

At this juncture in her significations, Miss Jane switches the mode from comedy to tragedy: "This world is so strange. Now, why a Katie Nelson? What good

is one? Why here with that little red nigger she called a husband? Why not
Baton Rouge? New Orleans? Why not the North? Huh? Tell me" (132). This
ending, "Tell me," engages the reader and is often used in black storytelling—
Hurston employs it frequently in her autobiography in the same way, in a series
of rhetorical questions, when she is describing her troubles with mathematics:
"Why should A be minus B? Who the devil was X anyway? I could not even
Imagine. I still do not know" (*Dust Tracks* 155).

The race drives Harriet mad: "Harriet was just laying there laughing and talking in that Singalee tongue. Looking at us with her eyes all big and white one
second . . . then all of a sudden just bust out laughing" (133); the people take her
to the state asylum at Jackson, and the bosses fire Katie. This section is mark-
edly like the ending of William Faulkner's *As I Lay Dying*, where Darl collapses
into mad laughter as he too is taken to a town called Jackson. But here the tragedy emerges from folk field ritual and color prejudice within the race. Hurston
spoke about this issue too: "I found the . . . blackest Negro, being made the butt
of all jokes—particularly black women. They brought bad luck for a week if they
came to your house of a Monday morning. They were evil. They slept with their
fists balled up ready to fight . . . even while they were asleep. . . . [They] dreamed
about guns, razors, ice-picks, hatchets and hot lye" (*Dust Tracks* 225). Gaines
thus indicates how the comic tradition Hurston describes in folk culture can
ultimately lead to tragedy.

I have discovered that the source for this episode must be Solomon Northup's *Twelve Years a Slave* (1853), a classic Louisiana slave narrative that is now
familiar to students because of the 2013 film. The slave Patsey is "queen of the
field": "such lightning-like motion was in her fingers as no other fingers ever pos-
sessed" (143)—yet Patsey is caught in a terrible dilemma, for her master repeatedly rapes her, leading to brutal lashings ordered by her mistress. The
name Gaines chooses for his version of Patsey is taken from that character's
best friend, Harriet. Eventually, Patsey is publicly beaten by Northup himself,
on orders of his master, and then by the master, so brutally that she is completely broken in spirit and body for life. Northrup published this episode sepa-
rately in northern newspapers, and it added substantially to the literature
against slavery as it was endlessly reprinted.

Gaines has told me in conversation that orally transmitted cultural memories
from the folk like these can be precious *lieux des mémoires*. Part of his planning for writing *Miss Jane* consisted of talking with the great black poet Alvin
Aubert about how Gaines's aunt Augusteen and her friends would have covered
the great events of their time in their "porch talk." One of the subjects they spec-
ulated about was the Great Flood of 1927, which was commemorated in varied
registers of the folk consciousness. Gaines also claims that folk-engendered
songs—particularly the blues—can encapsulate events:

> And though Mozart and Haydn soothe my brain while I write, neither can
> tell me about the Great Flood of '27 as Bessie Smith or Big Bill Broonzy

can. And neither can describe Louisiana State Prison at Angola as Lead-belly can. . . . William Faulkner writes over one hundred pages describing the Great Flood of '27 in his story "Old Man." Bessie Smith gives us as true a picture in twelve lines.   (Gaines, *Mozart* 27–28)

Here I ask students if they know of any songs that epitomize an event in this way—one response has been the song "Woodstock."

Another important Louisiana event, the assassination of Huey Long, forms one of Miss Jane's key memories and another of her succinct and ironic summations: "he did call the colored people nigger. But when he said nigger he said, 'Here a book, nigger. Go read your name.' When the other ones said nigger they said, 'Here a sack, nigger. Go pick that cotton'" (151). Miss Jane's account of the folk gathering, weeping, and praying for the dying Long echoes what the great sociologist St. Clair Drake told me, in a personal conversation, about being in a small Louisiana town square just after Long was shot: both poor whites and blacks were weeping over Long. Miss Jane's summation implicitly links Long with her Ned—"Look like every man that pick up the cross for the poor must end that way" (153)—a pronouncement that also looks forward to Jimmy's death and those of John and Robert Kennedy, Malcolm X, and Martin Luther King, Jr. This offers an opportunity to quiz students on similar figures and events in the history of the United States and to help them see different moments of change and improvements in racial history, which have often come at tremendous cost.

Miss Jane has more of a religious stance in the last part of the book, partly because she has found religion and partly because she has seen a connection between the biblical tales of bondage and liberation and the unfolding civil rights drama—a vision she is obviously better equipped for since her conversion. Her faith keeps her hoping for a Messiah, and one appears. Jimmy's birth in the quarters comes under a lucky star, for "Joe [Louis] had just tanned S'mellin [Max Schmeling]" (200). This is a useful teaching moment, for students learn about the initial advent of blacks into the American sporting scene and masculine folk culture, something today's youth often think has been a norm. I also tell them how the community will often single out a promising youth as "the one," a figure who will achieve literacy and go on to provide leadership for the community; I reveal that Gaines himself was "the one" for Cherie Quarters.

When Miss Jane decides to move out of the Samson house and into the quarters, she asks permission, causing a comic outburst on Robert Samson's part that is straight out of Faulkner: "You asking me? I didn't know I was still running Samson. I thought you was. I thought it was up to you to tell me when you wanted to move and where. And it was my duty to go down there and clean up the place for you. To run a special pipe down there. . . . To run a special line of lectwicity. . . . I thought that was my duty at Samson. Is I done missed out on a duty?" (201–02). The speech, while meant to be amusing, actually serves Robert's purpose, for it points to the absurdity of a servant who hasn't done much work in a decade receiving all these favors from the patriarch of the plantation. But at the same time, as I show the students, the comic tirade endorses the old formulaic fiction that a beloved servant is "like one of the family" and thereby fosters a benevolent, altruistic image of the employer/master. Students see that the exchange also offers evidence of a long-term joking relationship between master and servant, but one that is clearly not equal, for Jane has fewer options in their verbal duels because of her status. The white patriarch/employer, however, clearly enjoys the joking relationship in that it creates the illusion of kinship that joking relationships always suggest.

Miss Jane makes it clear that Jimmy becomes who he is by listening to the voices of the people as they pass the world through their mouths on the gallery, employing mockery and exaggeration. His precocious oratorical talents increase the certainty that he's "the one." We soon see that being "the one" establishes a set of rituals, such as keeping the initiate out of harm's way—no fighting, no reckless play. His role in reading the papers to the elders and writing their letters echoes that of Gaines when he was a young boy. Miss Jane relishes the funnies: "See what devilment they in this time." He also reads to her about baseball, which became a central fascination for African Americans when the game was integrated. Gaines uses Miss Jane to reveal what Jackie Robinson meant for the black folk: "Jackie and the Dodgers was for the colored people; the Yankees was for the white folks. Like in the Depression, Joe Louis was for the colored. When times get really hard, really tough, He always send you somebody" (203).

Jimmy's role as "the one" also gets established by contrast, as Miss Jane and the community signify on Jimmy's replacement while he is in New Orleans. Miss Jane refers to the sub dismissively as that "ugly boy there of Coon" (205). His dog, Dirt, echoes his nickname, for the children take to calling the dog "Monkey Boy Dog." His worst fault, however, lies in being literal when writing letters for the illiterate. He doesn't know how to embroider and embellish them the way Jimmy does, for Jimmy knows the people's dreams and aspirations, aligning him with other racial leaders such as King, who is referred to by Charles Johnson, in the title of his book on King, as "Dreamer." Indeed, the sub scorns embellishment and comments sarcastically and tellingly, "Let preachers tell them lies" (205), to which Miss Jane comments, "Oh, he was evil, that boy" (205).

When Jimmy returns to the community to enlist its aid in the civil rights marches, Gaines punctuates the very serious meeting at the church with a bit of byplay between Jane and Head Deacon Just Thomas, who resents Jane's telling him to shut up:

> He always kept a pocket handkerchief with him to wipe his bald head—keep it from shining all over the place. Now he started shaking that wet, dirty handkerchief at me. "That's why they took the mother from you," he said [Jane had been church mother]. "If you ain't arguing bout something you don't know nothing bout, you at that house listening to those sinful baseball games." (227)

Of course, Elder Banks—literally a doubting Thomas—is opposed to the people's involvement in the struggle and is castigated by the young as a "handkerchief head"—hence the sly hidden message in Gaines's seemingly irrelevant wordplay between Jane and Banks. This scene requires some foregrounding for it to fully resonate with students, but they respond to the humor and hypocrisy easily.

Miss Jane's attitude toward civil rights proves informative, for she engages with the movement only through Jimmy, not through his friend, the "long headed" boy with steel-rimmed glasses who clearly reveals his dictie-outsider status by affectedly wearing overalls and clodhoppers on Sunday and by praising the "good country lemonade" (228). Miss Jane bridles at his statement that "your mere presence at the demonstrations will bring forth multitudes": "'They teach you to talk like that?' I just looked at him. 'That's retrick,' he said. 'Well, I can do without your retrick here. . . . If you can't say nothing sensible, don't say nothing'" (230). Here, as students recognize, folk wisdom comically trumps "book larnin'."

In one of the key uses of humor in a doubled way, Jane tells us about the racist refusal to let colored folk try on clothes in Bayonne's stores. This is illustrated by Unc Gilly, who buys a pair of overalls "big enough for two people. . . . If the people didn't carry Unc Gilly a dog's life in these quarters. Robert Samson teased him as much as the colored did. Every time he saw Unc Gilly in them big overalls he started laughing. When Unc Gilly died, Matt Jefferson mentioned them overalls at the wake. Unc Gilly laying up there in his coffin and the people thinking about foolish things like that" (231). Students note that Robert's white laughter must be quite different from that of the folk. I observe that the people's making a joke out of the outrage of the fitting room instead of demonstrating offers a good example of what Rose Coser describes as disabling humor, when, for instance, mistreated patients at hospitals make jokes among themselves about the conditions without actually accosting the staff.

Miss Jane also uses folk humor to comment incisively on the racial aspect of World War II:

> The japs wasn't like the white people said they was. They was colored just like us, and they didn't want kill us, they just wanted to kill the white soldiers. If the colored soldiers was marching in front, the japs would shoot over the colored soldiers head just to get to the white boys. If the colored soldiers was marching in the back, the japs would drop the bombs shorter. It was this that made them integrate that Army and nothing else.   (207)

Miss Jane gets all this from Jimmy, "the one." Here, students can see that the purely black perspective offers a comic but quite telling corollary to received "official" history and, as such, echoes passages that Hurston's editors excised from her wartime autobiography, *Dust Tracks on a Road*, that were highly sarcastic about the imperialist aspects of American foreign policy.

Students are encouraged to see the thematic of moral instruction that is present both in communal orality and in the pronouncements of Miss Jane. Keith

Byerman and others have pointed to the central role played by teachers in *Miss Jane*, including Ned and Mary Agnes, as well as Jimmy as a teacher of justice. But surely Miss Jane is the best teacher of all. Rambling, tangential, but always folksy and often comic, she deeply instructs her readers into the history of her people and into the principles of communal involvement. In this aspect, her embrace of humor, folk culture, tale telling, and vernacular speech casts her in the role of Silenus, a figure from Greek myth who had a rough exterior but uttered profound truths. Further, her narrative "uncrowns" that of the white plantation owners she serves but also the pronouncements of the Lost Cause historians and white writers like Margaret Mitchell, who have seemingly cornered the market on southern history as seen through fiction.

As students soon see, Miss Jane and her fellow narrators encourage us to laugh at the pretensions of the white characters. Her humor creates an intimacy between her narration and the reader, while simultaneously creating a democratic community, for as the Russian philosopher M. M. Bakhtin asserts, only equals may laugh (92). Indeed, as many of Gaines's fictions delineate, white southerners did not permit their servants to laugh in front of them, as this would suggest disrespect and equality.

Gaines has stated that he purposely ended Miss Jane's narrative in 1962, the year before President Kennedy's assassination. I tell students this decision may have come from his commitment to making this novel a reflection of black folk memory, which was not powerfully attached to Kennedy until his death was linked five years later with those of Bobby Kennedy and King.

Unfortunately, many Americans know Miss Jane only through the film that was made for television, which was celebrated in its time and showered with numerous Emmy Awards, including Best Actress for Cicely Tyson. Sometimes I show the film or, more often, portions of it. Lorna Fitzsimmons, in an excellent and detailed essay, points out the many ways in which the power of Gaines's novel was significantly diminished by the filmmaker. In scene after scene, the oppressive actions and utterances of the white power structure are muted, softened, or cut; the disturbing interracial love affair between Tee Bob and Mary Agnes was eliminated altogether. I also show students how the salty humor—much of it using racial language—which gives the "piquancy" to the book's voices, was gutted.

Whether I have students view the film, I always show them the second disc of the thirtieth anniversary reissue of the movie on DVD (Korty), which features an excellent documentary; it stars Gaines himself, speaking of the writing of *Miss Jane*. This disc includes interviews with scholars, who describe the oral tradition in African American culture; conversations with the film's director and producer; comic traditions in African American discourse; and footage of the celebrated Emmy Awards broadcast, where the film swept most of the major honors. Viewing this documentary gives students a valuable set of tools as they ponder the implications and literary achievements of the novel.

Finally, in our concluding wrap-up discussions of the novel, students some-times wonder why Gaines employs humor when very serious issues are being dis-cussed. I then quote something he said about this: "I think in much black folk-lore and blues that even when things are at their worst there's often something humorous that comes through. . . . When people take advantage of people, or when people hurt other people, it's often just ridiculous and the humor comes through. Humor and joking are part of change" (Gaudet and Wooton, "Talking" 213). On another occasion he put this more generally: "I don't know how to tell a story without some humor. No matter what the problem is . . . because in daily life there is not only the grimness around us but there is humor as well. I don't go consciously to writing humor, it just evolves—it just comes into the writing . . . no matter how dark things seem, there's humor always somewhere around" (Saeta and Skinner 241). To his credit, Gaines amply demonstrated the truth of these statements in the text of his masterful *Miss Jane.*

NOTE

[1] This essay quotes from then 1972 Bantam edition of *Miss Jane.*

Whose Story Is This? Teaching
The Autobiography of Miss Jane Pittman,
Novel to Film

Margaret D. Bauer

Ernest J. Gaines's novel *The Autobiography of Miss Jane Pittman* fits well into my southern literature survey course, which begins with an introduction to plantation fiction. I like to open the class's final unit with one of Gaines's novels to show how the plantation system continued to be influential well into the twentieth century. *Miss Jane*, written in the tradition of slave narratives, so successfully depicts the voice of a woman who was about ten years old at the time of emancipation that the author has had to remind people ever since the book's publication that Jane Pittman is a fictional character. And when I teach the novel, I begin by establishing my students' understanding that it is, indeed, a novel. In recent years, I also make certain they understand that all *books* are not *novels* and that *novels* are *fiction*. When I teach *Miss Jane*, we discuss the novel first, and then we watch the 1974 television movie adaptation and consider the significance of the filmmaker's changes to the novel, just as we have examined how Gaines employs but changes the various tropes of the slave narrative and of plantation fiction.

To start, I direct students' attention to the fictional introduction to the novel, by an African American schoolteacher who has noticed the voices that are absent from his classes' history books and thus who seeks out 110-year-old Jane Pittman in order to add her story to the mix. In this element of the novel, as in all, we discuss how Gaines partially employs but then deviates from a traditional narrative element of slave narratives, which are often introduced by a white authoritative voice to validate the first-person black voice to follow. Gaines's novel's "editor" is presumably, like his subject, African American—according to John Callahan, he is "a figure for Gaines himself" ("Image-Making" 59), although one critic, Blyden Jackson, assumed he was white in his article on the novel (255). Gaines himself identifies his editor character as "a black schoolteacher from Baton Rouge" (Gaudet and Wooton, *Porch Talk* 31), but it is interesting to note to students that he is not racially identified in the novel, and relying on the author's assertion in an interview falls under the definition of intentional fallacy. We discuss, rather, why it is that most critics (including myself) have assumed he is black. I ask students for evidence from the novel that would support such a reading, directing them, if they are not certain, to consider the interaction between Jane and others and this man, which leads them to recognize how Jane and her guests are not discomforted by his presence in Jane's home, how they speak to him as they would to any (black) man younger than they are, that there is no special (even if only surface) respect or deference shown to him like what we witness in other black-white interactions in the novel.

After we have watched the movie, I explore with the students the significance of the choice to change this character from a black history teacher to a white journalist. They recognize the white voice of authority added for the predominantly white viewing audience, just as a white authoritative voice was used for the predominantly white reading audience of the nineteenth-century slave narratives. And yet, Callahan points out in his essay on the novel and movie, "The bitter social irony in all this is that Gaines' interlocutor is closer to the mass audience than [screenwriter Tracy Keenan] Wynn's. Everyone has personal knowledge of history teachers; how many of us have ever seen a feature writer?" (59). It is interesting to also note that while Gaines's history teacher fades out of the story, merely introducing it and then allowing Jane to take over, the movie's white journalist reappears between scenes, as though the viewer needs to touch base with this sympathetic white man as the movie progresses, and Jane experiences very little positive interaction with any of the white people in the stories she relates to him.

Turning to the overall structure of the novel, which begins toward the end of the Civil War and ends at the start of the civil rights movement, I ask the students to consider the central character(s) of each section of the novel. Of course Jane figures into every plotline, but is it always her story she tells? What is her role in each storyline? As I have discussed in my own earlier writing on this novel, Jane is often a witness to the actions of others.[1] The tragic figure of the first section is Big Laura, and like the heroic male characters of the rest of the novel, she pays the highest price for fighting back against the white man. But note how Big Laura dies, with a baby in her arms. She is defending her child, which allows the largely white readership to understand this woman's violence against white men—and, of course, Gaines depicts these men as pointlessly and savagely violent. I remind students that just before this raid on the newly emancipated slaves' campsite, Laura had also threatened violence against a black man who threatened Jane. She is colorblind when it comes to defending children against anyone who would harm them. We discuss how Gaines employs with Big Laura (beginning, safely, with a mother) a technique of the authors of slave narratives: humanizing his "other," showing the white reader what he or she would have in common with someone like Big Laura: the willingness to sacrifice herself for her children.

Witnessing this first death affects the ten-year-old Jane, who has also recently experienced a severe beating for asserting her right to call herself by that name. Throughout the novel, Jane is witness and chronicler—and survivor. She endures a hundred-plus years, living to tell the tale. But is it her story she tells? Whose story is this? I ask my class. A novel called *The Autobiography of Miss Jane Pittman* may seem (and even purport) to be the story of its narrator, but this narrator is really telling the stories of four men in her life: her husband, Joe Pittman; her adopted son (Big Laura's biological son), Ned Douglass; the sensitive white youth Robert "Tee Bob" Samson, Jr., who falls in love with a black woman and wants to marry rather than just lie with her; and the civil rights activist Jimmy, "the one" who would lead the quarters community.

Gaines summarized his novels' heroes and their conflicts in an interview with John O'Brien. I use this passage to introduce Gaines to students whenever I teach his books (I teach one every year, alternating between this one and *Of Love and Dust, A Gathering of Old Men,* or *A Lesson Before Dying*). In 1972, a year after the publication of *Miss Jane,* his third novel (but the point applies to the novels that followed as well), Gaines told O'Brien:

> You must understand that in this country the black man has been pushed into the position where he is not supposed to be a man. This is one of the things that the white man has tried to deny the black ever since he brought him here in chains. . . . My heroes just try to be men; but because the white man has tried everything from the time of slavery to deny the black this chance, his attempts to be a man will lead toward danger.   ("Ernest J. Gaines" 30)

This quotation is a good starting point for talking about Joe Pittman, Ned Douglass, and Jimmy. Joe Pittman's desire to assert his manhood in a world that would call him "boy" his whole life is dangerous. In this character's case, it is interesting that, in contrast to Big Laura and then later Ned and Jimmy, Joe is not killed by a white man, nor is his death overtly related to contentious race relations. We talk about how Gaines, like Frederick Douglass, to give just one example, is aware of his largely white audience and readers' possible discomfort with conflicts between black men and white men. Although we do witness one of Joe's white employers treating him unfairly, Joe does seem to win that battle and then moves to take a job in which his superior talent breaking horses allows him to stand out as an individual, as the "Chief," as he is called. Thus, Gaines's first tragic hero in this novel is *any* man, not just a black man, and, as the conjure woman tells Jane, "man is put here to die. From the day he is born him and death take off for that red string. But he never wins, he don't even tie. So the next best thing, do what you can with the little time the Lord spares you. Most men feel they ought to spend them few years proving they men" (95).[2] Like the authors of slave narratives, Gaines provides here a means by which his audience, *any* audience, can identify with Joe Pittman, even if he is a black man in the Reconstruction South.

Surprisingly, Jane herself is largely at fault for bringing about the death of her husband, which leads to a discussion about what happens when a woman (Jane) tries to protect her man (Joe) from himself. I ask the class if, by killing off the one man Jane says she ever really loved, Gaines is "punishing" Jane in the tradition of so many writers who punish female characters for stepping out of their place. As the class ponders this question, we talk about the author's agenda, his own humanness in critiquing a character he so evidently cares about. There are numerous essays and interviews in which Gaines talks about "Miss Jane Pittman," reflecting his respect for the women who inspired her characterization, particularly the woman who raised the author for many years between the time that his mother and stepfather left for California and when he joined them there, at age fifteen, having exhausted the educational opportunities for an African American in Louisiana.

And still it is the black *man's* story Gaines repeatedly tells; the black women of his fiction, including Miss Jane, are not so fully drawn, are rarely so heroic. Theirs is not the story that interests Gaines so much—*and that's okay,* I want my students to understand.[3] The writers among you, I note, will also discover the stories you are interested in telling. The writer gets to choose whose story he or she will tell. As readers, we just need to be aware of whose story is being told, to recognize whose story is not, and to explore the significance of who is telling whose story. What is the effect of Gaines here telling the story of these men through the voice of Jane? Mary Ellen Doyle points out that "Gaines has never been excoriated for crossing gender lines as William Styron was for crossing those of race in *The Confessions of Nat Turner.*" She suggests that this may be in part because "he had the good sense to be forthright about his viewpoint in creating a woman protagonist by also creating a male editor" ("*Autobiography*" 104). As we discuss the various levels of narration here, I ask, Is the black history teacher's quest to get Jane's voice into his narrative a desire for *her* story or the *community's* story? This brings us back to what is emphasized in his "introduction": how many people stepped in to help the centenarian tell the story of the events she had witnessed over a century of observing?

After Joe's death, Jane's surrogate son, Ned, returns, educated and ready to lead his people. I ask students to notice a few things at the start of discussing Ned's story in the novel (the second half of book 2). First, I point out that as soon as Ned returns, we learn that he will die. The only suspense, then, is how and when, which emphasizes the inevitability of death for men who act like Ned. Second, I direct them to the end of book 2, asking them to note the focus on the death of the Cajun Albert Cluveau and, to start our exploration of its significance, to remember who killed Ned's blood mother, Big Laura. The men Jane refers to as "Secesh" are the poorer whites who, historically, did the dirty work of the plantation owners—the overseers and the like who were usually the ones to go out in search of runaway slaves and the ones who inflicted physical punishment upon slaves, allowing the "genteel" master a more restful night's sleep, his conscience clear as he distanced himself from such brutality.

After Ned's return, Jane introduces us to Albert Cluveau, with whom she has a relationship not unlike friendship, except that they could never admit to being friends, which is probably a relief to Jane, who might not want to admit even to herself that she is friends with a known assassin. Albert is on the payroll of some unseen white authority who tells him when a black man needs killing, a black man like Ned Douglass, who is stirring up dissatisfaction with the way of life in this post–Civil War plantation South. Most of Gaines's novels explore the social dynamics in Louisiana between the Cajuns and African Americans, and within the various storylines, the discerning reader can recognize that these two groups of people had much more in common with each other than the Cajuns did with the white aristocracy. But typical of how racism is used to maintain the old order, the Cajuns were allowed some upward mobility, on the basis of their race, that the African Americans were not, and this inspired animosity between the two groups, the Cajuns asserting their supremacy as white men, the African Americans resentful of the preference shown to (white) Cajuns whenever plantation land was divided up for shares or even for sale, even though African Americans had worked the land the longest, albeit beginning during the time of slavery.[4] *Miss Jane* reveals where the real power is: Albert does not want to kill his fishing partner's son, but he feels he has no choice; killing for the white authority is his job, and he has been protected from prosecution for these murders. Now, it is a choice between killing Ned and losing that protection. All he can do is warn Jane that he has been hired. And when he does kill Ned, he of course kills his relationship with Ned's mother. Eating together—at the same time, even if separated (never at a table with each other)—was a step toward more civil relations between whites and blacks much closer to each other on the social ladder than either group was to the wealthy landowners, evidence as it was of two people interacting as individuals in spite of their otherwise segregated lives. Albert betrays his friend Jane; he kills her son. And then the guilt over killing a person, not just some black man but a man who was loved by his mother, turns Albert into a raging maniac by the end of his story.

Gaines then turns from the agonizing death of Albert to another white man who dies in emotional agony. Alvin Ramsey points out how, in this novel, "white people died too. But they did not die struggling against oppression, seeking freedom or higher levels of humanity. They died running away from their crimes, from their whiteness. Check out Albert Cluveau and Tee Bob. Died insane. Died by suicide." Ramsey continues: "In the midst of this white decadence, black life continued to struggle for survival and for triumph" (35), an interesting point of contrast to note as we begin discussing the next central tragic figure of the novel, Robert "Tee Bob" Samson, Jr.—though he is nothing like his father. Tee Bob learns early of both the humanity of black people and of social forces that would separate their lives from his own. I direct students to recognize both of Tee Bob's relationships with African Americans: first with his half brother, Timmy, and then with the Creole schoolteacher, Mary Agnes. Here again, the students recognize echoes of plantation fiction: white and black brothers playing together as children, then separated abruptly when the black brother acts out; the communal expectations about the only kind of relationship between a white man and a black woman.

The few privileges that Timmy, the black son of Robert Samson, Sr., has enjoyed as the playmate of the legitimate Samson son—indeed, also as a somewhat indulged (for a black boy) son of the plantation owner himself—have influenced his sense of self, and he dares to raise his hand to a white man who strikes out at him, which means he must leave before he is hurt or killed. Once again the "bad guy" in this scenario is the poorer white man who threatens Timmy's life, while Robert, Sr., "protects" his mulatto son by sending him away. But as Gaines sets up the altercation Timmy has with Tom Joe, he has his narrator note that Tom Joe "hated the Samson in Timmy much as he hated the nigger in him," and, similarly, she reports that Timmy tells Tom Joe, "I wouldn't call white trash Mister if I was dying" (143). Miss Amma Dean Samson, Tee Bob's mother, mounts a surprising defense of Timmy and challenges her husband's assertion that society dictated there was nothing he could do to Tom Joe. Robert argues that "[y]ou pinned medals on a white man when he beat a nigger for drawing back his hand." "Even a half nigger?" Miss Amma Dean asks, but Robert reminds her, "There ain't no such thing as a half nigger" (144). By this point in the semester, we have certainly discussed the one-drop rule that governed the slave South, and here the students recognize that such an attitude about racial identity continued well past slavery—and indeed, someone usually notes how even today the lightest-skinned Americans of mixed race are still identified as "black."

So Tee Bob loses his childhood playmate overnight. I ask students to consider the role Tee Bob's fond memories of Timmy—and his helplessness to do anything about the loss of his friend when he was such a young boy—might have played in the events that lead to Tee Bob's suicide. Timmy, they recognize, was not just some black boy to his brother. He was Tee Bob's friend, and he was taken away by a society that had rules about how black and white were to interact. Here again, I call students' attention to the fact that we are told at the end of this episode from Tee Bob's childhood, while he is still just a boy, that Tee Bob "killed himself before he learned how he was supposed to live in this world" (145). In this instance of removing suspense regarding a character's fate, though, I point out how Gaines then rebuilds the tension of suspense by interrupting Tee Bob's story with a couple of "aside" chapters about the Great Flood of 1927 and the Louisiana governor Huey Long, perhaps reminding us of how many years we are beyond slavery—and yet how little has changed in this still plantation South.

When Jane picks up again with the story of Tee Bob, college age now, we already know what will happen to this young man, and before we meet him again, we meet the answer to the question, What will drive Tee Bob to kill himself? It is Mary Agnes. His love for another person of mixed race, a beautiful woman he is allowed to rape with impunity but is not allowed to marry. Tee Bob simply does not want to live any longer in such a world. Here again, the person who emerges as the most villainous when the dust settles after the suicide is Tee Bob's white friend Jimmy Caya, a young man apparently not of the same aristocratic class as the Samsons. He is the one who tries to explain to Tee Bob that if he wants Mary Agnes he should just "take her" (171). Then he is the one who, after Tee Bob's death, blames Mary Agnes, even lies about her, saying Tee Bob told him "she wouldn't let him alone" (185). Jules Raynard, a friend of the Samson family, stops Robert from going after the young woman, reminding his friend that Jimmy Caya is "trash" but that "we know better" (185). Once again, "white trash" seems more demonized than the southern gentleman.

One thing that the students often find puzzling as this episode draws to a close is Jules's theory of who is to blame for Tee Bob's suicide—which includes all of them, including Jane and Mary Agnes. I ask students what they think of his theory. Jules sounds like a voice of reason after the horror of the suicide, and certainly he is effective in protecting Mary Agnes from Jimmy Caya's intent to scapegoat her for Tee Bob's death, but would Gaines use a white man as the authoritative voice in his novel, as Blyden Jackson suggests he does (272)? Jules's theory, once he spells it out for Jane, does not differ too much from Jimmy Caya's suggestion that Mary Agnes "know[s] her duty, and all she expect from you is ride the horse down there" and "take her" (171). Jules tells Jane that Mary Agnes "knowed the rules" and "was a hundred years wiser" than Tee Bob, and he believes that she even "led him on for just a second. . . . While he was standing there over her she invited him down there on the floor" (192). Doyle points out the objectionable nature of this suggestion, "which smacks of the assumption that black women somehow ask for their rape" (*Voices* 148). I caution students about falling for his authoritative voice themselves, directing them to Jane's question of Jules, "ain't this specalatin?" (192). Indeed, it is. Sometimes, when I have taught Faulkner's *Absalom, Absalom!* earlier in the same semester, I can remind the class of how we realized as we discussed that novel that most of it too is "specalatin" on Quentin's and Shreve's parts as they try to make sense of the Old South and its vital prevalence in the New South, which is exactly what Jules and Jane are trying to do after Tee Bob's death. But how would this privileged white man know anything about what was going on in Mary Agnes's mind as she was trying to deal calmly with an agitated man who could rape her with impunity if he were not as decent as she had told Jane she believed he was. The doubt Tee Bob likely saw in the face of the woman he loved was whether she might have misjudged him and was therefore in very great danger of being assaulted.

As I have indicated, the made-for-television movie is well worth showing to a class discussing this novel. The film adaptation provides numerous points of discussion, including what is left out of the movie and why. For example, the story of Tee Bob's fatal love for the black schoolteacher is left out, and I ask students to consider why and we discuss how interracial love might have been even more discomforting in the 1970s than white on black violence—how sex is still more strictly censored than violence. Also left out of the film is the beating that the child Jane receives when she asserts her new name, although the killing of both Ned and Jimmy by white men is in the movie (the latter "offstage" but referenced; Jane's beating is not referenced). The students recognize that there is no way to "explain" (and excuse) the beating that Jane receives as an innocent child, while Ned and Jimmy are agitators fully aware that their activities will likely get them killed. Indeed, as we have noted, Gaines tells us up front, upon Ned's return to Jane's life, that he will be killed.

Next, we examine what is changed in the movie and why. I've already mentioned the change from the black history teacher wanting Jane's story for his classroom of black students to a white reporter seeking Jane's story for his audience and, ultimately, for the movie's white television audience. Similarly, we discuss how the black stallion that kills Joe Pittman in the novel becomes an albino horse in the movie; the symbolism of a white horse killing a black man may be easy to interpret, but it is interesting to see how this question leads us to wonder why Gaines used a black stallion. In his essay on the novel, Albert Wertheim points out that "Gaines does not yield to a simplistic allegory that depicts Whitey as the devil, something he could easily have done by making the satanic stallion a white one. Instead, Gaines recognizes that the obstacles confronting and defeating the black man are not reducible to the whole white race" (225). So what does the black stallion symbolize? I ask. I share with students the provocatively titled review of the film "Through a Glass Whitely: The Televised Rape of *Miss Jane Pittman*," in which Ramsey summarizes what the white and black horses mean in the respective versions of the story, which brings us back to the discussion of the danger of asserting black masculinity in the oppressive South: "[The] black horse symbolized Joe's own Black manhood, his Black youth, and Black strength—all of which he was trying as best he could to maintain. It is important for us to see that Joe Pittman died while in pursuit of a *black* horse and for us to understand that this represented the essence of his life—seeking, struggling to maintain a grip on Black manhood" (33). Ramsey believes the movie's change oversimplifies the novel's more complicated revelations about racial oppression: "All of the meaning and symbolism surrounding Joe Pittman was cut out of the television production. They replaced the symbolic black horse with a white horse—a complete turnaround. There was no triumph in Joe's death. The image that was gotten across was one of a Black cowboy being destroyed by whiteness. And that was it" (34). One might contrast Ramsey's review for the periodical *Black World* with Pauline Kael's more positive review for *The New Yorker*. Kael refers to this seemingly simple change as "unfortunate" but explains it away without exploring what is "unfortunate" about it: "For photographic reasons (the sequence was being shot using day for night), an albino was used instead." Kael finds "the eerie white horse with a ghastly pink look around the eyes . . . mystically effective," but then, again without explanation, remarks that "the color switch suggests a racial symbolism that doesn't quite fit the situation" (75).

Indeed, it is interesting to have students contrast reviews of the film by black and white critics and between publications targeting particularly African American or mainstream audiences. Consider Kael's condescending tone in her *New Yorker* review of the film, for example, when she contends that "movies for blacks have something that white movies have lost or grown beyond. . . . I think it's something that whites miss; it's what they mean when they say that there's nothing to take their children to. It's a lost innocence, a lost paradise of guiltlessness, and some of the black movies have it" (73). In the subtitle of her review, "How to Make a White Film from a Black Novel," Vilma Raskin Potter argues that *Miss Jane* is a white movie. She and other critics like her who were not so enamored with the movie would certainly also disagree with Kael's assessment of the "moral complexity" of the movie (73). In his *Black World* review, Ramsey laments, for example, that African American "history was again filtered through that white lens that is constructed to keep Black truth from passing through with integrity" (31). It is interesting to also note the two different reviews in *The New York Times*: right after the television airing of the movie, John J. O'Connor's review is headlined "TV: Splendid 'Jane Pittman' Relates Black History," and then, about ten days later, Stephanie Harrington's review headline asks (presumably in direct response to O'Connor's headline), "Did 'Jane Pittman' Really Show Us Black History?"

In the same edition as O'Connor's laudatory review of the movie, *The New York Times* also published a related story by Charlayne Hunter, "'Jane' Show: Tale of Hope and Efforts," which focuses on the importance of the role of Jane Pittman for Cicely Tyson, since there were so few "scripts for women, period" and "less for black women" (68). Hunter begins her human-interest piece describing the roomful of African American celebrities after the screening of the movie. According to Hunter, as the movie ended, "Nikki Giovanni wept in the arms of Cicely Tyson." Since I have shown this movie to many classes, I can attest that it is very difficult to sit through the last scene without crying, but I ask my students: does its affectiveness make it a good film?

Perhaps the most significant change from novel to film is the melodramatic ending added to the movie, which is a pretty unforgettable scene for anyone who has seen the movie: Tyson, made up to look like a centenarian, walks past the big white sheriff and his deputies to the "Whites Only" water fountain, with Negro spirituals playing in the background for full effect. Once you have seen the movie, try not to picture this scene as you reread the much more subtle and quiet ending to Gaines's novel: "Me and Robert looked at each other there a long time, then I went by him," Jane reports, as she leaves the Samson plantation on her way into town. Jane acts. The end. She heads into town for the civil rights demonstration, even after Robert Samson, Sr., threatens no home to return to for anyone who participates in any such activities—the most courageous action Jane has taken since she asserted her right to her new name and rejected her slave name when she was ten years old. But such a subtle ending wasn't dramatic enough for a movie. In her review, Potter also suggests that the fairy-tale ending allowed the viewing audience to turn off the TV and go to bed believing all was right with the world: "If Jane can drink at the fountain, then America is safe . . . a cosy assurance to a white audience: *They've got what they wanted. You can all go back to sleep now*" (372).

Typical twenty-first-century students will not, of course, recall the phenomenon of *Roots*, even if they are familiar with the miniseries, and so may not be able to appreciate the fact that the film adaptation of *Miss Jane* preceded and perhaps prepared the (majority white) audience for the subsequent miniseries. I usually tell them about *Roots*—the record-breaking viewership, the use of familiar white actors from popular television series to remind the discomforted viewer that the cruelties enacted on the screen were part of a *movie*. I suggest that *Miss Jane* may have helped to make a case for a weeklong movie with African American characters in the lead roles. We also compare the tear-jerking ending of the film adaptation of *Miss Jane* with the supernatural elements that the author Charles Chesnutt used to not discomfort his audience too much in his Uncle Julius stories, in which the narrator tells of the horrors of slavery to the carpetbagger couple who have bought an old plantation vineyard. I usually teach Chesnutt stories in the same class, so we have discussed his majority white audience earlier, and Gaines's novel provides a way to show students how long that audience remained largely unchanged. Just as magic spells may have given Chesnutt's audience a way to dismiss the sad truths about mothers being sold away from babies, wives from husbands, Miss Jane's uninterrupted drink from the "Whites Only" fountain provides false comfort to the viewing audience. Gaines may have elected to leave us at the end of the novel with the image of Jane going into town in direct defiance of her landlord. But that short step past Robert Samson was a courageous act exactly because of what was imminent upon her return to what was still called "the quarters": this 110-year-old would likely find her possessions packed up, herself locked out of her home—which was not really "hers." Or perhaps we can hope as we close the book that Jane's brave defiance of this white authority will finally get through to Robert, who lost his son over the same issues Jane is going into town to protest against. Without a romantic, melodramatic ending, Gaines allows us this hope. The filmmaker elected instead for the cathartic tears and the false sense of certainty that all will be well, and history tells us differently. Many more Jimmys will be killed, many more Janes displaced. Hope for a future in which such is not the case is ultimately much more satisfying than a false depiction of the past.

NOTES

[1] My book *William Faulkner's Legacy* discusses echoes of Faulkner in several Gaines works in a chapter titled "Miss Jane Is Still Not in the History Books" (43–93). My argument is that Gaines is filling in a story marginalized in Faulkner's fiction—the story of the African American male, particularly in the post–Civil War South. And as Faulkner marginalizes African Americans in his work, Gaines to some extent marginalizes black women—even Jane, who watches and reports. This chapter would be particularly useful reading for a southern literature class that also includes readings by Faulkner.

[2] This essay quotes from the 1971 Dial edition of *Miss Jane*.

[3] I discuss Gaines's focus on male stories in more depth in *William Faulkner's Legacy* (45–53).

[4] It might be useful to share with students how Gaines responds to the question "What does the word *Cajun* mean to you?" in *Porch Talk with Ernest Gaines*. His response to Marcia Gaudet's observation that his "portrayals of Cajuns seldom show their positive characteristics and values" provides some history behind the contentious relations between African Americans and Cajuns in Louisiana (Gaudet and Wooton 82–83).

Media Adaptations and Gaines's Novels

Valerie Babb

It has become commonplace to note that we live in an increasingly visual culture. More and more, students come to know their world and history as much through screens as through texts. This trend has informed my teaching of the canon of Ernest Gaines. In addition to the well-known 1974 television adaptation of *The Autobiography of Miss Jane Pittman* (dir. John Korty), which won nine Emmy Awards, three other Gaines works have made the transit to the small screen: *The Sky Is Gray* (dir. Stan Lathan), based on the short story published in *Negro Digest* in 1963, collected in *Bloodline* (1968), and adapted for public television in 1980 as part of *The American Short Story Collection*; *A Gathering of Old Men* (dir. Volker Schlöndorff), adapted by CBS in 1987; and *A Lesson Before Dying* (dir. Joseph Sargent), adapted by HBO in 1999. Each of these adaptations provides an avenue for considering ideas of spectatorship and representation, ideas key to understanding how the currency of the visual shapes narratives of race.

Before considering the significance of specific adaptations of Gaines's works, I ask students to think about representations of blackness in visual culture. When one looks at the language of visual culture, it seems a mode of inquiry made for a literature heavily focused on seeing and perception, where the very concept of representation is central to narratives of race and culture. Visual culture theory's emphasis on image, representation, portrayal, iconography, and iconology, and its evocative terms such as "scopic regimes," "the spectacle," and "surveillance," seem to beg to be applied to works with titles such as *The Autobiography of an Ex-Coloured Man* (1912), *Their Eyes Were Watching God* (1937), *The Bluest Eye*

(1970), and *The Color Purple* (1982). Blackness is at its origins a visually defined quality. The lived experience of being black is constructed through the valuations given to seen phenotypic traits and sustained, among other modes, through visual manifestations.[1] Black literature has consistently offered commentary on the meanings of perceived blackness by questioning the relationship of what is seen to what is. These considerations assist my students in becoming aware of their stances as viewers of racial content, an awareness that makes their assessment of race and cultural elements in writing more self-reflective.

As my students and I consider the adaptations of Gaines's works, discussion of changing narrative form evolves into analysis of why he might choose particular modes. Gaines employs a variety of strategies—first person, communal, omniscient, and sometimes a blending of many of these—to create a storytelling voice that asserts the primacy of African American ways of telling. His overlaying the oral and vernacular onto the written and standard undercuts the privileging of one form and culture over another whose expressive practices were often deemed marginal within an American culture that has traditionally associated mastery of written discourse with social power. Comparing adaptations of his works to the novels themselves crystallizes Gaines's craft and his respect for the voices of his Louisiana parish as the foundations for compelling fiction. For instance, I ask students to consider the contrast of voice-over versus the multivocal narratives that Gaines often designs. We are then able to deepen our comprehension of the racial and cultural politics of narrative form throughout literary history. What associations accompany certain narrative modes? Why, traditionally, was the omniscient narrative privileged in western-European-derived discourse? Why was first person characterized as limiting? Why were forms incorporating orality deemed incapable of expansively conveying novelistic experience?

The first Gaines work adapted for television was *The Autobiography of Miss Jane Pittman* (1971). The novel is as much about the ways history is told as it is about the remarkable life of a fictionalized 111-year-old woman. I ask students to view this work as an instance of receiving history from an often overlooked perspective, that of a black female ex-slave. The invented autobiography symbolically remedies the silences that formal annals of history imposed when they focused on some voices to the exclusion of others. The character Miss Jane provides an interior view of enslavement that emphasizes the psychological impact on those enslaved as well as their ability to survive in spite of the institution. She lives through most of the significant periods of black history in the United States—slavery, emancipation, and the emergence of civil rights advocacy—and it is fitting that a history teacher opens the work with his desire to have Miss Jane's recollections fill the lacunae of formal historical records. Drawing upon the Works Progress Administration interviews of former slaves recorded in *Lay My Burden Down* (1945), Gaines imbues the novel with cadences of oral speech, and the act of recalling is a central trope, one that fosters class discussions of the role of memory in binding and sustaining a people's lives and culture.[2]

The televised movie, no doubt in an attempt to reach a wider audience, replaces the black teacher—a figure that means much in Gaines's fiction, because good teachers show students the existence of a world beyond their segregated parameters—with a white reporter. The difference in figures shows Gaines giving primacy to Jane telling her own story, as opposed to a reporter writing about Jane. Questions of the role of validating authorities' impact on black expression invariably arise, and the white reporter might be interpreted as part of the legacy of authenticating documents included in the extratexual material that introduced and often closed nineteenth-century narratives of the enslaved. One of the most compelling qualities of Miss Jane is that she validates herself through embodying individual, ancestral, and sociopolitical history, but the transition from page to screen seems to suggest that another site of validation is needed to appeal to a popular viewership.

The novel ends with a scene of quiet defiance as Jane stares down the owner of the plantation, who attempts to stop her from attending a protest march. The television movie closes with a scene that makes use of the familiar Jim Crow iconography of the segregated South, the "Whites Only" water fountain. Jane's ascendency to symbolic leadership is rendered through her being driven to town, where slowly she walks to take a drink from the "Whites Only" water fountain at the courthouse, the camera following her step by step. By the time of the novel's publication and the made-for-television movie, "White Only" or "White" and "Colored" labels attached to drinking fountains, restrooms, and station depots were part of the landscape for viewers of American cultural history, increasingly replicated in black-and-white news photography and televised broadcasts of the civil rights and post–civil rights eras.[3] They were at once familiar, if repellant (to most). Contrasting the novelistic and the televised versions of Jane's taking her stance allows for the consideration of what the making of icons signifies, particularly at a time when so much cultural meaning is rendered visually.

"The Sky Is Gray" was the next Gaines work to be made into a televised format. The short story tells of eight-year-old James's odyssey to the only dentist in the area who will treat blacks. James, accompanied by his mother, must journey from the relative safety of his rural community to the more racially hostile city of Bayonne. The security of what he knows decreases as he enters a world where he encounters those who are different from him, and he must learn the codes of behavior that will assure his survival. His mother, Octavia, momentarily rearing James on her own because his father is away fighting in the army of a nation that doesn't extend full citizenship to him and his family because of their race, is determined that her son learn these codes to be able to take care of himself should the need arise. James absorbs his lessons well, and he stoically refuses to acknowledge fear or even the intense pain of his toothache. In his interior monologue he tells himself that he can never be scared and can never cry. When the dentist leaves for lunch before seeing him, he and his mother are left to navigate a separatist environment in the bitter cold. They are unable to buy food because of their impoverishment; they are unable to find shelter because, being black, they cannot enter where they will. Three incidents serve as signposts against which the story illustrates James's developing awareness: the overhearing of a conversation between a college student and a minister, his watching his mother maneuver their segregated social world for his benefit, and his viewing his mother's interaction with a couple who own a grocery store.

While waiting in the dentist's office, James sees the interaction of a minister representing an old guard too timid to change the status quo and a young man who critiques the hypocrisy of American democracy. The interchange and the bearing of the young man provide James with a model of what his future might look like. This, combined with the lessons of his mother, allows him to realize that he is much more than the definitions his society seeks to impose upon him. When the dentist breaks for lunch and closes his office, Octavia must find ways to keep James from the cold while adhering to the strict laws of racial segregation. To keep him warm, she enters a white-owned hardware store and feigns the examination of an ax for purchase while she plants James in front of a woodstove. Her dissembling has allowed her not only to warm her son but also to maintain their dignity without pleading with the proprietor to let James stand at the stove. In another instance, a kindly white couple seeks to offer them food and a warm place to stay, but it is imperative to Octavia that James not accept charity. A strategy is devised between Octavia and the woman, as each appreciates the position of the other, in which James does chores to work off the "debt." He learns of both segregation and compassion in this moment. Observing his mother, James at one point vows that he will make all this up to her someday, and it is through this vow that readers ascertain his appreciation of her teachings.

Much of what we see of James's growing comprehension comes through Gaines's representation of interior thoughts. James's worries that his mother will spend the little money they have to feed him, and his determination not to give in to hunger, show his understanding of their financial constraints; his noting her uncertainty as she traverses a hostile environment reveals his intuiting the tenuousness of being black in segregated environs. All his epiphanies are conveyed through a first-person voice. While the televised version retains much of the story's plotline, this perspective is shifted. The black director Stan Lathan, who also created a television movie of James Baldwin's *Go Tell It on the Mountain* (1953), instead skillfully translates the inequities of segregation through the landscape of the quarters in which James (played by James Bond III) and Octavia (Olivia Cole) live.[4] He shows the internalization of separatism through blacks automatically walking to the rear of a bus when they enter and through the deference of averted eyes giving way as whites are encountered on the street. The action of the novel is vivified, but context for these actions is not always provided. The difficulty in translating James's thoughts to the screen highlights the centrality of interior narrative to the story's meaning. Without James's subsequent reflections, Olivia's punishment when he is unable to kill two pet redbirds so the family will not starve comes across as the actions of a harsh maternal figure. My students have often found this divergence instructive in understanding how perception changes as one moves from within the circle to without. They frequently remark on how important it is to consider the stance of the reader/viewer in the making of meaning.

What goes into constructing meaning and, even more important, understanding is a central theme in *A Gathering of Old Men* (1983). Originally titled "The Revenge of Old Men," the novel is constructed as a communal narrative detailing how claiming responsibility for an act of revenge restores self-esteem and humanity to men in their twilight years. The action takes place in Marshall Quarters in the 1970s, but racial conventions give the work a timelessness that evokes any era since Reconstruction. Little has changed for these tenant farmers. They are subjected to abuse by Cajun overseers and appear reconciled to their lot. When one overseer, Beau Boutan, is found shot to death, Candy Marshall, the young white owner of the plantation, seeks to protect Mathu, a man for whom she has a daughterly affection and whom she believes is the killer. She devises a plan where all the black farmers confess to the murder. The community is thrown into an uproar wondering how something so shocking could have been done by elderly men perceived more as part of the landscape than as men with agency. The segments constitute a whole, revealing a portrait of racial and economic subjugation. Each man takes advantage of the opportunity to "confess," for each has committed the same act in his mind, avenging psychically particular wrongs: the loss of a son refused treatment at a hospital because he was black; the rape and death of a sister; the return to the ignominy of segregation after fighting for liberty in World War I. Every voice gives a perspective on Beau that, when taken together, makes him a conglomerate of all the white men who have abused them.

Each section is named after a narrator, and two names are provided: the formal one that signifies how the person is perceived by the larger, more official world and the informal one that signifies how the person is known in the community or how each sees him- or herself. Robert Louis Stevenson Banks, a.k.a. "Chimley," is an example. This dual naming replicates the tension between one's self-conception and the societal value imposed upon one. As characters narrate their stories, individualities emerge in sharp contrast to the homogenization that social definitions effect. Some of the narrations move the action forward, while others provide reflection and context. The complexity of this narrative style is hard to develop in film form, and the screenplay for the televised *Gathering*, written by the playwright Charles Fuller, merges some of the segments into one, and this conflation contrasts with the panorama of injustice Gaines so deftly evokes. The television movie focuses more on action and makes particular use of visual setting. Shots of the cane fields, the Spanish moss hanging from trees, the bayou, and the local cemetery conjure the rural place Gaines creates. Discussion of the emphasis on action and the cinematography brings to the fore Gaines's technique of maximizing voice and minimizing description. For him, the why is ultimately more important than the what. The ending of the movie moves away from this emphasis by showing the retreat of white Cajuns who had come to avenge Beau's death. Their fleeing in the face of the black solidarity might be

more rousing to a popular viewership, but it deemphasizes the evocation of transformation that is the focus of the novel.

A Lesson Before Dying (1993) is the most recent Gaines work to be adapted.
The protagonist, Jefferson, is given the death penalty for murder. An innocent
victim of bad circumstances, he is caught in a store after a robbery standing near
the bloody bodies of his black friends Bear and Brother and the shopkeeper
Mr. Gropé, cash from the register and an open bottle of whiskey in his hands.
His defense lawyer, in his closing statement, frames Jefferson as an unwitting
brute, no better than a hog and lacking the intellect to plan such a robbery. The
analogy rankles Jefferson's godmother, and to restore his humanity she asks the
teacher Grant Wiggins to speak to her godson and make him realize he is not
the animal society frames him to be. As a pair, Grant and Jefferson influence
each other. Both exist as outsiders in the community, Jefferson because of his
race and subsequent trial, and Grant because he had been educated away from
the world of his birth. Both wonder if their lives are of value, Jefferson because
the social valuations he has imbibed have filled him with self-hate and cynicism,
and Grant because he wonders if his work educating students who can attend
school only from October to April, when not working the fields, will ever yield
meaningful results. Their growing bond, where each sees aspects of himself in
the other, allows both to find new meaning and resolve.

Lesson's narrative style breaks from other Gaines works somewhat. While the
speech, communal narratives, and oral cadences of his Louisiana world are still
present, also present is a visual narrative in the shape of a diary Jefferson writes. Its
nonstandard orthography is meant to convey meaning through the sight of words
as well as through their signification: "mr. wiggin you say write something but I
dont kno what to rite an you say I must be thinking bout things I aint telin nobody
an I order put it on paper but I dont kno what to put on paper" (226).[5] This passage
offers a unique opportunity for considering how Gaines uses the visual appearance
of words on a page to thematic effect. The spelling conjures voice, education, and
place, and the stream of consciousness arrangement suggests the awareness that
begins to overwhelm Jefferson, as he, for the first time in his life, contemplates his
own being. Writing, for Jefferson, is transformative, and his passages move from
halting descriptions of day-to-day events to eloquent reflections on the circumstances that have brought him to where he is. His last statement to Grant—"good
by mr. wigin tell them im strong tell them im a man" (235)—reflects the very realization his godmother hoped the interaction with Grant would bring about.

Short of having titles as part of the movie's visual mechanism, the multiple
ways of telling in *Lesson* are difficult to duplicate on the small screen. But the
filmed version keeps very close to the text and tries to reproduce some of its complexities. The beauty and ugliness of Gaines's segregated setting is rendered
through the Louisiana landscape, encompassing cane fields, antebellum mansions, and the courthouse as a symbol of a questionable justice. The actors Don
Cheadle (as Grant) and Mekhi Phifer (Jefferson) provide performances that reveal a complex portrayal of race that is a useful starting point for addressing

Gaines's consistent eschewing of broad characterizations in favor of depicting the intertwined nature of race in close southern quarters. Both the book and the movie provide opportunities for examining whether conceptions of race are changing even amid the continued existence of racism. *Lesson* was written at a time when cultural discourse surrounding race coincided with discourse on individualism. The binary of black and white is increasingly being challenged by arguments citing hybridity and fusions. Racial essentialism is being complicated by conceptions of cultural multiplicity. It is interesting to read Gaines, a writer so vested in the portrayal of a single community, against the backdrop of these developments, for his writing foreshadows many of these changes. His influences have always been wide ranging, including authors as varied as William Faulkner, Ernest Hemingway, Leo Tolstoy, and Ivan Turgenev. Writing of the complicated coexistences of black and white Americans, Cajuns and Creoles, made Gaines part of a very hybrid southern world of multiple fusions.

Adaptations of Gaines's works are part of a long history in which film and television have shaped how blackness is perceived. The space between novel and adaptation provides a useful site for engaging many of the themes and significances of his novels. The editorial decisions going into transferring a work of literature from the page to the screen encourages contemplation of changing or static cultural climate and how his writing implicitly comments on both. Considering what the term "adaptation" means and what kinds there are, from the loose to the faithful,[6] it becomes evident that issues of adaptation are intertwined with questions of racial authenticity, racial representation, and aesthetic choice. Gaines's works, via different means, afford significant examination of all these issues. The frequency of their adaptation is testament to the expansiveness with which they treat large racial, cultural, and historical themes while coupling these with skillful strategies delineating the minute details of a single imagined parish.

NOTES

[1] Studies in this area are many. Some that provide an introduction include Jessica Evans and Stuart Hall, *Visual Culture: The Reader*; Michael D. Harris, *Colored Pictures: Race and Visual Representation*; and Anne Elizabeth Caroll, *Word, Image, and the New Negro: Representation and Identity in the Harlem Renaissance*.

[2] For Gaines's comments on his use of the WPA collection, see Rowell.

[3] Access to these images and a cultural context for their understanding can be found at the University of Georgia Civil Rights Digital Library (crdl.usg.edu) and at the Digital Library of Georgia Freedom on Film Oral History Collection (russelldoc.galib.uga.edu).

[4] Lathan would also direct a 1987 adaptation of Harriet Beecher Stowe's *Uncle Tom's Cabin* for the Showtime network. It starred Avery Brooks as Tom and Phylicia Rashad as Eliza and attempted to imbue Tom with dignity and gravitas.

[5] This essay quotes from the 1993 Knopf edition of *A Lesson Before Dying*.

[6] Discussion of these technical aspects can be found in Brian McFarlane, *Novel to Film: An Introduction to the Theory of Adaptation*, and George Bluestone, *Novels into Film*.

Gaines and the Black Power
and Black Arts Movements

James Smethurst

Ernest Gaines has frequently distinguished his work from the protest tradition of African American fiction that he sees descending primarily from Richard Wright and flowering in the black arts and black power era of the 1960s and 1970s. In part this distinction has to do with aesthetics and what he saw as the limited palette of this protest genre. However, to a larger degree his reluctance to associate himself with this tradition has more to do with what Gaines sees as its privileging of the northern ghetto as the sole legitimate literary landscape of black life. In a similar vein, he has also told the story of how people influenced by the black arts and black power movements in the San Francisco Bay Area objected to the subject matter of *The Autobiography of Miss Jane Pittman* (1971), suggesting instead that he write on what was happening at that moment in the black communities of Northern California.

Yet Gaines has also insisted that he was deeply influenced by the cultural and political moment of the 1960s and 1970s and by both the civil rights and black nationalist currents of that era. This essay will discuss the teaching of Gaines's work, particularly *Miss Jane* and *In My Father's House* (1978), within the context of the black arts and black power movements, especially those manifestations of black arts that were closely linked to Texas, Mississippi, and Louisiana (principally New Orleans) and were institutionalized in journals (*Nkombo, Hoodoo,* the early *Callaloo*) and organizations (BLKARTSOUTH, the Southern Black Cultural Alliance [SBCA]) with close relationships with the civil rights movement in the South, specifically the Student Nonviolent Coordinating Committee, or SNCC (in Mississippi), and the Congress of Racial Equality, or CORE (in Louisiana). Much of Gaines's writing from the 1970s and early 1980s is closely related to—both influencing and influenced by—the southern black arts movement's efforts to create (or reclaim) a usable southern black history and a southern black artistic and intellectual tradition, and to a black power and black arts concern with the reconstitution of the black family through a reclamation of black manhood along the lines of the model associated with Malcolm X by those movements.

So what characterized the black arts movement in the South, particularly New Orleans? Like black arts everywhere, there was a general agreement that African Americans were a people, a nation, with the right or even the obligation to determine their own destiny. As was the case with almost every black power and black arts institution and organization everywhere, culture was seen as a crucial component of this struggle for self-determination, an essential part of breaking the ideological bonds of racism and white supremacy that were significantly transmitted to both black and white people through culture. There was also a tremendous emphasis placed on building black political, economic, educational, and arts institutions.

However, there were a number of ways in which southern black arts activists generally distinguished themselves from their northern and western counterparts. While the black arts movement in the South, as elsewhere, was largely based in urban centers and on college campuses, there was a greater sense of connection with the land and with black folk who still lived in the rural communities of the Black Belt than was generally the case in the North and West. Of course, many black arts and black power militants had spent time in the South during the civil rights movement. Still, few northern black theater troupes and black performing artists regularly traveled to the southern countryside and performed before rural and small-town black audiences as did the Free Southern Theater, based first at Tougaloo College in Mississippi and later in New Orleans. The southern black arts movement was also longer lived than the movement in many places, arguably surviving until the mid-1980s and the collapse of the SBCA.

The southern black arts movement activists, by and large, had a sense that their work, and the work of southern black artists generally, was not sufficiently valued by those in the northern and western centers of the movement, particularly New York City, Chicago, the Bay Area, and Los Angeles. Consequently, they were much concerned with building regional institutions and organizations, such as BLKARTSOUTH, the SBCA, and the Southern Coalition of African American Writers, and journals, such as *Nkombo* (based in New Orleans), *Rhythm* (based in Atlanta), and *Callaloo* (initially based in Baton Rouge), which would encourage the development of black art and artists in the South and help that art and those artists reach a wider audience. They were also often devoted to uncovering and promoting a local black cultural tradition in music, literature, theater, dance, and the visual arts. What this meant concretely is that they searched out and honored artists in what might be thought as "high" and "vernacular" genres (though the black arts activists often work assiduously to break down those distinctions) whose work preceded the black arts era, such as the poets Octave Lilly, Jr., and Marcus Christian in Louisiana, as well as pushing for the recognition of contemporary artists, such as the New Orleans musicians Ellis Marsalis and Alvin Batiste, whom they saw as on the forefront of contemporary black creativity, even if those artists were undervalued in the North and West (Salaam, "BLKARTSOUTH" and "Blk Art South"). They were also concerned with preserving and disseminating southern black cultural and social history. Tom Dent, a New Orleans native whose work was crucial in building a black art network in New Orleans and throughout the South, including such organizations as the Free Southern Theater, BLKARTSOUTH, the SBCA, and the Congo Square Writers Union and the journal *Nkombo*, spent considerable time collecting oral histories of civil rights workers, black musicians in Louisiana, and local black communities in Mississippi and Louisiana.

Finally, the southern black arts circles linked to New Orleans and the SBCA were generally resistant to anything they saw as a prescriptive "black aesthetic."

Despite the strong influence of Maulana Karenga's seven principles of Kawaida (the Nguzo Saba), especially in organizing black cultural and educational institutions, there was in the southern black arts movement a general sense of tolerance of ideological, spiritual, and even phenotypical variety that made people suspicious of what they saw as reductionist notions of blackness (or perhaps more forbearing: although aesthetic and ideological differences did not disappear, they did not split groups in the way they did elsewhere) (Dent, "New Theaters" and "Enriching").

As noted earlier, Gaines separates himself from black arts literature, which he sees as a manifestation of the urban protest tradition that derived, in his view, particularly from Wright. In fact, he generally claims that no black writer has had any significant impact on him, because he did not encounter the work of any black writers in his early childhood in rural Louisiana, his teenage years in Vallejo, California, or even his early college career at San Francisco State College in the 1950s. By the time he began to read such authors as Wright, James Baldwin, Ralph Ellison, and Zora Neale Hurston, according to Gaines, his style was set to an extent that allowed only minimal influence.[1] Though Gaines did assert that Hurston did influence him in the course of one interview (and denied any inspiration in others), the most he would generally allow about black literary ancestry is that Hurston and, especially, Jean Toomer would have made a mark on his work, had he read them in time, because of their representation of black rural folk. Instead, Gaines cites a number of white North American and European writers, particularly William Faulkner, Eudora Welty, Ernest Hemingway, and Leo Tolstoy (and other nineteenth-century Russian fiction writers) as his models, particularly in the writing of dialogue and the representation of rural landscapes and subjects.

Gaines did, however, suggest that black music (gospel, jazz, and the blues), black storytelling, and other black folkways had considerable impact on his writing. If he learned much about the rendering of literary dialogue and description of a particular sort of rural southern place from Faulkner and Welty, among others, his stance, presentation of this place, tone, and sensibility were much derived from vernacular southern black art (O'Brien, "Ernest J. Gaines" 28). In this, he had a lot in common with leading black arts originators, such as Larry Neal and Amiri Baraka. "Listen to James Brown scream. Ask yourself, then, Have you heard a Negro poet sing like that?" Neal famously asked in the afterword to the groundbreaking 1968 black arts anthology *Black Fire* (653). (It's worth noting here that James Brown was a southern, not a northern, soul singer.) Baraka laid out a similar argument at far greater length in his study *Blues People* (1963). The power of much of this music was that it was aimed at a black working-class and farm audience who were not, according to Baraka, Neal, and other black arts artists and critics, very interested in the approval or the aesthetic tastes of white people. Interestingly, though Gaines rarely, if ever, put it this way, his sense of the lessons of black music for the African American writer posited the importance of a black audience in a way not unlike that imagined by black arts activists.

Of course, one is inclined to take Gaines's claims about his early ignorance of other black writers and the lack of influence of African American writers on his work with a grain of salt. While it is possible that he had no access to books by black authors during his early childhood in Louisiana and his adolescence in California, it is hard to believe that no one suggested that he look at the work of other black writers during his time at San Francisco State College and Stanford University. He also mentioned on a number of occasions that he was aware of the Beat scene in San Francisco, which was a notably interracial milieu with the African American poet Bob Kaufman as perhaps its most prominent figure. The notion that Gaines's style and approach were so set that when he did read black writers, in the late 1950s and early 1960s, they had no impact on him seems a bit suspect, even if the impact was negative. It is also hard to believe that Margaret Walker's novel *Jubilee* (1966) did not have an impact on Gaines's *The Autobiography of Miss Jane Pittman*. As Ashraf Rushdy notes, besides sharing much subject matter, both novels straddle the boundary between the written and the oral, between the official records and transcripts and the oral tradition of black folk in their histories of slavery, the Civil War, Reconstruction, and the Jim Crow counterrevolution (91).

Of course, there were other influences on *Miss Jane*. As Gaines himself frequently notes about his work, the Faulknerian influence is pronounced. Certainly, the conceit of an older woman telling stories in fragments and fits to a younger male, whose consciousness filters those stories, recalls *Absalom! Absalom!* There is much of the same combination of often slapstick humor, vivid speech, horror, and intense introspection that marks Faulkner. Perhaps more than *Absalom! Absalom!*, *Miss Jane* resembles a sort of black *Light in August* if it had been told in old age by Lena Grove to a young (but less conflicted than Quentin Compson) would-be intellectual/writer.

However, having said that, Gaines was also following in the long black tradition of representing history and historical narration in a way that was seen as not simply supplementary but actually superior to most "mainstream" scholarship of the time. It is important to recall that Gaines wrote the novel not much more than a decade after Kenneth Stampp and other younger, revisionist historians of slavery, Reconstruction, and Jim Crow began to displace U. B. Phillips and the Dunning school of historians, which whitewashed slavery and distorted Reconstruction in many respects. It was a time when younger black historians associated with the civil rights and black power movements, such as John Blassingame, Sterling Stuckey, John Bracey, Jr., and Vincent Harding, were writing an even more revised history that drew on the testimony of black folk, as encoded in folklore, popular culture, literature, and direct testimonies, such as the Works Progress Administration slave narratives. This was a time, after all, when the admissibility of the WPA narratives as historical evidence was very much in question.

This sort of new history that drew on a variety of vernacular sources (and black art) was also close kin to the work that southern black arts activists, particularly

Dent, Nayo Watkins, Toni Cade Bambara (during her Atlanta days), and John O'Neal, undertook. They were tremendously concerned with ancestry, both in the collective sense of the cultural (and often oral) testimony of common black people in the rural and urban South as well as individual older artists and activists whose names were known, such as Lilly and Christian (both of whom were also political activists and historians).[2]

In other words, *Miss Jane* was very much in the vein and engaged in the same sort of project of demonstrating a southern black historical narrative tradition, which is to say a sense of black folk literature and art that expressed a historically constituted people. While Gaines notes that he learned much about dialogue and the telling of stories from Faulkner, the content of Gaines's writing and his artistic stance differ greatly from that of Faulkner, who tended to represent African Americans (at least dark-skinned African Americans) as being relatively static, virtually outside history, in their constitution.

So to teach the novel and more clearly grasp its meaning in the cultural moment, one needs to introduce students to a variety of modes of black storytelling and narration, particularly that of the rural and small-town South, and even introduce them to WPA slave narratives and other historical documents in a vernacular black voice. It is important to revisit or acquaint students with the debates within the professions of history and literary studies under the impact of black power, black arts, and black studies of what counted as historical evidence *and* as literature. It is also worth recalling and making available to students the southern black arts project of placing the black South at the center of the black nation's effort to look backward to a history of struggle and forward to liberation, of "the idea of ancestry," to quote Etheridge Knight's poem about a family reunion in Mississippi (*Essential* 12–13). As in Knight's poem, the dialogue between the teacher-artist and the southern black folk narrator in *Miss Jane* suggests the importance of this ancestry to younger black people, including those who joined or were the children of the Great Migration—of which, after all, Gaines was a member. In that sense, despite Gaines's focus on the rural and small-town South, the novel is a product of the Great Migration as seen after the advent of civil rights, black power, and black arts. This is true of not only *Miss Jane* but also much of Gaines's later work, including *A Gathering of Old Men* (1983), in which storytelling and oral history is rendered in a more communal manner, and *A Lesson Before Dying* (1993), which, like *Miss Jane*, features a dialogue between a more formally educated narrator and a folk subnarrator.

Another hallmark of the southern black arts movement, particularly in fiction and drama in what might be thought of as the late southern black arts era, from about 1977 to 1983, is a meditation on the meaning and functioning of the civil rights, black power, and black arts movements in and for the South, especially in the wake of the murder of Martin Luther King, Jr., in Memphis, Tennessee. Again, this focus on legacy that also deeply reflects on inheritance, history in which the personal intertwines with the public, and ancestry has a considerable resonance in Faulkner's work, specifically *Absalom! Absalom!*, *The Sound and the Fury*, and *Light in August*, but, like Baldwin's *Go Tell It on the Mountain*, differs greatly in its positing of a black subjectivity, a black history, and a black narrative tradition (or set of traditions) that are intertwined with, but not ancillary to, those of white southerners. Gaines's *In My Father's House* resembles Bambara's *The Salt Eaters* (1980) in that both consider this complex analysis of ancestry and legacy.[3] Like Baldwin's *Go Tell It on the Mountain* (and Toni Morrison's *Paradise* [1997]), *In My Father's House* features a generation gap that is more prominent than that in *The Salt Eaters*, replaying an apparent disjuncture between older civil rights activists and leaders and younger black power adherents. The protagonist, Phillip Martin, is much like John Grimes in *Go Tell It on the Mountain* in that he has undergone a conversion and leaves a life of poverty, violence, drinking, and womanizing to become a preacher. Or rather Phillip is what Grimes might have been had he stayed in the South and succeeded as a preacher, becoming (as his name connotes) a civil rights leader in the mold of a local King in the small Louisiana town of St. Adrienne. However, Phillip's position as a preacher, civil rights leader, and community pillar is doubly threatened, both by the present—the aftermath of King's assassination and what seems to be the failure of the sort of nonviolent politics aimed at black equality and racial reconciliation associated with King—and the past, with the appearance of Etienne, Phillip's son from a relationship of his earlier life, a son whom he had essentially denied.

Black power, in its various forms and rhetoric, haunts the novel. While in Baton Rouge, Phillip encounters Billy, who is trying to organize a black guerrilla army that will defend and ultimately liberate black people, an army that is a sort of mash-up of the Black Panthers, the Black Liberation Army, and the Republic of New Africa, all of which operated in the South—and, in the case of the Republic of New Africa, saw the future of black people as a nation in the South. One can find echoes of famous black arts works in Billy's rhetoric, notably the Last Poets' signature "When the Revolution Comes," with its closing repetition "and party and bullshit" (*Last Poets*): "'That's niggers for you,' Billy said to Phillip. . . . 'When they march them in the gas chambers niggers go'n still be just playing'" (159).[4]

Billy's point/counterpoint with Phillip over the morality and practicality of armed struggle in which Phillip remains dedicated to nonviolence, however confused he is in other things, generally reflects Billy's plans as ideological fantasy rather than practical strategy. However, Billy also echoes Malcolm X's argument that once you have stripped away formal Jim Crow you have the northern ghetto. Are Watts, the South Side, Harlem, West Oakland, and so on the promised land?

> Niggers can vote. Vote for what? Voting can't fill your belly when you hungry. Another nigger sit up there in the capital. Doing what? Another one go to Washington. For what? They put another couple on television to broadcast news—thems the changes you talking about? I'm talking about changes that keep white men from coming into South Baton Rouge and

shooting down our people. If it happen, we pick up guns, we pick up
torches, and we hit back.   (164)

This is a harder argument to dismiss, one with which King grappled at the end
of his life and with which Phillip is beginning to grapple in the original proposal
to protest the hiring practices of Chenal's store—though he remains significantly
dependent on white liberal or quasi-liberal supporters and is willing to betray
the movement to help his son, paradoxically betraying his paternal role in order
to assuage his guilt over his failure as a father. What does civil rights, then, mean
in the present following the assassination of King? How does it differ from liberation, from self-determination? How does one understand the past in the face
of this symbolic rupture, a rupture emphasized by the outraged uprisings of black
people in at least 110 cities, large and small, in all the regions of the United
States?

The past and present become strangely conflated in Gaines's novel, as Etienne
takes the name of "Robert X," after the manner of Malcolm X and the Nation of
Islam, before coming to kill his father for abandoning and essentially destroying
his first family. The "X" combines the missing African name (and ancestors) and
the missing father. Ultimately, it's not the father but the son who is physically lost
as Etienne / Robert X commits suicide rather than killing his father as he originally intended, leaving Phillip mourning the absence in his life (one that he had
denied or repressed before) and the destruction of his first family. He declares
himself to be lost (again). However, his wife, Alma, tells him, "We g'on have to
start again" (214).

Obviously, the figure of Malcolm X and the black power movement that he
helped inspire and inform loom large in the novel. In some important respects,
Phillip becomes more identified with Malcolm X than with King, despite his continued, if somewhat strained, belief in nonviolence and the likelihood of justice
with the polity of the United States. As many commentators have noted, Gaines's
work, both in this novel and in other pieces, often grapples with issues of black
manhood. However, it is Malcolm X and the black arts and black power understanding of his meaning for black masculinity that are at the center of the novel's
tragedy and possible redemption, more so than the more frequently cited generational conflict in Turgenev's *Fathers and Sons* (or *Fathers and Children*, in a
more literal, less masculinist translation). After all, much of Malcolm X's story,
particularly as told in *The Autobiography of Malcolm X*, turned on the loss of
his father to racist violence, the slower but sure ruin of his mother by the state,
the destruction of his family as metonym for a larger assault on the black family,
and his redemption by finding a new father in Elijah Muhammad and a new
family in the Nation of Islam. The meaning of Malcolm X for many in black
power and as expressed in black arts literature and art turned on him as a figure
of black manhood.[5] It is worth noting that this manhood was not identified with
a sense of machismo as we would normally understand it, other than in, perhaps,
the sense of Malcolm X's fearlessness and conviction that black people needed

to do whatever it took to defend and liberate themselves "by any means neces-sary."[6] However, that sort of fearlessness and conviction was not seen as the sole property of men in the black power and black arts movements. One of the key aspects of Malcolm X's iconic manhood was the notion of black male responsi-bility, of the role of the black male in the reclamation of the black family as the father. One might rightly see this as a normative heterosexual model of the family, but it is also one that emphasizes male responsibility, modesty, reason, intelligence, and restraint and the replacement of the original lost father with a new father—again, running against the stereotype of the supersexual, physically dominant, hyperaggressive black male.

In My Father's House is very much concerned, then, with the challenge of-fered by Malcolm X and his meaning for black manhood as presented by much of the black arts movement. The tragedy of Gaines's novel is that Etienne / Robert X, despite his name change, is unable to either reconnect with his birth father or find a new father after the manner of Malcolm X. Consequently, he is unable to reclaim his manhood and kills himself. This, in turn, seems to prevent Phillip from playing his role as father, precipitating his deep sense of failure, loss, and being lost. Phillip had been something like the macho stereotype of a black man, a "beast" he says himself, before his conversion. Even after his embrace of Chris-tianity, he retains much of that macho image, albeit in a different modality. He is described as a physically dominating masculine figure with a taste for the good life and a rumored interest in women other than his wife. None of that helps the crisis of manhood that he faces, particularly after his son's death. Interestingly, it is Alma and her friend Beverly, rather than a male figure, who assert and try to convince Phillip that it is not too late for him to start over and take his proper place, to be the father to his surviving family that he should have been to Etienne / Robert X and his mother and siblings. Of course, the idea of black women help-ing black men overcome their failures as men, as seen in Maulana Karenga's influential Kawaidist ideology (which exerted a great influence on the black arts and black power movements in Texas and Louisiana) and Amiri Baraka's work when he was most under the influence of Karenga, was an important facet of the more masculinist manifestations of black power and black arts.[7] While it is unclear that Phillip will succeed in playing his role, reclaiming his manhood in the sense of Malcolm X's meaning for black power and black arts, the framing of the problem and its possible solution is very much set in terms of black power and black arts, even if Phillip appears to reject other ideological and organizational aspects of those movements.

In order to give students a better understanding of how Gaines's work, par-ticularly In My Father's House, fits into the black power and black arts era and how his work resonates with radical black nationalist literature, rather than sim-ply critiquing or completely diverging from black arts writing, it is crucial to dis-cuss the issue of how black manhood figured in the black arts and black power vision of the liberation of the black family and, by extension, the black nation. In particular, the black arts casting of Malcolm X and his life as the quintessential embodiment of black masculinity and the restoration of a sort of family that was attained only after extreme crisis can be helpfully juxtaposed against, for example, Phillip's own crisis of manhood that is as yet unresolved at the end of *In My Father's House.*

In short, Gaines's work, to some degree with his encouragement, has been read against the black arts movement, tending to reduce the movement to a limited view of its manifestation in a relatively few northern and western cities, in part to emphasize the southern nature of his novels—with the South, especially the rural South, being seen as essentially antithetical to black arts. However, as Gaines's work itself notes, particularly *In My Father's House,* black power and black arts were no strangers to the South; in fact, southern events, figures, and institutions were crucial to the genesis and development of those movements. Thus, it is essential for any teacher of Gaines to read his work not only against the ideology and aesthetics of black power and black arts, but with them also.

NOTES

[1] See Fitzgerald and Marchant 13; Beauford 19; Carter 85; Rowell 91; Gaudet and Wooton, *Porch Talk* 33–34.

[2] For an example of this, see Dent's "Marcus B. Christian: An Appreciation."

[3] A sort of retrospective southern, black power, black arts, civil rights travelogue that takes up this question of ancestry and legacy is Dent's *Southern Journey.*

[4] This essay quotes from the 1983 Knopf edition of *In My Father's House.*

[5] For many examples of the association of Malcolm X with black manhood by black arts writers, see Randall and Burroughs's landmark black arts anthology *For Malcolm* and the poems in the "Malcolm" section of Bracey et al.'s *SOS—Calling All Black People* (309–23).

[6] Malcolm X first popularized this phrase in a speech at the founding rally of the Organization of Afro-American Unity in 1964. See Malcolm X, "Speech."

[7] For a study of Maulana Karenga and his US organization, see Scot Brown. For a study of Amiri Baraka's political and cultural organizing during the period when Baraka was heavily influenced by Karenga, see Woodard.

An International and Comparative Approach to Gaines's *Catherine Carmier*: The Influence of Ivan Turgenev's *Fathers and Sons*

Toru Kiuchi

The Influence of Turgenev and Other Foreign Writers

Ernest J. Gaines's *Catherine Carmier* presents an effective way of showing students how an international and comparative approach can readily be made, because no writer more openly and frequently admits in interviews that his less read and undertaught novel was written under the influence of *Fathers and Sons* by Ivan Turgenev (1818–83) and other Russian writers. If the author had not told us the relationship between the two novels, nobody would notice it. Class discussion of Gaines's novel in comparison with the Russian classic does, without doubt, lead to interesting insights.

Before the writing of his first novel, *Catherine Carmier*, under the influence of Turgenev, Gaines's literary apprenticeship began with reading other nineteenth-century Russian writers such as Anton Chekhov (1860–1904), Maxim Gorky (1868–1936), Leo Tolstoy (1828–1910), Aleksandr Pushkin (1799–1837), Nikolay Gogol (1809–52), and Fyodor Dostoevsky (1821–81). Gaines started to read them to know about how his people, the peasants, in Gaines's words, had been depicted by white writers, though he did not find the real life of his own people. Gaines was unsatisfied with the treatment of the peasants in John Steinbeck's books—the people in the Salinas Valley in *The Grapes of Wrath* and the Chicanos in his other works—and those of southern writers in the United States, because they were not treated as real human beings but only as "caricatures" and "clowns" (O'Brien, "Ernest J. Gaines" 28).

Gaines found nineteenth-century Russian writers, especially Tolstoy, Turgenev, and Chekhov, knew how to write about peasants: "When the white writers are writing about the blacks of the fields, they seem to make them caricatures rather than real people, but the Russian writers made their peasants real" (Fitzgerald and Marchant 7). Regarding the influence of Russian writers on him, Gaines said, "I think the thing I recognize in Russian writers, especially when they're writing about the peasant, is some of the same sort of thing that I've experienced in the Southern part of the United States" (6).

The peasants appearing in Russian novels are the same sort of people with whom Gaines was familiar in Louisiana. As Gaines says in an interview, "I would read about people from the earth, farm people like I was, like my people were" (Tarshis 75). In *Catherine Carmier*, Raoul Carmier and his father and his family are all from the earth, as Gaines is from Louisiana. Thus Gaines found a way to write while reading Russian writers who wrote about peasants and their outdoor life.

Gaines probably took an interest in Chekhov's short story "Peasants," which was based upon Chekhov's own experiences on his country estate; Gaines has admitted that he "also learned from Anton Chekhov" (Rowell 92). Chekhov is well known as a Russian playwright and short story writer, his most popular work the play *The Cherry Orchard* (1904). Chekhov also practiced as a medical doctor throughout most of his life. In 1892, he bought the small country estate of Melikhovo, where he lived with his family until 1899 and made himself available to the local peasants as a medical doctor. Along with helping victims of the famine and cholera epidemic in 1892, Chekhov built schools and a clinic for the peasants. Chekhov's direct contact with peasants made him witness to their unhealthy living conditions. Gaines might have been aware of the reality in Chekhov's peasant characters in "Peasants" and other works. Gaines's realistic representation of Raoul's farm is, like in Chekhov, apparently based upon his own life as a farmer in Louisiana, as in the naturalistic account of Raoul and his daughter Catherine driving home: "The car lights flashed on yellow ripe corn on either side of the road, then on tall green stalks of sugar cane that leaned toward the road like willow branches" (152).[1]

Tolstoy, an early admirer of Chekhov's short stories, is regarded as one of the greatest authors of all time. Born to an aristocratic Russian family, Tolstoy is best known for the novels *War and Peace* (1869) and *Anna Karenina* (1877), often cited as masterpieces of realist fiction. *Anna Karenina* tells the story of society's faults and includes an account by a landowner who, like Tolstoy himself, works together with the peasants in the fields in search of improvement of their lives. The theme of *War and Peace* is an investigation into Russian history itself. Gaines's historical philosophy is likewise evident in the portrayal of the Carmier family through Raoul's father, Robert; Raoul himself; and Catherine. At the beginning of the novel, Robert Carmier, a very proud farmer, repeats that "he could farm as well as any man and better than most" (8) in order to buy some land from a prejudiced owner. In spite of his hard work and fight against the Cajun sharecroppers, Robert is killed: "About three months later, Robert disappeared. No one knew how, nor where to. That morning he had gotten on his horse and left for Bayonne. Neither he nor the horse was ever seen again" (13). Gaines confesses that Robert is a little like his own great-grandfather: "My great grandfather was a bit like that. He had a conflict like that" (Sartisky 267). Raoul is set up to be approximately in his fifties in the novel and consequently born around 1900, for Catherine, born in the 1930s, is in her early twenties (about the same age as Jackson, who is twenty-two [69]) in the late 1950s or the early 1960s at the beginning of the civil rights movement ("Madame Bayonne wanted to hear [Jackson's] opinion of the Freedom Riders and the sit-in demonstrations by the Negro students in the South" [107]); Robert is accordingly born between 1850 and 1860, coming of age in the era of Reconstruction. During Reconstruction the Massacre of 1866 broke out in New Orleans, where police and armed white people assaulted more than a hundred people—Creoles and recently freed black American citizens—who had assembled outside the Louisiana Constitutional Convention. The massacre had a cultural impact by way of numerous editorials and poems published in *La Tribune de la Nouvelle-Orléans* that denunciated the violence and praised the French Revolution of 1789 and an uprising by Toussaint L'Ouverture in Haiti in 1798. The writers' use of these international incidents "became part of a Creole literary tradition that for generations had linked literary arts to political and social concerns" (Senter 277). (Gaines chooses "Toussaint," the Haitian hero's name, for Catherine's aunt Margaret Toussaint, who plays a role in helping Catherine from Bayonne.) Robert Carmier grew up during a time in which Creole identity and pride were heightened: "The idea that people of color had rights was present in the atmosphere, and Creoles [had] had political experience in the establishment of such rights in France and the French colony of Haiti" (Senter 280).

Russian writers thus initially influenced Gaines's development as a writer sensitive to the cultural history of Louisiana. Finally he found Turgenev, even among many other foreign writers including Gustave Flaubert and Guy de Maupassant: "I learned from the great nineteenth-century Russian stylist, Ivan Turgenev. His *Fathers and Sons* was a great influence on my first novel, *Catherine Carmier*; I used his novel as a Bible when I was writing *Catherine Carmier*" (Rowell 92).

When asked for advice about how to be a good writer, Gaines answered:

> If you are a writer, read good writers, whether they are white or black, Chinese or Japanese, or Russian, or writers from Mars or wherever. Read the best to see how they do things, because any writer can help you—any good writer can help you. . . . The great Russian writers (Tolstoy, Turgenev, and Chekhov) can help you. The great French writers, Flaubert and de Maupassant, can help you.   (98)

This kind of advice would be also applicable for students before they start to read Gaines, especially *Catherine Carmier*.

Catherine Carmier *and* Fathers and Sons

Gaines was born in 1933 on the River Lake Plantation near Oscar, Pointe Coupée Parish, Louisiana, where generations of his family had lived since the era of slavery. Pointe Coupeé Parish is the site where, in April 1795, "a conspiracy was formed for a general uprising of the slaves throughout the parish" (Dunbar-Nelson 16), after the news came of the successes of the French Revolution and the slave revolt in Saint-Domingue (now Haiti). At age fifteen, Gaines left there for Vallejo, California, where he developed a passion for reading novels by Turgenev and other foreign writers (African Americans were not allowed access to libraries in Louisiana at that time). As he told an interviewer, "Once I started reading, I used to read everything, and I suppose I just stumbled on them. Turgenev's *Fathers and Children* [*Sons*] was first" (Fitzgerald and Marchant 7). At age sixteen, he started to write an early version of *Catherine Carmier*, typing "by the use of one finger at a time," and he "wrote about a hundred and fifty or seventy-five or eighty or ninety pages, whatever" (Parrill 173). He put Turgenev's *Father and Sons* (1862) on his desk every day to use it as his Bible during the writing of the novel: "My *Catherine Carmier* is almost written on the structure of *Fathers and Sons*," he admitted (Laney, "Conversation" 61). He mailed the finished novel to a New York publisher but was rejected, so he burned the manuscript.

Fathers and Sons is regarded as one of the major Russian works of nineteenth-century fiction, with a universal theme of the generational divide between fathers and sons. Set in 1859 at the moment when the Russian autocratic society started to move gradually toward reform, the novel deals with the conflict between conservative fathers and their "nihilistic" intellectual sons. In the early nineteenth century, the German philosopher Friedrich Jacobi (1743–1819) used the term "nihilism" to negatively characterize transcendental idealism; however, it became popularized after Turgenev used it to characterize Bazarov as "nihilistic" in the novel.

As Gaines told an interviewer, "I left in '48, came back in '50. Auntie died in '53. I didn't come back then. I couldn't; I didn't have money. After that I came back in '58" (Gaudet and Wooton, *Porch Talk* 130). Gaines was in Louisiana when he began rewriting *Catherine Carmier*, and it took him about five years to finish it, reworking it about twenty times. However, it was "much longer in earlier versions and it had much more to do with Catherine and her family than it did with Jackson" (O'Brien, "Ernest J. Gaines" 33). At the last stage of writing, Gaines returned to "Louisiana, living in Baton Rouge for the first six months of 1963" (Estes, Introduction 3), and finished it. His tentative titles for the novel included "A Little Stream," "Barren Summer," and "Catherine," and he decided to choose "Catherine" and add the character's last name to the title at the suggestion of an editor. However, Gaines noted, "But I wish now that I had stuck to the title 'Barren Summer,' because it's a barren summer for them all. Nobody gets anything out of that summer" (Gaudet and Wooton, *Porch Talk* 117). *Catherine Carmier* was thus published in 1964.

Fathers and Sons, published about one hundred years before *Catherine Carmier*, begins with Arkady Nikolaevich Kirsanov's return to his father's provincial estate, Marino, after his graduation from St. Petersburg University. Arkady brings his friend Yevgeny Vasilyevich Bazarov. Arkady's father, Nikolay Petrovich Kirsanov, welcomes the two young men, but Nikolay Petrovich's brother, Pavel Petrovich Kirsanov, strongly disagrees with Bazarov's philosophy of "nihilism." After a while the two young men go spend a few days at Nikolskoe, the estate of Madame Anna Sergeyevna Odintsova. There Bazarov falls in love with Anna, and Arkady meets and comes to love Katya (Katerina) Sergeyevna Lokteva, Anna's sister. Arkady and Bazarov subsequently leave for Bazarov's home. Bazarov's parents receive them warmly and passionately, but the young men soon leave for Marino again, to the sorrow of Bazarov's parents. Arkady then goes to Nikolskoe to see Katya again, while Bazarov does scientific research at Marino. However, the relationship between Bazarov and Pavel Petrovich grows worse; Pavel Petrovich challenges Bazarov to a pistol duel only to be wounded. Bazarov returns home after the duel but accidentally contracts typhus. On his deathbed, he implicitly tells Anna how he loves her.

Students soon notice that there are many similarities between *Catherine Carmier* and *Fathers and Sons*, as Gaines himself admits: "The same thing happens in those two books; a young man educated in a different part of the country comes back to be with the old people for a short while, and he falls in love with a beautiful woman, and of course there's tragedy" (Lowe, "Interview" 299). Gaines's emulation of Turgenev leads students to a deeper understanding of *Catherine Carmier* in terms of the gap in the relationship between young and old generations. A comparative approach to Gaines's novel partly clarifies one of the reasons the protagonist, Jackson Bradley, returns home to Louisiana after being educated at school, since Gaines heavily depends on Turgenev's novel structurally and thematically. An international and comparative study of Gaines's work is indispensable from this point of view.

Catherine Carmier opens with a scene wherein Jackson returns home to Bayonne to stay at Aunt Charlotte Moses's house for a while. Brother, Jackson's childhood friend, is waiting for him, and one of the Cajuns at the store asks another Cajun friend of his if Jackson is one of those "demonstrate people there" (7), vaguely afraid of new social change as the civil rights movement reaches its height beyond the quiet world of Bayonne. Similarly, in *Fathers and Sons*, Nikolay Petrovich and Pavel Petrovich are sensitive to two nihilists, Bazarov and Arkady, symbols of the new, emergent era, because Turgenev wrote the novel as a response to the widening divide between two generations during the growing nihilist movement of the 1860s, a period in which the countercultural aspects of nihilism overwhelmed Russia. At that time, the Russian defeat in the Crimean War exposed the weakness of the regime. When Alexander II came to the throne in 1855 after Tsar Nicholas, the most urgent issue for him was the abolishment of serfdom. However, by 1859, there were still 23 million serfs in Russia; when Bazarov comes home, the emancipation of serfs, the so-called great revolution, is a big, unfinished agenda item for the regime. Alexander II eventually succeeded in his efforts and the emancipation of the serfs was thus issued in 1861. The freed peasants then bought land, causing the end of the landowners' aristocracy. Although Turgenev wrote *Fathers and Sons* in the late 1850s, before the emancipation of serfs was announced in 1861, the rumor of this great change was already spreading among the people, and as he was working on the novel, he strongly felt the wave of a new era approaching.

Bazarov's nihilism, with its concomitant tenet of belonging to no sides, emerges in the course of such a great revolution; it resembles Jackson's ambivalent position, vacillating between two possible futures: to remain in Louisiana as a teacher or leave for California. Not only is Jackson ambivalent, but so is Raoul Carmier, in that he claims the status of a Creole, denying being either black or white, although his daughter Lillian denies this position once and for all: "I can't stand in the middle of the road any longer. Neither can you, and neither can you let Nelson. Daddy and his sisters can't understand this. They want us to be Creoles. Creoles. What a joke. Today you're one way or the other; you're white or you're black. There is no in-between" (48). The definition of *Creole* is difficult; according to *The Harvard Encyclopedia of American Ethnic Groups*: "In the United States, in the 20th century, Creole most often refers to the Louisiana Creoles of color. Ranging in appearance from mulattos to northern European whites, the Creoles of color constitute a Caribbean phenomenon in the United States" (qtd. in Kein, Introduction xiii). Hundreds of slaves and free people of color from Saint-Domingue migrated to New Orleans at the dawn of the nineteenth century, especially after the revolution led by L'Ouverture in 1798. "Raoul" and "Carmier" are French names, and the Carmier family was likely meant to be descendants of these immigrants. Because Creoles of French and Spanish descent have a long history in the area—since the Louisiana Purchase in 1803—it is no wonder that Raoul Carmier, regardless of being outdated, is a man of great self-respect. Joseph Griffin interprets Raoul's position as "[l]ocked in a vision of social and racial superiority—and indeed his heroic gestures against the white people in a sense vindicate this vision—he will not submit to the place assigned him in the racial and social order established by the South" (35), just as Bazarov rejects being in the aristocratic class or succumbing to any categorization: "Aristocracy, liberalism, progress, principles . . . goodness, what a lot of foreign . . . and useless words! A Russian doesn't need them, even if they come free" (48–49).

Before the beginning of the main love story of Jackson and Catherine, Gaines has Antoine Richard, one of the quarters people, speak as an omniscient mouthpiece to narrate the history of the quarrel over the property between Catherine's grandfather Robert Carmier and the landowner Mack Grover: "Antoine Richard said there was silence after this, and he lowered his head to look at the floor" (9). Gaines admitted that he had a hard time narrating the story from an omniscient point of view: "*Catherine Carmier* was told from the multiple point of view at one time. It just didn't work" (Gaudet and Wooton, *Porch Talk* 130). Students who read both novels realize that Gaines learned from *Fathers and Sons* how the novel should be narrated; Gaines himself confessed, "But I think the major thing I liked about [Turgenev] was the structure of his small novel" (Laney, "Conversation" 60), and that "form is what I'm interested in" (Rowell 92). Like Antoine Richard, Arkady serves as a temporary narrator, talking from an omniscient viewpoint to persuade frustrated Bazarov into understanding Pavel Petrovich's personal history and to decrease the tension between these two people: "Arkady told him his uncle's story. The reader will find it in the following chapter" (28). This description begins as follows in chapter 7: "Pavel Petrovich Kirsanov was educated first at home, like his younger brother Nikolay Petrovich, then at the Corps des Pages" (28).

Awaiting Jackson's arrival at Aunt Charlotte's house in chapters 6 and 7, his aunt and his childhood friend Mary Louise are so restless to welcome him back home after going out "on the front porch for about the tenth time" (20) that at "two great blasts . . . [t]heir hearts leaped into their throats. They looked toward the door, then at each other. Charlotte nodded her head; Mary Louise smiled" (21–22). Charlotte goes inside the house to check the floors and her appearance in the mirror, and her heart beats faster. Then she throws her arms around Jackson, almost knocking him back into the car. Gaines explained how he based their encounter in the novel upon Turgenev's *Fathers and Sons*: "when Charlotte meets Jackson, it was the same as when Bazarov meets his parents. I didn't know how an older person could meet a young person" (Parrill 192). Similar to how Charlotte receives Jackson, in chapter 1 of *Fathers and Sons*, Arkady's father, Nikolay Petrovich, and his mother, Arina, cannot wait for their son to come back home, asking the servant Pyotr many times, "Well, Pyotr, can you see anything yet?" (25). Once Arkady arrives and comes close to his father, "[a] few moments later his lips were touching the beardless, dusty and sunburnt cheek of the young graduate" (8).

Bazarov's parents are even more enthusiastic to receive their son when he suddenly and unexpectedly returns home in chapter 20. Arina Vlasyevna, Bazarov's mother, cries her son's first name, "Yenyusha, Yenyusha," and "[s]he at once put her chubby little arms round his neck, pressed her head to his chest, and there was silence" (110). In chapter 27, Bazarov's second sudden arrival home without notice causes his mother to get excited in a rapture of delight, and she again gets "into such a state and scurried about the house so much that Vasily Ivanovich [Bazarov's father] compared her to 'a partridge'" (180).

It is not difficult for students to detect that both novels are not deriding old age but rather praising old people who have accomplished the virtue of making their lives end well. Lillian declares to her sister that their father's farming business will soon be overtaken by Cajuns: "Daddy's world is over with. That farming out there—one man trying to buck against that whole family of Cajuns—is outdated. Can't you see that? Can't you understand that? It's the same thing his sisters are trying to prove in the city. Can't you see that?" (40). Raoul's world is indeed almost over, but it is not possible for Catherine to admit it. She is unknowingly aware that a new society emerges after the old one collapses, but the ending world is not worthless, just following a new tendency of the times. Konan Amani is of the opinion that "change is not the mere replacement of the old with the new, the past with the modern, but a blending of the positive aspects from both" (263). In chapter 11, Nikolay Petrovich also notices and is surprised that his view of the world is now totally different from that of his son. Pavel Petrovich wonders why Nikolay Petrovich looks pale and is strongly against his brother's lamentation that they are already outdated, behind the times:

> "My brother says we are right," [Nikolay Petrovich] thought, "and setting all vanity aside, I do myself think they are further from the truth than we are, but at the same time I feel they have something which we don't, some advantage over us. . . . Youth? No, not just youth. Doesn't their advantage lie in their being less marked by class than we are?"   (55)

Nikolay Petrovich is shocked, unable to leave the darkness in the garden; Pavel Petrovich insists that they have "much more right on our side than these young gentlemen" (54). Raoul and Catherine, representative of the old times, versus Lillian and Jackson, of the new times, is the same relationship as that of old Nikolay Petrovich and Pavel Petrovich versus the young Bazarov and Arkady. The contrast is not only clear in human relations but also in place settings and landscapes. As Gaines has said, "The style of [*Catherine Carmier*] is based around Turgenev's *Fathers and Sons*" (Sartisky 265); in accordance with Gaines's admission, his story is limited to three main places: Charlotte's house, Catherine's house, and Bayonne. Comparably, the three places to which *Fathers and Sons* is limited are Marino, Nikolskoe, and Bazarov's homeland estate. The country estate or garden that Russian aristocrats built were called *usad'ba*. These three *usad'bas* each are landscaped according to the taste of the owners. Marino, the *usad'ba* of the Kirsanovs, has a vast territory with two hundred serfs and boasts an "elegant study, with its walls, papered in a handsome dark grey, displaying weapons hung on a multicoloured Persian rug" (40). Nikolskoe is as magnificent as the Kirsanovs' estate, standing on the slope of a low hill, with "a green roof, white columns and a pediment with a coat of arms" (78). The *usad'ba* of the Bazarovs is rather small and meager in comparison with the Kirsanovs' and the Odintsovas', consisting of "six tiny rooms" with "a leather couch, in places worn through and torn" (112).

Jackson Bradley and Yevgeny Vassilich Bazarov are characteristically alike in that they no longer believe in God. Bazarov intends to take over his father's medical practice and tries his best to do research, believing in the strength of science only and not believing in culture and arts. Jackson, a college graduate like Bazarov, is "incapable of merging successfully the influences of his Southern upbringing and his education in the North," because "acquiring the means to decipher the codes of the dominant culture is an enterprise fraught with danger and complexity" (Beavers 134). Charlotte asks Jackson to go pray at church in chapter 22, yet Jackson declines her request: "I haven't forgotten God. But Christ, the church, I don't believe in that bourgeois farce—" (100). Jackson is a kind of nihilist like Bazarov, not believing in God. Bazarov does not pray to God even on his deathbed in spite of his father's desperate demand:

> "Yevgeny," Vasily Ivanovich continued and fell on his knees in front of Bazarov although his son didn't open his eyes and couldn't see him. "Yevgeny, you are better now. God willing, you will recover. But take advantage of this moment, give comfort to your mother and to me and do your duty as a Christian! It's terrible for me to say this to you, it's terrible. But even more terrible . . . it's for eternity, Yevgeny . . . think, how terrible. . . ."   (191)

Bazarov answers his father indifferently:

> "No, I'll wait," Bazarov interrupted him. "I agree with you that the crisis has come. But even if you and I are wrong, it doesn't matter—they can give communion to the unconscious."
> "Please, Yevgeny . . ."
> "I'll wait. And now I want to sleep. Don't bother me."   (191)

Because students new to Russian literature can find it challenging, it would be easier to begin with Russian writers mentioned in Gaines's novel. Lillian is the third child of Raoul but was brought to New Orleans when she was very small, so she does not respect her father as much as Catherine does. She begins to read European and Russian novels at school: "Lillian started with Victor Hugo, whom she was reading at present, then she went to Dumas, whom she had read only recently. Dumas, like Pushkin, her favorite poet, was part Negro" (123)—Victor Hugo (1802–85), a French poet and playwright; Alexandre Dumas (1802–70), a prolific French playwright and novelist and a son of General Dumas (1762–1806), who was born in Saint-Domingue to a French nobleman and an enslaved African woman; and Pushkin, as mentioned above, a Russian poet and novelist of African descent, whose maternal great-grandfather, General Abram Petrovich Gannibal (c. 1696–1781), was born, according to Pushkin, in Ethiopia. Gaines has a feeling of intimacy with Dumas and Pushkin because of their African blood. Interestingly, though Gaines respects Pushkin and admires his narrative technique—"Look at how Pushkin starts his novels; that's how novels should begin" (Desruisseaux 114)—Pushkin is referred to as an out-of-date writer in *Fathers and Sons* when Bazarov finds Nikolay Petrovich reading Pushkin and tries to stop it: "Do please explain to him that that's no good. He isn't a boy. It's time he gave up that nonsense. And what a thing to be a romantic in this day and age!" (45). Bazarov criticizes Pushkin's romanticism, arguing that being romantic in his time is nonsense. Students should know that Gaines presumably intentionally reverses this structure: Lillian, daughter of the new generation, favors Pushkin; by contrast, Bazarov, also son of a new generation, does not care for the Russian poet. When students raise the issue of the difference, here is a good opportunity to recommend that interested students read Pushkin's *Eugene Onegin*.

The Use of Letters in Both Novels

Lastly, I would call attention to how letters are effectively used in both novels. Once he falls in love, Jackson is always thinking about Catherine and wonders what he should do after he has decided to leave Louisiana as soon as possible. Then Lillian's letter arrives: "Pardon me for not writing a long and formal letter. There's a dance in Bayonne Sunday night. Being held at the Catholic Hall. We'll be there. Hope you come. Lillian" (189). Jackson goes to the dance to meet and steal away Catherine in the car. They drop by her house to pick up suitcases and her child, Nelson, to leave Louisiana for good. Raoul, given the news by two African Americans that Catherine has run away with Jackson, rushes to his own house and bumps into Jackson and Catherine on the porch. Lillian's letter triggers the conclusive fight between Jackson and Raoul. Likewise, in chapter 10 of *Fathers and Sons*, the statesman Matvei Ilyich Kolyazin sends a letter to Bazarov and Arkady to invite them to the governor's ball, to be held two days later (46). At the governor's ball Mrs. Sitnikov introduces Madame Odintsova to Bazarov, who is immediately attracted to her. The letter prompts Bazarov's love for Madame Odintsova as a result.

Toward the end of *Catherine Carmier*, Raoul fights Jackson to take back Catherine, pointing a gun at him. Jackson knocks the gun from Raoul's hand, but Raoul clings to him so that Jackson cannot go away with his daughter. The violent fight ends with Jackson's punch, which cuts Raoul's mouth, making him bleed: "Then Jackson heard a sound, a sound that could have been made by man or animal, but which was definitely a sound of defeat" (241). Nevertheless, Catherine does not go with Jackson, saying that she cannot leave her father wounded like this and remarking, "It's not over with, Daddy. You have stood this long. You can keep on standing. I'll stand beside you" (244–45). Here, we can compare the situation to the duel between Bazarov and Pavel Petrovich. After Pavel Petrovich bears witness to the kissing of Bazarov and a servant, Fenechka, Pavel Petrovich challenges Bazarov to a pistol duel: "I have the honor to proposing to you the following: we fight tomorrow, early, let's say at six, behind the little wood, with pistols, at a distance of ten paces . . ." (148). Bazarov readily accepts the challenge and chooses Pyotr as a witness. The next morning, the two fight with pistols; Bazarov is left unwounded, and Pavel Petrovich is injured in the thigh. Bazarov leaves Marino for his homeland. He wins the battle, but he dies later of typhus. In this regard, the same thing happens to Jackson, who wins the fight against Raoul but cannot obtain Catherine.

To help students consider and appreciate the fate of Catherine and Jackson, I lead them to a suitable illustration. Jackson compares his fate to a fallen leaf while he talks with Madame Bayonne: "I'm like a leaf, Madame Bayonne, that's broken away from the tree. Drifting" (79). Bazarov shares the same opinion: "Look at that. . . . There's a maple leaf which has come off and is falling to the ground. Its movements are just like the flight of a butterfly. Isn't that odd? That something so melancholy and dead should be like something so happy and alive" (127). The example gives us the paradox of Jackson's and Bazarov's radicalism, informing two novels' critiques of a conventional and one-sided worldview. The grappling with *Catherine Carmier* through the lens of *Fathers and Sons* deserves to be tried to initiate an earnest debate about foreign literature viewed through the lens of American literature. Likewise, getting students through Russian literature may be challenging, and yet this approach provides a good perspective from which students can see a foreign culture's traces in a Louisiana bayou.

NOTE

[1] This essay quotes from the 1981 North Point Press edition of *Catherine Carmier*.

Of Love and Dust: Why Gaines's "Funnest" Novel Had to End in Tragedy

Reggie Scott Young

I will never forget a comment a student made about Ernest J. Gaines's *Of Love and Dust* in a class called Louisiana Literature several years ago. This was a student who seldom contributed to discussions and who had not shown a significant degree of interest in the previous works read from our syllabus, which included Walker Percy's *The Moviegoer*, Robert Penn Warren's *All the King's Men*, and Gaines's earlier novel, *Catherine Carmier*. At times I worried about her being bored. However, in the middle of a lively exchange about the novel's early chapters and its amusing portrayal of Marcus Payne, a man whose freedom becomes endangered by a plantation owner who has purchased his bond for the purpose of subjecting him to five or more years of labor, and his futile attempts to defy a plantation overseer (Sidney Bonbon), a hand shot up in the back of the room and a face that never seemed to smile said with grinning lips, "This must be the funnest novel Mr. Gaines has ever written."

I wasn't the only one who laughed that day, and I think we all laughed with this student instead of at her. We had been discussing the early antics of John and Freddie, two gay Christian field workers; Marcus's attempt to harvest corn wearing what another student described as "his pimp shoes and city hustling clothes"; and especially the slapstick depiction of a house fair brawl attended by Marcus and his appointed mentor, Frank James Kelly (Jim Kelly), the novel's narrator. Even though it was an English class, the student's tongue-in-cheek use of the word *funnest* would not have been as poignant if she had expressed it in standard English. After all, our school is located in Lafayette, a city and parish in south Louisiana that is only sixty-five miles away from the plantation where Gaines spent his boyhood. It is the same university where Gaines served as writer-in-residence for more than twenty years before he retired in 2005. Most of the students I teach are the Cajun, Creole, and black American descendants of people who served as models for the characters Gaines created for this novel as well as other works that depict life in this region of the country.

Similar to the students Grant Wiggins teaches in one of Gaines's better-known novels, *A Lesson Before Dying*—children who meet with Wiggins in a small 1940s backwoods church that also doubles as a schoolhouse during the week—many of the previous generations of my students' families did not have access to higher education during their youth or access to what we might today think of as quality educational experiences at the primary and secondary school levels, if they were able to attend high school at all. Some of the students I teach today from poorer areas of the parish and the surrounding bayous and rural areas of other nearby parishes are first-generation college students who were not afforded the same kind of preparation for college that students typically receive in many other states, and that is why the "funnest" statement sounded like a revelation to me. It told me that some aspect of Gaines's novel had engaged that student during her process of reading. It was not as if the student spoke like that all the time, and I am sure she knew her choice of words offered the best way for her to express what she desired to say.

There are obvious examples of humor students encounter in this novel, especially in the first half of the narrative, although this particular work may not appeal to all readers, especially those who are more interested in representations of urban and suburban life or works expressed through postmodernist experiments in narrative style and form. *Of Love and Dust* features a linear plot through a fairly straightforward narration, and none of the novel's folk characters, with one or two possible exceptions, has ever participated in anything more formal in nature than what the novel describes as Sunday termination services in the church housed in the plantation's quarters. In recent years the concept of gritty literary works set in the South has increased in importance to southern literary studies, and despite the exclusion of works by Gaines from the recent anthology *Grit Lit: A Rough South Reader* (Carpenter and Franklin), there is no better example of a rough, tough, and gritty southern novel than *Of Love and Dust*. It is a work that is steeped in the same country blues that evolved as a way of offering insights into secular dimensions of African American rural life that compelled both men and women to do the best they could for themselves without developing much of a reliance on others. According to Gaines in his essay "Miss Jane and I," from his collection *Mozart and Leadbelly: Stories and Essays*, the novel's plot was inspired, in part, by a Lightnin' Hopkins song, "Tim Moore's Farm," whose lyrics include the following lines:

> Yeah, you know Mr. Tim Moore's a man
> He don't never stand and grin
> He just said, "Keep out of the graveyard, I'll save you from the pen"
> You know, soon in the morning, he'll give you scrambled eggs
> Yes, but he's liable to call you so soon
> You'll catch a mule by his hind legs.

The song's lyrics, available online along with *YouTube* videos of Hopkins's recording, illustrate the manner in which Gaines drew inspiration from another medium in his effort to portray black rural life of the era when both Hopkins and Mance Lipscomb (anonymously) recorded versions of the song. There is lingering confusion concerning which bluesman deserves credit for its composition, but, like other folk-inspired songs and stories, "Tim Moore's Farm"—or "Tom Moore's Farm," as Lipscomb titled his version—should be viewed as a product of a collaborative process outside the world of artistic ownership and copyright laws.[1]

Of Love and Dust is, in part, a work that stems from Gaines's effort to offer a revised and greatly expanded rendering of the song's text. Gaines has stated that the better-known version, by Hopkins, was his source of inspiration.[2] Marshall Hebert offers a representation that is suggestive of the callous landowner Tim Moore.[3] The novel's plot owes a debt to the song's line, "[k]eep out of the grave-yard, I'll save you from the pen." Although Marcus is not literally kicked by a mule's hind legs, he suffers a similar fate in his dealings with Marshall. The over-seer, Bonbon, is in essence Gaines's substitution for the song's mule, although the song refers to "Mr. Tim Moore's man," someone who does not "stand and grin" and tells the speaker, "If you stay out the graveyard nigger, I'll keep you out the pen." Gaines has commented that Bessie Smith's mastery of language allowed her, in "The Backwater Blues," to describe the Great Flood of 1927 in twelve lines of poetic blues lyrics whereas William Faulkner took over one hundred pages to do the same thing in prose (Gaudet and Young xvi). Gaines does the reverse in revising a simple, four-verse song into an almost-three-hundred-page prose portrayal of a black man, Marcus, whose body is placed under the subjection of a plantation patriarch because of the acquisition of his bond. Because of the rights granted to white landowners in many parts of the South during Jim Crow, Marshall is allowed to assume ownership of Marcus's body and soul after Marcus's arrest for the fatal wounding of another black man in a bar fight. Despite the possibility that Marcus acted in self-defense, the novel offers an illustration of how involuntary or forced labor involving African American men helped supply landowners with a source of cheap labor in a manner remi-niscent of antebellum slavery.

In the spirit of fun and to approach the text from a different perspective, es-pecially in university classes made up of students who are predominantly non-English and non–liberal arts majors (this is also a great approach to the novel for high school students), I like to play clips of Morgan Freeman in his role as Hoke Colburn, the chauffeur in *Driving Miss Daisy*. Two decades ago it would not have been unusual to have students who had either seen the film or at least known about it, with a few being aware that *Driving Miss Daisy* won the Acad-emy Award for Best Picture in 1990, the same year Spike Lee's *Do the Right Thing* failed to receive a nomination. (A number of film critics, including Gene Siskel and Roger Ebert, proclaimed Lee's film the best from that year and said that the academy's decision was made to appease mainstream white audiences long before the #OscarsSoWhite controversy began in response to the exclusion of nonwhite nominees for Academy Awards in 2016.[4]) I then ask if there has ever been an actor who could play the role of Jim Kelly better than Freeman from that earlier time in his career, and there is usually near unanimous agreement that there is not. This is something I once discussed with Gaines, and he liked the idea of Freeman playing the role of Kelly so much that he would have supported casting today's older Freeman to play the part. (The idea of casting actors to play characters in *Of Love and Dust* came to me after I discovered an old screen-play that Gaines had stored in his personal archives, one he wrote for the novel not long after its composition.) After showing students the clips of Freeman in *Driving Miss Daisy*, I then offer them excerpts from commentaries by white and black film critics and viewers that are critical of both *Driving Miss Daisy* and Hoke Colburn as a character, especially Colburn's repeated use of the stereo-typical phrase "Lawdy." Of course, that can make some students feel a bit uncom-fortable, especially those who really like Freeman as an actor, but then I ask them to consider if their favorable responses to Colburn might somehow be related to why the film industry found more value in *Driving Miss Daisy* than in *Do the Right Thing*, especially since the latter was a much more innovative and cutting-edge work that set out to accomplish what many great works of art successfully do by shining a light on our frailties as human beings in a fallen world. That leads to a discussion about whether Gaines's novel also accomplishes this goal or if it fails for any specific reasons.

In showing film clips of Freeman, I want to encourage students who do not always have extensive literary backgrounds to consider *Of Love and Dust* as they might a movie—not to judge the novel or rate it in a manner like they would on the *Rotten Tomatoes* Web site; instead, I want them to analyze this highly cin-ematic novel the way a critic might analyze a film. This process allows us to ex-amine the similarities and differences between works in the two genres, and it often results in students gaining a better understanding of elements of craft re-lated to plot, setting, and characterization. I want to involve students in a dis-cussion about the novel's potential as a film that will engage them as both creative and critical thinkers as they consider ways to reimagine the work in a different medium. I place added stress on characterization, because it often leads to lively discussions after I ask students to think about the actors and actresses who might be best suited to play the roles of notable characters from the novel.

The film industry prospers from its adaptations of literary works and its cast-ing of leading actors to play the roles of important fictional characters, so when the opportunity presents itself I challenge students to do the same with this novel. It can be rather fruitless to ask students today to consider actors from the time of the novel's publication, since the middle of the twentieth century is like an-cient history to many of them; nevertheless, I tell them that Hollywood would have surely considered certain actors from that era such as Billy Dee Williams in the role of Marcus (someone they might recognize from the original *Star Wars* trilogy), Leslie Uggams as Pauline (whom they might recognize from her minor roles in *Deadpool* and television's *Empire*), Sidney Poitier as Jim Kelly, Sondra Locke as Louise, Warren Beatty as Bonbon, and Lee Marvin as Marshall He-bert, as well as other actors based on the films and roles they had appeared in. In classrooms equipped with audiovisual devices, I attempt to expose students to the actors' bios, films they appeared in, and clips of performances available online as a way of explaining my rationale for selecting them to play characters from the novel. That generally leads to a classroom debate about the merits of actors from today, and students in recent years have suggested the likes of Ter-rence Howard for the part of Marcus, Denzel Washington to play Jim Kelly, Beyoncé for the role of Pauline, and so on (these are by no means unanimous choices). In arguing for their selections, students are forced to dig into the text to find evidence to help support their choices. If an older student claims Will Smith would be a better choice for Marcus based on his role in *The Legend of Bagger Vance*, others who have seen that film may point out the stark differences between Bagger Vance's character and Marcus's and that the Smith of today is too old to play the part based on the novel's description of Marcus's character. The point of the exercise is to encourage students to use the language of the novel to help support their casting decisions, and in doing so it helps them to gain a deeper understanding of the text as well as the craftsmanship the author used in constructing a believable world full of authentic characters.

In discussions of this nature it is important to make sure students understand that an adaption is a revised version of an original work based on someone else's interpretation and artistic vision—an adaptation is not necessarily meant to offer an exact representation of the original. Since literary works and films about the past use history as a canvas for writers and filmmakers to explore relevant issues of humanity in relationship to their own present age, one could not expect an adaption of *Of Love and Dust* today to reflect every aspect of a novel that was written in the late 1960s, especially because filmmakers today might decide to let Marcus and his white lover, Louise (Bonbon's estranged wife), escape at the story's end, with Marshall, instead of Marcus, being the one to pay for his crimes of manipulation. Discussions of a possible director might raise the issue of whether the film should have a black director or simply the best director possible. Inevitably a student will shout out, "Tarantino would do an awesome job with this book," and I will jokingly suggest that there are not enough explosions in Gaines's narrative to suit Tarantino's style. (Is he the best director for this particular story, or simply someone whose films you have enjoyed?) For those who insist that only a black director should be used to film a work by an African American writer (a surprising number of nonblack students often join in and argue this point), I make reference to the playwright Romulus Linney's adaptation of *A Lesson Before Dying* for the stage that carries with it Gaines's blessing. Students are then asked to consider potential directors based on their cinematic vision and filmmaking style as opposed to their racial background: what would be the rationale for hiring a Spike Lee (*Malcolm X*) or John Singleton (*Rosewood*) for this particular film? What about Tate Taylor (*The Help* and *Get on Up*) or Marc Forster (*Monster's Ball*)? The subject of a possible film adaptation based on a close reading of the novel can lead to a paper assignment requiring students to discuss how they would adapt the novel and direct specific actors to play major and supporting roles.

In a special topics course I once taught titled The Blues Impulse in American Literature, I assigned students to read Gaines's novel in tandem with August Wilson's play *Joe Turner's Come and Gone*, because both offer depictions of the historical seizure and enforced bondage of African American men through the convict lease system that operated in several southern states during Jim Crow.[5] I asked students to consider Jim Kelly in relationship to Herald Loomis in Wilson's play; after all, they are both presented as men who have lost the very essence of their manhood. We debated the issue of black manhood while examining these characters and others from our reading list, since manhood and its essence is an important thematic concern of the blues. In fact, manhood as a universal concept, as opposed to its being a relative one, is one of the issues the readings led us to address, and it resulted in a discussion about the construction of identity in relationship to factors such as race, gender, and local culture. Using sources from feminist and queer theory as well as works that address race as a social construction, I used it as an opportunity to expose students to theoretical considerations of the issue in an effort to help them understand that their personal assumptions about manhood—assumptions often based on personal experiences and information received from family, friends, communal sources, and popular culture—are not necessarily comprehensive and authoritative.

In Wilson's play, the unsuspecting Loomis, a religious man from a devout Christian family, is kidnapped by the infamous Joe Turner and his men and subjected to seven years of hard labor despite not being suspected of involvement in any crime. When he is finally released and shows up at a boardinghouse in Pittsburgh in search of his wife and daughter, he is a shell of his former self, having lost what the play characterizes as his metaphorical "song." Similar to Gaines's novel, the play's plot and title were directly influenced by a blues song, an early tune that was known in parts of the black South in the 1890s. When a black male would fail to make it home at night in one of the areas under the influence of Joe Turney, the brother of Tennessee governor Pete Turney, the explanation given to loved ones about his disappearance was "They tell me Joe Turner's come and gone." Little is known about how Turney became Turner in folklore and song, but Turney was famous for running a chain gang for profit that used to prey on African American males who were suspected of minor crimes as well as unsuspecting innocent ones. In *Of Love and Dust*, although Marcus has not been convicted, the outcome of his legal defense is understood to be a foregone conclusion and therefore he is forced to begin his term of servitude under Marshall's control before the date of his actual trial. In resisting Marshall and his overseer, Bonbon, who is likewise a pawn under Marshall's control, the novel depicts Marcus's efforts to maintain possession of his song, whether song is interpreted to mean manhood, humanity, or freedom.

A consideration of the blues can offer important insights into the aesthetic that informs Gaines's work as a writer. In *Mozart and Leadbelly*, Gaines discusses how the authors of classic novels provided him with crucial insights concerning the genre as a literary form, but the people he wanted to write about and the culture he wanted to represent on the printed page could not be found in those works. He wanted to write about what he characterized as "[t]his Louisiana thing that drives me" (also the title of a photobiography about his life and career as a writer that I helped to compile and edit) and about a particular folk community, a blues cultural community. Although classic works of fiction might have taught him valuable lessons about how to structure stories on the page, it was blues music and the other sacred and profane cultural expressions he remembered from the plantation quarters where he was raised that helped to inspire the contents of his novels, short stories, and personal essays.

Gaines's essays are valuable for teaching his works because they offer insights about both his process of writing and his development as a writer. In published interviews, recorded talks, and Q&A sessions from public appearances, Gaines has resisted requests for him to speak critically about his own works, asserting that his only job is to write his books while leaving it to scholars and readers to interpret them. In the essay "Miss Jane and I," he explains what the character Miss Jane Pittman has meant to him while also providing insights into the process that led to her creation and her life off the page (including the television movie based on the novel, reviews of the novel that assumed Jane was a real person, and other interesting details); essays such as this one, along with the published interviews that are included in *Porch Talk with Ernest Gaines* (edited by Marcia Gaudet and Carl Wooton), *Conversations with Ernest Gaines* (edited by John Lowe), and various magazines, journals, and periodicals, should be considered important resources for anyone teaching his works.

In the title essay from *Mozart and Leadbelly*, for example, Gaines discusses how during a trip back to Louisiana one summer to do research and spend time with family and friends he visited the notorious White Eagle lounge in Port Allen, a small town just across the Mississippi River from Baton Rouge. While there his friends pointed out a man who had recently killed another man, referred to only as "H," but H's killer was sitting up in the White Eagle enjoying a drink as if nothing had happened (28–29). According to Gaines, the response he received after he asked, "Shouldn't he be in jail?" went as follows: "He was the good nigger. . . . You don't have to go to the pen when a good nigger kills a bad nigger. A white man can pay your bond and you work for him for five to seven years" (29). Gaines goes on to write:

> I could not get that image of this guy sitting there in his blue silk shirt, blue slacks, and two-toned shoes from my mind, and back in San Francisco one day while listening to Lightnin' Hopkins and "Tim Moore's Farm," I thought about this guy at the White Eagle who had killed H. Suppose now, just suppose, I said to myself, you take a guy like this and you put him on a plantation to work off his time under a tough, brutal white overseer: what do you think would happen between the two of them? (29)

The experience led to Gaines's composition of the story "Three Men," which appeared in his *Bloodline* collection, a work that he later developed into *Of Love and Dust* in an effort to explore the consequences a man such as H's killer might face under the subjection of a brutal white overseer. As a writer who teaches literature in addition to creative writing courses, I find that sharing Gaines's story about the experiences that led him to write *Of Love and Dust*, including his listening to the Lightnin' Hopkins song, can help generate curiosity in students concerning how authors come across ideas for their works and how stories and novels can develop out of source materials.

In a southern literature course I once assigned students to read *Of Love and Dust* right after our reading and discussion of Zora Neale Hurston's *Their Eyes Were Watching God*, a work that offers another depiction of African American grit lit—especially chapters that focus on protagonist Janie's life with Tea Cake in the area of the Everglades in Florida that characters refer to as "the muck." One of the most important aspects of our discussions about the novel was the debate we had about its merits as a work of literature among students with strong backgrounds in literary classics and the traditional canon. The dialect used in the first-person narration was a challenge, but of greater concern for students from strict religious backgrounds was Janie's act of walking away from her arranged marriage with another man without first obtaining a divorce. In response I read passages from Charles S. Johnson's 1934 study, *Shadow of the Plantation*, as a way to illustrate how people who were forced to live in plantation communities during the Jim Crow era were often excluded from full participation in the legal system, meaning they could not legally marry or obtain legal divorces from their common-law marriages. Johnson points out that to residents of many of these communities, the act of leaving a partner signified the fact that a divorce had taken place (54–55). Since laws forbade slaves from obtaining legal marriages or exercising basic human rights in most of the South during the antebellum era, many of the cultural practices that developed during slavery remained in place to varying degrees well into the twentieth century. Those practices play significant roles in several of Gaines's other works; for example, Sonny, the child narrator in "A Long Day in November," a story from *Bloodline*, watches as his mother considers marriage to another man on the same day she leaves the cabin she shares with her trifling husband and Sonny's father. Other examples are Jane's adoption of the orphaned Ned in *The Autobiography of Miss Jane Pittman* and her common-law marriage to Joe Pittman and her assumption of his last name, despite both being based on de facto practices. Works such as Johnson's study, which was published in the decade before the setting in *Of Love and Dust*, can help students gain a better understanding of the reality they will find themselves exposed to during their process of reading. Contextual works of this nature can also help students avoid reading the novel through the filter of their own lives and the cultural norms of the communities in which they live.

The first time I taught the novel, I knew much less about the blues as an expressive form and how blues expressions have served as a literary impulse that runs through works in both the African American and southern literary traditions (Werner). I attempt to offer students insights concerning the artistic value of the blues, which I consider to be an underappreciated art form. Kelly's measured cadences in narrating the opening chapters often help to pique students' interest in the text, motivating them to dig more deeply into the novel's construction of characters, its vivid plantation setting, and the way Gaines succeeds in offering multiple points of view through his use of Kelly as a single first-person narrative device. In some of the classes in which I have taught *Of Love and Dust*, I have found that a consideration of Gaines's methods as a storyteller can lead students to learn significant lessons not only about how literature works but also about important contextual matters that some instructors may prefer to dismiss as extraliterary (these are issues that may contribute to *Of Love and Dust* being one of the author's least taught works of fiction). But there are those, beside myself, who value the novel and consider it an underrated treasure. For example, in a poll of southern scholars, critics, and writers conducted by *Oxford American* in 2009 to select the "best southern novel of all time," *Of Love and Dust* did not make the list (*A Lesson Before Dying* was twenty-fourth in the voting, and *Miss Jane*, required reading for every high school student in France, did not receive any votes), but it did receive enough votes to be listed in the magazine's ranks of underrated books from the South. One of the judges, Susan Straight, commented about the novel: "I read this novel every year and use it in classes often, and I am always stunned by this entire world recreated in one isolated rural setting, and how an opera of love and hate and revenge is played out in the fields and small houses and dusty roads" ("Underrated Books"). *Of Love and Dust* may not offer the best demonstration of a metaphorical "Mozart" classical or formal influence on Gaines's work as a novelist, but one could argue that no other southern novel is as deeply steeped in a "Leadbelly" or Deep South blues aesthetic as this particular work.

This is a very southern novel from a writer who owes a great debt to William Faulkner, but an overemphasis of Faulkner's influence in discussions of Gaines's fiction can obscure other issues that merit consideration. During my first classroom encounter with *Of Love and Dust* as a college student in the 1980s, I learned much more about Faulkner's legacy as a great southern writer than I did about the novel by Gaines that our class had been assigned to read, and Faulkner was not on our syllabus. Although Gaines has spoken about the important role Faulkner and other southern writers had in his development, he has also attempted to show critics and scholars that his works have a very different agenda from Faulkner's. One example can be found in his statement about Miss Jane Pittman in relationship to Faulkner's Dilsey, in which Gaines said he did not have Dilsey in mind when he created his character and that "the difference between Dilsey and Miss Jane Pittman is that Faulkner gets Dilsey talking her story from his [the Compsons'] kitchen; the young schoolteacher in my book gets Miss Jane's story from Miss Jane's [own] kitchen. And it makes a difference" (Lowe, "Interview" 313). Gaines has also credited Russian authors such as Ivan Turgenev and Leo Tolstoy, the British novelist W. Somerset Maugham, and various American writers such as F. Scott Fitzgerald and Ernest Hemingway as important influences. In fact, Hemingway's well-known theme of "grace under pressure" is an important concept for students to understand in their consideration of Marcus in *Of Love and Dust* and other major characters from Gaines's novels and short stories; it is Marcus's demonstration of grace in the face of certain death that leads both Kelly and Bonbon to respect him. Although

Gaines has disavowed any direct influence from Richard Wright, it is important to keep in mind that their respective works, set in rural Mississippi and adjoining rural Louisiana, are cut from virtually the same cultural cloth, and *Of Love and Dust* depicts a world that is similar to the one conveyed in Wright's "Long Black Song," from his collection *Uncle Tom's Children* (1938), a story that also considers the tragic consequences of interracial sex in the South.

Since the narration in *Of Love and Dust* is written primarily in the blues-inflected folk language of Jim Kelly, someone who wails a tune about his feelings of grief for his past lover, Billie Jean, Kelly's role deserves considerable attention in class discussions. Whenever I teach Gaines, I find it useful to ask students to examine his constructing of a layered narration through his use of free indirect discourse and other narrative techniques, similar to what he does in other novels such as *Miss Jane* and *A Lesson Before Dying*. Unlike multivocal narrative works that offer fictional representations through the use of different narrators, Gaines uses Kelly as the sole narrator to represent the various voices and narrative perspectives of others on the plantation. The novelist John Edgar Wideman offers one of the earliest and best critical discussions of *Of Love and Dust* in an essay that appeared in a 1974 special issue on Gaines in *Callaloo*; in it Wideman discusses some of the possible oversights in the use of Kelly as a narrative device. After all, Kelly, even as the novel's first-person omniscient voice, provides insights into events and activities by other characters that he has no way of knowing, although most of the information he conveys is through speculation and hearsay. But Wideman states that because Kelly is such a compelling voice and a figure that most readers find easy to identify with, he is a narrator that we readily trust; therefore, readers are happy to overlook technical glitches in the writing that involve his narration.

It may be helpful to refer to Wideman's essay when very sharp student-readers ask questions about Kelly's role as storyteller that may be difficult to answer. It also provides an opportunity for discussion about how narrations work in fictional texts and the various ways authors make use of first-person narrators. One work many students already know and that Gaines has admitted learning from while developing Kelly as his narrator is Fitzgerald's *The Great Gatsby*. Since Kelly's disgust at Marcus's actions and demeanor in the first half of the novel likely mirrors the impressions that many students will have of the character (after all, students' impressions of Marcus are informed by Kelly, a character who is liked and respected by most others in this fictional world), when Kelly's opinion about Marcus changes—after Kelly admits that Marcus's actions have helped to change him for the better—students may begin to see Kelly as a more dynamic character, especially after his act of defiance at the novel's very end, when he walks away from Marshall's influence and control in protest of Marcus's death. Because it is so easy to like Kelly, students may want to view him as the novel's protagonist instead of Marcus, but I try to get them to question whether this is an analytical response to the narrative based on what we know about the principles of characterization or an emotional reaction due to their feelings about Kelly.

In the novel's closing scene, Marcus has already been killed by Bonbon, owing to the manipulation of Marshall and Marcus's refusal to take off and run without standing up for himself. After receiving a last meal from Aunt Margaret and giving her a consoling kiss on the jaw, Kelly departs from the plantation in possibly his first true act of agency, despite not knowing what awaits him in the future. In his conversation with Aunt Margaret, she reiterates the fact that Marcus and Louise were doomed to die because of their demonstration of courage as a couple willing to act on their love for each other in a place and time when a black man standing up for himself in union with a white woman was an intolerable taboo. Aunt Margaret is blind to the fact that, despite Bonbon's role in Marcus's death, Marshall is ultimately responsible, possibly because she and the other elders in the plantation community are fearful of any change that might disrupt the relative comfort of their lives. That is why they might be as relieved by Marcus's death as they are sorrowful, because Marcus as a character represents and anticipates the kind of change that will sweep the South and the rest of the nation in the second half of the century. Wideman notes Marcus's Roman name and that he possesses traits that are comparable to Cassius Clay before he became Muhammad Ali. Gaines, in fact, has admitted that Ali was one of the models for Marcus's character (*Mozart* 149–50). That is why it is always interesting to me when a student asks: if Marcus is meant to represent the most dynamic character in the story, or the novel's hero, why does Gaines let him die in the end?

It is not unusual even today for commentators on the novel to claim that because of the setting it was only natural for Marcus to die and that his death in the story was an unavoidable conclusion; after all, at that time in the Deep South, how could he have gotten away? That is why I make it clear to students that Marcus's dying and Louise's being institutionalized are not what happened in Gaines's original version of *Of Love and Dust*, because in it the two of them, not Bonbon and Pauline, escape to the North. In the title essay from *Mozart and Leadbelly*, Gaines reveals that his editor at the time told him the ending was a farce and that he would have to revise the second half of the narrative in order to get the novel into print (29). In discussing the essay with a class, I point out that one of the arguments made by the editor was that Marcus had killed a man, so it was unrealistic to allow him to get away free in the end, despite the fact that there are a number of characters in this particular fictional world who had already killed but did not have to die for the sake of maintaining a moral balance. Marshall and Bonbon had conspired to kill in the past, and in the revised, published version they both have a hand in killing Marcus, but in the end Marshall remains in control while the white Bonbon is allowed to flee with the black woman he had maintained an adulterous relationship with for many years. I like to point out that this is a novel that was written right before the release of such films as *100 Rifles* (1969), *Sweet Sweetback's Baadasssss Song* (1971), and *Shaft* (1971), each featuring depictions of interracial sexual relationships, so it could be that an editor's directive robbed Gaines's novel from being a visionary work, much more reflective of the time when it was written and also one that looks forward to later in the century, when lines of racial and sexual division began to erode. Students will obviously have different opinions about this issue, and there are often those who agree with the wisdom of Gaines's editor, but that is another reason *Of Love and Dust* is one of his "funnest" novels to teach and a novel that students can learn a great deal from about literature, the process of writing, and the world in which we live.

NOTES

[1] Although Hopkins is listed as the composer of "Tim Moore's Farm," an article in *Texas Monthly* reports that a farmer, Yank Thornton, composed the initial version of "Tom Moore's Farm" (Waller). Lipscomb, who lived on a neighboring farm, heard Thornton perform crude versions of the song at local dances and helped Thornton improve the lyrics while providing it with a musical arrangement on this guitar. Hopkins did not hear the song until years later, in 1949, and changed the title to avoid possible reprisals from the real Tom Moore and his brothers.

[2] Gaines has discussed his affinity for Hopkins's song in various interviews: for example, see Lowe, *Conversations* 3, 4, 100.

[3] For more about Moore and the Moore farm, see Schiche. The farm, which served as a work farm for parolees, in many ways mirrors the Hebert farm of Gaines's novel.

[4] On *Driving Miss Daisy* as one of the more controversial selections for best picture, see Levy; Bromley. Both Gene Siskel and Roger Ebert wrote positive reviews about *Do the Right Thing* at the time of its release: Ebert, in particular, noted its importance in helping the nation understand the plight of inner-city black residents in the 1980s. Despite early warnings by mainstream white critics who claimed the main purpose of *Do the Right Thing* was to promote racial hatred and violence, Lee's film is regarded today as an important work in the history of American cinema.

[5] There are numerous articles available on the practice of convict leasing in the South: for Louisiana, see Carleton. On convict leasing and the music that developed in folk communities in response to it, see "'They Tell Me.'"

His Foot in a Door That Slavery Built: History, Symbol, and Resistance in Gaines's *Of Love and Dust*

Richard Yarborough

Of Love and Dust appeared in 1967 to favorable critical response. Publications as varied as *The Nation, Negro Digest, The New York Times Book Review*, and *New Statesman* lauded Ernest Gaines's second novel as further evidence of his promise as a fresh talent on the American literary scene. However, *Of Love and Dust* was soon overshadowed by the release of his justly celebrated *The Autobiography of Miss Jane Pittman* in 1971 and its Emmy Award–winning film adaptation in 1974, both of which were greeted with widespread enthusiasm. Over the half century since its publication, *Of Love and Dust* has garnered relatively little attention from scholars, teachers, and general readers alike, despite the fact that it is one of Gaines's most emotionally compelling, provocative, and artfully constructed works. Furthermore, largely because of both Gaines's characteristically accessible prose and the novel's straightforward plot, there has been a tendency to underestimate the conceptual ambition, stylistic control, and structural complexity manifest in *Of Love and Dust*. This essay offers a range of pedagogical strategies designed to enable students to engage fruitfully a text that richly rewards in-depth analysis. I first focus on the requisite historical background for appreciating what exactly is at stake in the book. Second, I examine Gaines's masterful use of language and symbolic imagery. Third, I discuss dominant themes in the novel.

Early in *Of Love and Dust*, the African American narrator, Jim Kelly, refers to "this year—forty-eight" (10); later he remarks, "The war had been over three years already" (136).[1] Clearly, the book is set in 1948, shortly after the end of World War II. Thus, one cannot help but be taken aback by the odd lack of consensus among contemporaneous reviewers regarding when the events in the novel actually take place. A possible reason for this confusion (which students may experience as well) is the ambiance of temporal stasis that pervades the novel. To put it another way, one can imagine the action being staged ten, twenty, even thirty years earlier. The uncanny sense both of timelessness and also of the intrusive, suffocating burden of history locates *Of Love and Dust* in a long tradition of post–Civil War southern literature. Moreover, it is crucial for students to realize that this burden of history is inextricably tied up with the institution of chattel slavery and its lingering, traumatic legacy. It may be hard for today's readers to grasp the overwhelming social constraints that shaped race relations in the South after the abolition of slavery and that persisted for roughly a century. Yet without some awareness of the elaborate, dehumanizing de facto and de jure protocols governing black-white interactions in the region, there is little chance that students will understand why Gaines's characters behave as they do. While it may be impractical to attempt to survey all the issues regarding race, gender, slavery, and the American South that are referenced in the novel, there are several that merit comment, even if only in the course of directing students to reliable sources of additional information.

The first is the unrelenting, oppressive nature of the racial segregation, economic marginalization, and political disfranchisement that confronted southern blacks from roughly the end of Reconstruction through the mid-twentieth century. In the late 1940s, when *Of Love and Dust* is set, the vast majority of blacks in the South could not vote and thus lacked any real political representation and clout. And the withholding of the franchise left them with few options for safeguarding their rights and for affecting governmental policies to their own benefit. Most African Americans were also dependent on whites for employment and thus had to monitor their behavior with that reality in mind. One indication of the ways in which white state power enforced racial subjugation was the harsh treatment of blacks in the criminal justice system, an issue that has received increasing attention in popular media in the United States over the past decade. A case in point in *Of Love and Dust* is the presence on Marshall Hebert's plantation of Marcus Payne, the young black man who serves as the catalyst for the tragic events that unfold. His release from jail—where he had been awaiting trial for murder—so that he can work in Hebert's fields is a continuation of a practice known as the convict lease system that emerged in the late nineteenth century as part of the perpetuation of the quasi-slavery conditions under which southern blacks existed. Once Marcus arrives on the plantation, the extent to which he is controlled (or meant to be controlled) by unrelenting labor and the threat of violence reveals just how little has changed since the days when slaves were managed in a similar fashion. (Two excellent resources here are *The New Jim Crow*, by Michelle Alexander, and the award-winning documentary *13th*, by Ava DuVernay.)

The vulnerability of African Americans in such dire circumstances extended well beyond matters of politics, mobility, economics, and the law. One of the most controversial and pervasive aspects of black-white interactions during and after slavery was the unimpeded access that white males presumed to the bodies of black women. Rape and other forms of sexual exploitation were rampant in the slave South and far too common through much of the first half of the twentieth century. (Gaines alludes in the novel to the fact that Sidney Bonbon, the Cajun overseer, "laid with all and any" of the black female field hands [62].) Whereas white men could abuse black women with relative impunity, sexual contact between black men and white women was unconditionally forbidden and brutally punished. Indeed, in parts of the United States, there were laws proscribing interracial marriage until the Supreme Court's *Loving v. Virginia* decision in 1967, coincidentally the same year in which *Of Love and Dust* was published. Accordingly, Marcus's carnal relationship with Bonbon's wife, Louise, constitutes the violation of a taboo judged by the white South to demand the ultimate retribution. In contrast, Bonbon's long-running involvement with Pauline Guerin, a black woman on the Hebert plantation, is sanctioned as long as he maintains at least the semblance of a commitment to his white wife and child. Students might be referred here to Jeff Nichols's 2016 film *Loving*, which dramatizes the circumstances leading to the Supreme Court's landmark decision. It would also be beneficial to call their attention to the horrific killing of Emmett Till in 1955. Till, a black Chicago teenager visiting family in Mississippi, allegedly insulted a local white woman and was subsequently kidnapped, beaten, and shot. The case—particularly the acquittal of the two white men accused of Till's murder—received widespread publicity in the United States and abroad and helped to highlight the ongoing racist treatment of blacks in the South.

But why does Gaines situate his plot in 1948 in particular? Although it may be relevant that 1948 is the year when he left Louisiana for the San Francisco Bay Area, I would suggest that the primary significance of the date is that it lies in the transitional period between the end of World War II and the emergence in the national consciousness of the civil rights activism that would forever alter southern race relations. That is, 1948 marks a moment on the cusp of unprecedented, unsettling change, change that none of Gaines's characters in *Of Love and Dust* can possibly see coming. Thus, it is useful for students to recognize Marcus's resistance as a foreshadowing of the radical challenge to white hegemony in the South mounted by blacks and their allies in the 1950s.

Starkly drawn and stylistically spare, *Of Love and Dust* offers an excellent opportunity to examine the diverse ways in which writers enhance and complicate their narratives through the manipulation of language and figures of speech. Accordingly, I kick off class discussion by having the students dissect the first page or two and then several other selected passages. Doing so can put a preemptive brake on any tendency to read primarily for plot. Furthermore, this exercise helps make the students aware of how authorial choices with regard to diction, syntax, and the like can determine the impact that a text has on both the intellectual and the visceral levels. Jim Kelly's description of Miss Julie Rand's house (9–10) and of Bonbon's shooting of the hawk during Marcus's first day in the field (39–40) are excellent sites for conducting such close readings.

The classic American novelist with whom commentators most frequently link Gaines is, not surprisingly, William Faulkner. Indeed, Gaines himself identifies Faulkner as a potent influence in his early years as a writer. However, in terms of prose style, the far more appropriate figure to invoke is Ernest Hemingway, whose so-called hard-boiled approach has shaped so indelibly the development of American fiction in the twentieth century. What the two authors share (and Gaines readily acknowledges his debt to Hemingway) is a dedication to understatement, to an extraordinarily economic use of language that can convey taut emotional control and self-suppression on the part of the narrator. Distributing a sample of Hemingway's work when teaching *Of Love and Dust* drives this point home quite effectively. The following excerpt from *A Farewell to Arms* exemplifies the stark emotional landscape in much of Hemingway's fiction:

> When I was through with the *choucroute* I went back to the hospital. The street was all clean now. There were no refuse cans out. The day was cloudy but the sun was trying to come through. I rode upstairs in the elevator, stepped out and went down the hall to Catherine's room, where I had left my white gown. I put it on and pinned it in back at the neck. I looked in the glass and saw myself looking like a fake doctor with a beard. I went down the hall to the delivery room. The door was closed and I knocked. No one answered so I turned the handle and went in. The doctor sat by Catherine. The nurse was doing something at the other end of the room.   (318–19)

With both writers, for instance, we are struck by the scarcity of modifiers, especially adverbs, in their prose. This tactic compels the reader to play an active role in uncovering—indeed, in *generating*—the affective content of a passage. Gaines's approach is vividly evident in stretches of dialogue, as in the heated exchange between Jim and Marcus when the former realizes that the younger man has designs on Bonbon's wife: the word *said* occurs seventeen times, yet it is not modified adverbially once (120–23). Calling attention to literary strategies in this detailed fashion can encourage students to focus on not just *what* novelists say but *how* they say it.

Gaines's commitment to voice, to the vernacular, in *Of Love and Dust* leads to a number of fascinating effects. What we find when analyzing his writing is his consistent use of simple declarative sentences, often quite short in length; furthermore, Jim's vocabulary and that of the people whose stories he tells are extremely limited. Like many African American authors in the twentieth century, Gaines renders speech patterns as much through rhythm, repetition, and word choice as through any extreme manipulation of spelling, typography, and the like. In addition, the cultural diversity of Louisiana provides fertile ground for Gaines's experiments with language. Among the more striking is his decision to present Creole French phonetically—for instance, we get "wee" instead of *oui* (154, 157). Elsewhere Jim addresses how Bonbon pronounces his name when he observes that the Cajun calls him "Geam" versus "Jim" (5). On another occasion, Jim himself says "chimleys" instead of "chimneys" (42). Gaines's creative approach to representing oral expression on the page merits sustained discussion and can assist students in developing both an eye and an ear for the diverse tactics that can be adopted in order to write the spoken word.

The sparseness of Gaines's prose can cause what details we get in his fiction to resonate with considerable figurative force, a force that he is not reluctant to exploit. I would argue that *Of Love and Dust* is one of the most intricately worked novels at the level of symbol and structure in his entire oeuvre. Accordingly, students should be urged to keep track of key images and motifs and to be alert to the loaded nature of the relatively scanty descriptions that Gaines supplies.

It is hardly accidental that the reader encounters a compelling example of symbolism at the exact moment when one of the main themes in the text is explicitly advanced. As Bishop, Marshall Hebert's black butler, painfully relates his failure to prevent Marcus from forcing his way into the Hebert residence, he complains, "He just pushed his foot in there. . . . The house his great-grandparents built. The house slavery built. He pushed his foot in that door" (215). Most students can grasp here how Marcus's unruly insurgency is framed in terms of his physical violation of a racially privileged space. The goal is to slow down their reading process so that Gaines's charged prose can register. A second symbolic image that emerges at another key point is the scythe with which Bonbon kills Marcus in the violent climax of the book. Although perhaps not an unusual implement to find on a farm at the time, the scythe is an odd choice of weapon, given the several references in *Of Love and Dust* to guns. (Jim comments on Bonbon's insecurity this way: "He was a man who needed a gun no matter where he was" [144].) Calling students' attention to the long-standing association of the scythe with personifications of Death—particularly as an implacable and ultimately inexplicable entity—will facilitate an understanding of Gaines's gambit here. In a plot that seems to move inexorably toward its fatal denouement, the presence of the scythe reflects Gaines's striving to imbue his novel with the narrative heft of tragedy and myth. Indeed, he has mentioned the influential role of classical drama as he was learning his craft. (It may be telling that Wash Jones kills Thomas Sutpen with a scythe in Faulkner's *Absalom, Absalom!*)

In a particularly memorable scene, we see how Gaines skillfully stages a character's ironic use of a freighted metaphor to indicate the importance of perception in the book. After Bonbon assigns him the task of clearing the leaves from his yard, Marcus brashly wisecracks, "I'll rake it. . . . Give it the best raking it ever had" (132). Whereas Jim and thus the reader are aware that Marcus's sly, salacious double entendre refers to his plans for Lucille, Bonbon's neglected wife, the Cajun remains oblivious. Indeed, Bonbon's missing the veiled meaning of Marcus's impudent pledge is but one sign of the extent to which he is largely blind to the true intentions of those around him. In addition, Marcus's witty—though exceedingly dangerous—allusion to his sexual prowess exemplifies the braggadocio and the erotic indirection often manifest in the traditional black blues idiom. In this regard, Jim's being a blues guitarist is hardly incidental. Gaines actually credits a song by the African American musician Lightnin' Hopkins with providing some of the inspiration behind the novel. Hopkins's music is readily available online, and it is not difficult to find examples of the humorously nasty sexual innuendo that infuses his lyrics.

Although there will not likely be sufficient class time to analyze exhaustively the symbolic images and terms in *Of Love and Dust*, it is important to highlight patterns that the students can then trace on their own. For instance, the names of characters are occasionally quite suggestive—the most obvious are Marcus

Payne ("pain"), Sidney Bonbon (derived from the French word for "good"; also, a type of candy), and Bishop (see my later discussion of religion). We find myriad representations of movement and stasis throughout *Of Love and Dust*—note the number of cars, horses, and tractors as well as the frequency with which people are shown walking, running, or sitting. Striking too is how often individuals describe others as children and babies. In addition to suggesting the complex familial social relations in the world of the novel, this motif highlights the ways in which innocence, naïveté, and maturity are crucial vectors in Gaines's characterizations.

Of Love and Dust is replete with barriers and obstacles of various kinds, including doors, barbed wire, fences, and walls separating adjoining living quarters. The unwritten rules governing black access at the local white-owned grocery store stand in for the entire system of Jim Crow segregation designed to constrain black mobility and agency. And the harsh policing of such racial divisions is signaled by the fierce dog guarding Bonbon's yard as well as by comments made about the lynching of blacks. Once Gaines has established these markers of racial power relations, he then dramatizes the explosive consequences when a black character either is ignorant of the protocols or refuses to respect them. Related to this depiction of barriers are the number of houses in the novel and the amount of action that occurs in domestic spaces of one kind or another. Key scenes take place in the homes of Jim Kelly, Pauline Guerin, Sidney Bonbon, Marshall Hebert, Josie, and Miss Julie Rand; and Marcus is, unsurprisingly, the only person who gains entry—or attempts to gain entry—to all of these sites.

In terms of organization, the novel is packed with foreshadowing and mirroring. An example of the former that will be apparent to students only upon a second reading is the fact that the destination to which Jim drives Marcus early in the story—Miss Julie Rand's house—is located on Louise Street (7). Gaines's use of doubling is more easily discernible. We have the contrast between the rambunctious vitality of Willy and Billy, Bonbon's mixed-race children by Pauline, and the infirmity and literal lack of color of Judy ("Tite"), his white child by Louise ("They had all the life, Tite had none" [164]). Furthermore, Gaines consistently juxtaposes the relationship between Pauline and Bonbon on the one hand and that between Louise and Marcus on the other. Each begins as a symptom of the social dysfunction of racism; then, in spite of the initial motives of the players involved, each evolves into a kind of love. Finally, and perhaps most intriguingly, Marcus quickly becomes an object of desire for both Louise and Marshall Hebert, and he is perceived by both as a potential weapon to be mobilized against Bonbon. This desire is evidenced via repeated moments of surveillance, whether it be Louise's gazing at Marcus from her porch or Hebert watching the young man from his car. Students should attend carefully to the many occasions when characters observe each other or trade glances.

Also instructive is how Gaines deploys images of clothing in the text, especially in the case of Marcus, whose flashy, entirely inappropriate attire symbolizes his stubborn refusal to conform and to stifle his individuality. Upon arriving on the plantation, for instance, he contends, "I'll never put that convict shit on my back. . . . I'm used to silk" (31). Then, toward the end of the novel when Marcus is preparing to flee with Louise and Tite, Jim provides us with a detailed description of the young man's colorful, flamboyant wardrobe (246). Indeed, it is tempting to view this passage as an homage to the well-known sequence in *The Great Gatsby* when Jay Gatsby flusters the enraptured Daisy by filling the air with shirt after vividly hued shirt that he exuberantly pulls from his cabinet. (Gaines himself has linked Jim Kelly and Nick Carraway, the narrator in Fitzgerald's novel [Gaudet and Wooton, *Porch Talk* 28].)

The most insistent image in the text and the symbol likely to be first identified by students is, of course, the ever-present dust. In one interview, Gaines explains, "Dust is the absence of love, the absence of life" (Rowell 90); in another, he says, "It is a symbol of death" (O'Brien, *Interviews* 91). However, the manner in which he manipulates this image is more complex and intricate than his succinct statements might suggest. It would actually be helpful for the students to circle or highlight the word every time it occurs as the initial step in unpacking the ways in which it conveys Gaines's thematic aims. For instance, as part of the examination of the opening paragraph of the novel that I recommended earlier, students should consider what Jim's reaction to the dust reveals about his personality. Dust is also associated with the leaves in Bonbon's yard, which, Jim remarks, "had been laying there ten, maybe twenty years; leaves on top of leaves on top of leaves; leaves that weren't leaves any more, but had turned back to dust" (133). It makes sense then that Marcus is the character who attempts to clear these leaves, the physical representation of the sedimented racism and violence of the South's slave past. The price that he pays for doing so is suggested when Jim observes drily that "[e]ven if Marcus used a shovel and even if he dug six feet in the ground he would never reach the bottom of all those leaves" (133). This indirect reference to the depth of a grave echoes an earlier exchange between Aunt Ca'line and Pa Bully. The latter comments regarding Marcus, "That one won't be here long. . . . And on the other hand he might." Aunt Ca'line asks, "Six feet under, you mean?"; Pa Bully replies, "Six feet under" (74).

As is the case with figures of speech generally, it is important that students resist the temptation to seek a single meaning for dust in the book and instead sensitize themselves to how Gaines generates a cluster of freighted associations around the image, all of which add nuance and power to the symbolic valence of the term. While dust is linked to the disintegrating leaves on Bonbon's property, it is also connected to the oppressive, stifling heat that persists throughout the novel (see Jim's mention of "hot corn dust" [117]). As a result of the dust and the heat, some characters utilize a range of defenses (again, barriers) that, in turn, can indicate status. For example, both Jim and Bishop have access to umbrellas that shelter them from the sun and thus distinguish them from other blacks on the plantation: in terms of rank, Jim is situated between the overseer, Bonbon, and the common field laborers; Bishop works in the Hebert household. We should not be surprised to learn that such attempts to protect oneself in this fashion prove futile in Gaines's fictive universe.

It would not do *Of Love and Dust* justice to attempt to boil this ambitiously conceived novel down to a single dominant theme. For this occasion, I will focus on but two of the major tensions that Gaines sets in motion. The first is that between religious faith and a despairing skepticism regarding the existence of a caring God, whom Jim cynically dubs "the Old Man" (note that Hebert is called "the old man" in this same passage [133]). Like countless American writers, Gaines peppers his narrative with a slew of Christian allusions. Early on, Jim references the several pictures of Jesus in Miss Julie Rand's home (10). Later, we observe the older woman cooling herself with a fan imprinted with an image of Christ on one side and an advertisement for a funeral home on the other (111). The association of religious belief with age, resignation, and death is reinforced by the depiction of the aptly named Bishop, who fails miserably in his attempt to safeguard Hebert's house, the preeminent site of white power, from the intrusive Marcus. Among the few superficially drawn individuals in the book, Bishop is the solicitous latter-day house slave whose pathetic plea to Hebert ("Your people . . . say long as I was a good boy I could stay here" [236]) manifests his pitiful dependency and lack of self-esteem.

Jim's ongoing internal conversations with himself reflect the crisis of faith that, for some characters, accompanies the breakdown of the social order catalyzed by Marcus's reckless, transgressive acts. The sense of impending destruction is underlined by Aunt Margaret's reference to the end of the world, to the apocalypse (138). In this regard, one should examine the myriad images of fire and burning, especially when connected to Marcus. For example, he brags to Jim about his power over women by touting his "blazing kisses" (110). Later, on the day of Marcus's initial sexual encounter with Louise, Jim reports that "Bonbon's yard was red. . . . When we went by the house I saw him [Marcus] standing against the fire" (167). Finally, Bishop's humiliating, futile confrontation with Marcus at the Hebert house leaves the older man's body, in his words, "on fire" (210). Thus, it is appropriate that the young man is explicitly linked to the devil (118, 210) and that when he visits the local black church, he never enters the building (126). Ultimately, however, Marcus's death can also be viewed as martyrdom. That is, his sacrifice models what the novel implies is a heroic resistance to oppression, thus rendering him something of a Christ figure. (Complicating this reading is the fact that Jim is thirty-three years old, the age at which Jesus Christ was crucified. See also Faulkner's Joe Christmas in *Light in August*, who is thirty-three when he is killed.) Again, students would be well served to consider that Gaines is intentionally not providing us with an easy interpretive scheme. To draw upon Fitzgerald's novel once more, just as Jay Gatsby is portrayed as driven by romantic idealism and also associated with criminality—that is, he is simultaneously innocent and guilty—Marcus is a similarly polarizing antihero. And given that Jim's religious faith is never ultimately resuscitated even as, in the end, his belief in the human capacity for courageous action is strengthened, it is fitting that we are offered a character whose behavior troubles any reliance on reductive ethical categories and straightforward moral choices.

Marcus's depiction as a person whom others find, by turns, irresponsible, appealing, selfish, intrepid, vulgar, frightening, lovable, immature, and provocative is tied directly to his role as the primary embodiment of and catalyst for change in the text. Grappling with his portrayal enables an engaging of a second major thematic tension in *Of Love and Dust*: that between rebellion and passivity, youth and age, risk and security, freedom and oppression. In their readings of Marcus's development, students might identify the diverse ways in which he stands out, violates convention, and disrupts order. On the one hand, Marcus's impact on his fellow blacks on the plantation is demonstrably unsettling. For instance, his instigation of the raucous fight at Josie's suggests how he seems to bring chaos with him wherever he goes. In addition, he constitutes a quite real danger for the black community, which is liable to be punished for his sins. On the other hand, he is likewise a threat to the white authority structure, and it is crucial to gauge the precise ways in which Marcus presents himself as a renegade, contentious force with whom those in control must deal. That is, just how does the young man stake his claim to selfhood and mount his audacious challenge to white patriarchy?

In *Narrative of the Life of Frederick Douglass, an American Slave, Written by Himself* (1845), Douglass describes how his captivity leads to his near total dehumanization. In a famous passage, he recalls, "I was broken in body, soul, and spirit. My natural elasticity was crushed, my intellect languished, the disposition to read departed, the cheerful spark that lingered about my eye died; the dark night of slavery closed in upon me; and behold a man transformed into a brute!" (74).[2] The activating factor in the reclaiming of his humanity is Douglass's desperate determination that he will no longer allow himself to be whipped, even at the cost of his life. The physical fight that culminates in his besting a white slave-breaker brings about the following radical change: "This battle with Mr. Covey was the turning-point in my career as a slave. It rekindled the few expiring embers of freedom, and revived within me a sense of my own *manhood*" (79; emphasis added). In discussing *Of Love and Dust*, it can be helpful to give the students this section of Douglass's autobiography for two reasons: first, to indicate just how far back the dramatizing of the struggle for self-respect and agency goes in African American literature; and second, to facilitate a comparison of Douglass's rebellious turn and that of Marcus, who on more than one occasion refers to himself as a "slave" (225). Furthermore, Douglass's employing the word *manhood* here should, in fact, be interpreted as gender-specific, for both he and Marcus connect a sense of their humanity to their assertion of power as men. However, an important distinction between the two is that whereas Douglass's insurgency is expressed through hand-to-hand combat, Marcus's strategy involves defeating Bonbon in another stereotypically masculine arena of contestation—that of sexual competition over women. Once the concepts of manhood and masculinity are put on the table, it takes little prodding for students to come up with various moments in the text that manifest Marcus's obsession with his male potency. For instance, his complaint about the apparent passivity of Jim and the other blacks on the plantation is couched in explicitly sexual terms; he brags, "Shit. . . . They don't nut this kid like they done nut all the rest of y'all round here" (30). For Marcus, castration is an apt symbol for what, in his opinion, is a cowardly and shameful accommodation to degrading, oppressive treatment. (However, many students will need to be alerted here and elsewhere to the meaning of slang expressions like "nut.")

It is also telling that Marcus's aggressive masculinity is juxtaposed in the novel with homosexuality, which he sees as a sign of weakness and perverse dysfunction. When Jim considerately offers Marcus a bath after his brutal first day in the field, the young man insultingly asks, "You a freak or something?" (44). Later, when Marcus feels Marshall Hebert's gaze on him as he cleans the plantation owner's yard, he says to himself, "If you one of them fat old punks, you better go mess with somebody else" (186). Then, right before his aborted escape attempt, he shares with Jim aspects of his troubled past that serve both to explain how he became the person he is and to elicit sympathy from Jim and the reader. An important part of that story involves his decision while in jail to stand up for himself, and the violation that he vows to rebuff, regardless of price, is being compelled to perform oral sex on another man. He tells Jim of a bullying prisoner named Horse Trader: "[He] even made people suck him off. Not me, some other cats. If he had ever tried that on me, I woulda killed him while he slept" (252).

What complicates the representation of Marcus's attitude here is the problematic portrayal of the black gay field workers John and Freddie. Described by Jim as "punks" (25, 37), the men never rise above the level of two-dimensional types. The distance that Jim feels from them is all the more striking in light of the intimacy evident in his interactions with nearly every other black person on the plantation with whom he comes into contact. One can argue that the extraordinary proficiency of John and Freddie at picking corn undercuts somewhat the highlighting of their effeminacy. After all, Marcus remains completely incapable of keeping up with them, even after he gains experience in the field. Unfortunately, however, we never have access to the thoughts of these two men. In a book full of individualized black voices, John and Freddie say little that does not relate to labor or to their apparently willing servitude in the face of white power. In sum, the flatness of their portraits renders them caricatures that weaken the narrative.

These derogatory references to homosexuality constitute a daunting challenge when engaging *Of Love and Dust* in the classroom. Indeed, they might well lead one to avoid assigning the book altogether. However, as in the case of many texts that require a similar cost-benefit calculus when gauging their potential pedagogical utility, the instructor choosing to teach *Of Love and Dust* must be committed to confronting its problems directly. One's strategy for doing so can depend, in part, on the initial student responses to this aspect of Gaines's novel.

At times, I have had class members raise the issue of possible homophobia without prompting. On other occasions, students have failed to read "freak" and "punk" as derogatory terms for gays and have thus missed the allusions to homosexuality (see my earlier comment regarding the need to explain slang terms in the text). Once this thematic thread has been teased out, a fruitful conversation regarding the construction of manhood can ensue. Without question, Marcus expresses the most thoroughgoing endorsement in the book of heterosexual masculinity as a mark of power and self-possession and as a weapon to be wielded against white male privilege. Furthermore, although Jim disapproves of Marcus's crude, explicitly sexual condemnation of him and other blacks on Hebert's plantation for what Marcus perceives as their resignation in the face of racist treatment, Jim ultimately does not reject the standards informing Marcus's judgment. At this point, the matter of where Gaines himself stands may arise. While this is not an unproductive topic, it is crucial to highlight how the fictive use of homosexuality as a foil for a male hero's striving for manhood is hardly unique to Gaines's work and indeed can be found throughout American literature. Key issues to consider here might include the following: Can one celebrate a male character's courageous rejection of oppressive forces without endorsing the gendered terms in which his insurgency might be framed? What are the consequences of a novel's focus on conventional expressions of masculinity for figures who are depicted as failing to meet mainstream criteria for normative male behavior? Can the seductive appeal of an irrepressible rebel like Marcus make it difficult for readers to mount a critique of the sexual nature of his transgressive struggle for self-determination? These questions evade easy resolution. However, when posed with regard to this and other novels, they can encourage students to develop analytical strategies for responding to problems like those encountered in this book.

Although Marcus is the text's primary and most controversial figure of resistance, students should identify other possible agents of change in *Of Love and Dust*, no matter how seemingly minor. For example, Willy and Billy, Pauline and Bonbon's twins, are blessed with a frenetic energy that is difficult to corral. Indeed, Aunt Ca'line reports that the "two little mischievous mulattoes" refuse to be sequestered on their side of the porch that she shares with Pauline, even after she installs a barbed-wire fence (60). Another character who contests boundaries is Louise, whose decision to enter into and then embrace a sexual relationship with Marcus reflects her desire to flee her virtual imprisonment at no small risk to herself (she has not left the Bonbon property in a year). Given the gender protocols of the time that mandated the dependence of a white woman like Louise on the will of her husband, she has few alternatives when confronted with Bonbon's open, adulterous relationship with Pauline. Jim mentions how Louise had run away at one point, only to be returned by her male relations; on that occasion, her father had advised Bonbon, "Next time she try that you beat hell out her" (163). In crafting the evolving bond between Louise and Marcus, Gaines emphasizes the extent to which both of them harbor a deep resentment as a result of Bonbon's controlling, dehumanizing behavior. Indeed, a compelling sign of Marcus's growing ability to connect with others is his recognition that Louise is as "much slave here as I was" (261). Ultimately, not only does Louise dare to reject limits imposed on white women of her day, but she even attempts (if naïvely) to repudiate her own racial privilege by adopting a grotesque, tragicomic blackface disguise for herself and her daughter as she plans her escape with Marcus. (Louise's use of soot to darken her skin may be connected to the dominant images of dust and fire in the text.) As Marcus's accomplice in his assault on white male hegemony, Louise comes to play a central role in the novel; however, her portrayal lacks the depth and nuance of most of the other women in *Of Love and Dust*. Part of the problem is the extent to which her immature, childlike nature is established as her main trait. She is frequently viewed as an adolescent; Jim describes her this way: "Louise was about twenty-five, but she was the size of the average twelve- or thirteen-year-old girl" (119; see also 155). Moreover, as in the case of John and Freddie, her interactions with Jim are scanty, which blocks our access to her subjectivity. Finally, her ultimate fate is decidedly unheroic when compared with that of her lover, Marcus. Emotionally stunted and apparently bereft of any nurturing support system, she lacks the psychological resources necessary to survive the trauma of Marcus's death. In two curt sentences, Jim informs us that Louise is taken first to a hospital and then to an asylum.

Instructing students to monitor carefully Jim's shifting attitude toward Marcus will enable a ready interrogation of just where our narrator ends up and thus where exactly the reader is left at the conclusion of *Of Love and Dust*. One key to appreciating Jim's psychological growth is marking the character's tendency at the outset of the novel not only toward a wary avoidance of trouble and disturbance but also toward nostalgia, cynicism, and inertia. It makes sense, therefore, that early on he often complies with the wishes of others, despite serious misgivings. Here is where examining Jim's ongoing inner dialogue with himself can again be productive, for he at times delivers a harsh critique of his own lack of pride and self-respect that leads the reader to arrive at a similar assessment.

Given the heightened narrative force with which the circumstances surrounding Marcus's death are presented, Jim's decision to leave the plantation might strike students as anticlimactic and perhaps even as a flight from conflict that replicates Jim's cautious reaction to the dust in the opening pages of the book. Three crucial moments later in the novel suggest otherwise. The first is his admission that he has come to respect Marcus: "I didn't blame Marcus any more. I admired Marcus. I admired his great courage" (270). The second is his refusal to accept a letter of recommendation from Marshall Hebert as he departs. The third involves Gaines's skillful staging of the final scene, in which Jim's walking into an uncertain future is juxtaposed with Aunt Margaret's return to the quarters and, effectively, back into the past. Jim may not have a clue as to where he is heading; however, his embracing movement and risk constitutes a repudiation of his prior life, one marked by a reluctance to take control of his destiny. Although Jim's subtle metamorphosis is hardly as dramatic as Marcus's grand, tragic defiance, there are unmistakable signs that he is no longer the person whom we met at the outset. As is the case with much of Gaines's fiction, *Of Love and Dust* is a book in which small gestures ultimately matter a great deal. Not only has Jim Kelly been forever changed by what he has experienced, but the novel suggests the unleashing of energies that, while destabilizing and even dangerous, will ensure that the days of the inhumane southern racial regime are numbered.

NOTES

[1] This essay quotes from the 1967 Vintage edition of *Of Love and Dust.*

[2] This essay quotes from the 1993 Bedford Books edition of *Narrative of Frederick Douglass.*

Falling Down Is Getting Up: Shame, Redemption, and Collaborative Change in *In My Father's House*

Herman Beavers

The obvious place to begin when teaching Ernest J. Gaines's 1978 novel, *In My Father's House*, is to devote attention to the novel's title. Though a study done in 1997 by Marie Goughnour Wachlin concluded that the Bible plays a very small role in public school education, it is nonetheless important to ensure that students understand that the title for the novel comes from John 14.2. The verse reads in its entirety, "In my father's house are many mansions: if it *were* not *so*, I would have told you. I go to prepare a place for you." And as will become clear, the plot of Gaines's novel is beautifully summed up in the next verse, John 14.3, which reads, "And if I go to prepare a place for you, I will come again, and receive you unto myself; that where I am, *there* ye may be also" (*King James Bible*). Though the words are attributed to Jesus, the novel's protagonist, the Reverend Phillip Martin, has usurped them and made them integral to his own sense of accomplishment. His desire for reconnection and redemption with his estranged son, Etienne, rests on the declaration "where I am, *there* ye may be also." But his patriarchal desires come into a direct state of conflict with his imperatives as a civil rights leader tasked with challenging the last vestiges of discrimination in his town. When the novel begins, Phillip is a man who is widely respected as a leader, father, and shepherd. But by novel's end, Phillip has come crashing to earth. Having overcome the waywardness of a youth filled with bar fights, drinking, and children by multiple women, Phillip is a man who embodies rebirth.

In this respect, teachers developing a pedagogical approach to *In My Father's House* would do well to emphasize that its larger imperative is to provide an extended deliberation on the nature of conversion. Whether they take the form of a religious experience or a secular triumph over adversity, teachers can point out that conversions are fraught with uncertainty, because the rhetoric of conversion is so prone to being characterized as a total transformation that involves the shedding of a past self to embrace a newer, stronger version of a reformed self. As Fred Hobson observes, the conversion narrative is often thought of as being a product of the Puritans' arrival in the New World, but its roots can be traced as far back as *The Confessions* of Saint Augustine. According to Hobson, "Almost all conversion narratives, religious or secular, bear essentially the same form— the description of a journey from darkness . . . to light, from sinfulness to a recognition of sin and consequently a changed life" (*But Now* 2). Just as the theologians Cotton Mather and Jonathan Edwards characterized their lives prior to entering the ministry as "wretched" and "loathsome," with Edwards declaring that he harbored "the bottomless depths of secret corruption and deceit" in his heart (qtd. in Hobson, *But Now* 2), so too does Phillip believe his own life prior to being saved was fraught with debauchery and wretchedness.

It is also important to point out that one of the main features of the conversion narrative, namely, its chronicling of the journey from sin to salvation, also turns out to be one of its potential blind spots, since conversion narratives often describe a solitary journey undertaken by a single individual. Though conversion may lead to membership in a larger community of believers and converts, one cannot gain entrance except through one's individual effort. The "changed life" that comes with a conversion experience requires converts to demarcate between the life they lived prior to "seeing the light" and the one they step into afterward. Hence, there is often little in the way of discussion about how friends and loved ones are expected to handle the conversion. If they are believers themselves, then perhaps it involves welcoming a new member into the fold, incorporating the convert into their everyday lives such that the distractions or disruptions the convert may once have caused are a thing of the past. But if they are not, if they remain fixed in the convert's past life, they can become casualties, discarded along with the other, now obsolete artifacts of the old life.

It is essential for instructors to point out, then, that when *In My Father's House* ends, it is not Phillip who has the final word but rather his wife, Alma, who responds to Phillip's resigned declaration, "I'm lost, Alma, I'm lost," with the reassuring words, "We just go'n have to start again" (211).[1] Her words mark the beginning of what has the potential to be a radical change in the life of Phillip and in the community in which he has served. Having been stripped of his title as president of the St. Adrienne Civil Rights Committee, Phillip's future as a leader is very much in doubt, which also means that the Martin family is in the precarious position of losing its previous level of prestige. Alma's insistence that Phillip's confusion and despair signal the need for a new beginning likewise points to Gaines's estimation that conversion narratives can lead to turmoil, since they so often involve discarding the past indiscriminately, as if there is nothing from the previous life worth sustaining.

Note, however, that Alma does not use the pronoun *you*, but rather *we*, as if to suggest that Phillip's redemption is not a solitary endeavor but a collaborative one she and Phillip will share. That Gaines opted to end the novel in this way points to what I would suggest is an important assumption, one that the master narrative of the civil rights movement is prone to assert, namely that the movement was a drama that took place on a *national* stage. Teachers can deemphasize this aspect of the movement in favor of a more local perspective, where the events unfold in a particular place, with actors whose achievements never become widely known (preferably motivated to achieve ends specific to that location) and who are less prone to see "the struggle" as being relevant to their small-scale efforts. Phillip's experiences as the leader of a local movement should remind teachers and students alike that it is perhaps more apt to talk about the civil rights *movements* that were taking place concurrent to those being witnessed on television screens. In this respect, *In My Father's House* is a novel that contemplates the vagaries of leadership and, in so doing, makes an implicit critique of monolithic characterizations of leadership in the civil rights movement.

Instructors may or may not be aware that one of the controversies that arose in the wake of the civil rights movement was that the death of Martin Luther King, Jr., also sounded the death knell of the national civil rights movement; so closely were the two intertwined that it became nearly impossible to separate them. Because *In My Father's House* seeks to highlight this problem on a smaller scale, teachers can point out how the novel juxtaposes the patriarchal desire of a father seeking to reconnect with his son against his civic desire to create an equitable and inclusive body politic. Gaines poses the question as to whether these conflicting imperatives—one personal (and spiritual), the other social (and secular)—can function conterminously. For beyond the weight of his grief and humiliation, there yet lies the question as to whether Phillip's efforts have liberated the black inhabitants of St. Adrienne or simply fixed their gaze on yet another figure using the rhetoric of racial progress to further his own designs.

For example, at the start of the novel, Virginia describes Phillip as "our civil rights leader round here" and also declares that he "[s]ure done some wonderful things here for us." She tells Etienne (who has adopted the name Robert X) that Phillip has done "such a good job here, people thinking 'bout sending him on to Washington" (10). When Etienne asks what Phillip has actually done, Virginia is emphatic in her response:

> "He's done everything," she said. "Everything. That's what he's done— everything. Changed just about everything round here, 'cept for old Chenal up there. But it won't be long 'fore Chenal fall too. He'll fall just like all the rest. Old white man we got uptown don't want pay the colored nothing for working. Own the biggest store up there, everybody go in his store, still he don't want pay nobody nothing for working. He'll change his tune when *Phillip get through with him*—you mark my word."   (10; emphasis added)

Though Virginia makes clear that hers is not a universally accepted assessment, she has the sense that "most of the people [of St. Adrienne] all for him." Virginia's characterization suggests that the triumphal narrative regarding the demonstration planned for later in the week has already been written. However, the language she uses to describe what is, in actuality, a struggle carried out by many suggests the ways that Phillip is credited as the sole catalyst for change in St. Adrienne. Indeed, for Virginia to say that Phillip is responsible for changing "just about everything round here" attributes an unrealistic level of authority and intentionality to all that he does.

Further, her declaration that Phillip will "be a good man in Washington" (10) fails to take into account the onset of a profound shift in power relations. As the first black person to run for a federal office from Louisiana, Phillip would hold a singular distinction. (Though Louisiana is noteworthy because two black people had held significant elected posts, lieutenant governor and governor, no black person from the state had been elected to the national legislative bodies of the United States Congress.) And it is here that *In My Father's House* sounds a cautionary note. The act of sending Phillip to Congress is certainly significant on multiple levels that are symbolic, political, and practical. But his election would also mark the shift from unelected leadership, from the theocratic elites who directed the civil rights endeavors in a number of southern communities with a spiritual mandate, to an elected leadership established and sanctioned by the vote. Moreover, it would signal the decision on the part of the St. Adrienne community to shift its tactics; rather than engaging in acts of protest and nonviolent resistance, the people would have to put their faith in the vote, hoping that Phillip's presence in Washington will transform that faith into tangible results back in St. Adrienne. What complicates this, of course, is that as a member of Congress, Phillip would represent a larger body of interests than his hometown. Finally, the ability to witness and experience Phillip's influence directly, as he uses it to overcome local forms of discrimination and exclusion, will become purely symbolic, since the shared task of confronting racist obstacles would be but one of the multiplicity of tasks he would need to focus attention on in Washington. And in light of the fact that new arrivals in Washington are at the bottom of the hierarchy of committees and procedural initiatives, Phillip would become a man whose main purpose would cease to be that of bringing change to St. Adrienne and would be inured in the task of seeking reelection.

It might be worthwhile, then, for instructors to spend time delineating the difference between protest politics and electoral politics; the former is often driven by emotion and public displays of discontent, while the latter is driven by compromise and the need to build consensus. Though Virginia's comment is purely speculative, instructors should not gloss what the shift might mean to the inhabitants of St. Adrienne. Furthermore, the novel uses this underlying tension as a way to invite the reader to ponder the nature of leadership, especially in terms of the ways that the locations in which leaders exercise power often present unforeseen consequences. Given the immediacy of local demands, is it always exercised in the service of the people's wishes? Or is it a product of the leader's own impulses and preferences exercised under the guise of working for the people? Though it is clear that Phillip has worked hard on behalf of the black inhabitants of St. Adrienne, it is equally the case that, as a consequence of the public visibility his leadership has garnered for him, his ranch-style brick house is the most expensive and elegant owned by a black family in St. Adrienne. The house sits behind a thick green lawn of St. Augustine grass about fifty feet away from the road. A driveway covered with seashells runs along the right side of the yard, ending under a canopy beside the house. The minister's big Chrysler and his wife's smaller station wagon are parked there.

Phillip's rise to leadership has resulted in an improvement of his material circumstance, but that improvement has not spread across the breadth of the black community. In this regard, *In My Father's House* seeks to limn the nature of identity as it occurs at the intersection of regret and aspiration. As we discover, Phillip was not always a black man living in the most expensive and elegant house in town. His humble beginnings on the Reno Plantation, where he grew up in a house with "the same rusted corrugated tin roof with a brick chimney sitting in the center" (106) as the other houses in the quarters, is a far cry from his present situation. But on a figurative level, Phillip's rise to the status of civil rights leader has to be considered against his climb out of poverty and waywardness. In a number of respects, *In My Father's House* is as much a narrative about the doubts that accompany the self-made man's successful act of pulling himself up by the proverbial bootstraps as it is a novel about Phillip's fall from grace. What distinguishes the novel, however, lies in the way that Gaines reverses the polarities associated with rising in prominence and falling from grace.

Ending the novel with the voice of Alma has everything to do with precipitating the reader to believe that Phillip's fall is actually *toward* grace. Gaines's critique of the civil rights movement is never overt, but it is clear that in the press for basic human rights, which requires a manifestation of heroic temper writ large, what is lost is the intimacy that should exist between a father and son or between a husband and wife. Alma's disaffection, which she expresses at various points in the novel, is a reaction to Phillip's independence of spirit. But it is also her way of asserting that for all the status he provides her, Phillip eschews intimacy with her, leaving her outside of any discussion regarding the civil rights struggle. As a self-made man, he feels little in the way of obligation to her or to the men who serve with him on the St. Adrienne Civil Rights Committee. In ways reminiscent of Frederick Douglass's *Narrative of the Life of Frederick Douglass* and his description of "how a slave became a man" (69),[2] Phillip understands his life prior to becoming a minister and civil rights activist as brutish. As such, he places a negative connotation on everything that came before, as if it means nothing to the man he has become. Rather than understanding his memories of hard physical labor and bar fights as being constitutive elements of his personality, as being the product of personal characteristics that have been repurposed for political struggle, Phillip has cut all ties to his past, as if his life did not begin until he entered the clergy. The clearest evidence of this is that even as he recognizes Robert X as one of the three children he fathered with his former lover Johanna, he cannot remember his real name or the names of his other two children.

Numerous commentators have pointed out that a major feature of Gaines's fiction is its constant effort to foreground the problematic of fathers and sons as a major obstacle to the achievement of a viable state of manhood. Philip Auger, for example, notes that "Gaines consistently writes about black men who face the problem of being denied the dignity and self-worth found in the status of 'manhood'" (qtd. in Hinds 648). Though there are numerous instances in Gaines's fiction where young black men are guided toward responsible manhood by women, most notably Ned in *The Autobiography of Miss Jane Pittman* and James in the short story "The Sky Is Gray," the author is nonetheless cognizant of the ways that the inability of black men to achieve their dreams is a major source of crisis, leading them to "brutalize other things near them, *at home*, when they cannot fulfill" those dreams (648–49).

If acts of conversion are most successful when they allow converts to integrate aspects of their former life with the newfound insight and clarity of purpose that come with the transformation, then what happens when a convert fails to integrate the past with the present? Clearly one form the past assumes comes in the form of Etienne, who has returned to St. Adrienne for the purpose of killing Phillip. Neither Virginia nor Elijah, as loyal members of Solid Rock Baptist Church, equate Phillip with his past; they see him only in terms of his accomplishments and his potential for greatness beyond the confines of St. Adrienne. But it becomes increasingly clear as the novel progresses that Phillip himself sees what he has done as proof of his worthiness. After his unilateral decision to call off the demonstration of the racist department store owner, Albert Chenal, that had been planned for later in the week, he is removed as president of the civil rights committee. The men who vote to remove him do so on the grounds that he is not "fit to be president" (129). The problem is that Phillip sees his duties as a father and his role as a civil rights leader as inextricably linked. For him, civil rights activism is not an end in itself but something he does in search of a greater reward. Though his decision to opt for his son over the wishes of the people planning to demonstrate seems arbitrary, it is clear that Phillip had hoped to reconcile with his son, to show him that he is a man whose accomplishments render him worthy of filial respect.

When Etienne accuses Phillip of treating his mother "like a common whore," of using and then discarding her, Phillip fends off the charge by declaring that they loved each other, that their feelings were mutual. Etienne characterizes Phillip's act of putting three dollars in his hand as an effort to assuage his guilt: "A dollar for each of us. That's what you paid. A dollar for each one of us" (101). What is evident in the exchange is that neither Phillip nor Etienne can find a vocabulary that will allow them to narrate the event outside of the context of slavery. Hence, Phillip's only defense for giving Etienne the three dollars is "That's all I had in the world. . . . I didn't even own myself then. Nothing. Nothing else but the rags on my back" (101).

In Phillip's mind, his climb into the clergy and from there to civil rights leader is most easily understood as an escape, a journey from slavery to freedom. His conversion, then, seems on its face to be a total one, because he draws such a marked distinction between his life before the conversion and the one after. When Etienne questions the validity of Phillip's version of his departure from the plantation, citing the fact that Phillip made no effort to prevent Johanna from leaving, we need to pay close heed to Phillip's reply when he insists,

> I couldn't bit more leave that room, that woman I didn't care nothing in the world for, than I can right now carry this here car on my back. I was paralyzed. Paralyzed. Yes, I had a mouth, but I didn't have a voice. I had

legs, but I couldn't move. I had arms, but I couldn't lift them up to you. *It took a man to do these things and I wasn't a man. I was just some other brutish animal who could cheat, steal, rob, kill—but not stand.* Not be responsible. Not protect you or your mother.   (102; emphasis added)

Phillips's conversion narrative is predicated on the notion that it was only by escaping from slavery that he could become the kind of man able to be responsible enough to care for a family. But his description of his feelings for Johanna reveals that such a characterization is specious. Though he may look back on his life and see a brute, that she carried such deep feelings for Phillip, deep enough to have three children by him, suggests he had to have been more than that. When Etienne accuses him of raping Johanna in the fields, that their couplings were simply a product of lust, Phillip replies, "Yes, we loved in the fields. But the fields was not dirty. The fields was clean. Clean as any bed" (101). Reading this, it is important for instructors to recognize that the task for them and their students is to reconcile the paradox that inheres between Phillip's sense that he was totally bereft of agency and his sense that his feelings for Johanna were substantive. Infidelity notwithstanding, Phillip cannot bring himself to the conclusion that Johanna brought out the best parts of who he was at the time. His act of giving Etienne three dollars, then, is not as the boy surmises an act of paying Johanna to take them away. Rather, it is a measure of his inability to manifest even the mere semblance of self-worth when it comes to remembering the man he was prior to being "called."

Further, the only hermeneutic Phillip has available to him to interpret his inability to act is slavery: "They had branded that in us from the time of slavery. That's what kept me in that bed. Not 'cause I didn't want to get up. I wanted to get up more than anything in the world. But I had to break the rules, rules we had lived by for so long, and I wasn't strong enough to break them then" (102). There is certainly merit in this categorization of past events. But it means that Phillip's life post-conversion is caught in a cycle of compensatory acts that need to become larger and larger in scope, seek increasingly more expansive transactions to complete. By opting for the life of a civil rights leader, a life that rests on the constant act of asserting his voice in public spaces, Phillip seeks to prove that he has a voice he can use to alter any circumstance that arises. But when he goes to bail Etienne out of jail, Sheriff Nolan refuses to take Phillip's money, a move that stymies Phillip's ability to draw on his present status and use his voice to persuade Nolan to accede to his wishes. Nolan's unwillingness to set a price for Etienne's freedom returns Phillip to a moment when the exchange of money was both inadequate and inappropriate. Ironically, Nolan's act of forcing Phillip to cancel the demonstration outside Chenal's store in exchange for Etienne's freedom likewise forces him to make the choice he declined to make twenty-one years prior, to opt for intimacy over his status as a leader. The situation is further complicated by Nolan's declaration: "This personal, not political" (90). Hence, Phillip makes the *correct* choice, but he does so at the wrong time, and his choice rests on putting family on par with public displays of voice. Phillip has made a severe tactical error: he has forgotten that the power of men like Chenal has long been buttressed by the state-sanctioned violence of the police, used to coerce blacks into submission. He refuses, moreover, to consider Nolan's assertion that the movement has sustained a fatal blow with the death of King: "That whole damn thing is over with. . . . Over with. When they nailed the coffin down on King that demonstrating thing was over with. All you doing now is bullshitting the people, that's all. It's over with" (92). Here, it would be worthwhile to pause and reflect on the fact that Phillip may indeed be a change agent in St. Adrienne, but he is limited in his ability to change men like Sheriff Nolan, whose view of the civil rights movement is refracted through his experience having to confront protestors imbued with a mandate endorsed by measures undertaken outside the city limits.

Compromised by his desire to free Etienne, Phillip makes no effort to refute Nolan's claims, in part because he has subscribed to the model of leadership that places so much emphasis on one individual but also because he has never sought to engage the loss of faith in the community. This development is in evidence in the novel's second chapter, when a group of teachers gather to drink and talk after work. When the teacher Elijah Green comes in and relates that Robert X has come to St. Adrienne and is interested in the party taking place at the Martin house over the weekend, several of the teachers express their disinterest. One, Chuck Allen, declares, in a way that reflects Nolan's views, "That whole thing's over with. . . . He did some good work but it's all over now" (20). After another teacher, a woman named Beverly Ricord, insists that she would "give anything" to have Reverend Martin's courage and that teachers "ought to be the ones out there in front," Allen concludes, "That shit's over with, kiddo. Them honkies gave up some, because of conscience, because of God. But they ain't giving up no more. Nigger's already got just about everything he's getting out of this little town. Anything else he want he better go look somewhere else for it" (21). Allen's act of referring to Phillip as "Nigger" proposes that for all his efforts to lift the community out of the kind of self-abnegation and loathing he felt as a young man, its members have failed to understand that the struggle is not about "getting [things] out of this little town," but rather it is—and has always been—about standing up to those who seek to nullify their humanity. The teachers, as part of the succeeding generation, have already lost touch with one of the movement's most fundamental goals: to codify *acts* of resistance as assertions of coherent forms of selfhood, not necessarily to seek a proscribed result.[3]

One of the challenges to ascertaining the significance of Gaines's novel lies in the necessity of recognizing that what is identified as the likeliest source text, John 14.2–3, is not the only source Gaines opts to draw from.[4] When we consider John 14.10, Phillip Martin can be understood as a man who requires physical proof of God's presence; he is not, as one might expect, a man whose beliefs rest on faith.

In light of this, the return of Etienne leads us to Christ's parable of the prodigal son as an additional source. *In My Father's House* is certainly not the only one of Gaines's works of fiction that borrows from the parable, which appears in both the short story "Bloodline" and his National Book Critics Circle Award–winning *A Lesson Before Dying*, but where these texts focused on sons, *In My Father's House* focuses on the relationship between father and son.

In an ambitious and insightful essay on black men and fatherhood, the Howard Divinity School professor Jay-Paul Hinds asserts that there are few examples of biblical scripture "more revered than the parable of the prodigal son" (641). As the "quintessential feel-good" story, it becomes easy for believer and nonbeliever alike to identify with the parable's message of compassion and faith. But Hinds goes on to ask some very pointed questions about this parable—so often held up as an example of beneficence, unconditional love, redemption, and restoration—that seek to place the parable's references to shame in the foreground. Hinds cautions us that with closer scrutiny, the parable of the prodigal son might actually "dissuade [us] from celebrating too soon" (642).

For one thing, Hinds points out, there is the question of what constituted the seeds of the son's prodigality in the first place. Indeed, he suggests that the younger son's desire to have his inheritance while his father was still alive may be a sign that all was not well in the household between father and son; the younger son's disaffection might have grown out of seeds "planted in the tempestuous soil of the father-son dyad." In light of the fractiousness found in other father-son dyads (Hinds cites Abraham and Isaac as well as David and Absalom, and we might also consider Isaac and Jacob), what are we to make of the son's desire "to possess what the father has?" And further, what, Hinds asks, "was going on in the house between the father and son, to be exact, that would lead to such an offensive request?"[5] The text does little to assist us; we know nothing of what, if anything, in the father's behavior may have led to his son's unreasonable request. What seems clear, according to Hinds, is the sense of merriment the reader feels "as the father runs out to meet his son, puts his arms around him, and kisses him, welcoming him back home." Hinds resists this sentiment and offers a rationale that is worth quoting at length:

> Nevertheless, we should pause, yes, if only for a moment, to mull over the troubling but all too evident fact that as soon as the son expresses his shame—"I have sinned against heaven and before you, I am no longer worthy to be called your son" (Luke 15:21)—the communication between father and son ends without warning. Surely the son had more to tell with respect to what he had experienced during his time away from home, perhaps some of the trauma which had troubled his mind and unsettled his soul. Feeling shame before his father is one thing, but to believe that he had fallen short before "heaven" bespeaks a cosmic sense of *inner* inadequacy that warrants the father's full attention. But the father fails to do so.   (642)

What is called for, Hinds proposes, is a more intensive rumination on the nature of shame. Citing a range of thinkers, Hinds quotes the evolutionary theorist Charles Darwin and the cultural anthropologist Ernest Becker, respectively, that in shame "we turn away the whole body, more especially the face, which we endeavor in some way to hide," and that where "guilt lames the human animal, *shame stops him dead*" (649; Hinds's emphasis).

I share Hinds's concern over the nature and substance of shame as an intergenerational phenomenon. For when we turn to *In My Father's House*, we are faced with the question of what will happen in St. Adrienne now that Phillip has lost everything, including his faith. An even greater concern, perhaps, is whether the blasted life of his son makes Etienne the novel's negative reprise of the prodigal son, a variation on the original theme. If this is so, I wish to engage Hinds's bold assertion that Phillip is guilty of filicide, that it is his actions, and his alone, that lead to Etienne's suicide.

Etienne's return and subsequent decision to take his own life suggest that Phillip has failed to create what the philosopher Henri Nouwen refers to as a "secure base" (qtd. in Hinds 642) to which his son can safely return. Though it would seem that the father-son dyad in the novel functions at a remove from Phillip's work as a civil rights leader, when we look closer, we see that his failures as a leader are a function of his failure as a father. When he rationalizes his decision to cancel the demonstration by saying, "I wanted my boy—I wanted my boy, Mills. I wanted him bad. I didn't know no other way to get him" (122), Howard Mills, one of the deacons at Solid Rock Baptist Church and a member of the committee, puts his desire into the larger context. "That's what we working for, Phillip, so our boys will come back home. So they won't have to leave home. That's why people like Chenal have to go" (125). In essence, the movement in St. Adrienne is deeply concerned with creating a stable base for all the prodigal sons to return. But to do so requires that the fathers confront their earlier failures to resist the racist status quo. Mills talks about knowing Chenal's father many years previous to the movement and describes how any "presentable black woman" who came into the store was liable to be raped. "I knowed it then," Mills states, "I was just too scared to say a word" (125). If this sounds familiar to readers of Gaines's fiction, it is because Gaines will reprise this sentiment in his 1993 novel, *A Gathering of Old Men*. And it is worthwhile for instructors to point students toward this connection, if only because it demonstrates how Gaines uses emotions like shame and regret as precursors to redemption. For Mills and the other men of the committee, it is clear that life in St. Adrienne has been largely mediated by shame. The movement is the product of their effort to channel shame into acts of resistance. Hence, Virginia has misrepresented circumstances in the town. It is *not* Phillip Martin who has inculcated change; rather he was on hand when a *community* elected to embrace a new version of itself and chose him to be its voice. In essence, he is *part of* rather than the progenitor of the black community's resistance effort. But Phillip's problem is that he believes his presence is of singular importance, when in fact the "president's vote [is] just one vote" (124), his voice one among many.

But this error is a function of a larger, more substantive miscalculation. The fact that his leadership in St. Adrienne lies beyond question has blinded him. When he sees Etienne standing in his home, he collapses, because he has never addressed what he recognizes as a failing he thought he'd left behind. By his lights, Phillip is "a man who walked upright before the Lord. He was redeemed . . . he was once a lost son—weak and wayward—who had spent all in the world, but he was now a man, a committed minister and community activist. But his overt status belies his inner brokenness" (Hinds 650).

As noted above, Phillip understands his acts as being the signs of his faith. Like the older brother in the prodigal son parable, who complains to his father that the hard work and loyalty he has steadfastly provided in the younger son's absence has never led to a feast that involved killing the fatted calf, Phillip believes that it is acts, not faith, that signal piety, which means in turn that he believes that God should reward him accordingly. Late in the novel, Phillip voices his expectation that his good work should result in the fulfillment of his desire when he states, "The last fifteen years I've given and gived and gived to my fellow man. I've taken my fellow man by the hand and led him the way you lead a small child" (211). Phillip believes his willingness to challenge Jim Crow conventions is proof of his commitment, as the one who "was ready to get the first blow" (211), but he conflates activism and patricentricity. Seeing his fellow activists as the equivalent of a "small child," Phillip's activism is an effort to get God's attention, which is confirmed when he states,

> 'Cause of Him. 'Cause of Him. 'Cause of Him I've been running after my son. I never woulda done it if it wasn't for Him. I woulda looked at my son going by the house, and I woulda forgotten him—if it wasn't for Him. But He changed me, and I can't forget my son. I can't forget my son, young lady. I can't ignore my son no more. That's why I say He owed me my son. Once He made me a human being *He owed me my son.*   (212; emphasis added)

If all his work has simply been the pretense for God to give him back his son, then Phillip's efforts can be reduced to being little more than an enactment of his hubris. And it confirms Alma's observation: "Ever since I met you, Phillip, you been running, running, and running. Away from what, Phillip? Trying to make up for what, Phillip? For what you did to that boy? For what you did to his mom? For other things you did in the past? The past is the past, Phillip. You can't make up for the past" (136). Seen from Alma's perspective, the father who greets the return of the prodigal son with a grand feast may have more to hide than the parable relates. If a father greets the son in a state of mind that is preoccupied with the task of mediating his own shame through acts of hubris, isn't it possible that nothing the son feels—even if it is murderous rage—will be important?

This is not to suggest that Phillip's life as an activist, as a minister who tends to his flock, cares for his family, and cares for his fellow man, is counterfeit. But the catastrophe of seeing Etienne at the party collapses the wall he has built between his present life and the shame he feels about his past one. It is no wonder that Etienne is a young man so ridden with shame and guilt; they are the inheritance he received from Phillip, who is himself conflicted about how a man should conduct himself in a world where black men are constantly under duress. His life as a civil rights leader and minister constitutes one approach. But his life prior to entering the ministry constitutes yet another.

Though drinking, violence (perhaps even murderous violence), and infidelity are central aspects of his past behavior, Phillip fails to understand that it might be these past behaviors that give him entrée to an understanding of the sins committed by his flock. Theologians like Mather and Edwards—and perhaps before them, Saint Augustine—sought to communicate that those who see that their lives have a divine purpose must eschew the notion that perfection is a state from which one can lead a flock. That is, a true spiritual guide leads from *behind*, as if to suggest unworthiness of the term "leader." Further, the seeds for Phillip's emotional trajectory from sin to salvation might well have been planted before the actual conversion; perhaps the very traits that lead him to view his past life as an anathema he would like to forget constitute the pivot upon which his career, in the wake of his life leading the St. Adrienne Civil Rights Committee, might turn. In other words, Phillip must learn how to make his sense of shame work *for him*. Hinds conjectures that the only way for sons to be able to reconnect with absent or compromised fathers may lie in men resorting to a different set of tactics. "What would happen," Hinds writes, "if shame were perceived not as an albatross, but as a source of innovation that inspires new ways of enunciating and understanding our manhood?" He continues: "Doubtless this much-needed reappraisal of shame holds great promise for black men who have suffered a number of castrative acts, be they sociopolitical, discursive, or otherwise. Could shame not *quickly* alleviated but *patiently* understood, facilitate a more salubrious bond between black fathers and their sons?" (644). Hinds's point should spur reflection on the counterintuitive value of shame. As he sees it, shame is not indicative of those parts of a life that need to be jettisoned; rather it is fuel for what lies ahead, a bonding agent necessary to cement ties between fathers and sons, and a healing balm whose effects are felt over a period of many years. The later stages of the novel seek to dramatize Phillip's rethinking how to use shame in these ways.

When he drives to Baton Rouge, looking for his friend Chippo Simon, Phillip learns of the young man who was killed when police raided his house after he stole food from a store. At a small diner, he meets an old man who turns out to be a minister like him. The difference is that this man—described as "a thin brown-skinned man who could have been in his seventies or even eighties," wearing an "old black overcoat . . . much too big and hanging too far to one side" (150)—looks disheveled, tired, with watery and bloodshot eyes. The woman working the diner counter warns the man not to bother Phillip, but soon the men commence talking. Noticing that the old man, whose name is Reverend Peters, is "holding the cup with both hands as you would a chalice" and looking at him over the rim of the cup, Phillip is suddenly uncomfortable. When talk turns to fathers and sons, Peters says, "He works in mysterious ways. . . . Keep the faith, man. Never doubt." Though this is a small word of encouragement, it is none-theless what Phillip needs to hear. He says to Peters, "There's a gap between us and our sons, Peters, that even He . . . even He can't seem to close." But Peters dismisses such talk, saying, "No such gap, man."

The contrast is a stark one: Phillip Martin, in his well-appointed attire and nice car, against this disheveled old man, Reverend Peters, but it demonstrates that for all Phillip's accomplishments, there is a man from much humbler cir-cumstances whose faith far outdistances his own. While Phillip has become a minister who is widely known, even by the people of Baton Rouge, this man is cold, hungry, and barely welcome to sit in the diner. However, what he models for Phillip is a quality of faith and reverence that does not depend on widespread admiration, the belief that he is an agent of change. Though the woman in the diner warns him that he needs to behave, because the diner is not a church, the old man's circumstances require him to minister to whatever souls cross his path. Though it would be a stretch to suggest that he is Christ incarnate, he demon-strates, nonetheless, that his faith in the God who resides in his Bible consti-tutes the beginning and end; he is a man free of all doubt. The irony, of course, is that for all his faith, he is neither prosperous nor revered. But Phillip's frus-tration at not getting Reverend Peters to come around to his position blinds him to the fact that Peters is a role model for him, a man whose precarious status does not prevent him from acts of ministering, even when the person in need is a member of the clergy.

At the liquor store, still looking for Chippo, Phillip encounters men who while away the evening hours gambling and drinking. In the process, he also meets a black Vietnam vet, a young man who is the sole survivor of a grenade attack and who has determined that the only way to rid the United States of its adherence to racial injustice is to create an army that will "burn [the] country down" (163). Even as Phillip tries to dissuade him from violence, we realize that the vet is in the midst of one way to deal with loss and grief, which requires meeting vio-lence with violence, using guerrilla tactics to overcome the establishment. The vet's anger, his sense that "[n]obody laughs more than niggers. . . . Nobody suf-fers more than niggers, nobody organize less than niggers—but nobody laughs more than niggers—nobody" (161), leads us to conclude that the young man is devoted to a "ministry" of his own.

And like Phillip, he too is an uneasy convert. But in the case of the young vet-eran, he has been convinced that violence is the only language that the powers that be will understand. What he wants to foment, by burning everything of im-portance, is an apocalypse: "This country here is the last crutch for Western Civilization—what *they* call civilization. . . . Burn it down, you destroy Western Civilization. You put the world back right—let it start all over again. Somebody got to pay for it, that's all" (162). His disillusionment leads him to conclude that voting, black faces on television, and black politicians do not constitute change of the sort that will prevent whites from killing blacks. When Phillip attempts to draw him out regarding his relationship with his father, the vet responds, "I don't bother him, he don't bother me" (165). At a time when the Black Lives Matter movement has, on the one hand, provided an impressive demonstration of how quickly large groups of young people can be mobilized to speak out against police violence, it also has, on the other hand, revealed the generational fault lines between veterans of earlier protest movements and the young people seeking to move beyond them. An instructor teaching Gaines's fiction at this moment, then, has an opportunity to link generational strife and protest, which is to say that the latter rarely happens without the former being manifest.

Gaines's decision to end the novel with Phillip's wife telling him that circumstances require them to "start again" begs the question: start what? He remains the pastor of Solid Rock Baptist Church, though with the ascension of Jonathan Robillard to president of the St. Adrienne Civil Rights Committee, it could be that his pastoral duties will soon come to an end as well. And Alma seems an unlikely figure to move to the forefront of a new branch of the movement. When we first meet her in the novel, the narrator describes her as "a small brown-skinned woman" who is "only thirty-five years old but [whose] calm, passive face and dark clothes made her look much older" (29). Twenty-five years younger than Phillip, she is accustomed to being overlooked and underappreciated, even by Phillip, and the narrator observes that at the party in the Martin home, when Alma speaks people "could hardly hear her over the noise in the room" (29). But if Phillip is going to find his way to the work he needs to be doing as the civil rights movement draws to a close, she is likely one of the few people—along with Beverly Ricord perhaps—who can set him back on the right path.

Phillip has experienced in Baton Rouge what all the people, including the locals in St. Adrienne, have experienced: the civil rights movement has failed to alter their circumstances. This does not mean that the movement's goals—ending discrimination, acquiring the right to vote, challenging unequal treatment—are specious. But it does mean that Phillip's investment in ministering has been compromised by the desire to be an instrument of change that can be seen and lauded. What he learns from Reverend Peters is that change comes one person at a time. Though Alma has been all but invisible up to this point, Phillip's fall *toward* grace means that he can draw on her perspective for clarity. It is she who explains that Phillip's behavior toward the men on the committee would no longer be tolerated and that they would no longer stand for being treated with such blatant disregard. Beverly Ricord provides him with a sense of all he has won through his struggle—not only for himself, but also for others in the community. She helps him to understand that the loss of Etienne does not mean that he has failed with his younger son, Patrick:

> "You wanted the past changed, Reverend Martin," she told him. "Even He can't do that. So that leaves nothing but the future. We work toward the

future. To keep Patrick from going to that trestle. One day I'll have a son, and what we do tomorrow might keep him from going to that trestle. That's all we can ever hope for, isn't it, Reverend Martin? That's all we work for, isn't it?" (213)

Implicit in Gaines's act of foregrounding the observations and opinions of women at the end of the novel rather than the beginning is his sense that though black women's contribution to the movement is often thought to be non-existent, what distinguishes what they have to offer is that they are oriented toward the future, while the men who stand in the forefront are motivated to seek redress for past injuries. This is in no way to suggest that Gaines is saying that women are immune to injury or that they are always the source of sage advice. But Alma's use of the pronoun *we* recasts the struggle, altering its emphasis on wiping away the past to one that is more oriented toward adopting an innovative posture in the face of failure. Collaboratively, Phillip and Alma (along with others) can create the secure base for their son and others like him to return from their travails in the world. Though she has been humiliated, shunted to the margins in the wake of Phillip's hubris, Alma's experience proves to be a source of insight. I am not suggesting that her role be solely oriented toward support; a collaborative venture in which political change is a distinct goal cannot succeed if women are relegated to behind-the-scenes roles. Instructors seeking to contextualize Gaines's novel as a way to ruminate on the failures of the civil rights movement need to confront the movement's marginalization of women directly. To be sure, it has long been understood that lacking women's logistical and organizational acumen, the black church would cease to function. Hence, I am also not suggesting that the Phillip Martins will become men sympathetic to a feminist agenda. But in the final analysis, it could be that *In My Father's House* constitutes an invitation for us to remember Proverbs 7.4, which states, "Say unto wisdom, Thou art my sister; and call understanding thy kinswoman" (*King James Bible*).

NOTES

[1] This essay quotes from the 1983 Norton edition of *In My Father's House*.

[2] This essay quotes from the 2000 Modern Library edition of Douglass's *Narrative*.

[3] In deliberations whether to adopt the strategy of nonviolent resistance, King and other leaders understood that their efforts to desegregate buses, lunch counters, and public facilities would be met with violent reprisals from angry whites. They understood that the act of asserting themselves would lead to failure in the form of beatings, jail, and overt acts of violence (as we see with the deaths of Medgar Evers, the little girls in the Sixteenth Street Baptist Church bombing, and Andrew Goodman, Michael Schwerner, and James Chaney). But what distinguishes the strategy is that it was understood as regenerative, inexhaustible, meaning that the movement proved to be every bit as relentless as Jim Crow racism and the discriminatory practices it engendered.

⁴ As I point out in *Wrestling Angels into Song* (9), Gaines's decision to name his protagonist Phillip has much to do with a moment later in John 14.8–10, when Philip, one of Christ's disciples, declares to Christ, "Lord shew us the Father, and it suffices us," leading Christ to challenge Philip's skepticism that to be in Christ's presence is also to be in the Lord's midst.

⁵ Hinds turns to the New Testament scholar Kenneth Bailey, who "contends that, per Middle Eastern custom, the son making such a request—while his father was still alive, no less—was tantamount to him saying, 'Father, I am eager for you to die!'" (648). What this means is that it is the younger son's act of filial impiety, if you will, that creates the circumstances for his eventual return.

Football and the Pastoral in
A Gathering of Old Men

Christopher Rieger

Ernest Gaines's *A Gathering of Old Men* is a novel that works very well in a variety of courses. I have taught it in upper-level undergraduate and graduate-level specialized courses, such as Southern Literature and Cross-Cultural American Literature, as well as to nonmajors in general education classes. The novel's length, style, narrative techniques, and subject matter make it adaptable to a range of courses and students. Almost all students report enjoying the novel, and most find plenty of different topics to discuss and analyze in both class discussions and written assignments. This essay focuses primarily on approaches to teaching the novel to a wide audience, not exclusively English majors. However, the approaches could easily be supplemented and expanded upon for upper-level undergraduate and graduate-level courses. My approach to teaching the novel in this essay focuses on two main areas: nature and football. Ultimately, these two seemingly disparate areas can be linked together.

On the first day of teaching *Gathering*, I introduce the novel, author, and themes with the help of some video clips that can be found online. The Web site Academy of Achievement has an excellent 2001 interview with Gaines on the occasion of his induction into the academy (Gaines, "Ernest J. Gaines"). The entire interview is about an hour, and eight short excerpted clips from the early portions of the interview are also available. The first twenty-five minutes or so feature Gaines discussing his childhood in the rural community of Oscar, Louisiana; his educational background; and his move to California because his parish of Louisiana had no high school for blacks. Later in the interview Gaines talks about *Gathering* (26:30–30:00).[1] The biographical information Gaines recounts about children working the fields relates to the novel's setting and themes. For instance, Gaines talks about how the houses his family members lived in were originally built as slave cabins, as well as the fact that his family had lived on that land for six generations. This information helps students envision the rural neo-plantation setting that is the basis for the fictional Marshall Quarters of the novel, while the nearby town of New Roads is the model for the fictional town of Bayonne in the novel's city-country pastoral axis. Gaines's family history on the land prepares students for the attitudes of the novel's black laborers about their home. There is a deep attachment the characters feel toward their natural environment that might seem at odds with the history of slavery, injustice, and exploitation that also defines this landscape. As Frank Shelton says in his excellent article "Of Machines and Men: Pastoralism in Gaines's Fiction": "Gaines sees it [the southern plantation] as a force for entrapment and dehumanization that must be changed, yet paradoxically the plantation is at the same time a source of strength and continuity for his black characters" (14).

In the Academy of Achievement interview, Gaines also discusses the fact that children attended school for less than six months each year so that they could help work in the fields. As he discusses his own educational journey, Gaines explains that blacks were not allowed in public libraries in Louisiana and that there were no high schools for blacks in his rural area. This sort of segregation eventually led his parents to move to Vallejo, California, where Gaines could continue his schooling. These stories not only help students better understand the rural Louisiana setting of the novel but also illustrate the pervasive and substantial racial discrimination confronting African Americans in the early twentieth century. Although *Gathering* is set in the 1970s, the novel emphasizes that this place and culture are in many ways relics from an older era, and students, in fact, often assume the novel's setting is much earlier. Though Gaines grew up in the 1930s and 1940s, the continuity of his experiences with many of the incidents in the novel can help emphasize the slow pace of racial change, especially in the rural South, as well as illustrate the theme of the continuing influence of the past on the present.

Another video that works very well in class is from a 2010 CNN story that discusses Gaines's work cleaning and restoring the old cemetery on the former plantation where generations of his family lived (Drash). This moving clip (and the accompanying text) features Gaines and his wife discussing the importance of the past and ancestors, as well as their reasons for wanting to save the cemetery. It allows for a nice biographical connection to the scene early in the novel in which the old men gather at the plantation cemetery before heading to the Marshall plantation with their shotguns, though it works best if students have read through the graveyard scene (44–57)[2] before being shown this video.

This graveyard scene allows for an introduction of an ecocritical approach to the novel. Specifically, the concept of the pastoral is useful, because it entails the uneasy combination of culture and nature and also the complicated relationship of past and present. Traditional versions of the pastoral mode posit the pastoral place as a middle ground between country and city, nature and culture, often a place where one from the city (frequently the author or his or her fictional counterpart) can retreat and become reacquainted with the "authentic" and the "natural" and, from this perspective, critique the "artificial" or "unnatural" metropolitan realm. As Leo Marx says in his classic study of American pastoral, *The Machine in the Garden*, the rural world in this pastoral equation often is presented as possessing an "alleged moral, aesthetic, and, in a sense, metaphysical superiority to the urban, commercial forces that threaten it" (99). Marx warns that this type of privileging of the rural can lead to a popular, sentimental pastoral that produces a "simple-minded wistfulness" and "escape from reality" (10) of the type seen in, say, Thomas Nelson Page's fiction or even the essays of the Southern Agrarians in *I'll Take My Stand* (1930). Marx favors instead an "imaginative and complex" pastoral (5) that attempts to blend elements of both urban and rural poles in a balanced middle ground.

The leading ecocritic and pastoral theorist Lawrence Buell echoes Marx in his description of complex pastoral's multiple frames or competing centripetal and centrifugal forces: "So American pastoral has simultaneously been counter-institutional and institutionally sponsored" (50). Terry Gifford, in his 1999 study, *Pastoral*, summarizes best the inherent complexities of this literary mode:

> So the pastoral can be a mode of political critique of present society, or it can be a dramatic form of unresolved dialogue about the tensions in that society, or it can be a retreat from politics into an apparently aesthetic landscape that is devoid of conflict and tension. It is this very versatility of the pastoral to both contain and appear to evade tensions and contradictions— between country and city, art and nature, the human and the non-human, our social and inner selves, our masculine and our feminine selves—that made the form so durable and so fascinating.   (11)

It is important to at least familiarize students with these descriptions of the different varieties of pastoral. To many, the term "pastoral" has a solely pejorative meaning and only refers to the escapist or sentimental variety. Gaines's pastoral formulation in this novel, though, is quite complicated. The black characters feel deep connections to the land and their natural environment, often through multiple generations. Thus, the land is linked with the past, and links to the past are important sources of strength and inspiration for the old men. However, the past and the same land are also strongly identified with the violence, shame, and injustice of racial oppression. For that reason, we might expect black characters to reject the rural place of the past in favor of the change and progress we might normally associate with the city.

The segregated graveyard where the old men gather is shaded by protective pecan and oak trees, but it is also on the verge of being engulfed by the ever-encroaching sugarcane crops and the tractor threatening to "plow up them graves" (92)—their symbolic connection to the past. This relates to another prominent theme of the novel: the threat of the erasure of black history and identity. Johnny Paul's monologue later in the novel (90–92) suggests that the whites and Cajuns are conspiring to wipe out the multigenerational history of black workers on the land of the Marshall plantation (using disappearing flowers as a metaphor). This connection of blacks to their land, and their nostalgia for a past when that connection was deeper and more authentic, raises some complex and interesting issues for class discussion. Given the novel's focus on change and progress in race relations, shouldn't we expect the black characters to be aligned with the future rather than the past? Why might these men look fondly, even romantically, on a past associated with oppression and even slavery? How do the blacks, whites, and Cajuns have different connections to this same land? Are some connections more authentic than others, and how do we define authenticity?

On one level, the novel does utilize an apparently traditional pastoral dichotomy of past/present and nature/culture, with the black characters aligned with the past and nature. Specifically, the tractor is a symbol for the white ruling class and its dominant culture, while the blacks are represented by more natural imagery and symbols. In the graveyard scene, Dirty Red gives Snookum (a small child representing future generations) a handful of pecans to eat just after they all hear the tractor, followed by an owl from the swamp. The voice of nature is calling to them from the past, and it drowns out the mechanized tractor and spurs Dirty Red to pass on the strength of the past to the future generations, rather than the passivity and cowardice of the present (55). Later in the novel, we do, in fact, see Snookum inherit this strength and display bravery, when he joins the old men standing up to Sheriff Mapes (70).

The tractor is also a symbol of modernity. It runs noisily beside Beau Boutan's body (5); its sound is ever present in the background, like the racial oppression that has been endured and even accepted but is now no longer to be ignored. In its first appearance it seems to be running with no human control, a machine in the garden operating by itself. Appropriately, the opening of the novel alludes to the biblical Adam and Eve story, a state of innocence in nature spoiled when Snookum's brother "[catches him] and Minnie playing mama and papa in the weeds" (3). This reference suggests that the pastoral place is not a paradise free from the issues and problems of the larger culture. Rather it is a battleground where these forces clash. One of the older black women, Bea, when she still thinks Candy shot Beau, says, "About time she shot one of them Cajuns, messing up the land with those tractors" (23). This idea of whites and Cajuns "messing up the land" also links the tractor to the idea of unnatural ownership of land. Mat and Chimley complain that they have hardly any place left to fish on the river they've been using for years: "The white people, they done bought up the river now" (27). Cajuns now control land that blacks had worked for generations. True ownership comes through working the land, the novel suggests, not legal titles. The fact that it's only leased, not owned, by Beau underscores his questionable possession. The cane fields are like lonely houses, like an empty shell without true inhabitants, only "ghosts" (43).

Gaines mentions multiple times that the tractor continues to run in place as everyone begins to gather at the site of the killing (52, 55, 60, 64). In fact, when Lou Dimes arrives, he notes that as one of the old men nonchalantly claims responsibility for killing Beau, the man stares at the tractor instead of either Lou or the sheriff: "With the stock of the gun on the ground and the barrel across his knee, he was looking out at the tractor in the road. He showed so much more interest in that damned tractor than he did me that I almost turned around to look at the damned thing again myself" (60). Sheriff Mapes finally has to direct one of his deputies to turn the tractor off, the first indication that perhaps the events of the day will lead to a diminution of white power. Shelton's essay on Gaines's use of the pastoral reads this symbolism similarly and argues that healthy black characters are the ones in tune with the earth while the whites of the book are linked to the unnatural machinery of the tractor: "While Gaines certainly feels that social change is necessary, such mechanization of agriculture is portrayed as dehumanizing, and it does not bring with it improvement in the lot of his black characters. In fact, the whites' devotion to machines and technology is associated with the compulsion to own and manipulate and with an insensitivity to the natural rhythms of life" (21).

In the novel's pastoral formulation, there is a privileging of knowing nature through labor. That is, those who have actually worked the land are more in tune with it and are therefore more deserving inhabitants than the legal owners, whose association with machinery indicates estrangement from nature. Johnny Paul has an extended speech that students often find puzzling where he says he killed Beau to "protect them little flowers" (90). His memories of long-gone plants and flowers are as strong as those of dead friends and relatives. He laments the flowers that no longer grow, and their loss is the loss of a way of life, including men plowing with horses instead of tractors. As he continues, Johnny Paul claims that he killed Beau because the tractor—and white culture by extension—threatens to destroy and wipe out all traces of the true inhabitants of this land, who will vanish forever like the flowers that no longer grow in their yards:

> I did it 'cause that tractor is getting closer and closer to that graveyard, and I was scared if I didn't do it, one day that tractor was go'n come in here and plow up them graves, getting rid of all proof that we ever was. Like now they trying to get rid of all proof that black people ever farmed this land with plows and mules—like if they had nothing from the starten but motor machines. . . . And I did it for every four-o'clock, every rosebush, every palm-of-Christian ever growed on this place.   (92)

This speech is a good opportunity to discuss with students why these characters feel such a strong connection to the land that has been a place of subjugation, toil, and exploitation. I often suggest that knowing nature through labor can provide a more intimate connection than certain conventional environmental attitudes, which see nature as wholly separate from human beings and as something to be protected and admired from a distance or as a place for recreation. Raising such issues can lead to productive debate or discussion of environmental and land-use issues, and rural students (in particular those from farming backgrounds) often have different perspectives on how human beings should use, interact with, and appreciate nature.

Johnny Paul's speech prompts another of the old men, Tucker, to voice explicitly the idea that cultural racism has impacted the natural realm of the farm, perverting the supposed pastoral middle ground into simply another bastion of the dominant culture's hegemony:

> After the plantation was dying out, the Marshalls dosed out the land for sharecropping, giving the best land to the Cajuns, and giving us the worst— that bottomland near the swamps. Here, our own black people had been working this land a hundred years for the Marshall plantation, but when it

come to sharecropping, now they give the best land to the Cajuns, who
had never set foot on the land before.   (94)

Tucker then goes on to relate the highly symbolic story of his brother Silas and
his mules racing in a plowing contest against Fix Boutan on his tractor. His description of the race emphasizes the bond between man and animal forged
through working the land, as well as the doomed, quixotic nature of the contest:

> Them two little mules did all they could, like my brother did. They knowed
> it was the end if they couldn't make it. They could hear the machine like
> everybody else could hear the machine, and they knowed they had to pull,
> pull, pull if they wanted to keep going. My brother and mules, mules and
> my brother. . . . How can flesh and blood and nigger win against white man
> and machine?   (96)

Silas is prophetically referred to by his brother as "the last black man round here
trying to sharecrop on this place. The last one to fight against that tractor out
there" (93). But even though he wins the race, the machine of racism mows him
down anyway: "because he didn't lose like a nigger is supposed to lose, they beat
him" (97). The game is rigged by the whites who control it; even when the black
man wins he really loses. Even when his people have farmed the land for a hundred years, those same sugarcane stalks are used to beat him into submission,
and the best farmland is given to the Cajuns "who had never set foot on the land
before" (94). Mules and men are both treated as disposable commodities; when
all the value has been extracted from their bodies they can be forgotten and cast
aside, and the white authorities call it "progress" (99). So even though the novel
rejects traditional pastoral ordering of the landscape in some sense, it also replicates the traditional pastoral formula by aligning the men with a lost past and
setting them against the tractor, which symbolizes both the mechanization of
modern industrial farming and the machine of institutionalized racism, both of
which have intruded on the garden and tainted it: the plantation ironically can
be both debilitating and empowering.

In traditional versions of southern pastoral, both from the antebellum and Reconstruction eras, the cleared, domesticated land of the plantation is figured as
the ideal pastoral middle ground, a harmonic combination of nature and culture. The harsh and even dangerous extremes of the wilderness and the city are
tempered in the bucolic, agrarian setting. However, in the decades preceding
Gaines's body of work, many southern writers had already challenged and revised the traditional genre formulae. The farm or plantation, as well as farmers
themselves, became problematized, as Maria Farland argues in an article about
the pastoral in modernist poetry and as I argue in *Clear-Cutting Eden: Ecology
and the Pastoral in Southern Literature*. Additionally, Melvin Dixon points out
in *Ride Out the Wilderness* that African Americans have always had a very different understanding of this pastoral nature/culture dichotomy. Beginning in

slave narratives, the pastoral garden has been full of threat and violence, while the wilderness is often a place of refuge and potential salvation. In literature, Dixon argues, black writers have had to create "alternative landscapes where black culture and identity can flourish" (2). Consequently, the plantation particularly and the farm and the rural more generally are typically rejected by black authors, who therefore also reject the white male pastoral formula of the country farm as a place of escape from the outside world. However, as Shelton argues, Gaines finds much to admire in the traditional pastoral setting, and he displays the enormously complex relationships among nature, race, and class: "Among contemporary black Southern writers, Gaines provides the most complex and comprehensive adaptation of the pastoral mode to black fiction since Toomer. He vividly dramatizes the negative side of the pastoral, but part of his importance arises from the fact that, rather than completely dismiss the mode, as did Wright, he provides a version including all of its complexities" (13–14).[3] Thus, Charlie's initial reaction after killing Beau is to run away and to ask his godfather, Mathu, to take the blame. Appropriately enough, Charlie says he is "go'n run and try to reach the North" (192) and winds up in the swamps just outside the plantation borders, a traditional landscape of refuge in slave narratives. Again, Gaines does not follow the traditional rejection of the pastoral place in black literature (that is, he does not conform to Dixon's formula), instead returning Charlie to the plantation in order to find salvation. Charlie reports that he had crammed dirt in his mouth in an attempt to kill himself while in the swamp and then had heard a voice calling his name. "I knowed that voice was calling me back here," he says of the plantation (193).

Just as Charlie prepares to turn himself in to the sheriff, Luke Will and his gang of redneck racists show up seeking vigilante justice. In the ensuing firefight, Luke and his cronies fittingly hide behind the tractor firing their guns, while the old men use the weeds and bushes as cover. Charlie kills Luke Will but is mortally wounded in the process. As he lies dying "like a big old bear looking up at us" (209), the men gather to touch him, "hoping that some of that stuff he had found back there in the swamps might rub off on [them]. . . . Then the women. . . . Then Glo told her grandchildren they must touch him, too" (210). While Charlie perhaps must travel to the wilderness to find his missing courage and the connection with nature that has been tamed, the resulting strength must be enacted and lived out in the plantations and towns. A connection to the past is also reestablished (as it is in the graveyard scene), and through the conduit of Charlie, generational strength and courage are passed on to new generations.

So Gaines both adopts and significantly alters the pastoral mode in this novel. His black farmers and workers occupy the traditional pastoral middle ground of the rural farm or plantation, yet they live there in a state of servitude and subjugation. The black characters also are opposed to the modern symbol of the tractor because it also represents the destructive, inexorable machinery of racism. Manual labor, actually working the land, supplies the pastoral connection to nature that is threatened by the tractor both as technology that takes jobs from black workers and as racism that denies the men access to the land their families have worked for generations. It is not coincidental that Charlie, the youngest of the old men, is also the hardest worker. Charlie says, "I can work longer than any man I ever met. Pull a saw, swing a axe, stretch wire, cut ditch bank, dig postholes better than any man I ever met" (189). Knowing nature through labor allows people to build empowering connections to place and with other people. Elizabeth Jane Harrison's *Female Pastoral* provides a guide for understanding this process in Gaines's novel. Harrison argues that southern women writers had to create a new version of pastoral, a female pastoral, that did not reduce women's identities to "a narrow association with the southern garden. . . . [Women's] interaction with land changes from passive association to active cultivation or identification" (10–11).[4] Gaines employs a strikingly similar process with race replacing gender as the traditionally limiting factor. That is, rather than have his characters reject the pastoral place for the supposed freedom of wilder landscapes, Gaines has them turn a negative association with the southern garden into an enabling force to counter a debilitating culture. While the swamps and wilderness may serve as sites of temporary respite and inspiration, Gaines recognizes that social change must occur where the people are.

Thus, it is perhaps fitting that we see change in the novel occurring in the city of Baton Rouge, more specifically in Louisiana State University's Tiger Stadium, which even prior to its 1978 expansion to 78,000 seats contains more people on game days than all but three cities in the state.[5] Gil Boutan and Cal Harrison's partnership on the LSU football team as white and black teammates represents the possibility for racial cooperation. Only through the races working together, Gaines is saying, can success be achieved, whether in athletic competition or in the larger southern family. The interdependence of white and black is something understood by the younger generations of Boutans who, although they may have selfish goals, push for progress in a still-segregated 1970s Louisiana. The novel's use of football allows for wide-ranging discussions with students of all backgrounds about the role of sports in American society (can it be a force for change and progress?), branching out into the history of famous athletes who have broken color barriers at different times and in different sports. Depending on the particular class and how much time is available, one might show brief videos from *YouTube* of the struggles and triumphs of figures such as Jack Johnson (boxing), Jesse Owens (track and field), and Jackie Robinson (baseball). Lively discussions are possible about whether sports are more or less progressive than society as a whole. For example, Robinson became the first black Major League Baseball player in 1947, and President Harry Truman signed the order to desegregate the armed forces in 1948. More recently, the widely publicized case of Michael Sam, who became the first openly gay professional football player in 2014, might suggest that professional sports can be slower to accept social change. I have found a useful parallel to the novel's depiction of racial integration and the resistance to it through the example of the 1966 NCAA Men's National Basketball Championship game. This game was the first to pit an all-black starting team against an all-white team. Coach Don Haskins of Texas Western College (now the University of Texas at El Paso) fielded an all-black starting lineup for his team, which took on the legendary coach Adolph Rupp and the University of Kentucky. Texas Western's victory at the height of the civil rights movement was a watershed moment in American sports, and the University of Kentucky signed its first black basketball player to a scholarship offer in 1969.[6]

I often have student-athletes in general education (nonmajor) classes, and this aspect of the novel has been a way to have fruitful discussions about race, sports, and society. Students often have enlightening tales of how sports and race intersect, sometimes in ways that parallel Gaines's novel. For example, discussions often turn to how sport promotes egalitarianism in its emphasis on performance over identity. Student-athletes attest to the fact that sports, because of their emphasis on performance and results, are often more of a true meritocracy than American society as a whole, a point that can challenge stereotypes some may have of athletes and sports teams as backward and small-minded. Students will often, with some prompting, reflect on how their own experiences in sports led them to meet and build friendships with people they might never have otherwise come to know, especially across racial lines.

Depending on how much class time is available or the specific course, there are several films that address similar themes of racial prejudice in sports, including *Glory Road* (2006), a dramatic rendering of Texas Western's 1966 championship game triumph over Kentucky. Of course, films might be assigned outside of class or short clips might be utilized from such other choices as *42* (2013), the story of Robinson breaking the color barrier in baseball, or *Remember the Titans* (2000), based on the true story of a football team formed by the forced integration of a high school in Virginia in 1971. Shorter, documentary-style clips about these topics abound on sites like *YouTube*, and teachers can find ones that suit their purposes and the amount of available time they have.

A related discussion can be had about black masculinity in sports during the same time period. This also relates to the novel's portrayal of elderly men who have been denied recognition as men or at least as men who are as masculine as their white counterpoints. One theme of Gaines's text is the rediscovery and reassertion of black masculinity in the face of dominant white masculinity. Black masculinity as a threat can be seen in the sports world of the era. A *Sports Illustrated* cover story from 31 October 1977, titled "Nobody, but Nobody, Is Going to Hurt My Teammates," details the trend of "enforcers" in the National Basketball Association (NBA) (Papanek). These "enforcers" were essentially the toughest guy on any given team, often designated to retaliate against the rough play of opponents, though occasionally inserted into games specifically to start fights. As Jack Ramsay, then coach of the Portland Trail Blazers, says in the article, "It's important for your team to let it be known that you will not be pushed around, will not be intimidated." This line is one that could easily be applied to the old men in Gaines's novel. Five of the six "enforcers" profiled in the article are black, and the implicit threat of these types of players to white audiences eventually became a major problem for the league, with at least six teams facing possible bankruptcy in the early 1980s. According to a 1984 *New York Times* article, "buyers were nowhere to be found, and attendance, television ratings and corporate sponsorship were flagging—all because of basketball's sorry image" (Gross). In the article, which touts the league's efforts at rebuilding from its 1970s image problem, then rookie NBA commissioner David Stern framed the situation in racial terms: "Our problem was that sponsors were flocking out of the N.B.A. because it was perceived as a bunch of high-salaried, drug-sniffing black guys."

To give students a better sense of these issues, it is helpful to use the most notorious case of NBA on-court violence as an example, a fight that changed public opinion and forced the NBA to change its product. The 9 December 1977 game between the Houston Rockets and Los Angeles Lakers descended into yet another on-court brawl. As the white Rockets player Rudy Tomjanovich rushed toward the combatants, the Lakers' Kermit Washington, a black man and one of the "enforcers" profiled in *Sports Illustrated*, instinctively turned and punched the onrushing player in the face. The impact from the punch and from Tomjanovich's head hitting the floor nearly killed the Rockets player and turned Washington into a threatening villain who received the longest suspension in NBA history at the time. A documentary about the incident and its aftermath, *Searching for Redemption: The Kermit Washington Story*, is available in seven parts on *YouTube*, as well as numerous shorter clips of the incident (Davachi). Connections can be made between the NBA culture of the time and other instances of black masculinity in sports that were seen as threatening by white America, including the outspoken Muhammad Ali (né Cassius Clay) and the track-and-field athletes Tommie Smith and John Carlos and their black power salute on the medal stand at the 1968 Olympics. The point here is to illustrate how sports can be a vehicle for social change and to demonstrate how the football scenes of the novel relate to those at the Marshall plantation. The discussion could even be extended to contemporary issues of race in sports, including low graduation rates for black college athletes, double standards for black players' in-game celebrations, numerous high-profile athletes showing support for the Black Lives Matter movement, and the refusal of the San Francisco 49ers quarterback and others to stand during the pregame playing of the national anthem.[7]

In a sense, the well-tended grass of the football field can be seen as the improved garden of the pastoral, a middle landscape that combines culture and nature, providing a space from which the norms of society can be critiqued. Arguably, the white-black partnership between Gil Boutan and Cal Harrison on the football field provides a model for racial cooperation and solidarity that is more productive than the confrontational model that occurs at the Marshall plantation. While the old men of the novel (and African Americans in general) are denied full access to the supposed harmonic middle ground of the plantation fields, the athletic field provides more of the ideal balance and equality than the traditional pastoral locales of the South can. Gil's refusal to join his father in a lynch mob to avenge Beau's death because he does not want to jeopardize his football career is paralleled by the decision of a third brother, Jean, who also wants no part of vengeance because he feels it will imperil his business in Bayonne that sells to both white and black customers. Events on the football field, in fact, directly and indirectly affect the "real world" and illustrate that the stadium turf can fulfill what Gifford calls the essential paradox of the pastoral: "that a retreat to a place apparently without the anxieties of the town, or the court, or the present, actually delivers insights into the culture from which it originates" (82). In this case, through his on-field partnership with Cal, Gil sees that the antagonism, suspicion, and hatred that have driven southern race relations in the past need not be the only model for the future. His brother Jean has much the same insight, and Candy Marshall's attachment to Mathu as a surrogate father leads her to push the old men to their armed rebellion initially. I often ask students whether Gil, Jean, and Candy are acting out of purely selfish motives, and many students agree that they are. However, I am quick to point out that Gil, Jean, and Candy's acting out of selfish motives is not necessarily reason to demean their actions. In fact, true change often happens only when people have a personal stake.

NOTES

[1] The most useful and relevant portions of the interview include the first four minutes, as well as portions dealing with his time in Louisiana and his move to California (12:42–15:05, 19:15–21:01, and 23:15–25:50). Depending on how much time is available and the nature of the course, instructors may also find valuable what Gaines says about his audience, his influences, and his advice for aspiring writers (34:12–41:50).

[2] This essay quotes from the 1992 Vintage edition of *Gathering*.

[3] Similarly, Mark Sandy examines how conventions of the pastoral are used and altered in African American literature as he interprets Morrison as reworking Wordsworth's pastoral places and characters.

[4] Peggy Barlett suggests that modern farmwork has become associated with masculinity through its connection both to outdoor physical labor and to technology: "Farming today is tied intimately to knowledge of engines and machine repair, and such machinery management is especially associated with male gender" (51).

[5] According to the official Web site of LSU athletics, Tiger Stadium's capacity in the early 1970s was more than 67,000 people, and the current stadium holds more than 102,000.

[6] There are many videos on *YouTube* about this famous game. I often show one called "History Day Documentary (Kentucky vs. Texas Western 1966)," which is a good length for class (about ten minutes) and is well researched and well produced (Peloff). Interestingly, the 2014 NCAA Men's Basketball Tournament semifinal featured an all-black Kentucky starting team versus an all-white Wisconsin starting team. The reasons for this and the meaning of it might also prove good fodder for discussion.

[7] In 2016 ESPN launched *The Undefeated*, a Web site that seeks to explore the intersections of race, sports, and culture.

Beyond the Weeds:
Teaching the Significance of Cajuns in
A *Gathering of Old Men*

Maria Hebert-Leiter

Much like the weeds that cover the ground in A *Gathering of Old Men*, to which most of the fifteen narrators refer, the link between Louisiana's past and future is one of twisted, tangled roots not easily unknotted by adherence to simple racial dichotomies or the usual American ethnic studies. At one point, Sheriff Mapes says to Johnny Paul, "I see," referring to the African American men's plan to stand together and protect Mathu, the assumed killer of the Cajun Beau Boutan. Johnny Paul replies, "No, you don't see" (88).[1] This assessment could also refer to readers who have been raised beyond the south Louisiana world of which Gaines writes, those who may not comprehend the complexity of Louisiana ethnicities and thus miss significant moments in Gaines's novel. To understand the full implications of Louisiana racial dynamics in *Gathering*, one must see between the lines printed in the novel and etched on the memories of the Louisiana folk. The weeds must be cleared, or, to be more literal, assumptions must be put aside.

While the novel focuses on the aging African American population of the Marshall plantation, it also offers insight into another Louisiana ethnicity: the Cajuns. Popular stereotypes have created false notions of what being Cajun signifies, as one student proved when she asked me if I was referring to the seasoning mixes sold in the grocery store when I used the term "Cajun." For this reason, I open my class discussion of Gaines's novel with the basic question: what do you think a Cajun is? Within this general discussion, I guide the students through the flawed representations in such films as *The Waterboy* (1998) and such TV shows as *Swamp People*, which emphasize how different, even backward, the Cajuns have become in the mainstream American imagination. This conversation naturally leads to my explanation of why and how such stereotypes were perpetuated, using textual evidence and interviews of Gaines to prove my argument. For example, when begging his father, Fix, to allow the law to guarantee justice for his brother's death, and thus to avoid the lynching party everyone expects, Gil Boutan says, "But I would like people to know we're not what they think we are" (143). Indeed, Cajuns, more often than not, are not what we think they are. Even Gaines admits as much when he explained in an interview that *Cajun* meant "a white who would give [African Americans] hell on False River" (Gaudet and Wooton, *Porch Talk* 83). It was not so much an ethnicity as a label for the white folk in the area who treated the black folk cruelly. Thus, an image of racism replaces what should be a story of survival and pride.

I do not intend to claim Cajun innocence. The truth, however, is more complicated than it may seem—a major theme of the novel. While Gaines also explained in the interview that "Cajun" to him meant "a white man who spoke

French" during the mid-twentieth century (Gaudet and Wooton, *Porch Talk* 84), the term actually refers to the large groups of Acadian descendants who traveled to Spanish colonial Louisiana from some of the thirteen British colonies or from France during the second half of the eighteenth century, a history I share with the students. The Acadians originally lived in Acadia, French settlements in what is now known as Nova Scotia, Prince Edward Island, and New Brunswick, but beginning in 1755, the British colonial government forced the Acadians of Grand Pré and other villages onto ships and destroyed their houses and farms to guarantee they could not return to their homeland. Once economically stable because of their agrarian skill, the Acadians found themselves scattered throughout the North American colonies, possessing little with which to make a livelihood. Roughly ten years later, groups began to migrate to south Louisiana, where they began settling in large groups and creating a new homeland (Brasseaux; Hodson). As word spread regarding the potential of this new home, others who had returned to France rejoined their relatives in the New World. Henry Wadsworth Longfellow even referred to Louisiana as an Eden in *Evangeline*, his sentimental epic poem about the deportation and the most famous literary depiction of the Acadian dispersal and subsequent survival (862). Using passages from this nineteenth-century poem, I explain the Acadian journey to Louisiana and its significance in the creation of a unique American ethnic group, the Cajuns. For a more detailed and accurate description of Acadian and Cajun history, along with explanations of Louisiana racial and ethnic categories, I draw from the studies of Carl A. Brasseaux, James H. Dormon, and Christopher Hodson into the Acadian dispersal, among others.

Louisiana was not always the Eden of Longfellow's romantic imagination for the Cajuns. To demonstrate this disconnect for the students, I map out the various branches of Louisiana ethnicities, which are often entwined with popular notions of race in the state's history, an elaborate system that maintained a power structure that benefitted neither the Cajun nor the African American. This lesson begins with basic definitions of ethnic terms, using Gaines's interviews and textual evidence as supporting clues. For example, I explain how "Creole" has shifted from referring to a person born in colonial Louisiana, regardless of race, to a racial signifier (Dormon x). While "Creole" has been used to refer to Louisiana colonists and to demarcate racial communities, Gaines uses the term as a class marker to refer to white landowners. He explains how the big house of the plantation where he grew up was "owned by the Creoles," which in this context refers to the white population of Creole descendants who were in positions of social and economic power (Gaudet and Wooton, "Talking" 228). Though "Creole" does not arise as a label for the characters in this particular novel, the term is significant because of its distinction from "Creole of color" or those who are from "the old Mulatto Place," or mulattoes, as Gaines refers to them in the story (38–39).

To further complicate the matter, "Creole of color," which Gaines abbreviates to simply "Creole" in interviews, creates yet another division and became a means of asserting superiority. While discussing this use of the term in the twentieth century, Gaines explains how the label was used to claim, "I'm not black, I'm not white, I'm Creole," though Gaines dismisses this concept as "falseness in itself because the Creoles were either French or Spanish" (Gaudet and Wooton, "Talking" 230). One of Gaines's narrators, Matthew Lincoln Brown, a.k.a. Mat, alludes to this racial and ethnic divide when he introduces Jacob Aguillard to the reader and mentions that "his kind didn't have too much to do with darker people" (39). In a later chapter, Grant Bello, also known as Cherry, relates Jacob's story about his sister Tessie, "who messed around with the white man and the black man," leading to her family's denying responsibility for her dead body because they were "against her living here in the first place round the darker people" (45). His next revelation is telling: "I'm light as them, but I'm not French, not quality" (45).

This sort of hierarchy frays once set against Mathu, because he, unlike the other old men, takes pride in how African he continues to be within such a racially mixed population. According to Cyril Robillard, a.k.a. Clatoo, Mathu is "one of them blue-black Singaleese niggers. Always bragged about not having no white man's blood in his veins" (51). Unlike Jacob's family and its pride in being more white than the black folk, Mathu prides himself on being 100 percent African. The other men fall somewhere in between Mathu and Jacob, with their "yellow" skin tones, "Indian and black" heritages, and other various shades of ethnicity, adding American Indian to this already complicated ethnic gumbo.

If Creoles of color resided between black folk and white folk in twentieth-century Louisiana, then the Cajuns lived between anyone of black or colored identity and the landowners. In fact, the proximity of Creoles of color to white Creoles reinforced the need for Cajuns in the racial hierarchy. Gaines emphasizes this interstitial positioning of the Cajuns when he explains, "I've lived in that interracial, or ethnic, mixture of the Cajun, and the big house owned by the Creoles—not Cajuns, but Creoles—and the blacks" (Gaudet and Wooton, "Talking" 228). This statement establishes the hierarchy at work in this novel as well as in his other fiction.

Additions must be made to the above ethnic groups, including the Anglo-Americans—those of American origin without French or Spanish ancestry—and those of Acadian descent whose families had ascended to a higher, more Creole-like level of prominence in south Louisiana, thus erasing the connection with their Cajun kin. Like the white Creoles in Gaines's fiction, however, both of these groups owned the land that the African American and Cajun men farmed. Furthermore, Spanish and American Indian ancestries, among others, also play prominent roles in the state, and the demarcation between ethnic groups is compromised by a history of interracial relationships and slavery. For example, one of the African American women in the novel claims a popular Acadian, thus Cajun, surname: Hebert. Glo, Snookum's grandmother, may have married an Hebert, a man whose family was once owned by Acadians. Or, perhaps, her ancestors were owned by such. Regardless, her use of the name demonstrates the degree to which the racial and ethnic lines in south Louisiana have become hopelessly entangled, as does Cherry's internal monologue regarding the light skin of his family, though they were not French. Yet both the Cajuns and the African Americans, whether they claim French ancestry or not, use *parrain* instead of the English *godfather*, reflecting the degree to which French—Creole and Cajun—has influenced all of these Louisiana communities.

To help the students navigate the intricacies of this system, I have them write brief descriptions of the characters introduced in the initial chapters of the novel. They quickly discover that Cherry is lighter than Chimley, called such because of his darker skin (39). At one point, Clatoo lists such descriptions to prove that Mathu "look down on" those whose skin was lighter, proving their racially mixed heritage: "Rooster was yellow, with nappy black hair; Clabber was milk white, with nappy white hair" (51). Surnames and the various shades used to describe the old men prove the paradoxical nature of this system, a significant rationale for the cooperation Gaines calls for in the story, since unraveling the paradox means comprehending the irony that has kept such a hierarchy in place from the beginning.

As complicated as this system may at first seem, this very structure reinforced the Cajun space between the aristocratic white landowners and their tenant farmers well into the twentieth century and the supposed need for it, which Gaines records in the novel. Basically, the Cajuns were considered white, but barely. Gaines clearly emphasizes the popular concept of Cajuns as "white trash" (Brasseaux 104). These descriptions of the old men are particularly telling when contrasted with the initial descriptions of the Cajuns. For example, Aunt Bea exclaims, "Why we ever let that kind on this land, I don't know" (23), at the beginning of the novel. "That kind" clearly indicates that the Cajuns are not *her* kind of people and had no right to the land except that bestowed by the superior landowners. Later, Cherry explains that "Beau Boutan was leasing the plantation from the Marshall family" (43), and while he does so to argue that the Cajuns took the best lands from the former sharecroppers, the black folk, in truth his statement also claims the land for the Marshall family, the white landowners, and not the Cajuns. Furthermore, the reporter Louis Alfred Dimoulin, a.k.a. Lou Dimes, describes Beau as "dirty" when he first views the dead body lying in the field (64). This detail contrasts his description of Uncle Billy, one of the old African American men who have gathered. According to Lou Dimes, Uncle Billy "was a clean-shaven old fellow," with his head "shaved as clean as his face" (67). During the 1970s, Cajuns were still considered trash by most of the wealthy white population. Thus, the African American men, finally ready and willing to stand against the injustices perpetrated by such "dirt," are viewed by Lou Dimes as cleaner, perhaps as more innocent and thus harmless.

Another way in which I guide the students to a more comprehensive understanding of this multifaceted hierarchy is to study the multiple narrators who frame the story of Beau's death and the larger history to which it relates. First, I require the students to research "polyphonic narration" and to apply the term to the novel. While other literature they read for the course may have included multiple narrators, Gaines's use of fifteen different narrators offers more viewpoints than usual. Then I divide the chapters among student groups for further study, which leads to a larger class discussion about the significance of this variation, of this layering, in terms of telling this particular story about the South. Initially, the discussion pertains to the different age groups (child, adult, elder) and identifications (white, black, mulatto) that are evident as the story shifts from person to person. The fact that the key characters in the story are never given their own chapters also becomes evident through a close discussion of this narrative technique. For example, we never hear the story from Mathu's perspective or Gil's. While the students are familiar with first-person narratives told by the protagonist, *Gathering* gives voice to those on the periphery of the story and, symbolically, of the population of which Gaines writes.

I guide this discussion of individual chapters with questions about the identities of the narrators and the storytellers that prompt student consideration of racial tensions. For example, Tucker relates the story of Silas, his brother who raced his plow against the Cajun tractor and won. He says, "Here, our own black people had been working this land a hundred years for the Marshall plantation, but when it come to sharecropping, now they give the best land to the Cajuns" (94). After, he calls Mapes's deputy a "little no-butt nothing" and "boy," claiming the power with which telling his story has bestowed on him (94–95). Later, he confronts Mapes directly: "Law said he cut in on the tractor, and he was the one who started the fight. That's law for a nigger" (97). Following this accusation, the narrator, Rufe, relates that Tucker "wanted Mapes to face him. Mapes wouldn't" (97). Such stories continue with Gable sharing the story of his mentally challenged son's botched execution for supposedly raping a white woman (100–02) and Coot's experience with discrimination even though he served his country in World War I (103–04). Gaines himself explains how the people of the quarters thought of Cajuns: "anytime there was a problem on the river, and because so many of the whites there were Cajun, it would always be 'that Cajun,' whether one of them was involved or not" (Gaudet and Wooton, *Porch Talk* 83). In another interview he admits, "You find a scapegoat. You've got to find a scapegoat. And in the case of the people where I come from, if the scapegoat was white, then he was a Cajun. That's all there is to it, whether he *was* Cajun or not" (Rickels 123). In *Gathering*, the Cajun scapegoat is the notoriously racist Fix Boutan. Throughout the novel, the people—old men, women, Candy, and Lou Dimes alike—expect that "Fix coming here with his drove" to exact revenge for the murder of his son Beau (9). Janey, the Marshalls' servant, tells Snookum, the young boy who delivers the news of Beau's murder, that he is "too young to know Fix. But I know Fix" (9). When Mapes arrives on the scene, he tells Russell, one of his deputies, to "go back on that bayou and keep Fix there," because he, like the others, believes a lynching party will be formed to exact the so-called justice he is supposed to dispense (65).

By this point, the students comfortably assume they understand the clear animosity between the Cajuns and the African American community. The history related emphasizes the basic white/black dichotomy, making it an advantageous point in the lesson to take the pulse of the class and ask what students think might be the larger thematic strands in this novel. As Gaines constructs the beginning of the story, the Cajuns are, obviously, at fault, given the long list of crimes the men relate both orally and through internal dialogue.

The chapter narrated by Joseph Seaberry, a.k.a. Rufe, begins in a similar fashion, with the old men confronting Mapes and admiring Mathu's pride. After all, Mathu "was a real man" (84), a theme repeated in the earlier chapters. By the end of this chapter, however, everything changes for the reader, since this division between the African Americans and Cajuns shifts. Once the old men have been given the opportunity to speak, Mapes corrects their memories of the past, accusing them of blaming Fix and the Cajuns for crimes they did not commit: "And it's all on Fix, huh? Whether he had anything to do with it or not, Fix must pay for everything ever happened to you, huh?" (107). Moreover, he reminds Ding Lejeune that the "woman who poisoned your sister's child was Sicilian, not Cajun" (107). He tells them, "Then you blaming the wrong person" (108). Yet the men and Mapes still wait for the arrival of Fix and the other Cajuns.

Instead of Fix and the Cajun men, the narrative turns to something more familiar to the students: two undergraduates walking out of a science class. Gaines moves the reader from the plantation quarters and a way of life quickly fading, covered by the weeds that have taken over, to the modern college scene and the men who have left the plantations and their quarters behind them. Students expect Cajun retaliation and violence. Instead, they are given "Salt and Pepper." Gil, a Cajun, and Cal, an African American, form a football partnership at Louisiana State University (LSU) that calls into question the tensions and animosities laid bare in previous chapters. Their friend Thomas Vincent Sullivan, a.k.a. Sully, narrates the success of their partnership on the field. The students and I discuss Sully's description of the players, which shifts the narrative focus of the novel. He claims, "Gil blocked for Cal on sweeps around end, and Cal returned the favor when Gil went up the middle" (112). Later, Gil admits that "he needed Pepper and Pepper needed him" (171). By contrasting these descriptions of the present team with the old men's past sufferings, the students begin to question earlier conclusions about Cajuns in general and about everyone's forgone assumption of the lynching party.

Sully provides an objective perspective that allows for racial cooperation and, perhaps, more. By doing so, he becomes a guide for the students through the muddled history of Louisiana. While Mapes corrects the men's versions of the past, he also waits with them, as certain as they are that Fix will come. Sully's chapter, however, offers a glimpse into the future, beyond the weeds. He first introduces us to Gil's desire to become an all-American player (111). Sully says Gil would "shake a black man's hand as soon as he would a white man's" (131–32). Whereas the beginning of Sully's first chapter emphasizes this cooperation, it ends with Gil's confrontation of Candy regarding her assumed superiority: "You never liked any of us. Looking at us as if we're a breed below you" (122).

Breed refers to animals and is reminiscent of representations and stereotypes of African Americans in the South from slavery onward. The old men's stories demonstrate repeatedly this popular acceptance of their people as less than human by relating beatings with sugarcane stalks and, as Lou Dimes testifies to the reader, memories of white men speaking to them "as you would speak to a dog" (58). Cajuns, specifically the Boutan family, are accused of these crimes, for which they are often responsible, thus creating the African American assumption that they are responsible for all such crimes and are not capable of change.

By studying Gil's accusation along with the testimony of the old men, students begin to understand the hierarchy at work: a pyramid with the white landowners at the top and the African American laborers pushed to the wide bottom. The Cajuns remain safely between, a buffer that guarantees the assumption of a continued clarity between white and black in Louisiana. Even though Sully has redeemed Gil, as Gil has himself through his nonviolent confrontation of the African American men, Fix remains guilty, regardless of his lack of action so far. Recalling Mapes's earlier argument that Fix and his family were responsible for some but not every racially motived crime, I have the students carefully read Sully's second chapter, which relates Gil's arrival home and his encounter with his father and a group of Cajun men.

I open the reading with Sully's description of Fix, who wears a "clean, ironed white shirt" (141), and refer the students back to Beau's description as dirty contrasted with the old men's "clean" appearance. While Beau may have been "living in the past" (74), the present crashes through Fix's life through Gil and his success at LSU. As Gil admits to his father, "Those days are gone forever, I hope," referring to lynching and other violence against African Americans (143). In this same chapter, the students meet Luke Will for the first time. Unlike Fix and the Cajun men, he has "long brown hair," a "beer-belly," and "some of his teeth were missing" (141). Sully calls him a "red-neck" (141), placing the popular "white trash" image of the Cajuns onto him and his gang. Further separating him from the Boutans, Fix says, "You might have been a friend of Beau's. But you not a member of this family, and you don't speak" (136). Fix "looked at him awhile" before shifting his attention to Luke Will's cohort, "the other big, rough-looking guy in the brown shirt" (136). If Fix's white shirt disrupts the earlier assumption that, like Beau, Cajuns are dirty, thus guilty, then this scene transfers this guilt to Luke Will and his crowd. The command that Luke Will remain silent in this family argument, in addition to his non-Cajun name, places him outside the Cajun gathering. At the end of his argument with Gil, a tired Fix claims, "I'm too old for causes. Let Luke Will fight for causes. . . . Go tell your friend Mapes this old Cajun will come to Bayonne at the law's convenience" (147). Though incapable of envisioning and desiring a future of racial cooperation like his college-educated son, Fix relents, if reluctantly, to the pressure of change, thanks in part to Gil. In the end, Luke Will commits the crime, enacts the supposed Cajun revenge, and the Boutans remain separate from it.

Though the old men accuse Fix of past injustices committed against them, the responsibility for this racial tension also falls upon the Marshalls and white land-owners in general. Throughout the novel, various narrators repeat statements that indicate white paternalism remains in place on the plantation grounds. Though the Thirteenth Amendment abolishing slavery was passed in 1865, both Candy Marshall and the bar owner Jacques Thibeaux, a.k.a. Tee Jack, refer to the African American residents in terms of possession. Commenting internally on Beau and his "six trailers of cane," Tee Jack corrects his thought in terms of who actually delivers those trailers, referring to Charlie, the man who worked for Beau, as "his nigger Charlie" (155). And when the old men choose to discuss their next step without Candy present, she says, "This is my place" (173), and claims the right to be present, because "my people have always protected them," mean-ing the African Americans who live in the quarters (174). Mapes calls her out by claiming, "[Y]ou want to keep them slaves," and that at least "your people let them talk" (174). To unravel the character of Candy and her purpose in the novel, I turn back to Tucker's story about Silas and his race against the machine. At the conclusion of the story, Tucker "stopped and looked at Candy," who refuses to look back because, according to Rufe, "[s]he knowed Tucker was telling the truth" (94). And though "she was born too late to witness it," she repeats a similar form of discrimination by assuming the old men need her protection (94).

To expand on this point, I have the students discuss why Gaines places the reader in Tee Jack's store and bar. Tee Jack demonstrates that some Cajuns *are* guilty of being prejudicial, that they do, in fact, discriminate against African Americans. Though the "nigger room's been closed now some fifteen, seventeen years," Tee Jack narrates, "they soon found out they wasn't welcomed" to pull up a barstool and drink alongside his white customers (152, 153). He even calls it "that desegregation crap" (152). More telling, however, is Tee Jack's descrip-tion of Jack Marshall, Candy's uncle. According to him, Jack views his inheri-tance, the Marshall plantation, as a burden. He cannot escape the weight of the white patriarchal past, and thus he lives "[f]eeling guilty about this, guilty about that" (154). But Jack chooses to drown himself in alcohol rather than do some-thing to change the situation. The Tee Jack chapter, in addition to offering an-other perspective on Louisiana Cajuns, also sheds light on the core problem of an enduring system of inequality and injustice. This guilt-ridden, ineffective ver-sion of Jack Marshall belies his own role in the system, yet Clatoo admits all the old men have gathered to stand with Mathu because he "always stood up," even to Jack Marshall (179). In fact, Clatoo explains, "That's why Jack Marshall don't like Mathu today" (179).

Aunt Bea, Candy, Jack Marshall, even Miss Merle cannot change the system because they benefit from it. As Fix argues, Gil's education has led to his advice that the family "don't move" (145), but his education embodies more than his time in LSU classrooms. Because of his partnership with Cal, Gil becomes a hero to the region, even if his actions are prompted by the selfish desire for success on the field. Russ, the deputy assigned to watch the Boutan family, convinces him that playing in a football game will be the best revenge for his brother's death: "Sometimes you got to hurt something to help something. Sometimes you have to plow under one thing in order for something else to grow. . . . You can help this country tomorrow. You can help yourself" (151). A Cajun, the old men's archenemy, offers hope by proving he can create a more promising future by playing alongside an African American man. This racial cooperation should be celebrated, but it comes at a price, as when Fix emphasizes how "All-American" Gil has become.

In Sully's second chapter, he captures the English influenced by Cajun French spoken by the Boutans. I have the students discuss Fix's pronunciation of Gil's full name: "Gi-bear" (138). This begins a larger discussion of other Cajun French linguistic influences that Gaines scatters throughout this scene, such as *parrain* and the affectionate "Tee" to refer to Beau's son, Tee Beau. A corruption of *petite*, Tee is still used in Cajun communities to refer to sons and other namesakes. Gaines also writes the names as they would be spoken, as with "A-goose." To provide a stronger sense of this dialect, I have the students watch the 1987 film version of the novel to hear the pronunciations. Yet Gil's speech patterns, his LSU all-American status, and his answering to both Salt and Gil demonstrate his ability to bridge this gap of difference, which makes him key to progress and change in the novel.

In the end, Mathu did not shoot Beau; his godson, Charlie, did. The nasty Boutans stay home, while Gil plays with Cal and wins the big game. What makes this novel different is the more complicated addition of the Louisiana racial and ethnic system that pits neighbors against each other to serve the land that has never belonged to any of them. And thus, Gaines reverses assumptions and teaches those outside the state borders about a layered history simultaneously in need of remembrance and change. As Gaines has explained, "the only ones who live in the present are Salt and Pepper. They're the ones living in the present and they're the ones who must make this America work. We've got to block for each other and do all kinds of things to get to the goal. The football players are a symbol for how we must do this together" (Saeta and Skinner 250). *A Gathering of Old Men* teaches us that we have to put aside assumptions to make way for such cooperation. We must all cheer for Gil and Cal and their success in offering a new, hopeful lesson to both south Louisiana and the nation at large.

NOTE

[1] This essay quotes from the 1992 Vintage edition of *Gathering*.

Who Done It? Gaines's *A Gathering of Old Men* as a Parody of Richard Wright's "The Man Who Was Almost a Man"

Virginia Whatley Smith

Certainly, parody—or the act of "signifying upon" another author's work by "in-direction" (Gates, *Figures* 242)—exists when an instructor arrives at teaching Richard Wright's short story "The Man Who Was Almost a Man" (1961) along with Ernest Gaines's novel *A Gathering of Old Men* (1983). The short story additionally functions as a "call" text in which the novel acts as its "response" (Stepto 1, 32). Parody or call-and-response enables black writers to upgrade history; in this instance, Gaines's novel extends the publication timeline of Wright's short story, which was published posthumously in the 1961 collection *Eight Men*. The publication date can be problematic, since parody is not always evident to students unless the comparative texts are taught sequentially or chronologically in an African American literature course. Furthermore, the time period of the setting is also significant, since it often differs drastically from the publication date. "Almost a Man" takes place in the mid-1930s. The key scene concerns the seventeen-year-old African American Dave Saunders being "called" by his Mississippi employer, Jim Hawkins, the plantation owner and the most powerful white man in the southern community, to "respond" to charges of killing Hawkins's mule. Gaines's novel takes place in the 1970s, and it not only exemplifies parody but also how historical racism and oppression are resistant to or slow to change in the Deep South. The paradigm of a "community gathering" in "Almost a Man" repeats in *Gathering*, but this time it concerns the "response" of eighteen seventy- to eighty-year-old African and African American men who have answered the "call" of a white female plantation owner to meet on her property in Louisiana in order to account for the murder of a powerful white man. Teaching the pedagogical connections between these two works requires a number of theoretical frames. Overall, the person or persons "who done it"—-i.e., who committed the crime in both cases—is problematic.

Gnosis: Knowing about Subjugated Knowledge

Any time an instructor teaches African American literature at the undergraduate or graduate level, the complex transnational cultural traditions will require that person to provide students, regardless of race, some basic knowledge about the narrative techniques utilized by black writers. I usually start the course by introducing some key terms and definitions, one being that of "gnosis," meaning "to know," which has been magnified as a key word by V. Y. Mudimbe in his work *The Invention of Africa: Gnosis, Philosophy, and the Order of Knowledge* (1988). Mudimbe's purpose has been to recover the "subjugated knowledge" about African traditions (ix). European American colonizers and slaveholders forbade their human cargoes of captive Africans to recall or speak about their customs once the invaders transported them to the New World and recodified the bondaged lots as nonhumans without histories or cultural traditions. Since the 1960s civil rights and black arts movements, however, scholars and writers transglobally have sought to "know" the truth about African customs. They have worked assiduously to recover the narratives, artworks, scientific studies, and histories of continental and diasporic African people that had been deliberately suppressed, omitted, or misrepresented in European American records and textbooks through the 350 years of American slavery (1619–1865) and Jim Crow segregation, to the miseducation of both black and white American students. Only with the 1954 *Brown v. Board of Education* decision abolishing unequal, segregated schools and then the 1964 Civil Rights Act mandating equal rights for African Americans in employment, wages, housing, and public facilities did misrepresented historical records begin to be widely corrected and disseminated.

It is important for students to recognize the ancient African traditions that became muddled, distorted, decimated, or lost during or after colonization and slavery and that, although altered, have continued to influence the identities of continental and diasporic Africans. The misrepresentations require the instructor to correct these distortions and to teach students to understand how Mudimbe's theory of gnosis works in recovering "subjugated knowledge." I start the course by providing three handouts: a map of early Africa when it was demarcated by kingdoms or provinces, a map of colonial Africa showing how fourteen European nations arbitrarily cut through customary territorial lines and divided continental Africa among themselves, and a map of present-day postcolonial Africa, which still largely maintains the boundaries set by Europeans. Like Humpty Dumpty broken to pieces after his fall, it is impossible for Africans to reconfigure present-day nation-states into their former ancient territories, since present-day Africa is greatly hybridized. The Europeans' laws and customs have been irreversibly integrated into or mixed within the social structures of indigenous Africans, including traditions of naming, styles of dress, manners of speaking, and religious practices, to name a few. Throughout the course, I additionally show film clips to assist students in visually assessing, contextualizing, and grasping periods of history, the customs of the people, and the physical contours and territorial limits of the lands being studied that would seem remote from their lives.

Students need to "know" and understand that during the 450 years of Anglo-American supreme control, they, along with their European counterparts, disseminated biased propaganda worldwide that claimed blacks to be intellectually inferior to whites. The gamut of perverted "historical truths" spread globally lay solely in the hands of the limited collectives of powerful European and then Anglo-American political, religious, and governmental agents who maintained hegemonic control over African, European, Caribbean, and South and North

American cultures. Christopher Columbus, for example, inaugurated the slave trade with his voyage to the Caribbean in 1492 and then trips around Africa in 1500 that, by 1502, resulted in the extermination of Caribbean Indians and the displacement of Africans off the continent to the Caribbean (Conniff and Davis 71). Moreover, following the lead of John Locke in his 1698 "Essay Concerning Human Understanding," eighteenth- and nineteenth-century philosophers and scientists inclusive of David Hume of Scotland, Immanuel Kant of Germany, Georges Leopold Cuvier of France, and Thomas Jefferson of the United States all perpetuated racist propaganda by touting the superior intellects, melanin absences, and physical characteristics of Caucasians over the inferior people of color—the Mongoloids and Negro Africans—in order to support the slave trade (Johnson and Lyne 49–51, 52–53, 54–57, 43–48). The 1960s and '70s marked the revolutionary and disruptive periods when African Americans finally became self-governed and proclaimed their freedom to control, name, historicize, and publicize their own cultural traditions from their own perspectives. Mudimbe merely augmented the cultural theories first marginalized and then later publicly espoused by African American scholars, writers, and theorists whose ideas about and pride of black cultural traditions started as far back as the Harlem Renaissance in the 1920s and '30s, began to burgeon in the civil rights and black arts movements of the 1960s and '70s, and continue to the present day.

I also introduce other significant theories in order to assist students in their critical readings of the texts. Students learn that the bulk of "found" subjugated works or newly etched narratives released about the lives of Africanist people reached the public domain owing to massive (re)publications during and after the 1960s and '70s in the forms of oral and written texts related to music, art, literature, history, and science. These works have conveyed the "historical truths" and corrected misperceptions about African and African American people from their own perspectives. More often than not, these works formed a chain of knowledge and even "talked," being "speakerly texts" (*Figures* 242)—the description the scholar Henry Louis Gates, Jr., has assigned to define oral-based narratives such as Nat Turner's *The Confessions of Nat Turner* (1831) or Zora Neale Hurston's novel *Their Eyes Were Watching God* (1937). James Snead has noted that the "repetition" of certain patterns or tropes between and among texts written or spoken by blacks is a fundamental construct linking oral and/or written narratives (59–60). Gates also formulated the theory of "parody," or "pastiche," as an important structural device (*Figures* 242–43). Its tendency of mimesis has been traced and seems to recur intertextually between and among texts spoken or written by black writers, composers, or performers.

By "black," I mean the sparse pre-eighteenth- and more prolific nineteenth-century African or diasporic African American slaves, fugitives, or freepersons who were semiliterate or literate and sufficiently skilled in the spoken and written forms of the English language to tell their stories. These skilled authors, composers, or performers have included creative artists, since the "call" motif extant between and among "speakerly texts"—both fully oral or micro-oral texts embedded within written works—illustrates how the "talking" narrative mode practiced by preachers, singers, composers, and writers works when a "response" is expected from the audience. One can easily turn to Ralph Ellison's "speakerly" as well as "writerly driven" novel *Invisible Man* (1952) and recall the blind southern preacher's sermon and his audience's response and then, years later in New York, Invisible Man's own spontaneous street corner oration upon witnessing the eviction of an elderly black couple from their Harlem tenement (122, 277). Robert Stepto specifically developed a formal theory about the African-cum–African American "call" and "response" tradition in *From Behind the Veil* (1991). In his study, Stepto identifies the African call-response pattern as existing between and among several slave narratives (1, 32). Gates additionally augmented his studies of parody by assigning the colloquial term of "signifying" to the practice. He expounds upon the African mode of "signifying upon" another person by calling out the person's name by "indirection." As an oral art form, the speaker's remarks can become caustic and demeaning since never is the target's name called outright (*Figures* 242–43). This form of "signifying" is skillfully demonstrated in Toni Morrison's 1970 novel, *The Bluest Eye*. Mrs. MacTeer lambasts the suspected milk thief in her home without ever directly calling out Pecola Breedlove's name.

Generally, other texts precede "Almost a Man" and *Gathering* in my African American literature classes, and depending upon the level of the course, I select historical works to illustrate how Africanist people became transplanted to the New World. For example, I teach Maryse Condé's novel *Segu* (1987), which reflects the history and culture of the Bambara Kingdom of Segu in the seventeenth century. It focuses upon Dousika Traoré, a royal council member; his polygamous circle of wife, cowives, and concubines, who have provided him with multiple children and four royal sons; the council frictions that lead to Traoré's downfall; and the socioreligious and political factors that cause the dissolution of his male dynasty. His particular disastrous experiences only magnify the larger cultural frictions affecting the general population that also cause the dismantling of the Bambara Kingdom. Personally, socially, and culturally, all the horrific actions initially stem from the king's arrogance and blindness regarding the ongoing internal secular and religious tribal wars, which compound rapidly owing to the external disarray already being induced by Europeans implementing their practices of colonization and slavery. This historical novel illustrates how Africans became transplanted about the continent or off site to England, the Caribbean, South America, or North America, thereby resulting in the hybridization of identities for the exiles.

Another text I often teach—whether fully or only the first chapter—that reflects ancient life in Guinea, West Africa, is *The Interesting Narrative of the Life of Olaudah Equiano; or, Gustavus Vassa, the African, Written by Himself*

(1789). It shows how Equiano became hybridized and Europeanized as a privileged slave. He reports his travels all over the world, including the Arctic Circle, as a captive slave, seaman, freedman, and slaver. Eventually, he chooses London, England, as his new home and becomes an activist fighting against slavery and colonization. The film *A Son of Africa* (1996) is an excellent scholarly work that recognizes Equiano's importance and provides visual representations of the British and American slave trades taking place in the aforementioned locations (Riley). Short clips from the film *Ship of Slaves: The Middle Passage* (1997) also enable students to recognize the horrors of the transatlantic passage (Harty). Moreover, the film *Sankofa* (1993) reveals the brutality of slavery on land for Africanist men and women in America as well as their labor assignments as house servants or field workers (Gerima). Against the foregrounded or backgrounded acts of slave owners in victimizing and dehumanizing their properties are scenes portraying slaves plotting revolts or acting upon their schemes—the consequences of failure being greater abuse and frequent killings of the revolutionaries.

The genres of slave narratives, novels, histories, autobiographies, and poetry form the bulk of the readings in my African American literature courses. Slave narratives written by Frederick Douglass, Harriet Jacobs, Harriet Wilson, and Nat Turner selectively provide great insights into the colonial and slave systems in both the South and North. W. E. B. Du Bois's 1903 sociohistory *The Souls of Black Folk* assesses the treatment of blacks before and after the Civil War and during and after Reconstruction as well as their turn-of-the-century struggles with neo-slavery and the backlashes arising from the Supreme Court's 1896 *Plessy v. Ferguson* decision mandating Jim Crow segregation of blacks from whites. The film by Richard Dormer entitled *The Rise and Fall of Jim Crow* (2002) is another excellent visual aide to supplement novels such as Frances Harper's *Iola Leroy* (1892), Charles W. Chesnutt's *The Marrow of Tradition* (1901), Jean Toomer's *Cane* (1923), James Weldon Johnson's *The Autobiography of an Ex-Colored Man* (1912), and Wright's *Native Son* (1940) and *Black Boy* (1945) that bring the "gnostic" knowledge of the students to or through the 1940s. For a two-semester survey course, or a course that focuses on mid-twentieth-century events, I frequently use *Invisible Man* as a transitional piece. This encyclopedic, folkloric, autobiographical, historical, modernist novel (whichever one chooses to call it) illustrates the travesties and sufferings that acculturated African Americans experience owing to the daily message that white society conveys to them: that they are noncitizens. The nameless African American protagonist, who starts out as a cultural amnesiac and stumbles gullibly and fearfully through life in the mid-1930s, finally, after a fifteen-year hiatus of living underground in the name of civil disobedience and consciousness raising, emerges in the 1950s to lead African Americans to freedom. Ellison's work prepares students for their readings of "Almost a Man" and *Gathering*.

Black Atlantic Boy-Men

Like the delayed civil rights activism of Ellison's hero, African Americans wholistically must answer two questions: what have we done to deserve such dehumanizing treatments in America? And why has it taken many African Americans so long to react to or revolt against slavery and neo-slavery, especially the men who are supposed to be protectors of the black family? These are the questions raised by Wright in his works, which he has signified upon by indirection over and over since the 1930s in his canon of male-oriented novels, novellas, short stories, poems, and plays as well as his autobiographical speeches, travelogues, and essays. He inserted his voice and opinions on the racial matters plaguing America starting in the 1930s and long before Ellison. Gaines, signifying upon Wright's work, interrogates the same questions in *Gathering* but provides lengthier explanations in a novel form, which Wright's short story appears minimally to address. I stress the word *appears*, because a text issued to the public always has a behind-the-scenes production history. Before the short story was first published as "Almos' a Man" in the January 1940 issue of *Harper's Bazaar*, it had functioned as a fully blown novel entitled "Tarbaby's Dawn," which Wright, already a successful poet with a penchant for fiction writing and a young communist living in Chicago, Illinois, wrote in 1934/35. He sent "Tarbaby's Dawn" out to publishers for consideration several times, but it received only rejections. Finally, after gaining national attention for the publication of "Big Boy Leaves Home" in 1936 and earning a contract with Harper and Row to publish his collection *Uncle Tom's Children* in 1938, which would garner the Story Prize, Wright laid "Tarbaby's Dawn" aside. Then, having won a Guggenheim fellowship to complete *Native Son* in 1939, he severed the last three scenes of "Tarbaby's Dawn," revamped it as the short story "Almos' a Man," and released it to *Harper's* as prepublication publicity for his acclaimed Book-of-the-Month Club novel *Native Son*, due out in March 1940. Unfortunately, the excised short story is filled with confusing gaps, such as to whom Dave Saunders is referring when he calls out the name Bill just before he jumps onto a train to escape two more years of neo-slave labor on Hawkins's farm. In the latter part of 1959, Wright assembled the collection *Eight Men*, changed the short story's title to "The Man Who Was Almost a Man" to be in sync with the titles of other works in the collection, and made minuscule changes in names and colloquial expressions.

The unpublished novel "Tarbaby's Dawn," the first of a trilogy that Wright had planned, fell into silence. But its suppressed presence in the *Harper's* and *Eight Men* versions of "Almost a Man" and in *Gathering* is being signified upon, even though both Wright's and Gaines's acknowledgments of the novel as a base text are absent. I add another vocabulary phrase of "absent/present markers" to the students' list of terms at this time, because authors do not necessarily reveal all of their writing sources or habits. However, Wright's penchant for intratextual repetitioning of or signifying upon his unpublished works or fragmented notes by indirection has been noted by critics, whether through apparent converted or obverse storylines. Wright also engages in intertextual signifying upon works by some admired or censured white authors, whom he acknowledges in *Black Boy* (293–95). Wright scholars for years have explored his writings in depth and drawn parallels to those resources. Just by providing brief comments about the habits of authors to borrow from other authors' works lets students know that mimesis, borrowing, or signifying is a common practice between and among black and white writers. Gaines's novel is a good model for teaching students how to recognize, explore, and prove authorial borrowings, especially if no correspondence exists as proof. Whether Gaines went to the Beinecke Rare Book and Manuscript Library at Yale University to read Wright's manuscripts, revisions, and working notes on "Tarbaby's Dawn" is uncertain. An excellent quiz assignment for students is to have them go online to the Beinecke Library Web site, locate the James Weldon Johnson collection, under which they will find the Richard Wright Papers, and trace and scrutinize the records pertaining to "Tarbaby's Dawn." Foraging through the files on Wright's manuscript and then taking brief notes about Wright's writing habits will enable the students to grasp how parody works both intratextually and intertextually by indirection. In addition, I also provide brief descriptions of Wright's plot devices that reflect an abundance of parallels between his works and Gaines's book.

For example, nowhere in "Tarbaby's Dawn" or the two short story versions does an African character exist. None appears in any of Wright's works until after his trip to the Gold Coast (now Ghana) in 1953 and the publication of his travel book *Black Power* in 1954, along with other autobiographical writings, essays, novels, and short stories. In *Eight Men*, Wright's short story "Man God Ain't Like That" is set in Kumasi, Ghana, and includes an African character, Babu. Gaines inserts an African protagonist, Mathu, in *Gathering*, but actually Gaines's representation is a partial composite of Wright's Tarbaby, with differences. Wright's terse description of seventeen-year-old Tarbaby is that the adolescent is over six feet tall, husky from plowing, and very, very black—the reason for his nickname. By his dark skin coloring, he seems to differ from his mother, father, and brother. On the other hand, Gaines's Mathu, noted to be a Senegalese African, is also described as being tall and "black as pitch," according to Miss Merle (19).[1] However, he is eighty-two years old and still the only full-blooded African on the Marshall plantation or in the area, according to remarks by other characters in the novel. Since the time period is the 1970s, and Mathu has served generations of Marshalls, it is probable that he was born in the 1890s, and by the mid-1930s, he would have been in his midforties like Bob Saunders, Tarbaby's father (183). However, by being a partial composite of Tarbaby, he has continued to act in the fiery spirit and dissident mode of his youth. Even though he has been reared on the Marshall plantation and surrounded by a culture imbued with Ku Klux Klan activism, Mathu has survived his acts of rebellion although whites still distrust him and think first of him when trouble arises in the black community. Candy Marshall, Sheriff Mapes, and Fix Boutan, father of the victim, all assume that Mathu is the culprit who again has risen up against the master and this time killed Beau Boutan at the novel's opening.

As *Gathering* proceeds, it seems to be more complex in character and plot developments than "Almost a Man." However, "Tarbaby's Dawn" provides the fundamental complexity of events that recur in *Gathering*. For example, Wright addresses the racial disparities and inequities that whites impose upon the African American community that appear in *Gathering*. Certain slave laws devised in colonial America have transcended time and remain applicable in the Deep South even during the 1960s and 1970s. It is here that I provide students with another vocabulary term, "Black Atlantic," invented by Paul Gilroy to describe the fractured psyches that Africans incurred upon being involuntarily transported to strange lands ("Black Atlantic" 11, 15). The film *Middle Passage* helps to illuminate factual evidence that most kidnapped Africans suffered from mental depressions, nervous breakdowns, and thoughts of suicide after their forced removals. Gilroy defines their common mental states, regardless of former tribal affiliations, as being representative of "the Black Atlantic fractured psyche." They formed a new nation of traumatized Black Atlantics by being housed together in the darkened bowels of slave ships, where they were chained, half starved, beaten, and raped (for women) during the journey to their New World destinations. Moreover, once they landed, these Black Atlantics were further traumatized, because their European American slave masters forced them to forget their African customs, to assume new, strange identities and names, and to temper their proclivities to dissent or face death.

"Almost a Man" and *Gathering* fully illustrate how African and African American men evolved into full-fledged Black Atlantics. They literally and symbolically became castrated "boy-men" who, out of fear and suffering, acceded to cultural amnesia about manhood practices in Africa. Mathu the African has remained the exception. Two handouts on slave laws help students to understand how the male-governed African household was deliberately changed in the New World to emasculate black men. To buttress their power over powerless people, the slave masters, within forty years of the landings of indentured servants and African slaves in 1619 and then in 1621 at the Virginia colony, passed two decrees to keep them contained and controlled. The first, the Virginia Slave Law of 1662, was passed to disempower the African male by changing the state of authority in the household from patriarchal to matriarchal. It required children issued henceforth from a slave woman to define their lineage by her identity, thereby nullifying any attempt of the father to claim lineage or to possess a sense of male pride for siring an African-type dynasty of sons. The politicians and slave masters instilled the fear of death in slaves for defiance by reenforcing the first law with a second known as the Virginia Slave Law of 1669. It allowed any slave master or his agent to "kill off" with impunity any dissident slave who dared to raise a hand in revolt. This meant, of course, that the black male could not defend his female dependents against the master's or his agent's acts of raping his female relations. It is not difficult for students to identify the passive, effeminized, and emasculated African American males in the texts. They have become Black Atlantic boy-men—males who have been trained to remain stunted boys forever, regardless of their age.

For example, Tarbaby/Dave addresses his father as "Pa" ("Man" 9). How stunted is his manhood? you may ask students. Bob Saunders has sired two sons, but as far as white society is concerned, he is a perfect boy-man: he works away at another plantation six and a half days a week, similar to absentee fathers in the olden days of slavery. On Sundays, Saunders comes home to mete out punishment upon his wife and two sons, particularly Tarbaby/Dave in the prime years of his adolescence. Indeed, Saunders's true nature as an emasculated African American male is evident at the "community gathering" near the ending of the work, which is related at Tarbaby/Dave's trial. The frequently absent, rarely present father figure capitulates without question to Hawkins's edict for Tarbaby/Dave to work another two years in order to pay for his decrepit mule. And, being racially powerless to dispute Hawkins but needing to express a modicum of male authority, Saunders masks his impotence by berating both his wife and son like children before the community. The trickling down of power from whites to blacks works briefly. The public humiliation increases Tarbaby/Dave's anger toward his parents and motivates him to flee the unjust decrees of his employer, his family, and his community. Since this sequence in "Tarbaby's Dawn" is also in "Almost a Man," students should be able to identify how Wright is signifying upon the Virginia Slave Laws of 1662 and 1669. Hawkins publicly nullifies Saunders's manhood; in turn, Saunders demeans both his wife and son to save face.

In a more elaborate parody of the Black Atlantic father figure trope, Gaines also draws distinctions between Mathu, the African father figure, and the other African American boy-men who have gathered on the Marshall plantation. At this point, it is important for students to identify another composite of Tarbaby/Dave in the guise of Charlie. In size, he too is over six feet, stocky, "jet black" and even "black as tar," according to Lou Dimes's description (186, 189). Because of the time difference between the 1930s and 1970s that allows for the aging process, Charlie at age fifty is understandably heavier than he would be as a youth like Tarbaby/Dave. Even so, the sociopolitical conditions in Louisiana have remained as static as they were in Mississippi in 1935. And similar to his youthful counterpart, Charlie has also used a weapon—a shotgun instead of a revolver—to kill his tractor-driving employer Beau Boutan. He thereby has broken the southern decree forbidding black men to arm themselves against white society. This law also has stunted the will of the African American men on the Marshall plantation and in the surrounding communities. Because of direct statements or allusions in the texts, however, students can easily pick out the significance of black men retaliating with weapons to see how the Deep South deals with their breaking a known taboo. Tarbaby/Dave's accidental shooting of the mule Jenny functions, by means of parody, as Charlie's killing of Beau in self-defense because of Beau's tirade of verbal abuse and then determination to murder, or "1669," Charlie for talking back and then independently resigning his job. Charlie does not wait around for a community trial; instead, he immediately runs into the swamps after his deadly action. Additionally, Tarbaby/Dave's second occasion of shooting his weapon occurs the next morning when he, in defiance of his father, decides to fire the rest of his bullets. In order to appease his rage, Tarbaby/Dave, this time, deliberately fires at Hawkins's house, fantasizing his power and satisfying his wish to "1669" his employer. This action is the reason Tarbaby/Dave self-declares his "manhood" by calling out Bill's name just before he leaps onto the train. Bill, a school dropout just two years older than Tarbaby/Dave, had introduced him to smoking and drinking when they snuck away to Natchez, some fifteen miles distant. Bill had also initiated Tarbaby/Dave into the mysteries of sex, which he acts upon and blunders by impregnating his girlfriend. In essence, Bill has taught Tarbaby/Dave the adolescent to "man up," even though Tarbaby/Dave seems to commit errors that get him into trouble after each initiation. These are the reasons Bill's gun and its symbolism of manhood are so important to Tarbaby/Dave. When Tarbaby/Dave meets Bill in a field one night, Bill informs him that the sheriff and local Klansmen have been searching for a black youth who has been conducting sexual assignations with a white prostitute in town. Bill has chosen to defy the law and arm himself with a gun, thereby creating both admiration and envy in Tarbaby/Dave's mind. Thus it is Bill, the armed rebel and father figure, who is the only person who could understand Tarbaby/Dave's action of defying Hawkins's work order.

This scenario becomes Charlie's parody. He returns from the swamps and tells Mathu, the gathered old men, the sheriff, and Candy that he refused to be degraded by Beau and shot him in self-defense. The action instills pride in Charlie for standing up like a man, because he finally has adhered to the tutelage of his "Parrain." Here, Charlie differs from Tarbaby/Dave. Before Charlie has his second gunfight with the Klansman Luke Will, he, unlike Tarbaby/Dave, asks for his "Parrain" (183, 186). *Parrain* is the Cajun term for "godfather," according to Gaines's depiction. It is Mathu's role, owing to his additional composite representation of the young man Bill, Tarbaby/Dave's idol, father figure, and guide. Tarbaby/Dave's mishaps with the revolver become Charlie's debacles with his shotgun. And Mathu, who, like Bill, believes in standing his ground, functions as Charlie's biological father and guide as well. Mathu has trained Charlie to face the consequences of his actions, but Charlie has broken his father's edict, like Tarbaby/Dave with that of his father. Mathu, on the other hand, has never acted like Bob Saunders, even though Mathu has married, fathered a son, and, at age eighty-two, has become a widower. A father, though, he remains.

The instructor must point out these reenactments to students, since they would not have access to the "Tarbaby's Dawn" manuscript. Another term to introduce to students is "existentialist hero." This character continually recurs in Wright's crime fictions, which, as a short story, "Almost a Man" falls into the category of and which Wright magnified as a genre. The protagonist finally revolts against unjust laws and devises his own amoral code that enables him to function as a man. Moreover, the existentialist, having been reared in a violent society, reacts violently with a gun, which violates the Virginia Slave Law of 1669. Tarbaby/Dave reflects a minuscule composite of the existentialist hero when he defies Hawkins, symbolically shoots and kills him, and leaves town on his own volition. Similarly, Charlie discovers his manhood as an existentialist hero. After Charlie returns from the swamps to confront Sheriff Mapes, he demands that everyone call him "Mr. Biggs" out of deference to his risen stature as a man (188). Like former slaves, Charlie demands his entitlement of being addressed like whites do to each other. A quiz assignment to list Tarbaby/Dave's blunders and then to identify them as the horrific deeds that the three Boutan brothers have committed against members of the black community supports why a formal salutation is important to Charlie. It is important to others. The seventeen elderly African American rebels who have shown up to take credit for killing Beau, until now, have acted as timid boy-men for thirty to forty years and refused, out of fear, to retaliate against the perpetrators lest the whites "1669" them as well. Indeed, Mathu, according to Miss Merle's and Clatoo's narratives, has been the only "man" to violate the 1669 law, stand his ground, and live another day. In their closed meeting on the plantation, Mathu finally tells the army of seventeen why he has always held contempt for them as castrated African American males. It is he who has kept alive the African concept of manhood, which means acting like a warrior and commanding respect.

Who Done It? Society's Ramifications and Remediations

Certainly, the "community gatherings" and trial scenes reveal that Tarbaby/Dave in "Almost a Man" and Charlie in *Gathering* are the African American male culprits who shot Hawkins's mule and Beau the tractor-driving land leasee, respectively, in the two plantation cultures. However, beyond their particularities, both Wright and Gaines illustrate that they are interrogating larger social issues as a whole and exposing the political factors affecting the social determinism of whites from blacks. Both authors signify upon historical patterns of slavery and neo-slavery still operating in the Deep South states of Mississippi in the 1930s and Louisiana in the 1970s by means of their rebel heroes in order to illustrate how southern systemic racism operates. The instructor can assign term papers just on the topic of gender power operating in the two works. For example, white women play a key role in supporting patriarchy in both "Tarbaby's Dawn" and *Gathering*. In the former, the seventeen-year-old Tarbaby performs domestic chores such as milking cows, collecting eggs, and waiting table for the Hawkins family before he leaves for school. It is Mrs. Hawkins at breakfast one morning who suggests to Tarbaby that he drop out of school and work full-time for her husband. Too sleepy to learn in his fifth grade class because of labor duties starting at dawn, Tarbaby quickly accedes when Hawkins buttresses his wife's suggestion by offering Tarbaby a salary higher than his father's. And being anxious to escape school and possibly handle his own money, Tarbaby never thinks of the consequences of his sinking deeper into the quagmire of neo-slavery as a full-time plowman. Mrs. Hawkins is just as pernicious as her husband in keeping blacks in eternal bondage.

Similarly, Gaines's gender parody in *Gathering* is equally effective, even with a larger range of characters. Pointing out to students that Candy is a composite of both Mr. and Mrs. Hawkins enables them to extrapolate physical signs of her masculine attire and hairstyle, as noted by Miss Merle. Candy is heir to the Marshall estate and a staunch patriarch. Despite attempting to appear liberal, she exercises her power in the same conservative mode of her living relatives, deceased parents, and Marshall ancestors dating back to the Civil War. For example, in calling together the community gathering of elderly males to come armed with discharged shotguns, she is merely preparing her line of defense before Sheriff Mapes arrives. She tells Miss Merle that she will not allow anyone to harm "my people" (19). Her first reaction has been to assume blame for Beau's death because she believes that Mathu is the culprit. In a chilling repetition of history, Candy and Miss Merle reveal how the paternalistic practice of burdening a male slave and a white family member with the responsibility of rearing an orphaned child has not ceased from the times of slavery. Both Candy and Miss Merle speak about or reflect upon Mathu's role in becoming Candy's surrogate father figure and male protectorate—a ludicrous assignment since, in reality, Mathu has no power over a white person— while Miss Merle has functioned as the mother surrogate. The pining for the antebellum days has not left the mind-sets of Candy, her drunken aunt and uncle, and even Miss Merle. Despite her claims of loyalty to protect Mathu, Candy flexes her power as the plantation owner and demands that she be allowed to be present during the closed meeting of elders in Mathu's cabin. Moreover, nowhere has she improved the lifestyles or poor diets of her "people," who still live in the dilapidated slave cabins on the property that are hampered by the surrounding tall weeds. Miss Merle is a hypocrite as well. The fact that she brings Janey's pies to feed the gathering exemplifies how she had been reared on the festivities of picnicking and eating that frequently accompanied lynching rituals, which everyone anticipates from Luke Will and the Klan. Both Candy and Miss Merle are merely contemporary forms of Wright's neo-slave icons Mr. and Mrs. Hawkins.

Is there hope for change in Deep South bondage practices? That is another question students can explore in "Almost a Man" and *Gathering*, according to the disparate endings portrayed by Wright and Gaines. "Tarbaby's Dawn" / "Almost a Man" has a bleak ending for Tarbaby/Dave's relatives, but for Tarbaby/Dave there is hope. Tarbaby/Dave smartens up finally, figures out that it will take him two years at neo-slave labor to pay for Hawkins's mule, and runs away to Memphis, Tennessee. Wright's plans for his second book in the trilogy, entitled "Tarbaby's Sunrise," predict his rise as a successful boxer in the footsteps of his idol Jack Johnson. Back home, however, with Hawkins remaining unpaid for a dead mule, it is for certain that the Saunders family will have to pay for Tarbaby/Dave's breach of contract. Perhaps Mrs. Saunders will become the cook for the Hawkinses as Janey does for Candy's Aunt Bea and Uncle Jack Marshall. Perhaps little Sal, under age six, at first will become a runner on the Hawkins plantation (as Snookum is for Candy) until he grows old enough to gather eggs, milk cows, feed chickens, and plow fields like his big brother Tarbaby/Dave. Attending school will not be an option (Snookum does not under Candy's authority). As for plowing, most likely Hawkins will extract some extra labor duties from Bob Saunders until Sal is old enough.

A bleak outcome occurs in *Gathering* as well, despite the glitter and glare from the outcomes of the court trials. Because events occur in the aftermath of the 1960s civil rights movement, it appears that some racial practices have changed in *Gathering*. For example, Gaines inserts the trope of generational shifts to show that the youth, like Tarbaby/Dave, prefer to transcend racist traditions. Cal, the son of Fix Boutan, is an example. Having formed a bond with his black teammate on the Louisiana State University football team as the formidable duo "Salt and Pepper," he chooses not to follow the path of racial hatred and Klan backlash arising from Beau's murder. Candy, however, seems unable to emancipate Mathu, but he takes his freedom himself. After the court trial, she begs Mathu to ride back to Marshall with her. However, he publicly refuses and chooses to ride back home in the truck with his elderly comrades. He is finally free, but is he? The court trial, a formal repetition of the plantation trial held by Mapes, reflects that the wheel of justice is slow to change in terms of granting full freedom to blacks. Cloaked in humor because of the age of the rebels involved in trial testimonies about Beau Boutan's and Luke Will's murders at the hand of Charlie Biggs, the judge sentences the eighteen dissidents to five years probation and prohibits them to arm themselves with a weapon during that time. In essence, while there is levity in the impossibility of the situation repeating itself—of old men gathering in armed rebellion—the judge's stipulation is not humorous. Instead, it is as bleak as the ending of "Tarbaby's Dawn" / "Almost a Man." As Gaines implies, the shackling of liberty recurs because the off-staged Virginia Slave Laws of 1662 and 1669 will still keep African American males operating as powerless boy-men in Louisiana, much as in 1930s Mississippi. The slave laws are subtle, still alive, and deeply entrenched within the infrastructure of the 1970s Louisiana sociopolitical system.

To be sure, Wright's "Tarbaby's Dawn," which was published as the short stories "Almos' a Man" and "The Man Who Was Almost a Man," is rich for teaching the art of parody along with Gaines's *A Gathering of Old Men*. A challenge, yes, because both works are crime fictions that pose similar problem/solution issues of "who done it" that have greater social ramifications beyond the two individuals guilty of the deeds. Indeed, both Wright's and Gaines's texts enhance the students' acquisition of new theoretical modes of gnosis, subjugated knowledge, the Black Atlantic fractured psyche, and cultural amnesia. This is what Wright says and by repetition Gaines parodies in their individual works. They show how racism in the Deep South is slow to change, with its policies dating

back to 1662 and 1669 Virginia and its enforcements functioning in a chrono-
logical trajectory from the mid-1930s in Wright's text through the 1970s in
Gaines's work. Consequently, with the actions of a black youth rising up to challenge the system and to declare his manhood, Tarbaby/Dave's revolt reverber-
ates across time and space to impel a fifty-year-old and eighteen seventy- to
eighty-year-old men belatedly but finally to stand up for justice. Overall, the two
works, when taught sequentially or chronologically in an African American literature course, will teach students the meaning of *gnosis*, for they will "know"
that excavating subjugated knowledge is an enlightening process.

NOTE

[1] This essay quotes from the 1984 Vintage edition of *Gathering*.

A *Lesson Before Dying* and the Culture of Surveillance

John Wharton Lowe

A *Lesson Before Dying*, a masterpiece many readers have yet to discover, concerns several stories, but all of them revolve around a black man awaiting his execution on death row, a burning metaphor of southern history that remains relevant today; unfortunately, this "scene of inscription" that inspired Ernest Gaines's narrative also speaks for America as a whole, in a postmodern age when more black men are in prison than in college. As a prosperous nation edges closer to an unthinkable apartheid, we would do well to ponder the significance of this narrative, its semiotics, and its relevance to the world we wish to shape in the new century.

One might miss these reverberations on a first reading; the story, after all, is set in 1948. The narrator, Grant Wiggins, teaches in a barely funded school in rural Louisiana; he hates living there, hates teaching, and seems to hate his students. Although the story quickly moves beyond Grant to focus on the aforementioned prisoner, Jefferson, a parallel between their lives emerges quickly: both live imprisoned lives, one that seems hopeless (Grant), another that will inexorably—and quickly—lead to death (Jefferson).

I asked Gaines why he decided to set the book in 1948 rather than 1988, as he had originally planned; it had always seemed to me that he has never been interested in merely glossing history but rather wants history to speak to our own time. He replied that the story had some dimensions to it in the earlier period it would not have had in 1988; that in our age, attorneys would fight some of the battles the book's characters have to wage on their own. Further, 1948 registers as a kind of *annus mirabilis* for Gaines personally, as he left Louisiana that year to live with his mother and stepfather in California, a move that he credits as a kind of salvation. Interestingly, a year or so before, a young man had been sent to the electric chair twice because the chair had malfunctioned the first time. Gaines read about the story and became intrigued with the powerful icon of the portable electric chair that was used at the time. Finally, Gaines wanted the story to relate powerfully to the rural black schoolchildren of the time, who got to go to school for only five and a half to six months, in rather rudimentary conditions. Anyone familiar with Gaines's biography, or who has visited Cherie Quarters in Oscar where Gaines grew up, knows that the building that serves as both church and school in *Lesson* is the very one Gaines attended, so the powerful pull of personal narrative must have directed him to relocate *Lesson* in the earlier time as well. Still, Gaines did agree that "the whole thing comes back to probably help us—I should hope so" (Lowe, "Interview" 307).

I begin teaching this novel by showing film clips from interviews Gaines has given, which include remarks he made while standing in his childhood church/school (Korty). I also read comments he made in response to questions I have asked him about this novel and the way it developed in his imagination (Lowe, "Interview").

I tell students that Gaines likely felt that setting the story in a period when racial feeling was far more virulent and exposed than it is now would uncover things that have been muffled in our own age, despite the statistics that tell us that an old story continues in horrifying fashion. Indeed, Gaines revealed to me that the little powder-faced white woman who is rude to Grant when he picks up Jefferson's radio is based on a woman in New Roads, Louisiana, who twenty-odd years ago turned away when Gaines asked her to recommend a coffee shop: "she looked at me and just turned away from me and spoke to Schlöndorff [the director of the film adaptation of *A Gathering of Old Men*], who was standing aside. So it's the same sort of thing" (Lowe, "Interview" 310).

On another occasion, however, Gaines gave yet another reason for setting the story when he did: he was intent on using his memories of bitter black school-teachers.

> Grant's a pretty angry person. All Grant wants to do is leave. We're talking about the forties, too, remember . . . all he could do as an educated black man was to teach. . . . I suppose we have produced as many good teachers, percentage-wise, as anyone else has produced in this country, with much more feeling for their students. But many blacks who would have preferred some other position than just being a schoolteacher, may have been poor schoolteachers because they were forced—that was the only thing they could go into—they did it, but they hated it.   (Lowe, "Interview" 308)

Gaines also said that Grant must spend as much time in the prison as in the schoolhouse, implying not only symmetry but overlap. This overlap has meaning today as well, beyond the appalling numbers of black men in prisons in the United States. I remind students that the black underclass continues to grow, despite the nation's prosperity, and more children are going to bed hungry and poorly educated. Public schools continue to deteriorate, and indeed, in many ways, they could be thought of as virtual prisons. The former Speaker of the House Newt Gingrich, a few years ago, extended the concept of institutions as storage bins for problems, with his suggestion of a new building program for orphanages. Thus the embarrassing spectacle of the black underclass (the larger group of white poor conveniently gets left out of many discussions of poverty) is to be incarcerated, first in orphanages, then in substandard, dangerous prison-like schools, and then in prisons themselves. Surveillance, work, isolation, and punishment are hallmarks of all three "houses of correction." The French philosopher Michel Foucault lists a number of goals that prisons are supposed to accomplish and also accounts for the rationale behind them. As he notes:

> How could the prison not be immediately accepted when, by locking up, retraining and rendering docile, it merely reproduces, with a little more

emphasis, all the mechanisms that are to be found in the social body? The prison is like a rather disciplined barracks, *a strict school*, a dark workshop, but not qualitatively different. This double foundation—juridico-economic on the one hand, technico-disciplinary on the other—made the prison seem the most immediate and civilized form of all penalties.

(233; emphasis added)

Especially, one might add, in a racist-capitalist society, where "civilization" all too often means confinement and concealment of the poor.

I encourage students to see this overlap between the "strict school" Grant runs, working under white supervisors, and the prison by listing Foucault's "prison goals": 1. isolation (ranked rows, cells; silence in both); 2. work (lessons, work around the schoolroom/prison); 3. "modulation of penalty." Work is defined, with isolation, as an agent of carceral transformation—it is to instill the ideals of order and regularity and forces subjects to conform to a central and shaping power. Work is seen as the agent that takes the student/prisoner and transforms that person into a machine. The student/prisoner is both "the cog and the product." For as Foucault asserts, "What then, is the use of penal labour? Not profit; nor even the formation of a useful skill; but the constitution of a power relation, an empty economic form, a schema of individual submission" (243). Where the school and prison differ is in terms of the "modulation of the penalty." The modern equivalent would be parole, where the offender's original penalty is modified because the offender has been deemed reformed and can be returned into society.

I ask students to remember that Grant, reflecting on his own harsh days in this same school under the cruel regime of the mulatto teacher Matthew Antoine, mourns his peers who were "released into society" after they had "served time" in a school that taught them they were worthless and doomed. "Bill, Jerry, Claudee, Smitty, Snowball—all the others. They had chopped wood here too; then they were gone. Gone to the fields, to the small towns, to the cities—where they died. There was always news coming back to the quarter about someone who had been killed or sent to prison for killing someone else" (62).[1]

Accordingly, the white power structure regards Grant with deep suspicion; he has, after all, broken away from the circle of surveillance, and worse, during that time he has acquired an education, which is tacitly understood to mean mastery of techniques of resistance. As long as he can be confined, however, to the narrowly tolerated and barely nourished black school, a school necessarily inscribed within the black church (an institution, with its white God and "servants obey your masters" Bible, felt to be helpful for social control—at least up to the civil rights movement), Grant can be tolerated as a necessary evil; but his activities on behalf of Jefferson immediately arouse suspicion and resistance among the powers on the plantation and in the prison. He is constantly being watched, and the white superintendent's visit is only one telling example of this scrutiny.

Despite these travails, Grant's life is made somewhat bearable through his affair with his fellow teacher, Vivian Baptiste. Students often note that she too feels entrapped by her circumstances; she dares not leave the area because of her angry estranged husband, who has threatened to take her children.

Ironically, because Grant loves Vivian, it is chiefly she who keeps him in his "cage" at the school. Moreover, he in some ways still labors under the matriarchy; he lives with Tante Lou, who is in her seventies. Miss Emma Glenn, Jefferson's godmother, also past seventy, is her best friend. The two old women, operating in tandem, use sheer force, will, and burning looks to get Grant to do their bidding, which is to make Jefferson walk to his death with dignity rather than wallow in fear and self-pity like the "hog" the defense attorney says he is. More important, perhaps, the sweeping configuration of white gaze in the courtroom, somewhat like a ring of white spotlights centering on the accused, initiates the thematic of discipline as centered on separation, categorization, surveillance, and control.

The white courtroom, however, has its counterforce in Miss Emma and Tante Lou, who are present but not described. The wash of white gazes and white words has swirled about them and they have not been moved, and through their stoic and heroic power—and, interestingly, partly through a silent *black* gaze that has the power to command—they will an agent of transformation and resistance out of Grant. The women's wisdom may further be seen in their shrewd manipulation of the white folk, whose help they need to reach Jefferson. They confine themselves to essentials: speaking to Henri Pichot, the owner of the plantation, Miss Emma says, "The law got him, Mr. Henri . . . and they go'n kill him. But let them kill a man" (22). Pichot's sister owes much to Miss Emma, who raised her, and this stereotypical but common situation becomes useful for Jefferson's cause.

Students note that the story alternates between the plantation and the jail. The prisonlike quarters is dominated, as it was during slavery, by the "big house," not accidentally the colloquial name in modern times for the prison. Pichot, the contemporary version of "ole massa," lives in the gray antebellum manse and has no children. He maintains strict control over the quarters and relies on informers to extend his gaze. The link between this center of surveillance and control with that of the jail is signified by the fact that Pichot's brother-in-law is Sheriff Sam Guidry.

Similarly, Grant utilizes the principle of strict surveillance in his classroom and has students act as his lieutenants when he isn't present. In the quarters (hard by the big house), in the school, in the cell, the position of constantly being watched creates a disciplined and subjected person. Periodically, this position is reinforced through the device of the examination. *Lesson* is punctuated regularly with such moments, many of them involving Grant, who must "pass" inspection from his white superiors; the interrogations he endures in Pichot's kitchen, in the sheriff's office, and during the white school inspector's visit offer ample evidence of the kind of "examination" all African Americans had to face in the pre–civil rights South. As I tell advanced and graduate classes, Foucault calls such moments the "ceremony of objectification" (187); as such, they offer an opportunity for the dominant culture to exercise its privilege in performance.

In yet another variant of the examination, the school and prison, with endless documents and classifications for the students/inmates, "capture and fix" them. Particularly in the latter institution, written description of the inmate, which begins with the legal category of criminal that the inmate inhabits, places the person under an increasingly restrictive written definition of personhood. As Foucault notes, this development in categorization radically limits the possibilities of individuality, as one becomes grouped with others and described through the words and terms of the oppressor: "The chronicle of a man, the account of his life, his historiography, written as he lived out his life formed part of the rituals of his power. The disciplinary methods reversed this relation, lowered the threshold of describable individuality and made of this description a means of control and a method of domination" (191). Thus the brilliance of the device of Jefferson's death row diary, which inverts this method, restoring his individuality and voice and also offering security, for the sheriff, knowing Jefferson is engaged in this activity, fears the journal's power, sensing it could be used to annul his own official record of his prisoner's identity and daily life in the cell.

The plantation house as site of "slave labor" may be seen in the fact that Miss Emma was a cook there for many years and Grant had worked there too. The current yardman, Farrell Jarreau, is in his late fifties and has known Grant all his life; since the latter's university days, however, Farrell takes his hat off before him and calls him "Professor." The internally created hierarchy of the quarters increasingly is revealed as a mechanism for an alternative social sphere and, therefore, as a strategy of resistance. Since Grant clearly has been elevated within this realm already, he has virtually no choice but to be its champion in the community's campaign to infiltrate and then subvert the operations of the book's various "prisons."

The quarters/big house configuration echoes that of early factories, where huge walls were erected to maximize concentration of labor, to protect materials and tools, and, above all, to control the labor force, which is accomplished through order and constant surveillance (Foucault 142). However, the labor force must be divided within this concentration too; no large gatherings are to be encouraged, and each individual is to have his or her own space. It is commonplace to speak of the black church as the major locus for communal gatherings and social organization and as a site of resistance; Gaines underlines and deepens this here since the church, locus of Grant's school, is the only communal gathering place permitted in the quarters. Although it constricts him early on in the book, his acceptance of his mission there at the end, through the agency of Jefferson's transcendent and sacrificial death, transforms the concept of the school as individual straitjacket into dynamic center for communal unity, development, and revolution, the opposite of the individual cells in the prison.

The prison, similarly, must be transformed into a nurturing, communal space if Jefferson is to die with dignity and thereby unify, inspire, and instruct the children in particular and the people in general, in the quarters and in the larger black community. I ask students to pinpoint how this is done; they usually see that this seemingly impossible mission is accomplished gradually and somewhat magically by the narrative, as it inches forward from the initial gifts of home-cooked food to the final scene in the cell, in which the schoolchildren visit Jefferson en masse with Grant. To make the transformation transcendent, the initial squalor must be established dramatically. As Grant enters the jail, so do we, seeing it through his eyes. He is coldly searched; then the prisoners extend their hands through the bars, asking for cigarettes or money. Grant sees repellent things: "a toilet without seat or toilet paper; a washbowl, brownish from residue and grime . . . barred window, which looked out onto a sycamore tree. . . . We were standing, because there was no place to sit" (71–72). Jefferson's brutalization is seen in his indifference—"don't matter . . . when they go'n do it?"—but also in his crazed perception that Grant is the one "Go'n jeck that switch" (74).

More disturbing still is the manner in which Jefferson subsequently "performs" this script, actually making sounds like a hog and "rooting" at food on the floor to repel Grant. This self-loathing results from the assembled white gaze, first in the theater of the white courtroom and subsequently in the scornful watchfulness of the deputies. All these factors fill out our initial survey/surveillance of the penal space.

Clearly, a prison is meant to unmake the domestic, to isolate, to disorient, to punish; but Jefferson has had a history of rejection and marginalization earlier *within* the black community, and this is manifest in the final interview he has with Grant. He thanks his former teacher for showing him the way to die with dignity but also tells him,

> Y'all axe a lot, Mr. Wiggins. . . . Who ever car'd my cross, Mr. Wiggins? My mama? My daddy? They dropped me when I wasn't nothing. Still don know where they at. . . . I went in the field when I was six, driving that old water cart. I done pulled that cotton sack, I done cut cane, load cane, swung that ax, chop ditch banks, since I was six. . . . Yes, I'm youman, Mr. Wiggins. But nobody didn't know that 'fore now. Cuss for nothing. Beat for nothing. Work for nothing. Grinned to get by. Everybody thought that's how it was s'pose to be. You too, Mr. Wiggins. You never thought I was nothing else. I didn't neither. (224)

Further, students see that this is a devastating moment for Grant, for it damns his teaching up to his experience with Jefferson in a way even the scenes we have been privy to in his current schoolroom have not.

Our conversations about the novel consider the possibility that Gaines has enfolded in both Grant and Jefferson initial personifications of Job and subsequent transformations into Prometheus. Literacy is understood in this community, as it always was in the slave narratives, as the tool one needed for all the necessary tasks of the hero: education, empowerment, revolution, and, finally, spiritual transcendence. The black teacher, constantly suspect in the white community because of his potential for insurrectionary leadership, always contains the potential for Promethean donation but also for that figure's torments. Chained to the rock of the Jim Crow system in a rural hamlet, Grant is tormented daily by the endless and demeaning rituals and modes of white southern patriarchy, be it on the plantation, in the town, or, especially, in the prison. The bitterness he feels, however, becomes destructive to his mission; hating his life, he also hates his students. As he states to Miss Emma early on, "I teach what the white folks around here tell me to teach—reading, writing, and 'rithmetic. They never told me how to keep a black boy out of a liquor store" (13). As this passage indicates, his "fire" has become muffled, internalized, destructive; it is up to Jefferson, the "new Prometheus," although nearly illiterate, to demonstrate through his diary the power of language, self-expression, and communal forms of knowing and to thereby inspire Grant to redirect his passion into the truths that will empower his students.

I remind students of the powerful role literacy has played in the quest for freedom and identity for all peoples, but particularly in classic texts of the African American experience. Frederick Douglass's first great moment of illumination comes when he realizes the power of literacy: "From that moment, I understood the pathway from slavery to freedom" (Narrative 49).[2] Again, freedom can mean many things; as Gaines told me, the diary was Jefferson's acceptance and expression of his humanity (Lowe, "Interview" 305). I tell my class about the great transformation of Malcolm Little to Malcolm X by means of a prison library and the writings of Elijah Muhammad.

Literacy is no panacea, however; as Douglass stated, his growing knowledge of the depth of his degradation, acquired through reading, tormented him:

> The more I read, the more I was led to abhor and detest my enslaver . . . that very discontent which Master Hugh had predicted would follow my learning to read had already come, to torment and sting my soul to unutterable anguish. As I writhed under it, I would at times feel that learning to read had been a curse rather than a blessing. . . . I envied my fellow-slaves for their stupidity. I have often wished myself a beast. . . . Any thing, no matter what, to get rid of thinking.   (55)

This passage from the nineteenth century helps students see the source of Grant's bitterness and Jefferson's willingness to become a "hog"—a beast—to escape the torment of contemplating his execution. Again, early on in the book, Jefferson thus represents Job, the man of sorrows; practicing literacy, however, Jefferson then becomes, initially at least, a suffering Prometheus, passing on the "torch" of the "book" to Grant, who in turn abandons his Job-like passivity, accepting his role as agent of cultural exchange, signaled by his actual/figurative transmission of the book/"book" to his students.

I remind my class that all these stages—including those to follow after the book's conclusion—unfold under a baleful and often punitive patriarchal gaze, in the actual prison and in the prison-seeming church/school; the latter is dramatized at one point through the visit of a white school official. Job-like/Promethean torment comes in the form of the patriarchal gaze. As Foucault has noted, the exercise of discipline requires a mechanism of surveillance, one that employs its methods of seeing simultaneously to create modes of power (170–71). This system must be understood in its significance by the observed, and Gaines's narrative makes it clear how the white power structure has built such a system on the plantation, in the town, and in the prison. All public spaces become, in effect, variations on the "prison" in their closely monitored and regulated dimensions.

Presumably, the ancient racial code of the South, constitutive of another community of the dominant and the oppressed, may be characterized in a similar fashion, as *Lesson* amply demonstrates, in its endless inventory of patriarchal, legal, penal, servile, and subversive gazes. It behooves us to think about this aspect of Gaines's "lesson," in that this gaze has become a regular, public feature of contemporary life. Virtually every evening our local news programs feature images of young black men spread-eagled against police cars, standing silently in courtrooms as sentences are pronounced, marching in ranks in prison yards. Karla Holloway has asked what the intent of such a camera is as it pans to a child being taken in for a "voluntary" interview with the sheriff. She concludes:

> There is no text for this event, only the image, which in the United States we have learned to file away as the public prejudices of our culture direct us to do. We create a file of anticipation that black youth, especially and specifically black male youth, fit a stereotype of criminal activity and generalized lawlessness. The camera's "intent" is to solidify the imagery and the expectation of a national text that criminalizes black youth. Consequently, it suppresses even the reporter's voice-over.   (*Codes* 152)

I tell my students that this type of scene is not just an image but a communal gaze, a gaze of surveillance, categorization, and locking away. The "voluntary" interview is part of a ritual of examination that all too often takes the form of a subtle and ritualistic torture. Because Gaines's novel, set in 1948, presents these issues uncluttered by our contemporary modes of obfuscation, it helps students to read our present situation, making them think twice about our seemingly passive look that is actually a participatory act of surveillance, judgment, and filing away of human beings.

And yet the gaze outward can bespeak defiance as well; on another occasion Gaines spoke about regrets people have about failure, concentrating on the moment that a person accepts an insults and drops the eyes; Gaines wants his fiction to "make up for that" (Sartisky 271). As my students discover, gaze takes many forms in this novel; most involve the mechanism of power, which can be positive or harmful. As Gaines has stated:

> There's also silence from a glance, a look gives as much meaning as a word or a line. It's when you've lived in that community and the community is

very old—you don't have to speak a word. . . . You understand when these older women, whether they're black or white, look at you in a certain way or *don't* look at you in a certain way. . . . Grant slams that door hard when he's taking off to Pichot's house, and he gives a whole feeling, emotion just by not seeing his aunt look at him, but knowing that she's looking at him, and at what part of his body she's looking at the back of his head, the side of his face! . . . When you're part of the community, when there's even the slightest movement of the hand or a mere look, or *not* looking—it can mean so much.   (Lowe, "Interview" 310–11)

As Grant and Jefferson renegotiate their relation, Jefferson becomes armed against white interpretations of his being, learning to send his own gaze inward and outward; consequently, the cell becomes transformed: instead of a "cell" of separation, confinement, punishment, it is opened up to become the scene of instruction. The relentless gaze of surveillance in this novel becomes transformed as well, into a sense of shame and revelation. The white men who come into Jefferson's cell shortly before the execution have made a bet that he'll die terrified, debased. Their anxiety over the wager forces them to examine him in a new way—the gaze now becomes exploratory, not for sauciness, surliness, or outright insurrection, but for hitherto unsuspected virtues. Ultimately, at least for the sheriff and the deputy Paul, the gaze leads to shame and revelation, a total inversion of penal surveillance. I suggest to my students that Paul—and perhaps the sheriff too—have been the recipients of a deeply revelatory "lesson," taught by a lowly, virtually illiterate water boy, one they doubtless continue to believe is a murderer and a thief. This too becomes part of the lesson, one that transcends race, for Gaines operates against the dictates of class as well, particularly in terms of the equation between stupidity and peasant. He demonstrates Antonio Gramsci's point that

> [t]here is no human activity from which every form of intellectual participation can be excluded: *homo faber* cannot be separated from *homo sapiens.* Each man, finally, outside his professional activity, carries on some form of intellectual activity, that is, he is a "philosopher," an artist, a man of taste, he participates in a particular conception of the world, has a conscious line of moral conduct, and therefore contributes to sustain a conception of the world or to modify it, that is, to bring into being new modes of thought.   (9)

In advanced or graduate courses, I ask students to consider Paulo Freire's classic formulation that the oppressed must find life-affirming humanization not just in having more food but by ceasing to be "things" by fighting as men: "This is a radical requirement. They cannot enter the struggle as objects in order *later* to become men" (55). How is this to be accomplished? For Freire, only through a humanizing pedagogy in which the leaders set up a continuing dialogue with the oppressed. The method of instruction must express the consciousness of the students themselves. This eventuates a pedagogy designed to lead to the *mutual humanization* of the teacher and the student (55–56). The relation becomes one of partners, and in fact, this is precisely the evolution of Grant's relation to Jefferson. By the end of the novel, Grant has helped Jefferson transcend the limits of the cell and his terrorized soul, but in a kind of symbiosis, Jefferson has transcended Grant's model to become a true hero, "the one" who can take on "the cross" for the community. Indeed, in his last interview with Jefferson in the cell, Grant refers to him as his "partner" (219). When I discussed this relation with Gaines, he told me his intention for the diary: "I thought that the diary would elevate it. . . . I needed something to get into Jefferson's mind, to show you who this was, and what was going to happen. Who this simple little water boy, or cottonpicker, or whatever he was, was; it had to be clear he was the savior of Grant, so Grant could save the children" (Lowe, "Interview" 301).

Students need to probe the reasons for Grant's poor performance as a teacher. We therefore look closely at a negative influence, his old teacher Matthew Antoine, who had predicted most of his male students would

> die violently, and those who did not would be brought down to the level of beasts. Told us that there was no other choice but to run and run. That he was living testimony of someone who should have run . . . in him . . . we felt it . . . there was nothing but hatred for himself as well as contempt for us. He hated himself for the mixture of his blood [he is mulatto] and the cowardice of his being, and he hated us for daily reminding him of it.   (62)

One of the things that Antoine clearly does not impart to his students emerges from Jefferson's diary: namely, the potential of language and writing for developing a sense not only of identity and discovery but also of uniqueness and worth. I share with students a story Gaines once told me about a conversation he had with two clerks in a hardware store in Lafayette, where he teaches. One, who recognized him, introduced him to the other as an important writer. The second clerk, a young African American, responded, "If he's so important, what's he doing here?" For Gaines, this indicated how she saw herself as unimportant and the university there as unimportant. "What I'm always trying to do is show how this place and these people *are* important. They may think they're insignificant, but the great stories have been written about people who constantly question their significance. . . . I've always been an admirer of writers . . . who pick up people who seem insignificant and look at their essence" (Lowe, "Interview" 299).

To understand this concept, which leads to the "expansion" of Jefferson's cell, students need to peruse one of the novel's key early scenes, which takes place in Pichot's kitchen. Grant, Miss Emma, and Tante Lou, who seek permission to visit Jefferson, are kept waiting there for hours while the white folks eat. When the stuffed white men saunter in to discuss whether Grant can visit Jefferson, their gazes dictate the performance of an old script. None of the blacks is asked to sit, and Grant's thoughts show us this:

> I tried to decide just how I should respond to them. Whether I should act like the teacher that I was, or like the nigger that I was supposed to be. I decided to wait and see how the conversation went. To show too much intelligence would have been an insult to them. To show a lack of intelligence would have been a greater insult to me. I decided to wait and see how the conversation would go.   (47)

He knows he's in trouble for using *doesn't* instead of *don't* and recognizes a trap when the sheriff asks who's right about letting him see Jefferson, he (the sheriff) or his wife, Pichot's sister. When Grant, Solomon-like, replies, "I make it a habit never to get into family business, Mr. Guidry," the sheriff responds, "You're smart . . . maybe you're just a little too smart for your own good." On this, Grant stays silent: "I was quiet. I knew when to be quiet" (49). These scenes in the kitchen are in effect *torture* scenes, the site of interrogation, and as such find their parallel at the jail when Grant is played with by the white jailers. Throughout the novel, the white gaze is meant to be corrective as well. When Grant slips up and asks for Paul at the jail, rather than "Mr. Paul," he's immediately corrected: "he [the chief deputy] stood there eyeing me until he felt that I understood" (188).

I try to show students passages that sum things up for us; for example, Grant complains to his aunt:

> Everything you sent me to school for, you're stripping me of it . . . the humiliation I had to go through, going into that man's kitchen. The hours I had to wait while they ate and drank and socialized before they would even see me. Now going up to that jail. To watch them put their dirty hands on that food. To search my body each time as if I'm some kind of common criminal. Maybe today they'll want to look into my mouth, or my nostrils, or make me strip. Anything to humiliate me. Years ago Professor Antoine told me that if I stayed here, they were going to break me down to the nigger I was born to be. But he didn't tell me that my aunt would help them do it.   (79)

This complex union of kitchen, food, jail, and torture requires unpacking. In terms of the kitchen, Elaine Scarry has noted that "the unmaking of civilization inevitably requires a return to and mutilation of the domestic, the ground of all making" (45). Richard Wright, William Faulkner, and many other writers have played on this thematic by placing horrific scenes of torment in kitchens. The antidote to the "unmaking" of the black world is only in formulae for "remaking," and thus the importance of the food lines from the old black women's kitchens to the jail cells, and not just that of Jefferson. By the end of the novel, when the community visits Jefferson en masse and shares a meal with him, the jail

cell has become domesticated, inverted, transformed. Further, we should remember that this is one of many adjoining cells, and the regeneration of one
could perhaps, in biological symbolism, lead to that of many. The visits to the
jail take on a new quality after Miss Emma decides not to go. Grant resists again,
objecting that Jefferson's "no kin" (77), echoing Cain's cry, "Am I my brother's
keeper?"—but also denying the communal in favor of his wounded individuality. By contrast, Grant inadvertently, through his sarcastic humor, shows us
the opposite of this approach by observing that the bag of food that Miss
Emma sends in her stead contains "enough . . . to feed everybody in the jail" (79).
This reference suggests how what Grant represents—literacy, the community,
African American culture—could indeed, like Christ's loaves and fishes, feed
the multitudes.

The thematic of torture expands further when Jefferson finally begins some
bitter exchanges with Grant in the cell. He accuses him of "vexing" him and
makes disparaging remarks about Vivian, "that old yellow woman you go with . . .
her old pussy ain't no good" (129–30). But Grant restrains his anger, realizing
the act of a desperate man. His own interrogations by the sheriff and the deputies continue relentlessly, and it becomes plain that he too has been under surveillance when in Jefferson's cell: "I know you haven't done a thing yet. Boys on
the block tell me. . . . I doubt if you ever will" (134).

We note too that the sheriff, upset by the visits of the old ladies and students,
intones with menace, "This ain't no school, and it ain't no picnic ground" (134).
However, these remarks prepare us for the transformation of the prison, for it
indeed *is* a school, a scene of instruction, and becomes a picnic ground, as eventually the entire community sends representatives to communal meals with Jefferson. The traditional picnic ground for rural African Americans has been the
area around the church, which in this book is also the school, so the telescop-
ing/transforming of space accomplished in the novel's complex symbolism melds
prison, school, and church, collapsing metaphysical walls of separation, thereby
annihilating the key mission of penal incarceration.

Religion's greatest scene of torture, of course, is Calvary, and Gaines employs
several Christic references that students recognize as the novel builds to a powerful climax. The children at the school are preparing a Christmas pageant, and
Jefferson remarks, "It's Christmas? . . . That's when He was born, or that's when
He died? . . . That's right . . . Easter when they nailed Him to the cross. And He
never said a mumbling word" (139). This exchange, however, links his looming
execution with the school pageant, which is described in loving detail. Here the
constriction of Grant's cruel classroom becomes utterly transformed with the
help of sheets, cheap decorations, makeshift costumes. Gaines/Grant carefully
names all those who are there, giving them individuality and warmth. Grant,
ever critical, mocks the humble pageant, yet the wealth of detail he gives makes
us admire the scene despite the attitude of our narrator. Gaines, imprisoned by
the first-person narrator, finds a way to break free. This culminates in Grant's
failure to see the deep comfort of traditional repetition—"I was not happy. I had

heard the same carols all my life, seen the same little play, with the same mistakes in grammar. The minister had offered the same prayer . . . same old clothes. . . . Next year it would be the same, and the year after. . . . [W]here were they chang- ing? I looked back at the people. . . . I was not with them. I stood alone" (151)— thereby unconsciously validating the indictment of Reverend Ambrose.

As I point out to students, Gaines reaps what he has sown here as the execu- tion is slated for the second Friday after Easter. "Always on Friday," Grant fumes: "Same time as He died, between twelve and three. But they can't take this one's life too soon after the recognition of His death, because it might upset the sen- sitive few" (158). The execution itself skews this line of presentation somewhat, when the executioner Henry Vincent demands that Paul see to it that Jefferson be properly shaved so as to ensure a quick demise. "He said that this was an ex- ecution, not torture, that he had seen enough of that for a lifetime" (243).

As the deputies attend the shaving scene, Jefferson asks about Deputy Claude's wife and son. Claude "tried not to meet Jefferson's eyes" (245), a representative detail of the reversal of the white gaze through shame. The entire black com- munity has taken the day off in honor of Jefferson, a communal act of resistance that seems to have been accepted by the dominant whites. The original scene of instruction (the school), here serving as a church, yet still a school, again becomes enfolded with the space of the cell through Reverend Ambrose's simple sermon, which also makes the point of the soul as a constrictive cell.

My students and I focus on Jefferson's final conversion, which leads to his di- ary; it comes in a powerful scene that summons forth Grant's most eloquent rhe- torical effects. With Reverend Ambrose and the two old women, Grant comes to the day room to share a gumbo. When Jefferson refuses to eat, Grant walks him around the room privately and tells him what a hero is, revealing that he, Jefferson, is Grant's hero, that by standing and dying with dignity he can give direction to him; he can, in fact, revitalize myth for the entire community. The spatial expansion of the cell; the mobility; the circling around the vital center of communal life symbolized by the reverend; the two devout matriarchs and the steaming bowl of gumbo (profoundly Afrocentric, but also French Creole in ori- gin, and yet embraced by all in this culture)—all configure the scene as epiph- anic, as does the language employed. Jefferson's tears, however, are his only response before he joins the others at the table and eats. There are several lev- els of reference here, typologically. In a sense, Grant is John the Baptist to Jef- ferson, the savior. In this baptism of inspiring words and communal gumbo, Jefferson not only rejoins the community, but he finds the nourishment he needs to stand and walk. Significantly, his silence here sets the stage for the incandes- cent revelation of his diary, which is prefigured in his last interview in the cell with Grant.

Although Gaines does not develop music's role in Jefferson's awakening iden- tity as fully as he might, we should remember that the diary Jefferson eventually composes, his legacy to the children and the community, had a powerful coun- terpart historically in the magnificent blues songs that grew out of the African

American prison population. "Penal Farm Blues," "My Home Is a Prison," and, yes, "'Lectric Chair Blues" are some of those titles (Franklin 7).

That diary, my students feel, is a powerful piece of writing, despite its limited vocabulary and stilted prose. As I tell them, everything in the novel leads up to it; everything after is really "amen." Writing the diary gives Jefferson a way of consolidating the memories of the community's inspiring visits to his cell with his resultant new conceptions of himself, now that he knows he is part of a culture, indeed a kind of keystone—albeit perhaps a temporary one—of that culture. Writing also gives him a measure of security in his final days, for the sheriff, fearful that he will indict him for prior harsh treatment, waxes solicitous, his gaze no longer baleful but actually apprehensive.

Appropriately, after the revelation of the diary, Gaines takes the narrative in some ways away from Grant and lets many other characters—some of them new to the tale, but all part of the community—describe the day of the execution. This sequence of writing focuses on their views—their gaze—at the electric chair. White and black people react in varying ways, some with nervous jokes, others with feigned sarcasm, but many with fascinated horror. One of the jokes follows the ancient tradition of gallows humor: "A man said it did look gruesome, and that's why they called it Gruesome Gerty. The man told the woman that whoever sat in Gruesome Gerty's lap when she was hot never sat down again" (241).

Students note the dual endings of the book—the end of Jefferson's diary and the end of Grant's narration—are parallel in their settings, which express both men's release from the prison of self. The diary ends with Jefferson spiritually leaving his cell through his appreciation of the dawning day:

> I jus wash my face
> day breakin
> sun comin up
> the bird in the tre soun like a blu bird
> sky blu blu mr wigin
> good by mr wigin tell them im strong tell them im a man good by mr wigin
>   im gon ax paul if he can bring you this
> sincely jefferson.   (234)

Similarly, when Jefferson's moment of execution is imminent, Grant has his pupils kneel, but he cannot stay in the restricted space of the church/school with them—he wanders outdoors, oblivious to all until a flitting yellow-and-black butterfly alights on a grassy hill and makes Grant open up to the vista; somehow this event, where space opens up for Grant, coincides with his knowledge that Jefferson has just died. He stands (always a significant verb in Gaines), stretches, and notices "the river, so tranquil, its water as blue as the sky" (252)—images, as in Jefferson's reverie, of purity and immensity.

This scene is soon followed by Paul's arrival to give Grant the diary. Paul plays a key role in the novel, for he is a source of information for Grant and us regarding Jefferson's daily life, and Paul's own "conversion" also contributes to the mildly hopeful tone of the final section. In a moving sequence, Paul "testifies" as a "witness" to Jefferson's heroic courage. Truly, Paul Bonin—Paul the good—has been transformed too, expressing not only his wish to be Grant's friend but also his willingness to return someday and testify to the children as well. I tell students about another famous prisoner, Malcolm X, who read over and over, while in prison, how Paul on the road to Damascus, upon hearing the voice of Christ, was so smitten that he was knocked off his horse in a daze: "I do not now, and I did not then, liken myself to Paul. But I do understand his experience . . . truth can be quickly received, or received at all, only by the sinner who knows and admits that he is guilty of having sinned much. Stated another way: only guilt admitted accepts truth" (*Autobiography* 163). The biblical Paul, né Saul, was of course a brutal solider, and he found redemption, leading to his role as the principal evangelist of Christ's doctrine. Gaines commented on his Paul, stating that at the novel's end, he "has been changed, and his is going to make some point—at least I hope so" (Lowe, "Interview" 307).

I remind students that the first sentence of the book reads, "I was not there, yet I was there." Grant is telling us he wasn't there when Jefferson's sentence was pronounced, but the sentence aptly speaks as well to the community members' relation to Jefferson throughout. They were not there when fate involved him in a criminal script that was interpreted wrongly and against him; they were not there in the cell with him, yet all of them identify with him in his position as pariah and scapegoat. Here I read students Etheridge Knight's magnificent poem "The Idea of Ancestry"; as Knight peruses the photos of his family pasted on the walls of his prison cell, he declares, "I am all of them, they are all of me, I am me, they are thee, and I have no sons to float in the space between." It is Gaines's achievement to illustrate this principle in the amplitude of prose, as Jefferson's importance to the community emerges in a way that it never did in his unconfined state. The poetry of his heroism unites the community, inspires an act of resistance, and lifts hearts. Surely the same is true for all readers of this deeply moving novel, who leave it knowing "they are all of them, they are all of me."

I encourage students to think about the way in which the novel concerns the African American community's changing same, its ability to fashion dignity and even glory out of debased circumstances, inhumane treatment, and the constrictions of every kind of confinement, prisons of the body and the spirit alike. Gaines has stated, and this book illustrates, that

> this is the responsibility of man; taking responsibility for the whole, all humanity, is what I think manliness is. It seems that too many of the whites are afraid to take that kind of responsibility, and so many of the blacks have been denied that kind of responsibility, and refuse to accept it because of their long denial. I hope I'm not only speaking for blacks; you use the tools that you have, and because I am African American and most of my char-

acters are, I put the situation there. But I could do the same with white characters. (Lowe, "Interview" 321)

Jefferson is correct to claim he is "youman" as he faces death; he is ours, he is "you," he is "man." In unfolding these parables, *A Lesson Before Dying* becomes a deeply instructive book for the ages to come in its indelible presentation of the resilience of man's spirit.

NOTES

[1] This essay quotes from the 1994 Vintage edition of *Lesson*.

[2] This essay quotes from the 1968 Signet edition of *Narrative of the Life of Frederick Douglass*.

Teaching Criminal Law Issues in
A *Lesson Before Dying*:
"She Knew, As We All Knew,
What the Outcome Would Be"

Susan Ayres

In my law and literature class, I vary the reading list from year to year, but one staple is *A Lesson Before Dying*, Ernest Gaines's eighth novel and winner of the National Book Critics Circle Award. Set in Louisiana in 1948, the novel is the story of Jefferson, a young black man wrongfully convicted of murder and given a death sentence by an all-white jury and racially biased legal system. Awaiting execution, Jefferson learns from Grant Wiggins, the local teacher, how to face death with dignity.

I teach *Lesson* using James Boyd White's model of "constitutive rhetoric," which is "the study of the ways we constitute ourselves as individuals, as communities, and as cultures, whenever we speak" (35) and which has "justice and ethics . . . as its ultimate subjects" (39). Law is a branch of constitutive rhetoric and is both culturally and socially specific, since a lawyer responds to a client's particular problems (37, 35). Law is also a narrative process "because there cannot be a legal case without a real story about real people actually located in time and space and culture" (36). White emphasizes the ethical aspects of constitutive rhetoric, such as the power to create character and community using honest persuasion versus the power to destroy character and community using manipulation or deceit (3–5).[1] Accordingly, one of the primary questions lawyers must ask is: "What kind of community should we who are talking the language of the law establish with each other, with our clients, and with the rest of the world?" (34).

Constitutive rhetoric in *Lesson* may be taught by considering two examples that destroy character and community and two examples that create character and community. The two destructive examples of constitutive rhetoric are legal: the degrading closing argument delivered by Jefferson's defense attorney and Jefferson's unjust conviction and punishment. These two negative examples critique white supremacy, the felony murder rule, and capital punishment. The two positive examples of constitutive rhetoric are interrelational: Grant's persuasion as Jefferson's teacher and Jefferson's transformation through his diary. Both sets of examples include one spoken (the lawyer's and Grant's speeches) and one written (the criminal law and Jefferson's diary). In addition to White's theory of constitutive rhetoric, I also use Judith Butler's theory of vulnerability and the "unaccountable subject" to examine the interrelationship between Grant and Jefferson.

Even though it is set in the 1940s, *Lesson* is still relevant to a law and literature course, not just for its historical representation of legal and social systems but as an illustration of the remnants of continued legal and social practice today.[2] For example, racism haunts the treatment of blacks in the criminal justice system. Currently, black males are "incarcerated at a rate more than six times higher than white males" (*Prisoners*). Moreover, historians describe the rise of the prison system as a response to the end of slavery. As Katy Ryan explains in *Demands of the Dead*, prisons grew and shifted "from a mostly white to mostly black population" in an effort "to incarcerate and disenfranchise the newly freed" (Introduction 8). Many scholars have documented "[t]he continuities between slavery and penal practices," and this includes death penalty executions, of which 80 percent since 1976 have occurred in the South (8). Racism in the criminal justice system and larger society continues to exist; as Gaines indicated in an interview by John Lowe, not much has changed: racist views exist but are just "not said so openly" ("Interview" 310).[3] Racism in the criminal justice system is "more subtle" now than during the Jim Crow era: "Nearly 80 percent of those executed since 1976 have been convicted of killing a white person, though black Americans constitute more than half of all murder victims" (Ryan 10).

Lesson contains two examples of racism and injustice in the criminal justice system. Both the defense attorney's closing argument and the imposition of the death penalty for felony murder may be analyzed through the law and literature lens of constitutive rhetoric. The closing argument destroys community by degrading Jefferson through racist norms of white supremacy. Moreover, the lawyer's unethical speech fails to acknowledge Jefferson's humanity and exemplifies ineffective assistance of counsel. Constitutive rhetoric informs an analysis of Jefferson's conviction based on the felony murder rule. Jefferson, who had no intent to rob the store, much less kill the owner, is given the death penalty. The law itself is unfair, but the injustice of Jefferson's conviction also has parallels to Willie Francis's botched execution in Louisiana in 1946.

The next set of examples of constitutive rhetoric in the novel are the interrelationship between Grant and Jefferson as teacher and student and Jefferson's transformation as recorded in his diary. Their interrelationship, while not completely positive, may arguably be viewed as an antidote to the negative critique of the legal system by restoring justice on a transcendent level, healing the black community, and suggesting the possibility of mutual respect between the black and white communities in the novel.

Jefferson's Defense

The novel begins with openly expressed racism that destroys character and community. Ironically, it comes from Jefferson's own lawyer, who appeals to the all-white male jury to spare Jefferson's life. The attorney publicly degrades Jefferson as a "fool" lacking "a modicum of intelligence" who "stood by and watched this [robbery and shoot-out] happen, not having the sense to run" (7).[4] The attorney continues his closing argument as follows:

Gentlemen of the jury, look at him. . . . Do you see a man sitting here? . . . Look at the shape of this skull, this face as flat as the palm of my hand—look deeply into those eyes. . . . Do you see anyone here who could plan a murder, a robbery, can plan—can plan—can plan anything? A cornered animal to strike quickly out of fear, a trait inherited from his ancestors in the deepest jungle of blackest Africa. . . . No, gentlemen, this skull here holds no plans. What you see here is a thing that acts on command. A thing to hold the handle of a plow, a thing to load your bales of cotton, a thing to dig your ditches, to chop your wood, to pull your corn. . . . Ask him to name the months of the year. Ask him does Christmas come before or after the Fourth of July? Mention the names of Keats, Byron, Scott, and see whether the eyes will show one moment of recognition. Ask him to describe a rose, to quote one passage from the Constitution or Bill of Rights.   (7–8)

His defense attorney continues by asking the jury to consider that Jefferson is his godmother's "reason for existence"; he then begs the jury to "be merciful" and makes his final plea: "What justice would there be to take this life? Justice, gentlemen? Why, I would just as soon put a hog in the electric chair as this" (8).

The lawyer's degrading closing argument may be analyzed for its "ethical or communal character, or its socially constitutive nature," since "[e]very time one speaks as a lawyer, one establishes . . . an ethical identity . . . for oneself, for one's audience, and for those one talks about, and proposes a relationship among them" (J. White 34). The community the lawyer creates is encapsulated by the word Jefferson's godmother remembers: "Called him a hog" (12; see also Lowe, "Transcendence" 146).

Thus, although the lawyer makes a plea for justice, his argument is unethical and manipulative rhetoric that constitutes a community of exclusion and of racism. Specifically, his power to name Jefferson a "hog" constitutes Jefferson's identity as other, as subhuman animal or thing, and ties intelligence level to literacy. The defense attorney's argument "condenses many common tenets used to justify maintaining African Americans in an inferior social status," including references to phrenology and to chattel (Babb, "Old-Fashioned Modernism" 253). The closing argument also "encapsulates the horror of black people's enslavement. . . . As a 'hog,' the young black Jefferson becomes another thing for whites to slaughter, to consume, and to debauch" (Thompson 285).

This label of "hog" launches the novel and motivates the insistence of Miss Emma Glenn, Jefferson's godmother and Tante Lou's best friend, that Grant teach Jefferson to die as a man. Miss Emma says, "I don't want them to kill no hog. . . . I want a man to go to that chair, on his own two feet" (13). This first example of constitutive rhetoric reinforces the white community's sense of supremacy, which pervades the entire novel. For example, Grant must enter the back door of the plantation owner Henri Pichot's house when he asks to visit Jefferson in jail, even though when Grant went to university, his aunt, Tante Lou, promised, "Me and Em-ma can make out all right without you coming through that back door ever again" (18–19). Also, when Grant buys Jefferson a radio, the white saleswoman ignores him (176), and when the white superintendent of schools visits, he inspects Grant's students' teeth (56). One of the most disturbing examples of white supremacy occurs when several white men place bets on whether Grant can transform Jefferson before the execution (43).

In addition to reinforcing white supremacy, the lawyer's argument also unethically reduces Jefferson's identity to an animal. The label of "hog" has such power over Jefferson that he begins to act like a hog in prison. The first several times Grant, Miss Emma, and Tante Lou visit Jefferson in prison, they bring him Miss Emma's home-cooked food (fried chicken, yams, tea cakes), which he refuses to eat. He also refuses to talk to them, except to say, "It don't matter," and to ask Grant about the execution: "When they go'n do it? Tomorrow?" (73). Miss Emma leaves the visits in tears and eventually sends Grant to visit Jefferson alone. When Grant again takes the home-cooked food up to the prison, he offers some to Jefferson, who rejects it by asking if Grant brought some corn, because that's what hogs eat. Jefferson insists, "I'm a old hog. . . . Just a old hog they fattening up to kill for Christmas" (83). Even though Grant repeatedly tells him that he is a human being and a man, Jefferson gets down on his hands and knees, puts his face in the bag of food, and begins to eat it: "He knelt down on the floor and put his head inside the bag and started eating, without using his hands. He even sounded like a hog" (83). During another visit when Jefferson acts like a hog, he insults Grant's fiancée, claiming, "Her old pussy ain't no good," and knocks the entire bag of food all over the floor because "[m]anners is for the living" (130).

The defense attorney's closing argument is an example of unethical constitutive rhetoric not only because it refuses to recognize Jefferson's human dignity, thus reinforcing a racist community, but also because it prejudices the jury and constitutes ineffective assistance of counsel. Under the Sixth Amendment, effective assistance of counsel is guaranteed in order that defendants receive a fair trial. In 1984 the United States Supreme Court articulated the two-part *Strickland* test to determine ineffective assistance of counsel. The first part requires that "the defendant must show that the counsel's performance was deficient," and the second part requires that "the defendant must show that the deficient performance prejudiced the defense" (*Strickland* 687). Under the *Strickland* test, Jefferson's attorney provided ineffective assistance of counsel. His performance was deficient when he appealed to the jury's racist beliefs by referring to Jefferson as a "hog." Moreover, his performance prejudiced Jefferson's defense, because the jury quickly deliberated "after lunch" and returned a guilty verdict, after which "[t]he judge commended the twelve white men for reaching a quick and just verdict" (8).

A modern court would likely agree with the conclusion that Jefferson's attorney provided ineffective assistance of counsel. For instance, in 1987 the highest criminal court in Texas reversed a death penalty conviction in the case of *Ex parte Guzmon*. The defendant, an undocumented immigrant from El Salvador, was repeatedly referred to by his attorney as a "wet-back" during his trial for capital murder (*Ex parte Guzmon* 725, 730, 731).[5] Guzmon and his two friends tried to steal a car after theirs broke down, and in the fray, one of the three shot the owner of the car. During his trial, Guzmon denied that he shot the owner, but the jury found him guilty after deliberating only fifteen minutes (730). The highest reviewing court found that the "wet-back" references constituted ineffective assistance of counsel, in part because, as was made clear during the voir dire of the jury, "[s]ome members of that jury did not feel applicant was entitled to all the protections afforded United States citizens" (727).

In another case, decided in 1982, the Eleventh Circuit reversed Terry Lee Goodwin's death sentence for ineffective assistance of counsel. Although the court found many instances of deficient performance that prejudiced Goodwin's defense, the most relevant was the closing argument of his attorney, who called him "a little old nigger boy":

> Well if you decided to impose the death penalty today and you decide to sentence him, Terry Goodwin, to the electric chair, historically speaking, you have got a very likely candidate. He is a little old nigger boy, he would not weigh a hundred and fifty pounds. He has got two court appointed lawyers appointed by this court to represent him to do the very best we can for him. He is poor. He is broke. He is probably mentally retarded. I dare say he has not got an I.Q. of over 70. He is uneducated. Probably just unwanted. This is the kind of people that we have historically put to death here in Georgia.   (*Goodwin* 803)

In the more recent case of *Buck v. Davis*, the United States Supreme Court found ineffective assistance of counsel when a defense attorney called an expert psychologist during the sentencing phase of trial (after a finding of guilt). The psychologist testified that although it was unlikely the defendant would engage in future violent conduct, because this was a crime of passion, nonetheless, since the defendant was black, he was statistically more likely to commit future violent acts (*Buck* 767). The expert testified, "It's a sad commentary . . . that minorities, Hispanics and black people, are over represented in the Criminal Justice System" (769). This case, decided in 2017, held that the attorney provided ineffective assistance of counsel because he knew the expert's opinion regarding race and likelihood of violence even before he called the expert to testify (768–69, 775). No competent attorney would "introduce such evidence about his own client," the court concluded (775). And the consequences of this were dire: "when a jury hears expert testimony that expressly makes a defendant's race directly pertinent on the question of life or death, the impact of that evidence cannot be measured simply by how much air time it received at trial or how many pages it occupies in the record. Some toxins can be deadly in small doses" (777).

Like the defense attorney in *Lesson*, the defense attorneys in these cases failed to give their clients dignity and respect. Prejudicial name-calling, associating intelligence with literacy, or associating violence with race are all examples of negative constitutive rhetoric by lawyers who hold the power to make life-and-death decisions for the "uneducated . . . unwanted" people.

Jefferson's Conviction

Jefferson's conviction provides another example of constitutive rhetoric that destroys character and community. Even though the jury finds Jefferson guilty and the judge sentences him to death, Gaines has described the situation of the novel as "a young man being in the wrong place at the wrong time who would be charged with murder" ("Writing *A Lesson*" 770).[6] Jefferson's unjust conviction raises a second example of constitutive rhetoric, specifically the unjust and inhumane effects of the felony murder rule and capital punishment.

Although lawyers and law students are familiar with the concept of felony murder, which would allow a death penalty conviction for a young man in the wrong place at the wrong time, this result confounds the non-law-trained reader. One of the elements of a crime is mens rea, or criminal intent. It seems unjust and even ludicrous that a person, such as Jefferson, could be punished by death if he had no mens rea, or intent to kill. However, this is the application of the common-law rule for felony murder that was accepted up until 1973 in Louisiana and is accepted in other jurisdictions even today. The felony murder rule, analyzed as constitutive rhetoric, creates a culture that extends criminal liability to those who may be innocent.

At common law, the felony murder rule provided that a person "whose conduct brought about an unintended death in the commission or attempted commission of a felony was guilty of murder" (LaFave 785). And under the law of parties, a co-felon, even one who was not the triggerman, was liable for felony murder when the murder was a foreseeable consequence of the felony (789). Because of its harshness, many jurisdictions abolished or limited the application of the felony murder rule. England abolished it in 1957, and "[i]t never existed in France or Germany" (Dressler 556–57). More recently in the United States, the felony murder rule has been severely criticized, and many jurisdictions have limited it to violent felonies (LaFave 786–87) or have required an intent to commit the felony and an implied intent to kill (such as extreme or reckless indifference to the value of human life) (Binder 440–44). In the 1987 death penalty case of *Tison v. Arizona*, the Supreme Court held that a non-triggerman co-felon could be found guilty of felony murder and receive the death penalty as long as the co-felon was a major participant (i.e., was present at the murder scene) and exhibited "reckless indifference to human life," which is "implicit in knowingly engaging in criminal activities known to carry a grave risk of death" (*Tison* 157).[7]

Despite modern limits on the felony murder rule, in Louisiana in 1948,[8] when the novel takes place, and even today in three jurisdictions in the United States (Renken 914), a co-felon who is a non-triggerman in a robbery can be found guilty of felony murder and sentenced to death under the common-law rules for felony murder and the laws of parties. In other words, as long as the jury believed that Jefferson had an intent to assist in the armed robbery, he could be convicted of felony murder and sentenced to death. While the reader knows that Jefferson did not intend to rob the store with his two friends, circumstantial evidence of his intent exists—and most criminal cases are determined on circumstantial evidence. Criminal cases are a battle of stories, and in *Lesson*, there are two competing stories: the state's story, which is told, and the defense's story, which is not told. Jefferson does not testify, and not a single defense witness is called (12). So, a constitutive rhetoric analysis of Jefferson's conviction examines the injustice of the felony murder rule and the injustice in the legal proceedings. James White argues that justice requires the two stories "be told in opposition or competition" and that "[y]ou are entitled to have your story told in your language (or translated into it), or the law is failing" (42).

The law fails Jefferson because his story is not told during his trial. The state's story is that Jefferson went to the store with Brother and Bear, and after the owner would not give them wine on credit, Bear shot at the owner, who shot back, leaving only Jefferson alive. Jefferson panicked, drank some whiskey, and took money out of the cash register. "He was halfway across the room, the money stuffed inside his jacket pocket, the half bottle of whiskey clutched in his hand, when two white men walked into the store" (6). This looks like felony murder, especially to an all-white jury, when the prosecutor argues that Jefferson went into the store with the intent of robbing and killing Mr. Gropé. As Gaines has commented, "in Louisiana in the forties, if he had been caught on the premises where a white man had been killed, with a bottle of liquor in his hand and money in his pocket, that added up to guilt" ("Writing *A Lesson*" 775).

Moreover, the white community agrees with the jury's verdict that Jefferson is guilty. For instance, when Miss Emma goes to see Mr. Henri, brother-in-law to Sheriff Guidry, Mr. Henri agrees to ask the sheriff if Grant can visit Jefferson but reminds Miss Emma, "And I also know what he did. Or have you forgotten that? . . . He did it" (22). Likewise, on the day Jefferson is executed, a white bank clerk tells a customer what she had told her son: "the sheriff just had to put an old bad nigger away, and she didn't want him to worry about anything" (242).

In contrast, Clay, a black man running an errand at the bank, is so transfixed by the bank clerk's misrepresentation about Jefferson's guilt that he completely forgets where he is and what he is supposed to be doing. Unlike the white community, the black community believes that Jefferson did not intend to kill or to assist with the robbery. As Grant reflects,

> They sentence you to death because you were at the wrong place at the wrong time, with no proof that you had anything at all to do with the crime other than being there when it happened. Yet six months later they come and unlock your cage and tell you, We, us, white folks all, have decided it's time for you to die, because this is the convenient date and time.   (158)

Miss Emma's reaction to the trial captures the black community's sentiment: "She knew, as we all knew, what the outcome would be" (4). Jefferson's conviction invokes questions about the constitutive rhetoric of felony murder and the possibility of a fair trial by a jury of twelve white men, especially when Jefferson's story is not told, or not told "in opposition or competition" to the state's story (J. White 42). The laws of the white community result in grave injustice, both because of the felony murder rule and because of the failure to tell Jefferson's story.

Not only is Jefferson's conviction for felony murder unjust but so is his death sentence. As Gaines explains, "[W]hat has happened in the book is that a man could possibly be innocent . . . and sentenced to death. I don't know if you could get more cruel than that" (Sartisky 274). Indeed, it is difficult to teach the constitutive rhetoric in *Lesson* without discussing capital punishment, especially since the underlying case that Gaines researched was a botched execution that occurred in 1946, when Willie Francis sat in the electric chair in Louisiana, but not enough electricity was generated to kill him ("Writing *A Lesson*" 771; Denno 18). Another execution date was set but was stayed for the Supreme Court to decide whether a new death warrant violated double jeopardy or the Eighth Amendment. A divided court upheld the execution 5–4 in *Louisiana ex. rel. Francis v. Resweber* (466). A little over a year after the botched execution, Francis was executed (Denno 18).

The allusions to Francis have contemporary relevance to the botched 2014 execution in Oklahoma, when the convicted murderer Clayton Lockett did not die as planned during lethal injection, but rather suffered a heart attack after being stuck more than ten times for an IV line, which was ultimately placed in Lockett's groin and ended up spilling the drugs into his tissue instead of his vein (Stern 78, 80, 82; Eckholm).[9] The cocktail of lethal injection drugs did not kill Lockett; rather, he regained consciousness, "struggled violently," and finally called out, *"Man,"* before he "slowly and in apparent agony" died of a heart attack (Stern 82–83). The botched execution of Lockett and others show that the question of cruel and unusual punishment, in terms of method of execution, is ongoing.

Gaines was familiar with Francis's case and said he "use[d] some of the information from the case material" ("Writing *A Lesson*" 771), but he did not want to set his story in the same year and invite comparison (Lowe, "Interview" 307). Gaines acknowledged similarities between Francis and Jefferson, including that "[b]oth young men are black. Both are nearly illiterate. Both were involved in the murder of a white man. [Francis] confessed to the murder. [Jefferson] would always maintain his innocence, to the end. No defense witnesses were called in either case" ("Writing *A Lesson*" 771). Additionally, "Gruesome Gertie," the state's traveling electric chair, was used in both executions (Denno 43; Gaines, *Lesson* 235–45), and the novel's executioner alludes to Francis's botched execution when he tells the sheriff and deputy that "this was an execution, not torture, . . . he had seen enough of that for a lifetime" (243).

Another similarity between the two stories is that both Francis and Jefferson wrote about their experiences. After the botched execution, Francis collaborated with a local resident to write a pamphlet entitled *My Trip to the Chair*, which helped fund Francis's Supreme Court appeal (Denno 23). Although I have not discovered whether Gaines read Francis's pamphlet, the copy of the pamphlet held by the Library of Congress was "'lost' for decades," until it was found by the journalist Gilbert King while he was researching his 2008 book on Francis (Stupp 52). Francis's pamphlet contains several parallels to Jefferson's death row experience. Like Grant and Miss Emma's plea for Jefferson to walk to the chair like a man, the day before Francis's first execution, a priest similarly pleaded with Francis: "I had a new life to start when I got up from that chair the next day, and I shouldn't start it like a little cry-baby. Even though I was only sixteen, he said, I had this one big chance to prove I was able to die like a man. It is one of the hardest things to make yourself learn how to die right" (Francis 36). Like Jefferson, Francis requested ice cream for his last supper (Gaines, *Lesson* 232; Francis 36). And the respective local sheriffs asked to be favorably portrayed in both Jefferson's diary and in Francis's pamphlet (Gaines, *Lesson* 233; Francis 35).

Francis's inhumane botched execution and second successful execution subtly influences *Lesson* and provides the opportunity to teach the constitutive rhetoric of the death penalty. The world constituted by law in the chapter about the execution is that of trauma, especially for the black community. The store owner's family attends the execution but is not mentioned otherwise in the novel—there is no call for death to avenge the victim, just a rendering of the traumatic effect. For the white community, the execution is more of an inconvenience than anything else. A white woman going into the bank tells her husband, "Oh, God, don't tell me that they have started. . . . But my God, the whole town can hear that thing [the generator]" (242). Another white woman complains that "she wished something like this could be done somewhere else. What about those poor [white] children up at the school?" (240). Even the sheriff tells his wife that "he wished this day had never gotten here, but now that it had, he had to do what he had to do" (238).

In contrast, the black community is paralyzed, like Clay at the bank. Everyone agrees to take shifts with Miss Emma the night before the execution and to take off work the next day in honor of Jefferson. Grant, who is too much of a coward to attend the execution, makes his students pray on their knees. Afterward, Paul, the jailer who brings Grant the diary, tells Grant to let the children know "he was the bravest man in that room today. I'm a witness, Grant Wiggins. Tell them so" (256).

Consequently, the novel may be read as a plea to abolish the death penalty through its example of an innocent man wrongly put to death. Gaines has said the book is not just about capital punishment but "is the product of a lifetime of nightmares about execution," and while he is not "a particular zealot against capital punishment, . . . he has long been obsessed with wondering what it must be like to know in advance the exact moment one is going to die" (qtd. in Ringle).

Indeed, some scholars, such as Jason Stupp, read the novel as primarily a prison and anti–death penalty novel (45, 56). Stupp goes as far as to claim that "[a] responsible mode of scholarship would combine [the] 'requirement to remember [the dead]' with the active pursuit of justice and the destruction, whenever possible, of discourse that attempts to hide or justify the barbarity of state-sanctioned death" (56).[10]

Engaging students in a debate about the constitutive rhetoric of capital punishment is one approach to *Lesson* but not the only approach. Other scholars see the main point of the novel as a lesson involving Jefferson's and Grant's transformations. This latter view finds support in Gaines's statements about the novel:

> I didn't want to write just another story of someone waiting to be executed, which had been done many times before. To make my story different, I made Grant also a prisoner, of his environment. . . . Eventually he becomes involved in Jefferson's plight, and in the end it will benefit both of them. He will teach Jefferson to live for a while and to die with dignity. Jefferson, in turn, will help Grant find himself.　　("Writing *A Lesson*" 774)

In terms of teaching the novel, student understanding can be enhanced by analyzing the constitutive rhetoric of the law of felony murder and of capital punishment. These issues foster robust debate about racism and justice in the novel and in the current criminal law system. The next two sections of this essay turn to two positive examples of constitutive rhetoric that rehabilitate and heal the community: Grant's persuasion as a teacher and Jefferson's transformation to "youman."

Grant's Persuasion as a Teacher

Constitutive rhetoric "includes *all* language activity that goes into the constitution of actual human cultures and communities" (J. White 39), so in addition to analyzing legal examples, students reading *Lesson* may also examine how Jefferson's conviction affects the community, including the community of women who persuade Grant to teach Jefferson to die with dignity. As part of the ethical analysis of Grant's teaching or persuasion, I incorporate both White's theory of constitutive rhetoric and Butler's theory of vulnerability and the "unaccountable subject," which provides another theoretical tool aligned with the philosophical questions Gaines raises in the novel.

In an interview, Gaines said the novel's primary theme is "What is a man?" (Gaudet and Wooton, "Talking" 239). Gaines has explored this question in several novels, which has prompted analyses of "new narratives of Southern manhood" in Gaines's fiction (S. Jones 31). As Gaines noted, "being a big tough guy" does not make a man, but rather "taking responsibility for the whole, all of humanity, is what I think manliness is" (Lowe, "Interview" 321). This idea of "taking responsibility for the whole" relates to Butler's call to give an account of oneself and recognition of the other—that "I" exist in relation to "you" (*Giving* 32–33). The relationship between Grant and Jefferson illustrates the view of a "relational ethic of contingency," for which "part of becoming human . . . is allowing for a social relationality that exposes our vulnerability to violence and in that provides the conditions for ethical responsibility" (Mills 145–46). While Jefferson's trial includes dehumanization, it becomes Grant's ethical responsibility to "refuse to return [that violence]" (Rigsby 404) by teaching Jefferson to be a man.

When the novel begins, Grant is a reluctant teacher, both to the parish children and to Jefferson. He did not want to return after college to Bayonne but did so for his aunt. He has no hope that anything will ever change[11] and sees his work as useless: "I wanted to scream at my aunt; I was screaming inside. I had told her many, many times how much I hated this place and all I wanted to do was get away. I had told her I was no teacher, I hated teaching, and I was just running in place here" (14–15).

However, using a rhetoric of silence and looks, Tante Lou and Miss Emma push Grant into teaching Jefferson to die with dignity. After they first bring up the subject, the two women stare silently and "looked at me as though I was supposed to figure out the rest of it." Miss Emma then says, "He don't have to do it," and Grant asks, "Do what?" As though it resolves everything, Miss Emma's final statement is "You the teacher" (13). In commenting on the power of these looks, Gaines emphasizes the importance of silence to convey meaning, as when old women "look at you in a certain way, or *don't* look at you in a certain way" (Lowe, "Interview" 310–11). Their looks create a community in which certain individuals are chosen to be "the one." As Gaines explains, "In a place like the Quarter where I lived, those old people, without you knowing, will concentrate on you, and they will choose you" (304). Miss Emma and Tante Lou choose Grant as Jefferson's death row teacher and turn a deaf ear to his refusal and protests.

Their persuasion is not as effective as that of Grant's fiancée, Vivian, who successfully persuades him to try to help Jefferson after he tells her that he does not know how to live, much less teach Jefferson.[12] He cruelly asks her, "Why not let the hog die without knowing anything?" (31). Vivian appeals to Grant by asking him to teach Jefferson "for us" (32). Vivian's approach is more persuasive than that of the older women because she is not appealing to him as the teacher—a role he rejects—but as her lover. As Gaines comments, "Vivian is there to keep Grant there, I think, without her he probably wouldn't have stayed long enough to really deal with Jefferson" (Lowe, "Interview" 302). Altogether, the three women's persuasion establishes a community in which men may accept their role of responsibility to the whole.[13]

A constitutive rhetoric analysis moves from the persuasion of the women to Grant's persuasion. As an extension of the violence already committed against Jefferson, the sheriff and others place a bet on whether Grant can transform Jefferson. And for over half the novel, it looks like they will win. Grant cannot get through to Jefferson. Even shortly before his execution, after Grant has given him a journal to write in, Jefferson records a visit from the plantation owner (Henri Pichot) and the school superintendent (Joseph Morgan): "I yer mr mo- gan say it aint fridy yet an mr picho say you want double that bet you want add that troter an mr mogan say it still aint fridy yet" (229).

How does Grant persuade Jefferson to die as a man? In the initial visits, Grant models and voices social norms, such as asking Jefferson to respect Nannan's feel- ings by eating the food she sends and being "kinder to her" (139); however, Jef- ferson ignores Grant's attempts to reach him and continues to act like a hog. Suzanne Jones believes that initially Grant cannot get through to Jefferson "for the same reason he is failing with his elementary school students. He does not want to teach, he is cynical about the prospect of making a difference, and thus he is angry about being forced into such a position" (42). I would add that Grant fails to teach his students and Jefferson until Grant learns the lesson that he ex- ists in relation to his students.

Pressure builds when Grant is called to Pichot's house in late February and learns that Jefferson's execution date is set for the second Friday after Easter, which Grant cynically views as convenient for whites (158). After Jefferson learns the date, two-thirds of the way through the novel, "all relationships are set into rapid motion" and "people increasingly look at each other and truly listen" (Doyle, *Voices* 217–18). A noticeable shift in communication is apparent during Grant's first visit after the execution date is announced. During this visit, the first thing Grant says is "How are you, Jefferson?" (169). Grant no longer appeals to man- ners and respect but relates to Jefferson "as a subject worthy of recognition" (But- ler, "Recognition" 141) when he offers to bring Jefferson whatever he wants:

> "I want me a whole gallona ice cream," [Jefferson] said, still looking out the window. I saw a slight smile come on his face, and it was not a bitter smile. Not bitter at all. "A whole gallona ice cream. Eat it with a pot spoon. My last supper. A whole gallona ice cream." He looked at me again. "Ain't never had enough ice cream. Never had more than a nickel cone. . . . But now I'm go'n get me a whole gallon." (170)

Grant describes Jefferson as looking at him "not as he had done in the past, in pain, with hate. He looked at me with an inner calmness now" (171).

During this visit, Jefferson recalls that "[w]e [Jefferson and his friend Gable] was suppose to go hunting that day," but he ended up going to the liquor store with Brother and Bear. When Jefferson sinks back into silence, Grant offers to bring him a radio. Gaines commented that "[t]he idea of the radio was not planned, but it turned out to be a most important turn in the story. From that moment on, there is some limited communication between the two of them" ("Writing *A Lesson*" 776). As indicated by his words and actions, Grant now rec- ognizes the face of the other, which provides the possibility for ethical respon- sibility (Butler, *Giving* 29). Grant does this by calling Jefferson "partner" and by telling the children to collect pecans and peanuts for Jefferson, which he brings to the jail along with some candy, apples, and comic books (184). Additionally, Grant tells Jefferson, "I want to be your friend. I want you to ask me questions" (185). Grant spontaneously comes up with the offer to bring Jefferson—who "is barely literate," according to Gaines ("Writing *A Lesson*" 776)—a notebook to "write your thoughts down" (185). Although Jefferson nods, he does not talk to Grant or ask him any questions. Before Grant leaves, Jefferson does manage to say, "[T]ell—tell the chirren thank you for the pe-pecans" (186). Grant's constitutive rhetoric serves to recognize Jefferson, to offer him "standing before the law" (Butler, "Recognition" 141). By humanizing Jefferson, Grant persuades him to serve as a hero for the community.

Chapter 24 contains one of the most important turns in Grant's persuasion, which Lowe describes as "a powerful scene that summons forth Grant's most eloquent rhetorical effects" ("Transcendence" 158). Grant asks Jefferson to be friends with his nannan and to eat her food. He also tries to persuade Jefferson by telling him about heroes and asking Jefferson to be a hero for the black community. After one of their earlier visits, Grant had stopped by the bar, where he overheard men talking about Jackie Robinson, and Grant remembered a story about a young black man who went to his execution crying out for Joe Louis to help him. Instead of this, Grant wants Jefferson to be a hero in order to disprove the myth of white supremacy. He tells Jefferson that "[a] hero is someone who does something for other people" (191). Grant confesses to Jefferson that Grant could never be a hero because he hates teaching and "want[s] to run away" (191). As he tells Jefferson, "I am not that kind of person, but I want you to be. You could give something to her, to me, to those children in the quarter. You could give them something that I never could. They expect it from me, but not from you. The white people out there are saying that you don't have it—that you're a hog, not a man. But I know they are wrong" (191).

Grant explains the myth of white supremacy to Jefferson when he says, "White people believe that they're better than anyone else on earth—and that's a myth. The last thing they ever want is to see a black man stand, and think, and show that common humanity that is in us all" (192). Finally, he appeals to Jefferson by saying, "I need you much more than you could ever need me. I need to know what to do with my life. . . . [Y]ou can be bigger than anyone you have ever met. Please listen to me, because I would not lie to you now. I speak from my heart" (193). During this didactic monologue, Jefferson is crying, and Grant ponders if Jefferson is thinking, "I cry, not from reaching any conclusion by reasoning, but because, lowly as I am, I am still part of the whole" (194).

Although several scholars have praised Grant's speech about white myths and the call to be a hero,[14] others find it unsettling in light of Jefferson's unjust execution.[15] Is it ethical for Grant to ask Jefferson to become a hero for him and for the community? Is it another instance of violence by Grant to name Jefferson a "hero" and ask Jefferson to do something that even Grant, the "teacher," cannot do? This is open for debate, but arguably, the interrelationship between the two allows each to exercise ethical responsibility and mutual recognition. This is seen during his last visit, when Grant brings not a whole meal, but simply baked sweet potatoes. Jefferson is not slouching, as he has done before, but is standing tall. He tells Grant that yes, he is a human being, but that they are asking a lot of him to be a hero. Jefferson refers to Christ on the cross, who died without saying a mumbling word, and says that is how he wants to go. At the end of this visit, Jefferson offers Grant a sweet potato, which symbolizes an offer of friendship from one human being to another. Their interdependence opens a space for ethical responsibility through recognition of the other as "youman" and "friend," or, as Lowe describes it, as "mutual humanization of the teacher and the student" ("Transcendence" 154).

Jefferson's Transformation

A final example of constitutive rhetoric in *Lesson* is Jefferson's personal transformation and his writing in his diary. Despite the injustice of Jefferson's conviction under the felony murder rule, his punishment ultimately results in the community's redemption. While this redemption does not justify the injustice, bringing Jefferson back into the community as a man who dies with dignity allows for him to serve as a hero for the community[16] and for his own self-transformation from a "hog" to a member of the human community.

Jefferson's transformation from being labeled a "hog" at his trial and acting out as a hog in his prison cell to standing as a man occurs in small stages, as indicated above. He tells Grant to thank the children for bringing him pecans, and he tells Nannan he is strong and loves her. The night before his execution he writes in his diary: "when i was a little boy i was a waterboy an rode the cart but now i got to be a man an set in a cher" (234). He demonstrates his dignity and strength when his head is shaved and he asks one deputy, Claude, how his wife and son are. His final act of dignity is walking to the electric chair. Paul, who observes the execution, later reports to Grant that "[h]e was the strongest man [there]. . . . When Vincent asked him if he had any last words, he looked at the preacher and said, 'Tell Nannan I walked.' And straight he walked, Grant Wiggins. Straight he walked" (253–54).

Although we see Jefferson's transformation through his actions, it is Jefferson's diary that gives us insight into his mind. Many readers have praised the chapter containing Jefferson's diary as the poetic centerpiece of the novel (Lowe, "Transcendence" 159; Gaines, "Influence" 88). Gaines has said that he did not know the novel would contain a diary but that it evolved, and he viewed it as an "epiphany" ("Influence" 90). Gaines stated, "We don't know him, I think, until he starts his diary. We don't know him until we hear him speak. We don't know a man until he speaks. He's trying to say something, to show who he is. We have these pictures of him provided by Grant, but we don't know what's inside of him. And that's what I needed to do" (88).

Jefferson's diary is the mode in which he gives an account of himself in response to Grant's call. Jefferson addresses his thoughts to Grant ("mr wigin"):

> mr wigin you say you like what I got here but you say you stil cant giv me
> a a jus a b cause you say I aint gone deep in me yet an you kno I can if I
> try hard an when I ax you what you mean deep in me you say jus say whats
> on my mind so one day you can be save an you can save the chiren . . . an
> you look so tied sometime mr wigin I just feel like tellin you I like you but
> I don't know how to say this cause i aint never say it to nobody before an
> nobody aint never say it to me.   (228)

Jefferson has never thought or written so much: "I try an think what you mean I got mo cause I aint done this much thinkin and this much writin in all my life befor" (229). Grant's responses influence Jefferson's questions about what it means to love Nannan; what it means to act like a human being by crying when Bok gives him a marble and his little cousin kisses him; and how Paul is decent, but Clark is not. Moreover, Jefferson apologizes to Grant for "how I talk that day when I was mad at you an say them nasty things bout her [Vivian]" (232). He also explains that during Grant's last visit, he cried because "you been so good to me mr wigin an nobody aint never been that good to me an make me think im somebody" (232).

The night before his execution, when he is sleepless (along with the entire prison), Jefferson thinks about the fateful day he went off with Brother and Bear and accepts his responsibility: "I aint had no bisnes going ther wit brother an bear cause they aint no good an im gon be meetin them soon" (233). Jefferson's diary is an example of constitutive rhetoric described by White because Jefferson's entries reflect and shape his relationship with Grant and with the community. The diary entries also demonstrate a relational ethics of vulnerability and interdependence described by Butler:

> In speaking to another, and at another's request, about how one has lived,
> one is responding to a request, and one is attempting to establish or re-
> establish a certain bond, to honor the fact that one has been addressed
> from elsewhere. . . . Giving an account is thus also a kind of showing of one-
> self, a showing for the purpose of testing whether the account seems
> right, whether it is understandable by the other, who "receives" the account
> through one set of norms or another.   (*Giving* 131)

Gaines has similarly described the aim of the diary "to show that he [Jefferson] had been trying to say something, that he had accepted his position, not being able to express his humanity, and now he was called upon to do so" (Lowe, "Interview" 305). Under the norms of the black community, Jefferson is innocent, and he transforms from a "hog" to a human being who stands tall, as his last diary entry promises: "good by mr wigin tell them im strong tell them im a man" (234). His transformation reflects a norm deeply valued in Gaines's work and echoed in the dedication of *The Autobiography of Miss Jane Pittman* to his aunt Augusteen Jefferson, "who did not walk a day in her life but who taught me the importance of standing."

Jefferson stands because he is uplifted, and that uplifts the community and the reader:

> He's talking about dying, and "I'm gonna die," and says the bluebird is sing-ing, and he pauses for a while, and says I hear my teeth hitting, and my heart, but I'm strong. . . . All these things—that is the uplifting in his mind. He's not going to be this coward. . . . He's not going to eat a whole gallon of ice cream with a pot spoon. He's going to eat a little Dixie cup. All of these little things elevate him—to salvation, to the uplifting of the soul of that person.   (Gaines, "Influence" 90)

The interaction between Jefferson and Grant demonstrates constitutive rhetoric that allows Jefferson's voice to be heard and allows both men to develop an ethi-cal responsibility to the community. Just as Jefferson accepts the call to be a hero, Grant accepts the call to be a teacher, which Paul, the white deputy, ac-knowledges when he brings Grant the diary and tells him, "You're one great teacher" (254). Perhaps Grant is one great teacher because he has recognized the other and realizes he exists only by virtue of his students.

As Jones imagines, Grant will accept the identity as the community's teacher and will relate as teacher in a more authentic way, shown by his statement to Jefferson that he had never previously taught about dignity, identity, or loving because the whites wanted him to teach only "reading, writing, and arithme-tic," but that he hated himself for doing so (S. Jones 45; Gaines, *Lesson* 192). The likelihood that Grant will accept the role of teacher for the plantation is also shown by his invitation to Paul to come to the class and "tell his students about Jefferson's dignity and courage" (S. Jones 48). As a result of his interrelationship with Jefferson, Grant cannot leave, as Gaines indicated in an interview: "Grant must go back to that school and that's when he turns around to his kids and he is crying in the very last sentence. He's gonna put everything now into being a better teacher and try to save these kids" (Gaines, "*MELUS* Interview" 205).

In conclusion, from the perspective of constitutive rhetoric, the racist and un-just community created in *A Lesson Before Dying* by the negative ethos of la-beling Jefferson a "hog" and convicting him of felony murder is transformed through a healing and positive rhetoric. Jefferson stands as a man at the end of the novel, and his transformation results in at least one white man, Paul, accept-ing their common humanity.[17] Paul not only tells Grant that he is "one great teacher," but Paul also says, "Allow me to be your friend" (254–55). The greater positive effect of Jefferson's transformation impacts the black community, which gains a teacher and a hero. Finally, as Lowe observes, Grant and Jefferson be-come "partners" through Jefferson's diary, which results in Jefferson being the "savior of Grant, so Grant could save the children" (Lowe, "Interview" 300).

NOTES

[1] White gives an analysis of different types of persuasion in *Philoctetes*, in which both Neoptolemus and Odysseus try to convince Philoctetes, who is living alone, to return to the community with the magical bow and arrow Heracles gave him. Neoptolemus's honest persuasion recognizes Philoctetes's full worth by trying to convince him to return so that his foul-smelling wounds may be healed and his fate may be fulfilled, whereas Odysseus's manipulative persuasion uses Philoctetes as a means to an end by trying to convince him to board the ship where they may steal his bow and arrow (4–7).

[2] Lowe discusses Gaines's decision to set the story in 1948 rather than 1988, as Gaines had originally planned ("Transcendence" 142–43).

[3] The part of the novel in which Grant is ignored by the white saleslady when he buys the radio is based on a similar event that happened to Gaines when he was filming one of his short stories, as he tells Lowe ("Interview" 310).

[4] This essay quotes the 1994 Vintage edition of *Lesson*.

[5] Guzmon's counsel made the following argument about mistaken identification during the guilt phase of the trial: "Now, you know, understand this man is, as I said, an unauthorized immigrant, a wet-back, whose hair is brown, and whose skin is probably about the color of mine, . . . but they all look like that, all three of them look like that. . . ." During the punishment phase of trial, his counsel reminded the jury that the defendant was "a wet-back, an illegal alien," and argued, "We also had [a psychologist] tell us about the attitudes . . . of the Latin Americans, wherein they can't take responsibility. They have to pass away everything as somebody else's fault. . . . I'll be frank with you. No sense hiding it from you. I think you knew it. [The defendant] was taking the position that [the psychologist] pointed out. He wouldn't take the responsibility" (*Ex parte Guzmon* 730, 731–732). I thank my colleague Malinda Seymore for directing me to the *Guzmon* and *Goodwin* cases.

[6] This essay quotes from the version of "Writing *A Lesson Before Dying*" published in the *Southern Review*.

[7] Many legal scholars, such as Friedman, McCord, and Renken, have criticized the felony murder rule and *Tison v. Arizona*.

[8] The law in Louisiana in 1948 can be gleaned from E.L.E.'s note that in 1942 Louisiana adopted the felony murder doctrine to dangerous felonies such as robbery (326). Bennett explains that Louisiana codified the common-law rule for felony murder and for parties, in "that all those who participate in any way in the commission of a crime are liable as principals" (249–50). Moreover, under the modern Louisiana criminal code, amended in 1973, in order to be convicted of a first-degree murder (capital murder), a defendant who is a party to felony murder must have the specific intent to commit the felony and that the victim be killed. See the historical notes to La. Rev. Stat. Ann. 14:30 (*Louisiana Laws Revised Statutes*).

[9] According to news reports, after European manufacturers banned the United States from using their drugs for executions, several death row convicts suffered barbaric deaths when prison officials turned to new drug cocktails that were kept secret (Levs et al.).

[10] By this, Stupp means the requirement to remember Jefferson as an individual and not in the coerced role of hero.

[11] At the Christmas pageant, Grant reflects, "I was not happy. I had heard the same carols all my life, seen the same little play, with the same mistakes in grammar. . . . Next

year it would be the same, and the year after that, the same again. Vivian said things were changing. But where were they changing?" (151).

[12] Gaines has similarly stated, "I don't know if I could tell anybody how to live. I don't know how to live" ("Lesson for Living" 33).

[13] For a discussion of masculinity in the novel, see S. Jones.

[14] Lowe describes the scene as "epiphanic": "Jefferson's final conversion, which leads to his diary, comes in a powerful scene that summons forth Grant's most eloquent rhetorical effects" ("Transcendence" 158). Doyle comments that "the central lesson of the novel [is] Grant's lesson to Jefferson on the nature of heroism" (*Voices* 220).

[15] Stupp argues that "Jefferson's diary . . . signals his resistance to the narrative the community fashions to coincide with his death" and that viewing his diary for its future use for the community overlooks "the voice of a human being facing death" (49).

[16] Stupp claims that scholarship that focuses on the redemption of the community turns Jefferson into an "animated corpse," rather than an individual (46–47).

[17] Ed Piacentino and Carlyle Thompson both emphasize the possibility of racial reconciliation in the novel, and Lowe notes that "the lesson . . . transcends race" ("Transcendence" 153).

The Car as a Vehicle for Teaching Gaines's "A Long Day in November"

Jennifer Nolan

The automobile is as ubiquitous in twentieth-century American literature as it became in twentieth-century American life, and its place there is equally central, from iconic American novels such as *The Great Gatsby, The Sound and the Fury, Native Son*, and *The Color Purple* to short stories by literary giants, such as Flannery O'Connor's "A Good Man Is Hard to Find" and Ralph Ellison's "Cadillac Flambé."[1] Indeed, locating examples is made difficult only by the number of options from which one might choose, and this ubiquity means that students in most American literature courses will have a built-in frame of reference for considering the car's symbolic function in American literature throughout the century. It is within this context that I teach Ernest Gaines's short story "A Long Day in November," in which the narrator, a six-year-old boy named Sonny, chronicles the day that his father's divided obligations to his car and his family come to a head.

While any number of works in which the automobile plays an important role could be paired fruitfully with "A Long Day in November" (Ellison's "Cadillac Flambé," also prominently featuring a car burning, may come to mind for many), I find using another 1960s short story, Joyce Carol Oates's "Where Are You Going, Where Have You Been?," to work particularly well in an undergraduate classroom. Each story takes place within a cultural milieu that is changing rapidly (in part) because of the mobility offered by automobiles. In "A Long Day," Eddie (Sonny's father) is enticed by the perceived freedom and mobility the car offers him as an African American man in the Jim Crow South, just as in "Where Are You Going," Connie (the protagonist) is enticed by the perceived freedom and mobility the car offers her as a suburban teenager. In each case, however, the car threatens these characters' places within their families, and the costs associated with the car ultimately outweigh the perceived benefits. Each story also raises discomforting questions about the relationship between the car and masculinity, as well as the perception of the automobile as a threat to women and family, both of which lead to lively classroom discussions. Students are also attracted to the youthfulness of the protagonists in these works; "A Long Day" features Sonny as our narrator, while "Where Are You Going" is related in the third person from a teenaged Connie's perspective. Further, the contrast between the immediacy evoked through Sonny's youthful voice and Oates's more distanced use of third-person limited provides a valuable point of comparison for discussing authorial uses of narration and point of view.

Before beginning discussion of either work, students should be provided with background regarding the role of the car in midcentury American life. The depth of this overview will depend on the content of the class, but at minimum it will be helpful to spend some time establishing the effects of the increasing availability of the car within each of the communities depicted. Perhaps the most useful resource for background material on the symbolic function of the car for African Americans is Paul Gilroy's "Driving while Black." As Gilroy discusses, despite, or perhaps because of, structural, social, and commercial attempts to limit black mobility, "cars seem to have conferred or rather suggested dimensions of citizenship and status that were blocked by formal politics and violently inhibited by informal codes" for African Americans (94). This, he contends, raises "the provocative possibility that their distinctive history of propertylessness and material deprivation has inclined them towards a disproportionate investment in particular forms of property that are publicly visible and the status that corresponds to them" (84).[2] As we will see, in "A Long Day" this is further complicated by the socioeconomic context, which makes the car, and the fact that Eddie was able to save up for it, both more meaningful for him and also more destructive for his family. In the postwar era, cars held increasingly symbolic importance for suburban teenagers as well. As cars became ever more ubiquitous with the rise of the suburb and the two-car family, Americans saw a resultant rise in the availability of cars to teens and in anxieties about the roles cars played in teen culture and the distance that increased access to mobility allowed from parental supervision, particularly for young women.[3] The association of the car with teenaged male identity and prowess and the perils these create for young women is reflected both in Oates's short story and the *Life* magazine article from which it was inspired, Don Moser's "The Pied Piper of Tucson," and it can be fruitful to include both if time permits.

Once the historical and symbolic function of the car in these communities is established, students are prepared to consider both texts. Our discussion of "A Long Day" begins with narration. Mary Ellen Doyle offers a useful analysis of Gaines's narrative techniques in his collection *Bloodline* in chapter 3 of her book *Voices from the Quarters*. As she explains, "though less attention has been given to the techniques of *Bloodline* than to its themes, Gaines himself has always insisted that technique is the central fact of literary creation" (46). According to Doyle, what is innovative about the narration of the first two stories in the collection is that they "are told not so much *by* as *through* the children, in what may be some of the most subtly nuanced points of view in American fiction. . . . In Gaines's stories, the children seem to speak in their own voices; readers are absorbed into their views, diction, limits of perception and explanation. Thus engaged, readers' emotions can be focused and sustained" (51–52).

With this in mind, I ask my students to look carefully at Sonny and consider why Gaines has chosen to use him as our narrator, which raises a number of fruitful questions: what is revealed through Sonny's narration? What is concealed? How are our opinions of the characters, and in particular Eddie, shaped by Sonny's narrative? I also find it useful to ask my students to consider how the narrative would be different had other characters told this story, which leads both to thoughtful considerations of what Eddie and his wife, Amy, would reveal and conceal, as well as a bit of humor when we reimagine the story through Gran'mon's eyes. By focusing on how Sonny depicts Eddie and contrasting this with how others would depict him, it becomes evident that Eddie is a good father whose priorities have become skewed. That Sonny loves his father is never in doubt; from his repeated reassurances to Eddie of this fact to his dislike of his Gran'mon for shooting at Eddie and trying to set his mother up with Freddie Jackson, Sonny's love for his father is amply evidenced. What has been cast into doubt are Eddie's priorities. This is perhaps best exemplified in the passage where Sonny admits to his father that he wet himself in school, which underscores both the close bond between father and son as well as how this relationship has become disrupted:

> "How come you not in school this evening?" Daddy asks.
> "I wee-weed on myself," I say.
> I tell Daddy because I know Daddy ain't go'n whip me.
> "You peed on yourself at school?" Daddy asks. "Sonny, I thought you was a big boy. That's something little babies do."
> "Miss Hebert want to see you and Mama," I say.
> "I don't have time to see nobody now," Daddy says. "I got my own troubles." (42)[4]

Through juxtaposing Sonny's admission to his father—and only to his father, despite having seen his mother, uncle, and grandmother directly after returning home from school—with Eddie's current focus on himself, Gaines simultaneously emphasizes the trust between father and son and how that trust has been ruptured through the introduction of the car.

This leads naturally to a discussion of Eddie's relationship with his car. That Amy sees the car as the cause for his changed behavior toward his family is evident in the way she characterizes Eddie's relationship with it during their fight on the morning she leaves:

> "I told you once," Mama says, "you not getting on me. Get on your car."
> "Honey, respect the child," Daddy says.
> "How come you don't respect him?" Mama says. "How come you don't come home sometime and respect him? How come you don't leave that car alone and come home and respect him? How come you don't respect him? You the one need to respect him."   (12)

As Valerie Babb has discussed, "[W]hile for Eddie the car is a symbol of masculinity and freedom within a society that traditionally has denied both to black men, Amy views it as an intruder usurping the attention Eddie should give to his family" (*Ernest Gaines* 17). Coupling this with Gilroy's analysis of the car as disproportionately meaningful for those who have less access to ownership of property and other material objects helps students to understand the reasons for the depth of Eddie's attachment and, importantly, for Gaines's mostly sympathetic depiction of him through Sonny's eyes. Placing the story within the broader context of the historical and symbolic meanings of the automobile for African American men struggling to define their manhood in a world that seeks to deny it provides a richer understanding of Gaines's use of narration in this work. Through Sonny, Gaines simultaneously demonstrates the detrimental effects of overemphasizing the car within this family and community and critiques larger societal values that created the context for the car's attractiveness to Eddie, whose "enthusiasm for the car and subsequent inability to see beyond its windscreen reveal how [his] conceptions of freedom have been transformed, compromised, distracted, and diverted" (Gilroy, "Driving" 86). Emphasizing the symbolic importance of the car within this historical context also helps students to understand one of their most frequently asked questions: why the car must be destroyed, not simply sold, to restore order. As Doyle explains, "the luring but threatening world outside his family nest is symbolized by the car, a false symbol of masculine freedom and control; when it is destroyed in the biggest communal fire of all, genuine masculine maturity, responsibility, presence, modeling, and support return to Sonny's life" (*Voices* 55). Thus, when Eddie asks Amy if she thinks they'll ever get another car, her response focuses on the symbolic rather than the physical: "When you learn how to act with one. . . . I ain't got nothing against cars." Eddie replies, "I guess you right, honey. . . . I was going a little too far" (77). She is not against cars, per se, but rather what they represent. Sonny's final reflections as he falls asleep, his long day over and his family complete, again reinforce the symbolic role of the car and its deleterious effects:

> We got Daddy's car and brought it all the way back here. Daddy and them turned the car over and Daddy poured some gas on it and set it on fire.

> Daddy ain't got no more car now. . . . I know my lesson. I ain't go'n wee-wee on myself no more. Daddy's going to school with me tomorrow. I'm go'n show him I can beat Billy Joe Martin shooting marbles. I can shoot all over Billy Joe Martin. And I can beat him running, too. He thinks he can run fast. I'm go'n show Daddy I can beat him running. (79)

Through the use of stream of consciousness, this ending offers one more opportunity for a discussion of Gaines's narrative techniques, and our focus on the car prepares students to understand the significance of Sonny's thoughts jumping from the car burning to his newly found confidence that he will be able to best his tormentor, Billy Joe Martin, when his father accompanies him to school.

The approach to "A Long Day" described thus far would easily fill a class period and can be successfully used as a unit unto itself. However, I find discussion of the story is richest when I pair it with one of many texts in which the car also plays a central role, such as Oates's "Where Are You Going." Though they are set in very different contexts, each of these stories raises similar anxieties about how the accessibility of the automobile threatens social and family life, highlights the relationship between the car and masculinity and the detrimental effects this has on women, and features youthful protagonists using different narrative styles.

Both Oates's story and the *Life* magazine article that prompted it illustrate how car-centric mid-1960s teen culture had become and how removed this culture was from parental influence, and thus I find it useful to assign at least the opening passages of Moser's article in addition to Oates's story in courses where I plan to focus on the role of the car.[5] As the article begins, the car is the central figure cruising through the world it has wrought: "At dusk in Tucson, as the stark, yellow-flared mountains begin to blur against the sky, the golden car slowly cruises Speedway. Smoothly it rolls down the long, divided avenue, past the supermarkets, the gas stations and the motels; past the twist joints, the sprawling drive-in restaurants" (23). In his easy acceptance by the teens and their willingness to keep his secrets, the murderer Charles Schmid embodied suburban parents' worst nightmares about the freedom cars allowed for their children. As Oates explained, "he may or may not have had actual accomplices, but his bizarre activities were known among a circle of teen-agers in the Tucson area; for some reason they kept his secrets, deliberately did not inform parents or police. It was this fact, not the fact of the mass murderer himself, that struck me at the time" ("When Characters" H1).

Once this background on Oates's story has been established, we begin our discussion by having students identify the thematic similarities they see between the stories, focusing particularly on the relationships between the main characters and cars. Like Eddie, Connie is enticed by the perceived freedom offered to her by the car. Though she herself cannot yet drive, she spends her summer nights at "a drive-in restaurant where older kids hung out" (60). Similarly, like Eddie, it is her participation in this car culture that comes between Connie and

her family; it is only through being at the drive-in that she comes to her tormentor Arnold Friend's attention and is ultimately driven away (literally and figuratively) from her family in his car. As in "A Long Day," the car creates a divide
between parents and children—in this case, an insurmountable one. One reason for this divide pertains to the relationship between the car and the man who
drives it. In both stories, the men believe that their masculinity is tied to their
cars. In Gaines, we see this through the attention that Eddie lavishes on his car
instead of on his wife, while in Oates, Arnold Friend derives almost all of his
power through his car, to the extent that he literally becomes less steady on his
feet the farther he gets from it. Thus both stories suggest a problematic relationship between cars and masculinity that poses a threat to women and family.
Focusing on these similarities, and how the authors depict them within the communities they have chosen, leads to lively classroom discussions and engagement with the texts.

Focusing on these similarities also leads naturally to a discussion about the
differences between the stories and the relationship depicted in each between
gender and cars. Several questions present themselves: why is Eddie able to be
successfully reunited with his family when Connie is not? What roles do family,
community, and gender play in the different endings of each story? What type
of masculinity does the car confer on Arnold Friend? How and why is masculinity defined differently in "A Long Day"? Ultimately, how similar and/or different are the messages conveyed by Oates and Gaines about the car (or, more
broadly, technology) and gender? What do the concerns expressed in each story
reveal about what is valued and/or feared in each of these communities?

Discussion of these thematic differences also prepares students to think critically about the different narrative techniques used by each author. Though both
stories focus on a youthful protagonist, Sonny narrates the events of his day as
they happen, while Oates uses a more distanced third-person limited narration
from Connie's perspective. As Doyle has noted, while most authors would use a
third-person limited viewpoint for a narrative in the present tense, Gaines employs the first person to do so, which "creates a 'now' effect and an instant immediacy and engagement with [Sonny] and his situation" without relying upon a
narrator separate from the child (*Voices* 51). Through using what Doyle has
termed "camcorder narration," in which "everything the child is aware of is re-
ported," including that which he "see[s] and hear[s] but could never understand,
remember, and repeat" (52), Gaines is able to present Sonny's perspective with
less visible authorial influence than he would had he used a third-person limited,
which is essential for building our empathy toward Eddie and our desire for him
to be reunited with his family. It is through Sonny's unfiltered thoughts that we
understand his love for his father and the importance of his family, as in the following observations he makes: "I like Uncle Al because he's good, and he never
talk bad about Daddy" (20); "I like Uncle Al, but I don't like old Gran'mon much.
Gran'mon's always talking bad about Daddy" (78); "I'm glad I'm not a bird. No
daddy, no mama—I'm glad I'm not a bird" (38). While Gaines's use of narration

can certainly be discussed absent an accompanying work, contrasting lines such as these to the more distanced, past-tense descriptions of Connie's thoughts and actions—e.g., "She thought, I'm not going to see my mother again. She thought, I'm not going to sleep in my bed again. Her bright green blouse was all wet" (74–75)—clearly draws attention to the immediacy evoked through Gaines's narration and helps students to better understand the technical accomplishments of his work.

Similar comparisons can be made with many other narratives given the ubiquity of the car in twentieth-century American literature and culture, and the techniques outlined above can be adapted successfully to a host of other pairings. Focusing on the symbolic function of the car in "A Long Day in November" offers an accessible lens through which to explore other thematic and narrative elements central to Gaines's oeuvre, such as masculinity, identity, community, and narration, while simultaneously placing Gaines in conversation with a broad range of works of twentieth-century American literature and culture.

NOTES

[1] For more on the role of the car in Faulkner, see Clarke. For more on Ellison, see Packer 189–230.

[2] See also Packer 189–230; Seiler 105–28.

[3] For further discussion about changing gender roles and the two-car family, see Packer 27–75. For further information about the fears and perils enabled through the role of the car in 1950s American teen dating rituals, see Dorr.

[4] This essay quotes from the version of "A Long Day" published in the 1968 Vintage edition of *Bloodline*.

[5] This choice is prompted in part by Oates's indication that these are the lines that most likely influenced her story, which seems borne out by the imagery from Moser's article mirrored there. As Oates explains, "I don't remember any longer where I first read about 'The Pied Piper'—very likely in *Life* magazine. I do recall deliberately not reading the full article because I didn't want to be distracted by too much detail" ("When Characters" H1).

"Blues Fallin' Down Like Hail": Reading "The Sky Is Gray" as a Blues Narrative

Qiana Whitted

Calloused fingertips easily mark Monsieur Bayonne as a bluesman in Ernest Gaines's short story "The Sky Is Gray." The young African American boy named James who narrates the story observes that "the tip of Monsieur Bayonne's finger is some hard, 'cause he's always playing on that guitar. If we sit outside at night we can always hear Monsieur Bayonne playing on his guitar. Sometimes we leave him out there playing on the guitar" (85).[1] "The Sky Is Gray" is one of Gaines's earliest published works, first appearing in *Negro Digest* in 1963 and reprinted five years later in the collection *Bloodline*, and while Monsieur Bayonne is a relatively minor figure in this story, the interminable sounds of his guitar resonate throughout the Louisiana writer's career. Again and again, Gaines's explorations of blackness, southern manhood, and religious conflict in the Jim Crow South are set against the aural landscape of the blues: from the restless evenings in *Of Love and Dust* (1967) when Jim Kelly strums "Key to the Highway" on his porch, to the consoling sounds of the little radio in *A Lesson Before Dying* (1993) that fill Jefferson's jail cell in the weeks before his execution.

Nevertheless, it is not the mere invocation of a guitar, a jukebox, a radio show, or even the hard tip of a finger that catalogs a work like "The Sky Is Gray" as a blues narrative. As a subgenre of African American storytelling and art, the blues narrative foregrounds the aesthetic, thematic, and emotional qualities of the oral musical tradition made famous during the first half of the twentieth century by performers like W. C. Handy, Bessie Smith, Robert Johnson, Ma Rainey, Lead Belly, Big Bill Broonzy, Muddy Waters, and Lightnin' Hopkins. Often blues narratives draw on the already rich figurative language and style of the song lyrics, with images of trains and traveling feet, desire and heartache, to capture a downhearted tone (though the blues can be exuberant and bouncy too). In adapting the music's lament about the troubles of the day, the creative writer's aim for the blues narrative is less about imitating sound and more about recalling the conditions of sorrow and survival that give the verses their plaintive, playful form. The writer Ralph Ellison speaks to the multiple registers of blues expression in his well-known description from a 1945 review of Richard Wright's *Black Boy*:

> The blues are an impulse to keep the painful details and episodes of a brutal experience alive in one's aching consciousness, to finger its jagged grain, and to transcend it, not by the consolation of philosophy but by squeezing from it a near-tragic, near-comic lyricism. As a form the blues is an autobiographical chronicle of personal catastrophe expressed lyrically. (78–79)

Here Ellison locates trauma at the center of the blues and characterizes its cathartic plea to wrestle with what pains us the most—"to finger its jagged grain"—as a narrative art. By tapping into this impulse, Gaines joins Ellison and a larger community of American writers that use the hard-won wisdom and tragicomic sensibility of the blues to deepen the reader's understanding of the existential questioning that is born out of individual and collective black suffering.

American literary studies and cultural studies scholarship has frequently explored the multidimensional relationships between blues music and African American writing, focusing particularly on individual works by Langston Hughes, Sterling Brown, James Baldwin, Amiri Baraka, Sonia Sanchez, August Wilson, Toni Morrison, Gayl Jones, Kevin Young, and Tyehimba Jess. Other critics take a broader, more conceptual view by identifying elements of the blues tradition in literary representations of spirituals and jazz, in the works of black women writers like Sherley Anne Williams, and in African American children's literature.[2] The exchange between blues music and literary discourse can also be reciprocal, as in Adam Gussow's analysis of Mamie Smith's "Crazy Blues," which draws upon critical readings of Rudolph Fisher's short story "City of Refuge" and Albert Murray's novel *Train Whistle Guitar* to argue for the song's social implications. Likewise, Ayana Smith reads elements of the African American signifying tradition (as articulated by Henry Louis Gates, Jr.) in the narrative lyrics performed by Charley Patton, Ma Rainey, and Robert Johnson.

In the classroom, reading "The Sky Is Gray" as a blues narrative can provide students with a profoundly immersive learning experience, one that calls upon a range of interdisciplinary material to advance the literary and cultural interpretation of the text. Steven C. Tracy's anthology *Write Me a Few of Your Lines: A Blues Reader* is a valuable resource for providing students and instructors with background on blues aesthetics, starting with debates over the historical roots of blues sound and instrumentation from West Africa and through the song and poetry of enslaved American blacks. The collection gathers together poetry, short stories, personal essays, liner notes, and cultural criticism on blues style, performance, and social content, along with an extensive discography and bibliography of primary and secondary sources. Particularly important for the study of Gaines is the section titled "Literature, Criticism, and the Blues," in which Tracy's introductory remarks list how literary works use and manifest blues music. Literary works

> seek to define the blues and its philosophy;
> celebrate the blues as a source of inspiration and transcendence;
> employ blues as an emotional, psychic, spiritual, community, political resource;
> use the traditional forms of the blues;
> experiment with the forms of the blues;
> use the traditional subject matter of the blues;

use nontraditional subject matter in combination with other identifiable
  blues elements;

pay tribute to a particular blues performer;

depict the exploitation and suffering of a performer or an archetypal blues
  figure;

depict the exploitation and suffering of a person or group of people;

challenge the currently prevailing notion of order, propriety, and
  morality.   (384)

Words of caution accompany this extensive list, as Tracy also notes that writers
may deploy any variation of these features literally or figuratively and combine
their understanding of specific blues forms with other tropes and vernacular traditions in African American culture. He concludes that "the literary critic, then,
must attempt to identify the nature of the oral blues tradition, and then open up
to the multiplicitous ways that those characteristics may be engaged, re-
envisioned, and utilized by a writer" (384). While only used copies of Tracy's
anthology are available as of this writing, Tracy's chapter on the "blues novel" in
the *Cambridge Companion to the African American Novel* offers a strong and
succinct explanation of these characteristics as well. The unit touches on Tracy's
eleven points, and though his primary focus is on the novel form, the chapter
offers critical reflections on theme, language, and structure, with examples that
are relevant to an analysis of Gaines's story.

More recently, Daniel Barlow's important essay "Blues Narrative Form, African American Fiction, and the African Diaspora" builds upon and productively
complicates Tracy's methods by arguing that the formal qualities of blues deserve more attention from students and scholars of literature. Through a survey
of one hundred novels and narratives, Barlow proposes his own "taxonomy of
techniques" (141) that extends the scope of the blues narrative into the rhetorical dimensions of texts that do not explicitly reference blues themes. The six terms
that he adopts to outline the blues narrative form include "multimedial combi-
nations," "intermedial references," "extended formal analogy or mimesis," "strategic variation," "vernacular delivery," and "participatory musicality." Barlow does
not overlook blues lyrics or performative elements in his analysis, but he suggests that a more narratological approach can help readers to understand not only
"what a given novel is about" but also "*how* narratives translate the blues and
why the history of that specific tradition of translation matters" (136). His essay
is particularly useful for exploring the distinctive voice and rhythmic structure
of "The Sky Is Gray."

And finally, our study should be mindful of—though not inhibited by—
Gaines's own observations about the role of the blues in his creative process.
He has said, for instance, "I think I have learned as much about writing about
my people by listening to blues and jazz and spirituals as I have learned by
reading novels. But the rural blues, maybe because of my background, is my
choice in music" (*Mozart* 15). Gaines calls attention to the value of the rural

blues as a storytelling medium in his personal writings, placing Bessie Smith's account of the Great Flood of 1927 alongside William Faulkner's (27, 132) and crediting the Lightnin' Hopkins song "Tim Moore's Farm" with inspiring both his story "Three Men" and his novel *Of Love and Dust* (15–16). Much of the scholarship on Gaines published since the 1970s acknowledges these influences, though critical discussions of "The Sky Is Gray" tend to place more emphasis on themes of black masculinity, religion, and coming of age; representations of segregation-era prejudice; and narrative voice.[3] Nevertheless, in their introductory essay to Gaines's 2006 collection, *Mozart and Leadbelly: Stories and Essays*, Marcia Gaudet and Reggie Young name singers like Smith, Hopkins, Lead Belly, and Big Bill Broonzy as Gaines's literary "relatives" who shaped "the cultural environment that permeated the plantation quarters where he spent many of his formative years and to which he returned to find his voice as a writer" (xvi).

Guided by Gaines's distinctive voice and his deference to the "sharp picture" that only the blues performer can create (Gaines, *Mozart* 132), my classroom discussion of "The Sky Is Gray" foregrounds the discursive interplay between literature and the blues by paying special attention to how the first-person perspective is crafted in the narrative. Next we shift to close textual analysis of the story through listening sessions of songs that explore the allegorical stages of the daylong journey James takes with his mother to the dentist. Rounding out our lessons are comparisons and contrasts with more recent blues narratives that include the comic book series *Bayou*, by Jeremy Love, and the hip-hop album *Good Kid, M.A.A.D City*, by Kendrick Lamar.

James's troubles begin with a toothache. The young boy tries unsuccessfully to hide the pain from his mother, Octavia, knowing the financial hardship that a trip to the dentist will bring their family if she misses a day's work in the field. The excursion that the pair comes to take into the nearby town of Bayonne— first on a segregated bus, then on foot in the cold—sets the narrative tempo of the people and the situations that James encounters in 1940s Louisiana. As the oldest child, James takes very seriously the responsibilities that his mother bestows on him while his father is away in the army: "I can't ever be scared and I can't ever cry" (84). He seldom speaks more than a line or two of dialogue at once, always careful to punctuate his responses with "ma'am" and "sir." Yet through the benefit of his first-person perspective, the reader is privy to the youth's unspoken anxieties and longings, from the fears he experiences when hearing another patient screaming in the dentist's chair to his wish to pick enough cotton in the summer to buy his mother a red coat. As a result, James's distinctive voice is central to any consideration of how "The Sky Is Gray" blends the joy and sorrow of the blues into an eight-year-old's worldview. While young James may not sing or play a musical instrument, it is the music of his narration, not Monsieur Bayonne's guitar, that becomes the fullest embodiment of a blues ethos.

Consider, for example, the scene when the dentist refuses to see James until after lunch, forcing him and his mother to wait outside on the cold sidewalk:

> "You hungry?" she says. She says it like she's mad at me, like I'm the cause of everything.
> "No, ma'am," I say.
> "You want eat and walk back, or you rather don't eat and ride?"
> "I ain't hungry," I say.
> I ain't just hungry, but I'm cold, too. I'm so hungry and cold I want to cry. And look like I'm getting colder and colder. My feet done got numb. I try to work my toes, but I don't even feel them. Look like I'm go'n die. Look like I'm go'n stand right here and freeze to death. I think 'bout home. I think 'bout Val and Auntie and Ty and Louis and Walker. It's 'bout twelve o'clock and I know they eating dinner now. I can hear Ty making jokes. He done forgot 'bout getting up early this morning and right now he's probably making jokes. Always trying to make somebody laugh. I wish I was right there listening to him. Give anything in the world if I was home round the fire. (106)

Though others rarely hear him speak, James's complex inner deliberations are crafted in a colloquial style that draws on the black southern vernacular of the people around him. What results is a conversation with the reader—a "participatory musicality," in Barlow's terms (146)—that is shot through with the kind of suffering that makes James sound much older and wiser than his years. There is levity here too, and a poignant wit and imagination that transforms his childhood vulnerability into hopefulness. The blues are made up of these seemingly contradictory forces of despair and transcendence, what the poet Kevin Young refers to as the series of "reversals": "survival and loss, sin and regret, boasts and heartbreak, leaving and loving, a pigfoot and a bottle of beer" (foreword 11). Thoughts of home, of laughter at his younger brother's jokes, become the resource that James relies upon to withstand the hunger and cold of this moment.

To fully appreciate the blues spirit of what James endures, however, our study of "The Sky Is Gray" cannot sit silently on the page. This is a story that benefits from being heard aloud, and in the classroom, I make time for a public reading of the two-page first section. Students are asked to listen for the rhythmic patterns of James's narration, to note the manner in which phrases, words, and sounds are repeated for emphasis through anaphora and epistrophe. Of the trip into town, James begins, "I'm go'n . . . we go'n . . . and go." Observing his mother: "I know what she thinking . . . she's thinking if . . . she's thinking 'bout. . . ." Of his toothache: "It's been hurting me and hurting me. . . ." and "Sometimes is just hurt, hurt, hurt. Lord, have mercy" (83–84). Together, the components of the young boy's narrative voice offer a strong example of what Barlow characterizes as "vernacular delivery," or "the textualization of flexible pitch areas, tonal patterns, and vocal texture; compositional traits like polyphony and tempo; and generic propensities of the blues such as second-person address, irony, and parody" (145). Inspired by the performance of bluesmen like Monsieur Bayonne in the quarter, James incorporates these devices throughout his telling, thereby creating an immersive experience for his own listeners.

Compare the vernacular delivery (form) and thematic reversals (content) of James's thoughts to a song from the 1940s like Huddie "Lead Belly" Ledbetter's "Good Morning Blues." Born in Louisiana and raised in East Texas, Lead Belly's experiences in and out of prison and as a farmhand led him to develop a singing style that incorporated plantation hollers and work songs into his music. The song also provides an excellent introduction to the style that Gaines refers to as the rural blues—also called "folk" or "country" blues—with the traditional vocal pattern and twelve-bar chord progression sound known as the "12-Bar Blues."[4] In the song's opening salutation and lyrical responses, Lead Belly uses apostrophe to directly address the blues as signifying a burden so relentless, it has become his unwitting companion: "When I got up this morning, with the blues walking 'round my bed, / Aww, with the blues walking 'round my bed, / I went to eat my breakfast, the blues was all in my bread" (lines 7–9). The song is suggestive of the unspoken weariness and clever determination that is James's own rejoinder to his throbbing tooth, his mother's strict demands, and the unknown trials of the day ahead. Even the young narrator's discouraging exchange with a pretty girl on the bus bears a correlation to the love troubles of the bluesman, though their banter draws only laughter from the adults seated around them. Race also plays an important role in "Good Morning Blues" that is relevant to Gaines's story. In the song's opening preamble, Lead Belly distinguishes his troubles from those of the white man, who has "nothin' to worry about," suggesting not only the social dimensions of his plight but the makeup of his target audience as listeners within the black community who can relate to his experience.

As a result, the blues that Lead Belly personifies in "Good Morning Blues" exhibits qualities that are both universal and particular to African American culture. To further reinforce this multilayered messaging, I introduce Sterling Brown's widely available seven-minute talk "What Are the Blues?," from the seventy-fifth anniversary celebration of the Thirteenth Amendment at the Library of Congress in 1940. Brown describes the music's deep melancholy tone and wry humor as "the spirit of good-bye, of 'it was better yesterday, it may be better tomorrow, but there's not much we can say for today, can we?'" While Brown recognizes that the wish "to be somewheres else" is not bound by any particular cultural tradition, he claims the blues as "the Negro's secular songs of sadness" and understands the music to be profoundly connected to the legacy of black enslavement and Jim Crow oppression in America.

Brown's remarks, like Lead Belly's performance, are a reminder that the blues impulse has traditionally been driven by a range of thematic content that can develop sociopolitical significance even when the stated subject is natural disasters, tired feet, or a lonesome night. I have argued elsewhere that Gaines follows suit by representing different types of unmerited suffering in his short story to better serve the parable-like structure of James's encounter with the problem of evil. As I point out,

> In a story like "The Sky Is Gray" in which moral evil is ever-present via the social, political, and economic brutalities of racial segregation and rural poverty, we must be attentive to the way Gaines chooses, instead, to foreground occurrences of bafflingly unprovoked suffering for which no one *person* or system can be blamed: the bristling cold, rain, and sleet of a Louisiana winter morning as well as the youth's toothache. . . . Clues throughout the narrative suggest that Gaines uses James's encounter with *nature's* brutal indifference to posit more constructive ways of responding to acts of *human* cruelty. (Whitted 232–33)

Venturing briefly into this philosophical conflation between physical/natural pain and moral suffering broadens our understanding of Gaines's efforts to represent a fuller range of black southern experience. In doing so, his creative approach aligns even further with oral blues traditions that refuse to separate the sacred and the profane. Despite the accusation that the unrepentant portrayal of sexuality and vice made the blues closer to "the devil's music," Gaines's work draws upon the music "to show that there is a sacredness in everyday life" (Gaines, *Mozart* 140).

For more advanced classes on blues aesthetics, I assign James Baldwin's 1964 essay "The Uses of the Blues," published only a year after Gaines's story. In an effort to chronicle the "state of being, out of which the blues come" (57), Baldwin focuses on the contradictions between the social realities of black life and the country's democratic ideals. His approach would seem to resonate with the heated exchange in "The Sky Is Gray" between the black preacher and the black student activist who refuses to believe in God or America's promises. Yet Baldwin's interpretation of Bessie Smith and Lead Belly can be applied just as well to the relationship between James and his mother in an antagonistic social environment. Baldwin explains Octavia's dilemma:

> I am talking about what happens to you if, having barely escaped suicide, or death, or madness, or yourself, you watch your children growing up and no matter what you do, no matter what you do, you are powerless, you are really powerless, against the force of the world that is out to tell your child that he has no right to be alive. And no amount of liberal jargon, and no amount of talk about how well and how far we have progressed, does anything to soften or to point out any solution to this dilemma. In every generation, ever since Negroes have been here, every Negro mother and father has had to face that child and try to create in that child some way of surviving this particular world, some way to make the child, who will be despised, not despise himself. (60)

These are the conditions that create the blues, Baldwin argues. Just as in his frequently anthologized short story "Sonny's Blues," Baldwin's essay insists that the truth-telling of the music forces us to confront hard, unspoken questions about black existence, turning what Ellison referred to as "personal catastrophe" into a challenge to the status quo.

Once our class has explored more conceptual approaches to the blues as a "state of being," it is important to return to the text of "The Sky Is Gray" and situate close readings of the story against discussions of specific songs and performers. What follows are four songs that track the theme of mobility in James's journey, highlight the story's depiction of his mother and of the tensions between blackness and manhood, and offer productive ways to interpret the story's conclusion. As Tracy points out, "blues is a form of poetry" that can benefit from the skills of literary interpretation (*Write* 383). Nevertheless, requiring listening sessions of these songs—above and beyond simply reading the lyrics—can urge students to engage in sustained aesthetic analysis and reflect upon the configuration of sound, pacing, inflection, instrumentation, and the persona of the singer in ways that are vital to unpacking the aims for which the blues narrative is striving.

Robert Johnson, "Hellhound on My Trail" (1937)

Johnson's song captures one of the most popular themes in the blues tradition through his focus on movement as resistance (or escape) and, more specifically, by deploying figures of mobility to convey the indefatigable progress of life. The walk James takes through the cold and sleet is a fitting accompaniment to Johnson's lament: "I got to keep movin' / blues fallin' down like hail / blues fallin' down like hail" (lines 1–3). Johnson's metaphorical use of the blues and the song's subsequent reference to the "hellhound on [his] trail" (line 7) encourages students to pay attention to the symbolic dimensions of the journey in "The Sky Is Gray." Consider that by the time James and his mother begin their trek, his toothache has been hounding him for nearly a month. Neither his auntie's aspirin nor Monsieur Bayonne's prayers has helped. Readers learn in the story's first five sections about his family's economic hardship and the responsibility that his mother places on him as the eldest boy to be self-sufficient, dignified, and strong. The walk that James takes through town in the story's second half, then, is but a literal manifestation of a greater journey toward his inner growth and development as an adolescent. The hellhounds driving their movement can even be extended to signify the social injustices being debated in the dentist's waiting room, where the civil rights activist insists that black people should "[q]uestion everything. Every stripe, every star, every word spoken" (95). Other blues songs, such as Mississippi Fred McDowell's "You Gotta Move" (1965), reenvision the theme of mobility in religious terms, while Bessie Smith's "Backwater Blues" (1927) and Johnson's "Crossroad Blues" (1936) reflect upon the crisis of immobility, homelessness, and confinement. All speak to the resolve that James expresses in his most profound moments of personal anguish: "My hands numb in my pockets and my feet numb, too, but if I keep moving I can hold out. Just don't stop no more, that's all" (107).

Ida Cox, "Wild Women Don't Have the Blues" (1924)

Cox joins Bessie Smith and Ma Rainey as one of the pioneering women blues singers who helped to define the form's early style and subversive reputation. Her song not only introduces students to the formative role that women played in classic blues traditions, but it also draws attention to James's mother, Octavia, as a blues figure. Many of the songs that blueswomen made famous focus on romantic relationships, with topics that address sexual freedom and pleasure as well as the disappointment and loneliness of infidelity. While the army and not "another gal" is the reason Octavia's husband "done left this town," as Smith sings in "Gulf Coast Blues" (1923), the narrative makes clear that the absence of James's father has placed added burdens on Octavia and their extended family. The assertiveness, pride, and sense of agency depicted in the songs of blueswomen are integral to Gaines's depiction of her character. But referencing Cox's idea of "wild women" also allows the class to reflect upon Octavia's resourcefulness in light of gendered expectations: "You never get nothing by being an angel child, / You better change your ways and get real wild, / . . . / 'Cause wild women don't worry, wild women don't have their blues" (lines 16–17, 20).

To Cox, the wild woman is one who doesn't "sit around all day and moan" about her problems and instead finds strength in having "a disposition and a way of [her] own" (lines 3, 11). Likewise, through James's perspective in "The Sky Is Gray," we see the careful negotiations and sacrifices that Octavia makes to guide her son through his own crossroads experience. She steers him into a hardware store after being locked out of the dentist's office and pretends to shop for ax handles while James warms himself by the heater (105). Later she deliberates over whether to spend their return bus fare on his food: "She flips the quarter over like she's thinking. She must be thinking 'bout us walking back home. Lord, I sure don't want walk home. If I thought it'd do any good to say something, I'd say it. But Mama makes up her own mind 'bout things" (110). Furthermore, Cox's refusal to spend time with a man "if he don't act right" speaks to Octavia's decision to ignore the man who whistles at her (104) and pull her knife on the man who acts like a "pimp" at the café (111). Strict and watchful with her son, Octavia's actions resonate with the ingenuity of Cox's wild women, the "only kind that really get by" (line 19).

Big Bill Broonzy, "I Wonder When Will I Get to Be Called a Man" (1957)

Broonzy extends our concern with the intersections between race and gender in "The Sky Is Gray" by focusing on the anxieties about black manhood. Each stanza charts the speaker's fifty-three years of indignity under a system of oppression that treats him like a "boy" despite his military service and lifetime of labor: "Now I've got a little education, but I'm still a boy right on / . . . / I wonder when will I get to be called a man / Do I have to wait till I get ninety-three?" (lines 22, 24–25). I use Broonzy's song to underscore what is at stake for Octavia in placing so much trust in her eight-year-old son, leading James to say early in the narrative: "I'm the oldest and she say I'm the man" (84). The same images of manhood from Broonzy's song appear in Gaines's story, including James's father as the soldier serving his country, Monsieur Bayonne as the farmworker, and the civil rights activist with "a little education." James seems most intrigued by the last, going so far as to admit, "When I grow up I want to be just like him. I want clothes like that and I want keep a book with me, too" (100). And yet the aspirational desires that the student activist represents in the narrative are in tension with the realities of second-class citizenship that are expressed through the segregated spaces on the bus, at the dentist's office, and in the restaurants of Bayonne that seem to declare, in Broonzy's words, "Black man's a boy, don't care what he can do" (line 17).

The song helps to stress a key irony in "The Sky Is Gray," given Octavia's final words to her son after she prevents him from trying to turn up his collar in the cold: "'You not a bum,' she says. 'You a man'"(117). Coming at the story's end, after the storms the two have weathered during their journey to the dentist, being a "man" in these final lines is no longer measured by age, as James once asserted. Instead it represents his mother's efforts to recognize his worth, to reward his responsibility, and, recalling Baldwin, to "try to create in that child some way of surviving this particular world, some way to make the child, who will be despised, not despise himself" (60).

Lightnin' Hopkins, "Trouble in Mind" (1960)

Recorded by several blues and jazz performers, including Jelly Roll Morton, Big Bill Broonzy, Nina Simone, and B. B. King, "Trouble in Mind" demonstrates that the blues are, as Richard Wright once wrote, capable of transforming their meditation on suffering "into an almost exultant affirmation of life, of love, of sex, of movement, of hope" (Foreword xv). The blues narrative that Gaines constructs contains poignant expressions of affection and altruism, from James's endearing thoughts—"I look up at Mama. I love my mama. I love my mama. And when cotton come I'm go'n get her a new coat" (99)—to the elderly white couple that stops the pair on the sidewalk to offer shelter from the cold (112). Hopkins, one of Gaines's favorite performers, repeats the refrain: "Trouble in mind, I'm blue, / But I won't be blue always, / You know the sun gonna shine in my backdoor some day" (lines 1–3).

Even as Hopkins admits, "I ain't never had so much trouble in my life before" (line 12), his guitar maintains a lively tempo that can be used to call attention to the hints of optimism in James's narration. James knows, for instance, that he will be returning to school one day and be asked to pick up where he left off by reciting "Annabel Lee" (112). He continues to follow his mother's lead as she accepts the unexpected offer of food and warmth from the white store owner while maintaining her dignity as a customer. And in keeping with Hopkins's idea that he "won't be blue always," James's observations acknowledge the potential for individual and collective change: "I'm still getting cold. But I can see we getting closer. We getting there gradually" (112). Sentiments such as these, combined with the musicality of the storytelling, are why Barlow makes a case for treating literary works such as "The Sky Is Gray" as more than written derivatives of the blues, but as "a constituent of the blues musical genre" itself (139).

Combining textual analysis of "The Sky Is Gray" with listening sessions of blues songs like the ones described above helps students to better understand how the blues narrative features outlined by Tracy and Barlow can be applied to Gaines's work. Though actual intermedial references to music in the story are limited to Monsieur Bayonne's guitar and the jukebox at the café, the sound and cadence of James's narrative voice "experiment with the forms of the blues" to the extent that even the *ummm-ummm* of his toothache pain recalls Robert Johnson's cathartic hum. Likewise, the tale draws on the pain and suffering that have been traditionally associated with the blues and their use as "an emotional, psychic, spiritual, community, political resource." And by reading the young boy's trip to the dentist as symbolic of life's blustery journey and of the nation's odyssey toward social and political progress, "The Sky Is Gray" undoubtedly "challenge[s] the currently prevailing notion of order, propriety, and morality" (Tracy, *Write* 384).

For further study, Gaines's story benefits from close comparisons and contrasts with blues narratives produced in the twenty-first century. Collections by African American poets such as Nikky Finney (*Head Off and Split: Poems*), Natasha Trethewey (*Native Guard*), Kevin Young (*Jelly Roll: A Blues*; *Book of Hours*), and Tyehimba Jess (*Leadbelly: Poems*) use blues-inflected verse to recall complex family relationships and coming-of-age narratives that connect with James's unique first-person perspective. There are also a growing number of visual narratives influenced by the blues. Comic books and graphic novels have focused explicitly on elements of performance, but most embody the blues as a way of being, combining the hard-edged wisdom of singers like Robert Johnson and Bessie Smith with a pastiche of trickster tales, pulp westerns, and the antiheroics of comics made popular by such writers as Alan Moore and Frank Miller. Derek McCulloch and Shepherd Hendrix's *Stagger Lee* (2006) unravels the late nineteenth-century history behind the songs of the infamous black bad man and folk hero. Rob Vollmar and Pablo G. Callejo's *Bluesman* (2006)—"a twelve-bar graphic narrative in the key of life and death"—tells the story of a struggling black musician who is wanted for murder in the Jim Crow South, while Robert Johnson suffers the loss of his soul for his uncommon musical talent in the manga series *Me and the Devil Blues* (2008), by Akira Hiramoto.

The title character of Jeremy Love's comic series *Bayou* (2010) is a swamp monster who plays the Delta blues with a crafty Brer Rabbit but also lives in fear of a white boss man along the Mississippi River. Love's comic is told from the vantage point of two children who share James's perceptiveness and courage: a black girl whose quest is to save her father from being lynched and a black boy who has himself been victimized by racial violence. The vivid color palette of fantasy and folklore in *Bayou* presents a stark juxtaposition to the grim, cold setting of "The Sky Is Gray," and yet both draw on the transcendent strains of the blues to represent the lives of black southern children and their parents.

Finally, students more familiar with hip-hop music may also appreciate the comparison between the difficult journey depicted in "The Sky Is Gray" and the story Kendrick Lamar tells in his 2012 concept album, *Good Kid, M.A.A.D City*. Lamar's account of his time growing up in Compton, California, during the 1990s is nothing short of Ellison's "autobiographical chronicle of personal catastrophe expressed lyrically," and over the course of each track, he moves away from the violence, misogyny, and substance abuse of his surroundings to think more critically about his choices and the systems of oppression that try to limit them. The album takes place over the course of a single day that begins with him losing his girlfriend, being involved in a shooting that kills his friend, and receiving a call from a record producer. The narrative is framed by increasingly concerned voice mails from his mother, culminating in a message that, according to the critic Rachel Kaadzi Ghansah, "recalls the blues elegies of Son House and Robert Johnson." In songs such as "The Art of Peer Pressure," "Sing About Me, I'm Dying of Thirst," and "Black Boy Fly," students will undoubtedly hear echoes of James's voice in another generation of black youths who face the hailstorms and hellhounds of racial oppression and dehumanization without losing sight of their self-worth.

NOTES

[1] This essay quotes from the version of "The Sky Is Gray" in the 1968 Vintage edition of *Bloodline*.

[2] See Jimoh; Antonucci; and Tolson.

[3] A selection of these critical works on "The Sky Is Gray" includes Duncan; McDonald; Callahan, "Hearing"; J. Roberts, "Individual"; Meyer; Papa; Mallon; T. Harris, *Saints*; Doyle, *Voices*; and Whitted.

[4] To better acquaint students with blues forms, PBS has developed an online "Blues Classroom" in cooperation with the Experience Music Project to accompany the documentary film series *The Blues*. The site includes a teaching guide on the twelve-bar blues, along with a glossary of terms and a bibliography of additional sources (www.pbs.org/theblues/classroom.html).

"Three Men," Queer Studies, and Pedagogy

Keith Byerman

In his 2006 article on Ernest Gaines's "Three Men," Keith Clark makes a case for the author's ambiguity about homosexuality. He contends that Gaines, in the very process of reconfiguring black male subjectivity, "cannily disrupts a univocal narrative of same-sex desire" but simultaneously re-creates a black hypermasculinity that endorses homophobia and violence, especially against the gay "other" ("Que(e)rying" 239–40). "Ultimately, however, 'Three Men' is at best a rhetorical conundrum, a dialectical narrative that undermines its own attempts to witness against delimiting notions of black male subjectivity" (240). While this is a position that can be justified by the text, especially if we assume we can know the author's intentions, I would suggest that, for the purposes of teaching the story, queer studies offers other options for interpreting character and issues of identity.[1] While it may not be necessary to introduce students to Clark's sophisticated approach, precisely because the story can so easily be read as homophobic, it is essential to carefully consider possible alternative interpretations of the characters, their context, and their interrelationships if students are to move beyond this conclusion to a reading that complicates Gaines's representation of black masculinity.

Any classroom discussion of the story from this perspective must begin with not only a presentation of queer theory, but also a definition of the term *queer*. If it is understood, as it often has been, as applying only to gay and lesbian issues or the binary of heterosexual and homosexual, then the conversation will not get much beyond the character of Hattie, his relationships to the putatively nonqueer characters, and the author's attitudes toward gay black men. If, however, *queer* is presented in the terms offered by several queer theorists, then a number of other issues emerge. Robert McRuer, for example, contends that the term is a statement not only of sexual identity but also of difference and resistance. "Difference" carries with it an assertion of nonessentialism: there are no fixed categories of sexual or gender identity; therefore, in such an approach, binaries of male/female or gay/straight are not meaningful. "Resistance" can be understood as a performative aspect of a text in which characters refuse or strategically adopt such categorizations or act in a manner that repudiates them (2–5). Eve Sedgwick goes further by suggesting that it is possible to understand queerness in more expansive terms; she points out that "recent work around 'queer' spins the term outward along dimensions that can't be subsumed under gender and sexuality at all: the ways that race, ethnicity, postcolonial nationality criss-cross with these *and other* identity-constituting, identity-fracturing discourses, for example" (9).[2]

If we take *queer* to offer these multiple possibilities for expression of desire, then "Three Men" provides an intriguing instance of a text permeated with masculinist language that nonetheless breaks down any fixed notions of black male subjectivity. It is precisely the stereotyped definition of black men as violent beasts that the narrative seeks to break through, but it is compelled to use that vocabulary in order to do its subversive work. Most of Gaines's other work is primarily concerned with the meaning of manhood within a social order designed to deny that option to African Americans. Even *The Autobiography of Miss Jane Pittman* pays significant attention to how male characters resist submission to that emasculating order and are sacrificed because of that resistance. It is even the case that some of Gaines's female characters, such as the mother in "The Sky Is Gray," exercise traditional male authority. In virtually every case, female characters play an apparently subordinate role; "apparently" is important, because they often exercise power behind closed doors while wearing a guise of submissiveness.

This pattern of alternative masculinities is evident and even exaggerated in "Three Men." The narrator, Procter Lewis, decides to turn himself in to the police after stabbing a man with a broken bottle during a bar fight. The fight was over a woman whom Lewis approached despite the presence of the other man. He had managed to escape, but then chooses to surrender. His logic is that since it was only a "nigger" whom he injured (or killed; we never learn the outcome), then he will be turned over to Roger Medlow, for whom he sharecrops, rather than be sent to prison. The fact that he goes to the police is itself offensive to the officers, since it implies an ability to think and calculate, skills inconsistent with the image of black men necessary to justify racial oppression. An act of apparent submission is taken instead as an act of resistance and, implicitly, a revision of black male identity.

Lewis is placed in a cell with two others, Munford and Hattie. Munford, who is significantly older, has been in and out of the jail regularly for fighting. He is always freed after a few days. Hattie is in for fondling a man in a theater. Munford, and soon Lewis as well, refers to Hattie as "woman," "whore," "freak," and "thing." Munford also discusses the pattern of violence, incarceration, and freedom that has been his life and that, he argues, will become that of Lewis. He contends that the system of racial oppression needs such men so that whites can feel not only their own superiority but also their humanity. He includes Hattie among those who have been emasculated by the social order. This analysis constitutes the central portion of the story. What Munford wants is for Lewis to break the cycle by refusing his compromised freedom and accepting his punishment by going to prison; while incapable of such an act himself, the older man believes that this is the only path to true black manhood. Lewis initially rejects this option.

When Munford is freed, Lewis is momentarily left alone with Hattie, whom he continues to insult and tries to intimidate. He contemplates what Munford said and begins to worry that Roger Medlow is not going to have him freed, meaning that he will go to prison, which he sees as the ultimate suffering. A few hours later, an even younger man is thrown into the cell after being beaten by the police. Hattie attempts to care for him, but Lewis pushes him aside and forces the boy to smoke a cigarette. Lewis then claims that he is in fact going to go to prison and insists that the boy pray for him when the sheriff comes to punish him for his refusal to play the game of racial oppression. He attends to the boy's wounds and silently cries, in part because the beating of the boy gives him the courage to resist. He does not know if he can actually face the consequences of standing up, and so, like many of Gaines's stories, this one is open-ended.

On the surface, the story appears to affirm a hypermasculinist and homophobic model of black male identity, one that even confirms the racist stereotype of the black man as naturally violent, promiscuous, and irresponsible. Munford has been getting into fights and thrown into jail for forty years, and Lewis, though only nineteen, has been incarcerated several times. Even the boy at the end has been in jail before. It is important for students to have a grasp of the intersection of the stereotype and the self-fashioning of black men during the early twentieth century. Folktales about the "bad man" figure, such as Stagolee, and the stories and legends associated with the musicians Huddie "Lead Belly" Ledbetter and Robert Johnson, as well as analyses of race and gender images, can assist in clarifying the connection.[3]

Several instances in the text reinforce this linkage. Lewis persistently and consciously refuses to address the sheriff and the deputy as "sir" until he is reminded to do so. Even when Paul the deputy reveals himself to be more humane, Lewis does not acknowledge the difference between the two white men. When he is taken to the cell, the dynamic of the prisoners is quickly established. Munford expects a cigarette from the pack Paul gave Lewis, and Munford and Hattie make clear their mutual dislike through insults. Lewis feels like crying but knows that such an expression would make him seem vulnerable and subject to intimidation. He also re-creates the scene that got him into trouble. In it, he starts a conversation with a woman he knows is with another man. He takes her outside and tries to convince her to leave with him. When Bayou comes after him with a knife, Lewis tries to talk him out of fighting, though he knows that will not happen. He eventually stabs the other man with a broken bottle. In effect, he seeks to prove his manhood by identifying the woman as property that he can take away from another man. His desire, in other words, is for dominance, especially over men, and not for sex. Thus, from the beginning, the narrative is queered.

Lewis and Munford's shared attitude toward Hattie is a form of bonding based on a binary of male and female. But at the same time, Munford's demand for one of Lewis's cigarettes positions the younger man as subordinate. The older man then tells what amounts to a folktale that superficially distinguishes Hattie from them. It combines the tall tale with the bad man tradition. According to Munford, when he was presented for his christening,

> [t]his preacher going, "Mumbo-jumbo, mumbo-jumbo," but all the time he's low'ing his mouth toward my little private. Nobody else don't see him, but I catch him, and I haul 'way back and hit him right smack in the eye. I ain't no more than three months old but I give him a good one. "Get your

goddamn mouth away from my little pecker, you no-teef, rotten, egg-sucking sonofabitch. Get away from here, you sister-jumper, God-calling, pulpit-splitting, mother-huncher. Get away from here, you chicken-eating, catfish-eating, gin-drinking sonofabitch. Get away, goddamn it, get away. . . ." (140)

Lewis thinks that this is merely humor but then realizes that Munford is serious. He reads the initial characterization as applying to Hattie, but Munford has more in mind. He says that you sometimes escape the cradle intact, but "they catch you some other time. And when they catch you, they draw it out of you or they make you a beast—make you use it in a brutish way" (140). Such a black man abuses women, children, and other men and eventually commits murder.

For purposes of this analysis, Munford queers notions of masculinity and not just black masculinity. By way of introduction to his tale, he points out that the whites who encourage such behavior are themselves not truly men, because their own sense of manhood depends on the dehumanizing of black males. Moreover, he acknowledges a sameness with Hattie: "They think they men 'cause they got me and him in here who ain't men" (138). In the tale, the pedophilic behavior of the black preacher becomes part of the initiation into Jim Crow society. It is a queered version of a particular form of desire, in that its motivation is not sexual but racial. According to this logic, manhood is an inborn life force that has to be "sucked out" so that this boy-child will become the emasculated being needed to maintain Jim Crow society. The preacher acts out his part so that the black community will have some control over the child's destiny. Hattie, in this parable, is one who has been successfully unmanned.

But often the preacher fails, as in the cases of Munford and Lewis. Then the larger society queers black manhood in a different way, by reinforcing through stereotypes, punishments, and rewards a grotesque form of masculinity that can find expression only through violence, corruption, and a carefully delineated domination, restricted to weaker members of the black community. Any evidence of intelligence, leadership, or responsibility is subject to severe white retribution. Ironically, according to Munford's analysis, white men, through this process, distort and destroy their own manhood by structuring white masculinity as the opposite of black. They become, in effect, dependent on that which they reject; they need the black man in order to be white and masculine. Thus, racial oppression becomes a queered form of desire of one man for another.

If Munford represents failed black masculinity because of his violence, Hattie would seem to represent it because of his homosexuality. If this is in fact the case, then Gaines can be said to take a view consistent with the black arts and black power movements that dominated African American culture at the beginning of his career. A number of writers from the period read white society as being effete and sterile and used homosexuality as a metaphor for this condition. Eldridge Cleaver, who published *Soul on Ice* in 1968, the same year Gaines published his story collection, describes homosexuality as "[t]he product of fissures of society into antagonistic classes and a dying culture and civilization alienated from its biology" (177).

Hattie is certainly made to seem alien to Munford and Lewis on the basis of his sexual orientation. But it is important to consider as well the class aspect of Cleaver's comment. After all, Munford, in one of the odder moments of the story, offers Hattie a small amount of money for "a little whirl" (139). While his comment is intended as a joke belittling the other man, it implies that he can imagine engaging in such behavior. There is no suggestion of threat or repulsion from his perspective. They are simply two men (or not-men, according to his earlier analysis) bantering with each other.

What is significant in this moment is Hattie's response. He angrily rejects the proposal, in part because of the offer of money, which he recognizes as an insult, one intended to make him the "whore" the others have labeled him. But more than this, he sees Munford as beneath him, as truly the "beast" that they have been talking about. Their ensuing interaction marks a class difference:

> "Do you think I could ever sink so low?" he said.
> "Well, that's what you do on the outside," Munford said.
> "What I do on the outside is absolutely no concern of yours, let me assure you," the freak said. "And furthermore, I have friends that I associate with."
> "And them 'sociating friends you got there—what they got Munford don't have?" Munford said.
> "For one thing, manners," Hattie said. "Of all the nerve."   (139)

The difference in diction here is telling. Throughout the story, Munford employs several verbal registers, from folk speech to social analysis to humor to the slightly ungrammatical form of this exchange. In contrast, Hattie's speech is carefully middle class with a hint of the melodramatic. In effect, he claims a status difference between himself and people like Munford, thereby making his presence in the jail a fundamentally different situation.

In creating this class distinction, Gaines appears to be engaged in a critique of what has been called the black bourgeoisie. In the novels *In My Father's House* and *A Lesson Before Dying*, he joins other fiction writers of his generation, including Toni Morrison, John Edgar Wideman, and Clarence Major, who express a preference for working-class and folklike characters over those who have done whatever it takes to gain money, power, and status in society. In the process, the middle class has frequently distanced itself from its roots in the black community. Hattie's sexual identity, in the eyes of Munford and Lewis, is aggravated by his middle-class pretensions. His claim to have friends with "manners" links him to what they view as white values. In this sense he is scorned the same way that Munford scorns Lewis's uncle, who has a relationship with Medlow that will aid in getting the younger man released into the white man's custody, regardless of his crime.

Hattie's claims can be labeled "pretensions," because, despite his friends, he is caught fondling another man "at this old flea-bitten show back of town" (127). He lacks access to a secure private space in which to express his desires. This situation is probably the result of his race. Since we have no indication that he has a professional position, he would not own a home to which he could take another gay man of either race. It is also unlikely that he could safely enter the home of a white man, even one with a similar orientation. What is left for him is public space, and even that would be limited by Jim Crow rules. Thus, he is forced into spaces such as a run-down theater.

But a second fact suggests that Gaines may have a more complex view of Hattie. One of the pieces of information that Munford reveals is that the criminal behavior took place in the front row of the theater: "Up front—front row—there he is playing with this man dick" (127). Munford is bemused with the thought that someone engaged in illicit activity would be foolish enough to make it so easy to be discovered. But it is possible to consider Hattie's choice to be deliberate. His openness may well be an act of resistance; after all, in a dark theater, there are many options if he wants his activities to be concealed. This notion is reinforced by his refusal to defend or deny his sexual identity; he reacts only to the insults of Munford and Lewis. He repeatedly points out that, unlike the others, he does no harm to anyone; he is different from them in that he has not become a "beast" (139), to use a term that he and Munford agree on. Despite the fact that the others assert his lack of manhood, he is the only one who has not sacrificed his sexual identity. In this sense, it is Hattie rather than Munford whom Lewis could look to for a model of black male identity.

Munford and Hattie can be read as dialectical terms in the story, with Lewis in the middle having to choose his way. It is not that the two older men represent options in the story for what the younger man can become, since throughout Lewis is contemptuous of what Hattie signifies. Rather, they are apparent extremes of black masculinity under the conditions of the Jim Crow South. One seems to be white identified, in terms of the rhetoric of black power, while the other takes on the role of black brute, a figure often apotheosized in that same rhetoric. The question of the story is whether black male identity is limited by this binary. As we have seen, Gaines complicates these terms early in the narrative.

In examining the character of Lewis, it is important to introduce the fourth "man" in the jail cell, a character the author misdirects us from in the title "Three Men." If Munford and Hattie are binary figures, Lewis and the unnamed fourteen-year-old are doubles. When the boy is brought into the cell, having been beaten by the police, he is crying, just as Lewis had wanted to do when he entered this space. Hattie immediately goes to comfort him in the same way he had approached Lewis earlier. The protagonist now takes on the role of Munford, quizzing the boy about what had happened. Significantly, Hattie answers for him, using much of the language of his departed antagonist: "Just look at his clothes. The bunch of animals. Not one of them is a man. A bunch of pigs—dogs—philistines" (150). But this does not change Lewis's homophobia; if anything it intensifies it: "Hattie was holding the boy in his arms and whispering to him. I hated what Hattie was doing much as I hated what the law had done" (150). Shortly after this, he grabs Hattie and throws him to the other side of the cell. His initial reaction to the boy shows similar traits of hypermasculine performance. He forces a cigarette into his mouth and removes it only when the boy cannot stop coughing. Later, he asks him if he wants another, and though the boy refuses twice, he compels him to smoke it. This phallic gesture, combined with the verbal and physical violence against Hattie, indicates a desire to establish dominance in this situation of impotence. It serves as a reversal of the role of the cigarette found early in the story. There, Lewis felt compelled to give one to Munford; here he compels the boy to take and smoke more than one. Ironically, his gesture, while seeming to require the manly act of smoking, serves to reestablish his own manhood through compulsion. He also interrogates the boy, telling him that he should not steal, even if he is hungry and his parents fail to care for him. Such advice is hardly credible coming from Lewis, given his history of bad behavior.

But this attempt to assert his masculinity must be contextualized by the mental turmoil occurring at the same time. He begins pacing and smoking and cannot seem to stop either one. He notes that the jail had become very quiet: "Nobody had said a word since the guards threw that little boy in the cell. Like a bunch of roaches, like a bunch of mices, they had crawled in they holes and pulled the cover over they head" (151). Just before, he also had chosen silence, implying that he is becoming one of the roaches. At this point comes a cathartic moment for him:

> All of a sudden I wanted to scream. I wanted to scream to the top of my voice. I wanted to get them bars in my hands and I wanted to shake. I wanted to shake that door down. I wanted to let all these people out. But would they follow me—would they? Y'all go'n follow me? I screamed inside. Y'all go'n follow me?
>
> I ran to my bunk and bit down in the cover. I bit harder, harder, harder. I could taste the dry sweat, the dry piss, the dry vomit. I bit harder, harder, harder. . . .
>
> I got on the bunk. I looked out at the stars. A million little white, cool stars was out there. I felt my throat hurting. I felt the water running down my face. But I gripped my mouth tight so I wouldn't make a sound. I didn't make a sound, but I cried. I cried and cried and cried.   (151)

In this dark night of the soul, he comes to the decision to go to prison: "I didn't want to have to pull cover over my head every time a white man did something to a black boy—I wanted to stand" (152). Having come to the point where he sees and feels Munford's insight about the moral nature of black manhood, he makes a last gesture toward the old version, one that exaggerates his previous behavior. This is the moment when he throws Hattie across the cell, then again forces a cigarette on the boy: "'You big enough to steal?' I said. 'You'll smoke it or you'll eat it.' I lit it and pushed it in his mouth" (153). He seems to need to be clear that what he will do is in fact an expression of manhood, which he still in part identifies with aggressive behavior. But what comes next follows the pattern established by Hattie. He first requests ("I want you to") that the boy start praying every time the sheriff comes to get him to beat him for not going with Medlow. He acknowledges that he does not believe, but that he needs the boy to believe: "That's the only way I'll be able to take those beatings—with you praying" (153). He then asks about the boy's family, who have failed him, and about Munford, who seems to be kin to no one. This combination creates the possibility of a relationship between the two young men. By telling the boy to pray, Lewis places on him a responsibility, which he reciprocates by saying that he intends to make sure that the boy never goes to jail again. He then takes on a nursing role:

> I wet my handkerchief and dabbed at the bruises. Every time I touched his back, he flinched. But I didn't let that stop me. I washed his back good and clean. When I got through, I told him to go back to his bunk and lay down. Then I rinched out his shirt and spread it out on the foot of my bunk. I took off my own shirt and rinched it out because it was filthy.   (154–55)

In this ritual of cleansing, he performs acts usually associated with women, but in a manner that transcends gender. It is nothing like the competition with Bayou, the exploitation of women, the isolated individualism of Munford, or the pretense of Hattie. He has, in effect, queered all of them. When linked to his decision to go to prison, it implies a submission to authority that is also an act of resistance. His relationship with the boy creates a moral and even spiritual bond that questions all the previous definitions of manhood.

But this does not mean that Gaines is offering a sentimental and tidy conclusion to his narrative. One clue is the comment noted earlier about hating Hattie as much as the law for their behavior toward the boy. The ending of the story is open in the sense that Lewis is uncertain whether he can stand all the beatings, even with the boy's moral support. But it is open in a different sense as well. He remains blind to the extent to which both Munford and Hattie led him to the closing point of the story. He cannot allow himself to have any identification with a gay man, because he still cannot see such a person as a man. But the hatred and the violence he engages in are signs that he feels threatened by the possibility that his new desire, to be a different kind of man, one who needs and helps others, will mark him as weak and even effeminate. The unspoken question at the end of the text is not whether he has the courage to face death for the sake of true manhood, but rather whether he can live as a different, "queer" kind of human being.

NOTES

¹ I am not taking up the discussion about the sexual orientation of either instructors or students in a classroom in which LGBTQ material is part of the syllabus. Those interested in that pedagogical debate should look at Haggerty; B. Alexander; and Clark, "Are We Family?," among others.

² For commentaries specifically on homosexuality and black male writers, see Nelson; Nero.

³ See Cleaver; R. Jackson; Bryant; F. Davis; and J. Roberts, *From Trickster.*

NOTES ON CONTRIBUTORS

Simone A. James Alexander is professor of English, Africana studies, and women and gender studies; affiliate member of the Russian and East European Studies Program and Latin America and Latino/Latina studies; and director of Africana studies at Seton Hall University. Her book *African Diasporic Women's Narratives: Politics of Resistance, Survival, and Citizenship* won the 2015 College Language Association Creative Scholarship Award and received honorable mention by the African Literature Association. Alexander is also the author of *Mother Imagery in the Novels of Afro-Caribbean Women* and coeditor of *Feminist and Critical Perspectives on Caribbean Mothering*. Her current projects include "Black Freedom in (Communist) Russia: Great Expectations, Utopian Visions, and Bodies of (In)Difference: Gender, Sexuality, and Nationhood."

Susan Ayres is a professor at Texas A&M University School of Law and also writes and translates poetry. Her scholarly research primarily explores law, literature, and culture. Current projects include translating the poetry of the award-winning Mexican poet Elsa Cross and analyzing incest and trauma in the works of contemporary poets such as Marie Howe.

Valerie Babb is Andrew Mellon Professor of Humanities at Emory University. Among her publications are *A History of the African American Novel* and *Whiteness Visible: The Meaning of Whiteness in American Literature*. She coauthored the book *Black Georgetown Remembered* and developed the concept for and produced the video by the same name. From 2000 to 2010 she was editor of *The Langston Hughes Review*. She has been a scholar-in-residence at the Schomburg Center for Research in Black Culture and is the recipient of a W. M. Keck Foundation fellowship in American studies. She has lectured extensively in the United States and abroad and presented a Distinguished W. E. B. Du Bois Lecture at Humboldt University. Babb teaches courses in African American literature, American literature, and constructions of race. She is the recipient of a UGA NAACP Mary McLeod Bethune Educator Award for teaching and mentoring.

Margaret D. Bauer, a native of south Louisiana, is the Rives Chair of Southern Literature and Distinguished Professor of Arts and Sciences at East Carolina University (ECU). She has served as editor of the *North Carolina Literary Review* since 1997, and in 2017 she received the North Carolina Award for Literature. She is the author of four books, including *William Faulkner's Legacy* (2005), which includes a chapter on Ernest Gaines. In 2007, Bauer was named one of ECU's Ten Women of Distinction and received the Parnassus Award for Significant Editorial Achievement from the Council of Editors of Learned Journals. Her other honors include ECU's Scholar-Teacher Award, Centennial Award for Excellence in Leadership, and Lifetime Achievement Award for Excellence in Research and Creative Activity, as well as the R. Hunt Parker Memorial Award for significant contributions to North Carolina literature, from the North Carolina Literary and Historical Association, and the John Tyler Caldwell Award for the Humanities, from the North Carolina Humanities Council.

Herman Beavers is professor of English and Africana studies at the University of Pennsylvania, where he teaches courses in African American literature and creative writing.

He is the author of *Wrestling Angels into Song: The Fictions of Ernest J. Gaines and James Alan McPherson* (1995) and *Geography and the Political Imaginary in the Novels of Toni Morrison* (2018). He is also the author of two poetry chapbooks, *A Neighborhood of Feeling* and *Obsidian Blues*.

Ineke Bockting holds doctoral degrees from the University of Amsterdam, the Netherlands, and from the University of Montpellier, France (*habilitation à diriger des recherches*). She has taught at universities in the Netherlands, Norway, and France, and she is now professor emerita of the Institut Catholique de Paris. Her publications include works on various aspects of the American South, William Faulkner, ethnic literatures, travel narrative, autobiography, narratology, literary stylistics and pragmatics, and cognitive science and literature. She is a member of Unité de Recherche: Religion, Culture et Société of Institut Catholique.

Keith Byerman is professor of English and African American studies at Indiana State University. He is the author of eight books on African American literature and culture, as well as numerous articles on African American and southern literature. He serves as president of the John Edgar Wideman Society and treasurer and past president of the African American Literature and Culture Society. He is also associate editor of *African American Review*.

Maria Hebert-Leiter, originally from Louisiana, currently teaches at Lycoming College in Williamsport, Pennsylvania. She returns home through her writing, which includes *Becoming Cajun, Becoming American: The Acadian in American Literature from Longfellow to James Lee Burke* (2009) and *Images of Depression-Era Louisiana: The FSA Photographs of Ben Shahn, Russell Lee, and Marion Post Wolcott* (coauthored with Bryan Giemza, 2017), along with essays on Louisiana literature and culture. She also participated as a visiting scholar in the 2016 NEH Summer Scholar program, Ernest J. Gaines and the Southern Experience.

Toru Kiuchi was professor of American literature at Nihon University in Japan. His publications on African American and southern literature include *The Critical Response in Japan to African American Writers* (coedited with Yoshinobu Hakutani and Robert J. Butler) and *Richard Wright: A Documented Chronology, 1908–1960* (coauthored with Yoshinobu Hakutani). He edited *American Haiku: New Readings* and was a Fulbright Scholar at Yale University.

John Wharton Lowe is the Barbara Lester Methvin Distinguished Professor of English at the University of Georgia. He is author or editor of nine books, including *Jump at the Sun: Zora Neale Hurston's Cosmic Comedy*, *Conversations with Ernest Gaines*, and *Calypso Magnolia: The Crosscurrents of Caribbean and Southern Literature*. He is the recipient of the MELUS Award for Distinguished Contribution to Ethnic Literary Studies and has served as president of the Society for the Study of Southern Literature, the Southern American Studies Association, MELUS, and the Louisiana Folklore Society. He is currently writing the authorized biography of Ernest J. Gaines.

Jennifer Nolan is assistant professor of English at North Carolina State University. Her research focuses primarily on the cultural, material, and visual contexts surrounding literary publications in popular American magazines during the first half of the twentieth century, with emphasis on F. Scott Fitzgerald, the *Saturday Evening Post*, and influential but largely forgotten female artists and editors. Her articles on Fitzgerald and others, such as William Faulkner, Langston Hughes, and May Wilson Preston, have appeared in *Book History*, *The F. Scott Fitzgerald Review*, *Faulkner and Print Culture*, *The Journal of Modern Periodical Studies*, and *American Periodicals*.

Christopher Rieger is professor of English and director of the Center for Faulkner Studies at Southeast Missouri State University. He is the author of *Clear-Cutting Eden: Ecology and the Pastoral in Southern Literature* and the coeditor of five books, including *Faulkner and Hurston* (2017) and *Faulkner and Hemingway* (2018). He has published on a range of American writers, including William Faulkner, Erskine Caldwell, Ernest Hemingway, Larry Brown, Marjorie Kinnan Rawlings, Zora Neale Hurston, and Karen Russell.

James Smethurst is professor of Afro-American studies at the University of Massachusetts, Amherst. He is the author of *The New Red Negro: The Literary Left and African American Poetry, 1930–1946*; *The Black Arts Movement: Literary Nationalism in the 1960s and 1970s*; and *The African American Roots of Modernism: From Reconstruction to the Harlem Renaissance*. He also coedited *Left of the Color Line: Race, Radicalism and Twentieth-Century Literature of the United States*; *Radicalism in the South Since Reconstruction*; and *SOS—Calling All Black People: A Black Arts Movement Reader*. He is working on the forthcoming *Brick Songs: Amiri Baraka, Black Music, Black Modernity, Black Vanguard* as well as a history of the black arts movement in the southern United States.

Virginia Whatley Smith is retired as associate professor of English, University of Alabama at Birmingham. She received her PhD in English from Boston University, and completed postdoctoral training at the University of North Carolina, Chapel Hill; Dartmouth University; and Emory University Psychoanalytical Institute. Smith is widely known for her extensive research on Richard Wright and has also published on Frederick Douglass, W. E. B. Du Bois, Ralph Ellison, James Emanuel, Gayl Jones, Alice Walker, and Sonia Sanchez, in *Obsidian*, *African American Review*, *PMLA*, and *International Journal of Languages and Literature*. Her article providing a semiotic deconstruction of Wright's classic photographic text *12 Million Black Voices* remains seminal, and her published editions include *Richard Wright's Travel Writings: New Reflections* (2001) and *Richard Wright Writing America at Home and from Abroad* (2016). Smith currently is working on a biography of Wright.

Terrence Tucker is associate professor in the Department of English at the University of Memphis. He received his PhD from the University of Kentucky, specializing in African American literature. His work focuses on post-1945 African American literature and drama, twentieth- and twenty-first-century American literature, and popular culture. He is especially interested in representations of black masculinity, notions of community and class, as well as expressions of black militancy and black humor. He has published work on topics ranging from race and pedagogy to Walter Mosley to African American superheroes. Tucker's book *Furiously Funny: Comic Rage from Ralph Ellison to Chris Rock* was published in 2018.

Qiana Whitted is professor of English and African American studies at the University of South Carolina. She is a graduate of Hampton University and received a PhD from Yale University. Her research focuses on African American literary studies, southern studies, and American comic books. She is the author of *EC Comics: Race, Shock, and*

Social Protest (2019) and *"A God of Justice?": The Problem of Evil in Twentieth-Century Black Literature* (2009). She is coeditor of the collection *Comics and the U.S. South* (2012). Her most recently published essays explore race, genre, and comics in representations of historical figures such as Nat Turner, Stagger Lee, and Emmett Till. She is editor of *Inks: The Journal of the Comics Studies Society* and chair of the International Comic Arts Forum.

Richard Yarborough is professor of English and African American studies at the University of California, Los Angeles. His work focuses on race, representation, and American culture, and he has written on authors such as Frederick Douglass, Pauline Hopkins, Charles Chesnutt, Harriet Beecher Stowe, and Richard Wright. He is the associate general editor of *The Heath Anthology of American Literature*, as well as the former director of the award-winning Library of Black Literature series, published by the UP of New England. In 2012 he received the American Studies Association's inaugural Richard A. Yarborough Mentoring Award, which is named in his honor. He was the 2016 recipient of the Darwin T. Turner Distinguished Scholar Award presented by the African American Literature and Culture Society.

Reggie Scott Young served as professor of creative writing and American literatures at the University of Louisiana at Lafayette. With Marcia Gaudet he compiled and edited *Mozart and Leadbelly: Stories and Essays* and, with Marcia Gaudet and Wiley Cash, *"This Louisiana Thing That Drives Me": The Legacy of Ernest J. Gaines*. Young also served as guest editor of a special issue of *Obsidian* on the novelist and poet Jeffery Renard Allen. His critical essays have appeared in *Multicultural Literature and Literacies: Making Space for Difference, Contemporary African American Fiction: New Critical Essays, August Wilson and Black Aesthetics*, and various literary journals. Young's creative works include a volume of poetry, *Yardbirds Squawking at the Moon*, and his works of poetry, fiction, and creative nonfiction have appeared in publications such as *Louisiana Literature, Oxford American, Fifth Wednesday Journal*, and *African American Review*.

SURVEY RESPONDENTS

The following scholars responded to the MLA's survey on teaching works by Ernest J. Gaines. Their comments aided our preparation of the "Materials" section of this volume. Except when new information has been offered, the list indicates scholars' institutional affiliations at the time of the survey.

Simone A. James Alexander, *Seton Hall University*
Susan Ayres, *Texas A&M University School of Law*
Margaret Bauer, *East Carolina University*
Herman Beavers, *University of Pennsylvania*
Alison Bertolini, *Louisiana State University*
Joanne Braxton, *College of William and Mary*
Carolyn Brown, *Université de Montréal*
Lillie Anne Brown, *Florida A&M University*
Deborah Cains, *ITT Technical Institute*
Jerry W. Carlson, *City College, City University of New York*
Robert Donahoo, *Sam Houston State University*
Mary Ellen Doyle, *Spalding University*
Kendra Hamilton, *University of Virginia*
Maria Hebert-Leiter, *Lycoming College*
Monica F. Jacobe, *Princeton University*
LaToya Jefferson, *Southwest Tennessee Community College*
Tori Kiuchi, *Nihon University, Japan*
Leslie Lewis, *Ithaca College*
Robert M. Luscher, *University of Nebraska, Kearney*
David Magill, *Longwood University*
Chante B. Martin, *Savannah State University*
Beth Maxfield, *Henderson State University*
Sharon Mitchell, *Wilkes Community College*
Jennifer Nolan, *North Carolina State University*
Lynn Pifer, *Mansfield University of Pennsylvania*
Jessica Reeves, *University of Louisiana, Lafayette*
Katherine Rummell, *California Polytechnic State University*
Denise R. Shaw, *University of South Carolina, Union*
Virginia Whatley Smith, *University of Alabama, Birmingham*
Rosemarie R. Sonnier, *McNeese State University*
Jacob Stratman, *John Brown University*
Beth VanRheenen, *Lourdes University*
Sabrina Völz, *Leuphana University of Lüneburg, Germany*
Nancy Whitt, *Samford University*
Quiana Whitted, *University of South Carolina*
Lorna Wiedmann, *Wisconsin Lutheran College*
Roland L. Williams, Jr., *Temple University*
Richard Yarborough, *University of California, Los Angeles*

WORKS CITED

Alexander, Bryant Keith. "Embracing the Teachable Moment: The Black Gay Body in the Classroom as Embodied Text." Johnson and Henderson, pp. 249–65.

Alexander, Michelle. *The New Jim Crow: Mass Incarceration in the Age of Colorblindness*. New Press, 2010.

Alexander, Simone A. James. *African Diasporic Women's Narratives: Politics of Resistance, Survival, and Citizenship*. UP of Florida, 2014.

Amani, Konan. "Change in Ernest J. Gaines' *Catherine Carmier*." *Revue du CAMES*, vol. 8, no. 1, 2007, pp. 257–64.

Andrews, William L. "'We Ain't Going Back There': The Idea of Progress in *The Autobiography of Miss Jane Pittman*." *Black American Literary Forum*, vol. 11, no. 4, Winter 1977, pp. 146–49.

Antonucci, Michael A. "'Any Woman's Blues': Sherley Anne Williams and the Blues Aesthetic." *Cultural Sites of Critical Insight: Philosophy, Aesthetics, and African American and Native American Women's Writings*, edited by Angela L. Cotten and Christa Davis Acampora, State U of New York P, 2007, pp. 67–82.

Arroyo, Elizabeth Fortson. "The Asterisk Southerner." *Oxford American*, Aug.–Sept. 1996, pp. 26–28.

Auger, Philip. *Native Sons in No Man's Land: Rewriting Afro-American Manhood in the Novels of Baldwin, Walker, Wideman, and Gaines*. Garland, 2000.

Babb, Valerie Melissa. *Ernest Gaines*. Twayne, 1991.

———. "Old-Fashioned Modernism: 'The Changing Same' in *A Lesson Before Dying*." Estes, *Critical Reflections*, pp. 250–64.

Bakhtin, Mikhail. *Rabelais and His World*. Translated by Helene Iswolsky, Indiana UP, 1984.

Baldwin, James. "The Uses of the Blues." 1964. *The Cross of Redemption: Uncollected Writings*, edited by Randall Kenan, Pantheon, 2010, pp. 57–66.

Barlett, Peggy F. "Three Visions of Masculine Success on American Farms." *Country Boys: Masculinity and Rural Life*, edited by Hugh Campbell et al., Pennsylvania State UP, 2006, pp. 47–65.

Barlow, Daniel. "Blues Narrative Form, African American Fiction, and the African Diaspora." *Narrative*, vol. 24, no. 2, May 2016, pp. 134–55.

Bauer, Margaret D. *William Faulkner's Legacy: "What Shadow, What Stain, What Mark."* UP of Florida, 2005.

Beauford, Fred. "A Conversation with Ernest J. Gaines." Lowe, *Conversations*, pp. 16–24.

Beavers, Herman. *Wrestling Angels into Song: The Fictions of Ernest J. Gaines and James Alan McPherson*. U of Pennsylvania P, 1995.

Bennett, Dale E. "The Work of the Louisiana Supreme Court: Criminal Law and Procedure." *Louisiana Law Review*, vol. 9, no. 2, 1948–49, pp. 247–77.

Binder, Guyora. "Making the Best of Felony Murder." *Boston University Law Review*, vol. 91, 2011, pp. 403–559.

Blount, Marcellus. "The Preacherly Text: African American Poetry and Vernacular Performance." *PMLA*, vol. 107, no. 3, May 1992, pp. 582–93.

Bluestone, George. *Novels into Film*. Johns Hopkins UP, 1957.

Bockting, Ineke. "Aspects of Liminality in Vladimir Nabokov's *Lolita*." *Migration and Exile: Charting New Literary and Artistic Territories*, edited by Ada Savin, Cambridge Scholars Publishing, 2013, pp. 73–80.

Bracey, John H., Jr., et al., editors. *SOS—Calling All Black People: A Black Arts Movement Reader*. U of Massachusetts P, 2014.

Bradley, David. *The Chaneysville Incident*. Harper and Row, 1981.

Brasseaux, Carl A. *Acadian to Cajun: Transformation of a People, 1803–1877*. UP of Mississippi, 1992.

Brathwaite, Kamau. *Roots*. U of Michigan P, 1993.

Bromley, Patrick. "Sh!#ting on the Classics: *Driving Miss Daisy*." *F This Movie!*, 6 Mar. 2012, www.fthismovie.net/2012/03/shting-on-classics-driving-miss-daisy.html.

Broonzy, Big Bill. "I Wonder When Will I Get to Be Called a Man." *Big Bill Broonzy Sings Country Blues*, Folkways Records FA-2326, 1957.

Brown, Scot. *Fighting for Us: Maulana Karenga, the US Organization, and Black Cultural Nationalism*. New York UP, 2003.

Brown, Sterling. "What Are the Blues?" *Freedom: The Golden Gate Quartet and Josh White at the Library of Congress*, Bridge Records 9114, 1940.

Bryant, Jerry H. *"Born in a Mighty Bad Land": The Violent Man in African American Folklore and Fiction*. Indiana UP, 2003.

Buck v. Davis. 137 S.Ct. 759. 2017. *Westlaw*, 2018, Thomson Reuters, westlaw.com /Document/I912d50fbf8df11e6bfb79a463a4b3bc7/.

Buell, Lawrence. *The Environmental Imagination: Thoreau, Nature Writing, and the Formation of American Culture*. Belknap Press, 1995.

Butler, Judith. *Giving an Account of Oneself*. Fordham UP, 2005.

———. "Recognition and Critique: An Interview with Judith Butler." By Rasmus Willig. *Distinktion: Journal of Social Theory*, vol. 13, 2012, pp. 139–44.

Byerman, Keith E. *Fingering the Jagged Grain: Tradition and Form in Recent Black Fiction*. U of Georgia P, 1985.

———. *Remembering the Past in Contemporary African American Fiction*. U of North Carolina P, 2005.

Callahan, John. "Hearing Is Believing: The Landscape of Voice in Ernest Gaines's *Bloodline*." *Callaloo*, vol. 7, no. 1, Winter 1984, pp. 86–112.

———. "Image-Making: Tradition and the Two Versions of *The Autobiography of Miss Jane Pittman*." *Chicago Review*, vol. 29, no. 2, 1977, pp. 45–62.

———. *In the African-American Grain: Call-and-Response in Twentieth-Century Black Fiction*. U of Illinois P, 2001.

———. *In the African-American Grain: The Pursuit of Voice in Twentieth-Century Black Fiction*. U of Illinois P, 1988.

Carleton, Mark T. "The Politics of the Convict Lease System in Louisiana: 1868–1901." *Louisiana History: The Journal of the Louisiana Historical Association*, vol. 8, no. 1, Winter 1967, pp. 5–25.

Carmean, Karen. *Ernest J. Gaines: A Critical Companion*. Greenwood Press, 1998.

Caroll, Anne Elizabeth. *Word, Image, and the New Negro: Representation and Identity in the Harlem Renaissance*. Indiana UP, 2007.

Carpenter, Brian, and Tom Franklin, editors. *Grit Lit: A Rough South Reader*. U of South Carolina P, 2012.

Carter, Tom. "Ernest Gaines." Lowe, *Conversations*, pp. 80–85.

Cash, W. J. *The Mind of the South*. 1941. Vintage, 1969.

Chesnutt, Charles W. *The Marrow of Tradition*. 1901. Dover, 2003.

Clark, Keith. "Are We Family? Pedagogy and the Race for Queerness." Johnson and Henderson, pp. 266–75.

———. *Black Manhood in James Baldwin, Ernest J. Gaines, and August Wilson*. U of Illinois P, 2002.

———. "Que(e)rying the Prison-House of Black Male Desire: Homosociality in Ernest Gaines's 'Three Men.'" *African American Review*, vol. 40, no. 2, Summer 2006, pp. 239–55.

Clarke, Deborah. "William Faulkner and Henry Ford: Cars, Men, Bodies, and History as Bunk." *Faulkner and His Contemporaries*, edited by Joseph R. Urgo and Ann J. Abadie, UP of Mississippi, 2004, pp. 93–112.

Cleaver, Eldridge. *Soul on Ice*. Dell, 1968.

Cobb, James C. *The Most Southern Place on Earth: The Mississippi Delta and the Roots of Regional Identity*. Oxford UP, 1992.

Collins, Patricia Hill. *Black Feminist Thought: Knowledge, Consciousness, and the Politics of Empowerment*. 2nd ed., Routledge, 2000.

Columbus, Christopher. "Narrative of the Third Voyage, 1498–1500." Lauter, pp. 128–31.

Condé, Maryse. *Segu*. Penguin, 1988.

Conniff, Michael L., and Thomas J. Davis. "Africans in the Caribbean." *Africans in the Americas: A History of the Black Diaspora*, St. Martin's Press, 1994, pp. 71–85.

Coser, Rose Laub. "Some Social Functions of Laughter: A Study of Humor in a Hospital Setting." *Human Relations*, vol. 12, no. 2, Apr. 1959, pp. 171–82.

Costello, Brannon. *Plantation Airs: Racial Paternalism and the Transformations of Class in Southern Fiction, 1945–1971*. Louisiana State UP, 2007.

Costello, Brian J. *A History of Pointe Coupée Parish, Louisiana*. Margaret Media, 2010.

Cox, Ida. "Wild Women Don't Have the Blues." Paramount 12228, 1924.

Crenshaw, Kimberlé. "Demarginalizing the Intersection of Race and Sex: A Black Feminist Critique of Antidiscrimination Doctrine, Feminist Theory, and Antiracist Politics." *The Black Feminist Reader*, edited by Joy James and T. Denean Sharpley-Whiting, Blackwell, 2000, pp. 208–38.

Cuvier, Georges Leopold. "Varieties of Human Species." Johnson and Lyne, pp. 54–57.

Davachi, Reza. "The Kermit Washington Story—Redemption." *YouTube*, 4 Apr. 2008, youtu.be/WkvnKMZXtto.

Davis, Angela. *Women, Race, and Class*. Vintage, 1983.

Davis, Francis. *The History of the Blues: The Roots, the Music, the People*. Da Capo Press, 2003.

Davis, Thadious M. *Southscapes: Geographies of Race, Region, and Literature.* U of North Carolina P, 2011.

Denno, Deborah W. "When Willie Francis Died: The 'Disturbing' Story Behind One of the Eighth Amendment's Most Enduring Standards of Risk." *Death Penalty Stories,* edited by John H. Blume and Jordan M. Steiker, Thomson Reuters / Foundation Press, 2009, pp. 17–94.

Dent, Thomas C. "Enriching the Paper Trail: An Interview with Tom Dent." By Kalamu ya Salaam. *African American Review,* vol. 27, no. 2, Summer 1993, pp. 327–44.

———. "Marcus B. Christian: An Appreciation." *Black American Literature Forum,* vol. 18, no. 1, Spring 1984, pp. 22–26.

———. "New Theaters across the South Join Hands." *Black World,* Apr. 1973, pp. 92–95.

———. *Southern Journey: A Return to the Civil Rights Movement.* William Morrow, 1996.

Desruisseaux, Paul. "Ernest Gaines: A Conversation." Lowe, *Conversations,* pp. 112–18.

Dixon, Melvin. *Ride Out the Wilderness: Geography and Identity in Afro-American Literature.* U of Illinois P, 1987.

Dormer, Richard. *The Rise and Fall of Jim Crow.* 2002. TV miniseries.

Dormon, James H. Preface. *Creoles of Color of the Gulf South,* edited by Dormon, U of Tennessee P, 1996, pp. ix–xv.

Dorr, Lisa Lindquist. "The Perils of the Back Seat: Date Rape, Race, and Gender in 1950s America." *Gender and History,* vol. 20, no. 1, Apr. 2008, pp. 27–47.

Douglass, Frederick. *My Bondage and My Freedom.* Edited by John David Smith, Penguin Classics, 2003.

———. *Narrative of the Life of Frederick Douglass, an American Slave.* 1845. Edited by Houston A. Baker, Jr., Signet, 1968.

———. *Narrative of the Life of Frederick Douglass, An American Slave.* 1845. The Modern Library, 2000.

———. *Narrative of the Life of Frederick Douglass, an American Slave, Written by Himself.* 1845. Edited by David W. Blight, Bedford Books of St. Martin's Press, 1993.

Doyle, Mary Ellen. "*The Autobiography of Miss Jane Pittman* as a Fictional Edited Autobiography." Estes, *Critical Reflections,* pp. 89–106.

———. *Voices from the Quarters: The Fiction of Ernest J. Gaines.* Louisiana State UP, 2002.

Drash, Wayne. "Author Ernest Gaines Comes Home to Where His Ancestors Were Enslaved." *CNN,* 9 Nov. 2010, www.cnn.com/2010/US/11/09/ernest.gaines.cemetery /index.html?hpt=C1. Accessed 21 May 2014.

Dressler, Joshua. *Understanding Criminal Law.* 4th ed., LexisNexis, 2006.

Du Bois, W. E. B. *The Souls of Black Folk.* Dover, 1994.

Dunbar-Nelson, Alice Moore. "People of Color in Louisiana." Kein, *Creole,* pp. 3–41.

Duncan, Todd. "Scene and Life Cycle in Ernest Gaines' *Bloodline.*" *Callaloo,* vol. 1, no. 3, May 1978, pp. 85–101.

DuVernay, Ava, director. *13th.* Forward Movement / Kandoo Films, 2016.

Ebert, Roger. "*Do The Right Thing.*" Review of *Do the Right Thing,* by Spike Lee. RogerEbert.com, 30 June 1989, Ebert Digital, www.rogerebert.com/reviews/do-the -right-thing-1989.html.

Eckholm, Erik. "One Execution Botched, Oklahoma Delays the Next." *The New York Times*, 29 Apr. 2014, www.nytimes.com/2014/04/30/us/oklahoma-executions.html.

E.L.E. "Notes: Criminal Law—Felony-Murder Doctrine—Death Caused by Shot Fired by Person Other Than Felon." *Tulane Law Review*, vol. 22, 1947–48, pp. 325–26.

Ellison, Ralph. "Cadillac Flambé." *American Review*, Feb. 1973, pp. 249–69.

———. *Invisible Man*. Vintage, 1952.

———. "Richard Wright's Blues." 1945. *Shadow and Act*, Random House, 1964, pp. 77–94.

Equiano, Olaudah. *The Interesting Narrative of the Life of Olaudah Equiano; or, Gustavus Vassa, the African, Written by Himself*. 1789. W. W. Norton, 2001.

Estes, David C., editor. *Critical Reflections on the Fiction of Ernest J. Gaines*. U of Georgia P, 1994.

———. Introduction. Estes, *Critical Reflections*, pp. 1–11.

Evans, Jessica, and Stuart Hall, editors. *Visual Culture: The Reader*. Sage, 1999.

Ex parte Guzmon. 730 S.W.2d 724. Texas State Court of Criminal Appeals, 1987. *Westlaw*, 2018, Thomson Reuters, westlaw.com/Document/Ia5d7a614e79f11d99439b076ef9ec4de/.

Fabre, Michel. "Bayonne or the Yoknapatawpha of Ernest Gaines." Translated by Melvin Dixon and Didier Malaquin, *Callaloo*, vol. 3, May 1978, pp. 110–24.

Farland, Maria. "Modernist Versions of Pastoral: Poetic Inspiration, Scientific Expertise, and the 'Degenerate' Farmer." *American Literary History*, vol. 19, no. 4, Winter 2007, pp. 905–36.

Faulkner, William. "Dry September." *Collected Stories of William Faulkner*, Random House, 1950, pp. 169–83.

———. "The Fire and the Hearth." *Go Down, Moses*, 1942. Penguin, 1978, pp. 31–106.

———. *Intruder in the Dust*. 1948. Vintage, 1972.

———. *Requiem for a Nun*. 1951. Vintage, 1996.

———. *Sanctuary*. 1931. Vintage, 1993.

———. *The Sound and the Fury*. 1929. Vintage, 1984.

Faw, Bob, producer. "Ernest Gaines." *PBS Religion and Ethics Newsweekly*, 18 Feb. 2011, www.pbs.org/video/1799186954.

Ferguson, Moira. *Jamaica Kincaid: Where the Land Meets the Body*. UP of Virginia, 1994.

Finney, Nikky. *Head Off and Split: Poems*. TriQuarterly / Northwestern UP, 2011.

Fitzgerald, F. Scott. *The Great Gatsby*. Scribner, 1995.

Fitzgerald, Gregory, and Peter Marchant. "An Interview: Ernest J. Gaines." Lowe, *Conversations*, pp. 3–15.

Fitzsimmons, Lorna. "*The Autobiography of Miss Jane Pittman*: Film, Intertext, and Ideology." *Studies in the Humanities*, vol. 28, nos. 1–2, June–Dec. 2001, pp. 94–110.

Folks, Jeffrey J., and Nancy Summers Folks. *The World Is Our Home: Society and Culture in Contemporary Southern Writing*. UP of Kentucky, 2000.

Foucault, Michel. *Discipline and Punish: The Birth of the Prison*. Translated by Alan Sheridan, Pantheon, 1977.

Francis, Willie. "My Trip to the Chair." As told to Samuel Montgomery. 1947. Afro-American Pamphlets, Part 3 (1827–1948), Rare Book and Special Collections Reading Room, Library of Congress. Ryan, *Demands*, pp. 33–44.

Franklin, H. Bruce, editor. *Prison Writing in Twentieth-Century America*. Penguin, 1998.

Freeman, Morgan, performer. *Driving Miss Daisy*. Directed by Bruce Beresford, Warner Brothers, 1989.

Freire, Paulo. *Pedagogy of the Oppressed*. Translated by Myra Bergman Ramos, Continuum, 1983.

Freud, Sigmund. *The Uncanny*. Translated by David McLintock, Penguin, 2003.

———. "Das Unheimliche." *Imago*, vol. 5, 1919, pp. 297–324.

Friedman, Andrew H. "*Tison v. Arizona*: The Death Penalty and the Non-Triggerman: The Scales of Justice Are Broken." *Cornell Law Review*, vol. 75, no. 1, Nov. 1989, pp. 123–57.

Gaines, Ernest. "Aunty and the Black Experience in Louisiana." Gaines, *Mozart*, pp. 45–51.

———. *The Autobiography of Miss Jane Pittman*. Dial Press, 1971.

———. *The Autobiography of Miss Jane Pittman*. 1971. Bantam, 1972.

———. *Bloodline*. Vintage, 1968.

———. *Bloodline*. 1968. W. W. Norton, 1976.

———. *Bloodline*. 1968. Vintage, 1997.

———. "Bloodline in Ink." Gaines, *Mozart*, pp. 37–44.

———. "Boy in the Double-Breasted Suit." *Transfer*, vol. 3, 1957, pp. 2–9.

———. *Catherine Carmier*. Atheneum, 1964.

———. *Catherine Carmier*. 1964. North Point Press, 1981.

———. "Chapter One of *The House and the Field*, a Novel." *Iowa Review*, vol. 3, 1972, pp. 121–25.

———. "Christ Walked Down Market Street." *Callaloo*, vol. 28, Fall 2005, pp. 907–13.

———. "Ernest J. Gaines: Master of the Novel. " *Academy of Achievement*, 4 May 2001, www.achievement.org/achiever/ernest-j-gaines/#interview. Accessed 21 May 2014.

———. "From *The Man Who Whipped Children*: Chapter 3." *Callaloo*, vol. 24, Fall 2001, pp. 1015–20.

———. *A Gathering of Old Men*. 1983. Vintage, 1984.

———. *A Gathering of Old Men*. 1983. Vintage, 1992.

———. "I Heard the Voices of My Louisiana People: A Conversation with Ernest Gaines." Interview by William Ferris. *Humanities*, vol. 19, no. 4, July-August 1998, pp. 10–13.

———. "The Influence of Multi-Art Forms on the Fiction of Ernest J. Gaines: An Interview with Ernest Gaines." By Marcia Gaudet and Darrell Bourque. *Interdisciplinary Humanities*, vol. 20, no. 1, Spring 2003, pp. 76–92.

———. "In My Father's House." *Massachusetts Review*, vol. 18, 1977, pp. 650–59. Rpt. in *Chant of Saints*, edited by Michael S. Harper and Robert B. Stepto, U of Illinois P, 1979, pp. 339–48.

———. *In My Father's House.* 1978. Knopf, 1983.

———. *In My Father's House.* 1978. W. W. Norton, 1983.

———. "Just Like a Tree." *Sewanee Review*, vol. 71, 1963, pp. 542–68.

———. *A Lesson Before Dying.* Knopf, 1993.

———. *A Lesson Before Dying.* 1993. Vintage, 1994.

———. *A Lesson Before Dying.* 1993. Vintage, 1997.

———. "A Lesson for Living." Interview by Dale W. Brown. *Sojourners*, Sept.–Oct. 2002, pp. 30–33.

———. "A Long Day in November." *Texas Quarterly*, vol. 7, 1964, pp. 190–224.

———. "A Long Day in November." Gaines, *Bloodline*, Vintage, 1968, pp. 3–79.

———. *A Long Day in November.* Dial, 1971.

———. "Mary Louise." *Stanford Short Stories*, edited by Wallace Earle Stegner and Richard Scowcroft, Stanford UP, 1960, pp. 27–42.

———. "A *MELUS* Interview: Ernest J. Gaines." By Wolfgang Lepschy. *MELUS*, vol. 24, no. 1, Spring 1999, pp. 197–208.

———. "Miss Jane and I." Gaines, *Mozart*, pp. 3–23.

———. "Mozart and Leadbelly." Gaines, *Mozart*, pp. 24–31.

———. *Mozart and Leadbelly: Stories and Essays.* Edited by Marcia Gaudet and Reggie Young, Knopf, 2005.

———. "My Grandpa and the Haint." *New Mexico Quarterly*, vol. 36, 1966, pp. 149–60.

———. "My Uncle and the Fat Lady." *Callaloo*, vol. 30, Summer 2007, pp. 684–95.

———. *Of Love and Dust.* Dial, 1967.

———. *Of Love and Dust.* 1967. W. W. Norton, 1979.

———. *Of Love and Dust.* Vintage, 1997.

———. *Of Love and Dust.* 1967. Vintage, 1994.

———. "Old Jack." *Callaloo*, vol. 24, Winter 2001, pp. 69–70.

———. "The Revenge of Old Men." *Callaloo*, vol. 1, May 1978, pp. 5–21.

———. "Robert Louis Stevenson Banks, aka Chimley." *Georgia Review*, vol. 37, 1983, pp. 385–89.

———. "The Sky Is Gray." *Negro Digest*, vol. 12, Aug. 1963, pp. 72–96.

———. "The Sky Is Gray." Gaines, *Bloodline*, Vintage, 1968, pp. 83–120.

———. "Three Men." Gaines, *Bloodline*, Vintage, 1997, pp. 121–58.

———. *The Tragedy of Brady Sims.* Vintage, 2017.

———. "The Turtles." *Transfer*, vol. 1, 1956, pp. 1–9. Rpt. in Gaines, *Mozart*, pp. 77–86.

———. "A Very Big Order: Reconstructing Identity." Gaines, *Mozart*, pp. 32–36.

———. "Writing *A Lesson Before Dying.*" Gaines, *Mozart*, pp. 52–62.

———. "Writing *A Lesson Before Dying.*" *Southern Review*, vol. 41, Fall 2005, pp. 770–77.

Gates, Henry Louis, Jr. *Figures in Black: Words, Signs, and the "Racial" Self.* Oxford UP, 1987.

———. *The Signifying Monkey: A Theory of African-American Literary Criticism.* Oxford UP, 1988.

Gaudet, Marcia, and Carl Wooton, editors. *Porch Talk with Ernest Gaines: Conversations on the Writer's Craft*. Louisiana State UP, 1990.

——. "Talking with Ernest Gaines." Lowe, *Conversations*, pp. 221–40.

Gaudet, Marcia, and Reggie Young. Introduction. Gaines, *Mozart*, pp. ix–xxii.

Gerima, Haile. *Sankofa*. Channel Four Films et al., 1993.

Ghansah, Rachel Kaadzi. "When the Lights Shut Off: Kendrick Lamar and the Decline of the Black Blues Narrative." *Los Angeles Review of Books*, 31 Jan. 2013, lareviewofbooks.org/essay/when-the-lights-shut-off-kendrick-lamar-and-the-decline-of-the-black-blues-narrative. Accessed 15 Dec. 2014.

Gifford, Terry. *Pastoral*. Routledge, 1999.

Gilroy, Paul. " The Black Atlantic as a Counterculture to Modernity." *The Black Atlantic: Modernity and Double Consciousness*, Harvard UP, 1993, pp. 1–40.

——. "Driving while Black." *Car Cultures*, edited by Daniel Miller, Berg, 2001, pp. 81–104.

Gladney, Margaret Rose, editor. *How Am I to Be Heard? Letters of Lillian Smith*. U of North Carolina P, 1993.

Godden, Richard. "Quentin Compson: Tyrrhenian Vase or Crucible of Race?" Polk, pp. 99–138.

Goddu, Teresa A. *Gothic America: Narrative, History, and Nation*. Columbia UP, 1997.

Goodwin v. Balkcom. 684 F.2d 794. United States Court of Appeals for the Eleventh Circuit, 1 Nov. 1982. *Westlaw*, 2018, Thomson Reuters, westlaw.com/Document/Id793745992f811d9bc61beebb95be672/.

Graham, Maryemma, editor. *Cambridge Companion to the African American Novel*. Cambridge UP, 2004.

Gramsci, Antonio. *Selections from* The Prison Notebooks. Edited and translated by Quintin Hoare and Geoffrey Nowell Smith, International Publishers, 1971.

Griffin, Joseph. "Creole and Singaleese: Disruptive Caste in *Catherine Carmier* and *A Gathering of Old Men*." Estes, *Critical Reflections*, pp. 30–45.

Gross, Jane. "N.B.A.'s Rebuilding Program Is Showing Results." *The New York Times*, 23 Dec. 1984, www.nytimes.com/1984/12/23/sports/nba-s-rebuilding-program-is-showing-results.html.

Gussow, Adam. "'Shoot Myself a Cop': Mamie Smith's 'Crazy Blues' as Social Text." *Callaloo*, vol. 25, no. 1, Winter 2002, pp. 8–44.

Haggerty, George E. "'Promoting Homosexuality' in the Classroom." *Professions of Desire: Lesbian and Gay Studies in Literature*, edited by Haggerty and Bonnie Zimmerman, The Modern Language Association of America, 1995, pp. 11–18.

Harper, Frances E. W. *Iola Leroy; or, Shadows Uplifted*. 1892. Dover, 2010.

Harrington, Stephanie. "Did 'Jane Pittman' Really Show Us Black History?" *The New York Times*, 10 Feb. 1974, p. D17.

Harris, Michael D. *Colored Pictures: Race and Visual Representation*. U of North Carolina P, 2003.

Harris, Trudier. *Saints, Sinners, Saviors: Strong Black Women in African American Literature*. Palgrave, 2001.

———. *The Scary Mason-Dixon Line: African American Writers and the South*. Louisiana State UP, 2013.

Harrison, Elizabeth Jane. *Female Pastoral: Women Writers Re-Visioning the American South*. U of Tennessee P, 1991.

Harty, Chris. *Ship of Slaves: The Middle Passage*. History Channel, 1997.

Hemingway, Ernest. *A Farewell to Arms*. Charles Scribner's Sons, 1969.

Hess, Natalie. "Code Switching and Style Shifting as Markers of Liminality in Literature." *Language and Literature*, vol. 5, no. 1, 1996, pp. 5–18.

Hicks, Jack. *In the Singer's Temple: Prose Fictions of Barthelme, Gaines, Brautigan, Piercy, Kesey, and Kosinski*. U of North Carolina P, 1981.

Hinds, Jay-Paul. "Shame and Its Sons: Black Men, Fatherhood, and Filicide." *Pastoral Psychology*, vol. 63, nos. 5–6, Dec. 2014, pp. 641–58.

Hiramoto, Akira. *Me and the Devil Blues: The Unreal Life of Robert Johnson*. Del Rey / Ballantine, 2008. 2 vols.

Hobson, Fred. "The History of the Southern Gothic Sensibility." *Oxford American*, Oct.–Nov. 1996, pp. 15–19.

———. *But Now I See: The White Southern Racial Conversion Narrative*. Louisiana UP, 1999.

Hodson, Christopher. *The Acadian Diaspora: An Eighteenth-Century History*. Oxford UP, 2012.

Hoffman, Frederick John. *William Faulkner*. Twayne, 1966.

Holloway, Karla F. C. *Codes of Conduct: Race, Ethics, and the Color of Our Character*. Rutgers UP, 1995.

———. *Passed On: African American Mourning Stories*. Duke UP, 2002.

Hopkins, Lightnin'. "Lightnin' Hopkins—Tim Moore's Farm." *Metrolyrics*, www.metrolyrics.com/tim-moores-farm-lyrics-lightnin-hopkins.html. Accessed 14 Feb. 2014.

———. "Sam Lightnin' Hopkins—Tim Moore's Farm." Uploaded by Jazz Everyday!, *YouTube*, 10 Mar. 2016, youtu.be/BFQsBSrFuoE. Accessed 14 Feb. 2014.

———. "Trouble in Mind." *Autobiography in Blues*, Tradition TLP-1040, 1960.

Hughes, Langston. *The Collected Poems of Langston Hughes*. Edited by Arnold Rampersad, Vintage, 1995.

Hume, David. "Of National Characters." Johnson and Lyne, pp. 49–51.

Hunter, Charlayne. "'Jane' Show: Tale of Hope and Efforts." *The New York Times*, 31 Jan. 1974, p. 68.

Hurston, Zora Neale. *Dust Tracks on a Road*. 1942. Edited by Robert E. Hemenway, 2nd ed., U of Illinois P, 1984.

———. *Their Eyes Were Watching God*. Harper Perennial, 2013.

Jackson, Blyden. "Jane Pittman through the Years: A People's Tale." *American Letters and the Historical Consciousness: Essays in Honor of Lewis P. Simpson*, edited by J. Gerald Kennedy and Daniel Mark Fogel, Louisiana State UP, 1987, pp. 255–73.

Jackson, Ronald L., II. *Scripting the Black Masculine Body: Identity, Discourse, and Racial Politics in Popular Media*. State U of New York P, 2006.

James, Stanlie M. "Mothering: A Possible Black Feminist Link to Social Transformation?" *Theorizing Black Feminisms: The Visionary Pragmatism of Black Women*, edited by James and Abena P. A. Busia, Routledge, 1993, pp. 44–55.

Jefferson, Thomas. "From *Notes on the State of Virginia*." Johnson and Lyne, pp. 43–48.

Jentsch, Ernst. "Zur Psychologie des Unheimlichen." *Psychiatrisch-Neurologische Wochenschrift*, nos. 22–23, 1906, pp. 195–98, 203–05.

Jess, Tyehimba. *Leadbelly: Poems*. Verse Press, 2005.

Jimoh, A. Yemisi. *Spiritual, Blues, and Jazz People in African American Fiction: Living in Paradox*. U of Tennessee P, 2002.

Johnson, Charles. *Dreamer*. Simon and Schuster, 1998.

———. *Middle Passage*. Atheneum, 1990.

———. *Oxherding Tale*. Indiana UP, 1982.

———. *Shadow of the Plantation*. U of Chicago P, 1934.

Johnson, E. Patrick, and Mae G. Henderson, editors. *Black Queer Studies: A Critical Anthology*. Duke UP, 2006.

Johnson, James Weldon. *The Autobiography of an Ex-Colored Man*. 1912. W. W. Norton, 2015.

Johnson, Robert. "Hellhound on My Trail." Perfect 70956, 1937.

Johnson, Vernon D., and Bill Lyne, editors. *Walkin' the Talk: An Anthology of African American Studies*. Prentice Hall, 2003.

Jones, Edward P. *The Known World*. Amistad, 2003.

Jones, Suzanne W. "New Narratives of Southern Manhood: Race, Masculinity, and Closure in Ernest Gaines's Fiction." Folks and Folks, pp. 29–52.

Kael, Pauline. "Cicely Tyson Goes to the Fountain." *The New Yorker*, 28 Jan. 1974, pp. 73–75.

Kant, Immanuel. "On National Characteristics." Johnson and Lyne, pp. 52–53.

Karem, Jeff. *The Romance of Authenticity: The Cultural Politics of Regional and Ethnic Literatures*. U of Virginia P, 2004.

Kein, Sybil, editor. *Creole: The History and Legacy of Louisiana's Free People of Color*. Louisiana State UP, 2000.

———. Introduction. Kein, *Creole*, pp. xiii–xxiv.

King, Martin Luther, Jr. "I've Been to the Mountaintop." Mason Temple, Memphis, TN, 3 Apr. 1968. *American Rhetoric*, 2 Feb. 2017, www.americanrhetoric.com/speeches/mlkivebeentothemountaintop.htm.

King James Bible. Tecarta Bible app, version 5.0.

Knight, Etheridge. *The Essential Etheridge Knight*. U of Pittsburgh P, 1986.

———. "The Idea of Ancestry." *The Norton Anthology of African American Literature*, edited by Henry Louis Gates, Jr., and Nellie Y. McKay, W. W. Norton, 1997, pp. 1867–68.

Korty, John, director. *The Autobiography of Miss Jane Pittman: Thirtieth Anniversary Special Edition*. Sony / Warner, 2004.

LaFave, Wayne R. *Criminal Law*. 5th ed., West, 2010. Hornbook series.

Lamar, Kendrick. *Good Kid, M.A.A.D. City*. Aftermath, 2012.

Laney, Ruth. "A Conversation with Ernest Gaines." Lowe, *Conversations*, pp. 56–68.

———, writer and producer. *Ernest J. Gaines: Louisiana Stories. Louisiana Public Broadcasting*, www.lpb.org/index.php?/site/programs/ernest_j._gaines_louisiana_stories.

The Last Poets. Douglas, 1970. LP album.

Lathan, Stan, director. *The Sky Is Gray*. Monterey, 2005.

Lauter, Paul, editor. *The Heath Anthology of American Literature: Colonial Period to 1800*. Vol. A, 5th ed., Houghton Mifflin, 2006.

Ledbetter, Huddie (Lead Belly). "Good Morning Blues." Bluebird B-8791, 1941.

Lee, Spike, director. *Do the Right Thing*. Universal, 1989.

Leek, Frederike van der. "Significant Syntax: The Case of Exceptional Passives." *Dutch Working Papers in English Language and Linguistics*, vol. 27, 1992, pp. 1–28.

Levs, Josh, et al. "Oklahoma's Botched Lethal Injection Marks New Front in Battle over Executions." *CNN*, 8 Sept. 2014, www.cnn.com/2014/04/30/us/oklahoma-botched-execution.

Levy, Emanuel. "*Driving Miss Daisy*: One of Worst Oscar Winners." *Cinema 24/7*, 25 Dec. 2013, emanuellevy.com/review/featured-review/driving-miss-daisy-one-of-worst-oscar-winners/.

Linney, Romulus. *A Lesson Before Dying*. Dramatists Play Service, 2001.

Locke, John. "An Essay Concerning Human Understanding." Lauter, pp. 635–36.

Longfellow, Henry Wadsworth. *Evangeline*. 1847. Edited by Lewis B. Semple, Pelican, 1999.

Louisiana ex rel. Francis v. Resweber. 329 U.S. 459 (1947). *Westlaw*, 2018, Thomson Reuters, westlaw.com/Document/Id8dfe7319c1c11d993e6d35cc61aab4a/.

Louisiana Laws Revised Statutes. La. Rev. Stat. Ann. § 14:30. Editor's and revisor's notes. West, 2015. *Westlaw*, 2018, Thomson Reuters, westlaw.com/RelatedInformation/NA22036E049FA11E5B13ADCD0475974AF/riEditorialMaterials.html?.

Love, Jeremy. *Bayou*. DC Comics, 2009–10. 2 vols.

Lowe, John, editor. *Conversations with Ernest Gaines*. UP of Mississippi, 1995.

———. "From Yoknapatawpha County to St. Raphael Parish: Faulknerian Influence on Ernest Gaines." *Faulkner and the Black Literatures of the Americas*, edited by Jay Watson and James G. Thomas, Jr., UP of Mississippi, 2016, pp. 161–82.

———. "An Interview with Ernest Gaines." Lowe, *Conversations*, pp. 297–328.

———. "Transcendence in the House of the Dead: The Subversive Gaze of *A Lesson Before Dying*." Folks and Folks, pp. 142–62.

MacAndrew, Elizabeth. *The Gothic Tradition in Fiction*. Columbia UP, 1979.

Malcolm X. *The Autobiography of Malcolm X*. With Alex Haley, 1965. Ballantine, 1973.

———. "Speech at the Founding Rally of the Organization of Afro-American Unity." *By Any Means Necessary: Speeches, Interviews, and a Letter by Malcolm X*. Pathfinder Press, 1970, pp. 35–67.

Mallon, William T. "Voicing Manhood: Masculinity and Dialogue in Ernest J. Gaines's 'The Sky Is Gray,' 'Three Men,' and *A Gathering of Old Men*." *Southern Studies*, vol. 5, nos. 3–4, 1994, pp. 49–67.

Marx, Leo. *The Machine in the Garden: Technology and the Pastoral Ideal in America.* Oxford UP, 1964.

McCord, David. "State Death Sentencing for Felony Murder Accomplices under the *Enmund* and *Tison* Standards." *Arizona State Law Journal*, vol. 32, 2000, pp. 843–96.

McCulloch, Derek. *Stagger Lee.* Illustrated by Shepherd Hendrix, Image Comics, 2006.

McDonald, Walter R. "'You Not a Bum, You a Man': Ernest J. Gaines's *Bloodline*." *Negro American Literature Forum*, vol. 9, no. 2, Summer 1975, pp. 47–49.

McDowell, Deborah E. "In the First Place: Making Frederick Douglass and the Afro-American Narrative Tradition." *African American Autobiography: A Collection of Critical Essays*, edited by William L. Andrews, Prentice Hall, 1993, pp. 172–83.

McFarlane, Brian. *Novel to Film: An Introduction to the Theory of Adaptation.* Clarendon Press, 1996.

McKay, Claude. *Selected Poems.* Edited by Joan R. Sherman, Dover, 1999.

McLaurin, Melton. "Rituals of Initiation and Rebellion: Adolescent Responses to Segregation in Southern Autobiography." *Southern Cultures*, vol. 3, no. 2, Summer 1997, pp. 5–24.

McRuer, Robert. *The Queer Renaissance: Contemporary American Literature and the Reinvention of Lesbian and Gay Identities.* New York UP, 1997.

Meyer, William E. H., Jr. "Ernest J. Gaines and the Black Child's Sensory Dilemma." *CLA Journal*, vol. 34, no. 4, June 1991, pp. 414–25.

Mills, Catherine. "Normative Violence, Vulnerability, and Responsibility." *Differences*, vol. 18, no. 2, 2007, pp. 133–56.

Morrison, Toni. *Beloved.* Penguin, 1988.

———. *The Bluest Eye.* Vintage, 1999.

Moser, Don. "The Pied Piper of Tucson." *Life*, 4 Mar. 1966, pp. 18+.

Mudimbe, V. Y. Introduction. *The Invention of Africa: Gnosis, Philosophy, and the Order of Knowledge*, Indiana UP, 1988, pp. ix–xii.

Naipaul, V. S. *A Turn in the South.* Knopf, 1989.

"NEA Big Read: Meet Ernest Gaines." *National Endowment for the Arts*, 17 June 2010, www.arts.gov/video/nea-big-read-meet-ernest-gaines.

Neal, Larry. "And Shine Swam On." *Black Fire: An Anthology of Afro-American Writing*, edited by LeRoi Jones (Amiri Baraka) and Neal, William Morrow, 1968, pp. 638–56.

Nelson, Emmanuel. "Towards a Transgressive Aesthetic: Gay Readings of Black Writing." *James White Review*, vol. 11, no. 3, 1994, pp. 15–17.

Nero, Charles I. "Toward a Gay Black Aesthetic: Signifying in Contemporary Black Gay Literature." *Brother to Brother: New Writings by Black Gay Men*, edited by Essex Hemphill, Alyson, 1991, pp. 229–52.

Nichols, Jeff, director. *Loving.* Universal, 2016.

Northup, Solomon. *Twelve Years a Slave.* Derby and Miller, 1853.

Oates, Joyce Carol. "When Characters from the Page Are Made Flesh on the Screen." *The New York Times*, 23 Mar. 1986, pp. H1+.

———. "Where Are You Going, Where Have You Been?" *Epoch*, Fall 1966, pp. 59–76.

O'Brien, John. "Ernest J. Gaines." Lowe, *Conversations*, pp. 25–38.

——. *Interviews with Black Writers*. Liveright, 1973.

O'Connor, John J. "TV: Splendid 'Jane Pittman' Relates Black History." *The New York Times*, 31 Jan. 1974, p. 67.

O'Reilly, Andrea. *Toni Morrison and Motherhood: A Politics of the Heart*. State U of New York P, 2004.

Packer, Jeremy. *Mobility without Mayhem: Safety, Cars, and Citizenship*. Duke UP, 2008.

Papa, Lee. "'His Feet on Your Neck': The New Religion in the Works of Ernest J. Gaines." *African American Review*, vol. 27, no. 2, Summer 1993, pp. 187–93.

Papanek, John. "Nobody, but Nobody, Is Going to Hurt My Teammates." *Sports Illustrated*, 31 Oct. 1977, www.si.com/vault/1977/10/31/626402/nobody-but-nobody-is -going-to-hurt-my-teammates.

Parrill, William. "An Interview with Ernest Gaines." Lowe, *Conversations*, pp. 172–99.

Patterson, Robert J. "Rethinking Definitions and Expectations: Civil Rights and Civil Rights Leadership in Ernest Gaines's *The Autobiography of Miss Jane Pittman*." *South Atlantic Quarterly*, vol. 112, no. 2, 2013, pp. 339–63.

Peloff, David. "History Day Documentary (Kentucky vs. Texas Western 1966)." *YouTube*, 12 May 2012, youtu.be/GTzCjaNaB-Y.

Percy, William Alexander. *Lanterns on the Levee: Recollections of a Planter's Son*. 1941. Louisiana State UP, 1991.

Piacentino, Ed. "'The Common Humanity That Is in Us All': Toward Racial Reconciliation in Gaines's *A Lesson Before Dying*." *Southern Quarterly*, vol. 42, no. 3, Spring 2004, pp. 73–85.

Polk, Noel, editor. *New Essays on* The Sound and the Fury. Cambridge UP, 1993.

Potter, Vilma Raskin. "*The Autobiography of Miss Jane Pittman*: How to Make a White Film from a Black Novel." *Literature/Film Quarterly*, vol. 3, no. 4, Fall 1975, pp. 371–75.

Prisoners in 2015. Bureau of Justice Statistics, summary NCJ250229, Dec. 2016, www .bjs.gov/content/pub/pdf/p15_sum.pdf.

Ramsey, Alvin. "Through a Glass Whitely: The Televised Rape of *Miss Jane Pittman*." *Black World*, Aug. 1974, pp. 31–36.

Randall, Dudley, and Margaret G. Burroughs, editors. *For Malcolm: Poems on the Life and the Death of Malcolm X*. Broadside Press, 1969.

Renken, Melanie A. "Revisiting *Tison v. Arizona*: The Constitutionality of Imposing the Death Penalty on Defendants Who Did Not Kill or Intend to Kill." *St. Louis University Law Journal*, vol. 51, 2007, pp. 895–933.

Rickels, Patricia. "An Interview with Ernest Gaines." Lowe, *Conversations*, pp. 119–36.

Rieger, Christopher. *Clear-Cutting Eden: Ecology and the Pastoral in Southern Literature*. U of Alabama P, 2009.

Rigsby, Ellen. Book review of *Precarious Life: The Power of Mourning and Violence*, by Judith Butler. *Law, Culture and the Humanities*, vol. 1, no. 3, Oct. 2005, pp. 403–05.

Riley, Alrick. *A Son of Africa*. Aimimage Productions, 1996.

Ringle, Ken. "A Southern Road to Freedom." *The Washington Post*, 20 July 1993, www .washingtonpost.com/archive/lifestyle/1993/07/20/a-southern-road-to-freedom /1f56f206-39d5-4c23-aca7-e26b58e8139f/?utm_term=.75f6ebb775f6.

Roberts, Dorothy. *Killing the Black Body: Race, Reproduction, and the Meaning of Liberty*. Vintage, 1997.

Roberts, John W. *From Trickster to Badman: The Black Folk Hero in Slavery and Freedom*. U of Pennsylvania P, 1990.

———. "The Individual and the Community in Two Short Stories." *Black American Literature Forum*, vol. 18, no. 3, Fall 1984, pp. 110–13.

Rowell, Charles. "This Louisiana Thing That Drives Me: An Interview with Ernest J. Gaines." Lowe, *Conversations*, pp. 86–98.

Rushdy, Ashraf H. A. "The Neo–Slave Narrative." Graham, pp. 87–105.

Ryan, Katy, editor. *Demands of the Dead: Executions, Storytelling, and Activism in the United States*. U of Iowa P, 2012.

———. Introduction. Ryan, *Demands*, pp. 1–30.

Saeta, Elsa, and Izora Skinner. "Interview with Ernest Gaines." Lowe, *Conversations*, pp. 241–52.

Salaam, Kalamu ya. "BLKARTSOUTH/get on up!" *New Black Voices*, edited by Abraham Chapman, Mentor, 1972, pp. 468–73.

———. "Blk Art South New Orleans." *Black World*, Apr. 1972, pp. 40–45.

Sandy, Mark. "'Cut by Rainbow': Tales, Tellers, and Reimagining Wordsworth's Pastoral Poetics in Toni Morrison's *Beloved* and *A Mercy*." *MELUS*, vol. 36, no. 25, Summer 2011, pp. 35–51.

Sargent, Joseph, director. *A Lesson Before Dying*. HBO Home Entertainment / Warner Home Video, 2010.

Sartisky, Michael. "Writing about Race in Difficult Times: An Interview with Ernest J. Gaines." Lowe, *Conversations*, pp. 253–73.

Scarry, Elaine. *The Body in Pain: The Making and Unmaking of the World*. Oxford UP, 1985.

Schiche, Ericka. "Lightnin' Hopkins, Mance Lipscomb, and the Legend of Tom Moore's Farm." *Houston Press*, 15 Mar. 2016, www.houstonpress.com/music/lightnin -hopkins-mance-lipscomb-and-the-legend-of-tom-moores-farm-7702841.html. Accessed 23 Oct. 2018.

Schlöndorff, Volker, director. *A Gathering of Old Men*. Echo Bridge, 2009.

Sedgwick, Eve Kosofsky. *Tendencies*. Duke UP, 1993.

Seiler, Cotten. *Republic of Drivers: A Cultural History of Automobility in America*, U of Chicago P, 2009.

Senter, Caroline. "Creole Poets on the Verge of a Nation." Kein, *Creole*, pp. 276–94.

Shelton, Frank W. "Of Machines and Men: Pastoralism in Gaines's Fiction." Estes, *Critical Reflections*, pp. 12–29.

Simpson, Anne K. *A Gathering of Gaines: The Man and the Writer*. Center for Louisiana Studies, U of Southwestern Louisiana, 1991.

Siskel, Gene. "A Serious 'Right Thing' for a Frivolous Summer." Review of *Do the Right Thing*, by Spike Lee. *Chicago Tribune*, 30 June 1989, www.chicagotribune.com /news/ct-xpm-1989-06-30-8902130689-story.html.

Smith, Ayana. "Blues, Criticism, and the Signifying Trickster." *Popular Music*, vol. 24, no. 2, May 2005, pp. 179–91.

Smith, Bessie. "Gulf Coast Blues." Columbia A-3844, 1923.

Smith, Lillian. *Killers of the Dream*. 1949. Rev. ed., W. W. Norton, 1978.

Snead, James A. "Repetition as a Figure of Black Culture." *Black Literature and Literary Theory*, edited by Henry Louis Gates, Jr., Methuen, 1984, pp. 59–79.

Stepto, Robert B. *From Behind the Veil: A Study of Afro-American Narrative*. 2nd ed., U of Illinois P, 1991.

Stern, Jeffrey E. "The Cruel and Unusual Execution of Clayton Lockett." *The Atlantic*, June 2015, pp. 71–83.

Strickland v. Washington. 466 U.S. 668 (1984). *Westlaw*, 2018, Thomson Reuters, westlaw.com/Document/I235b05aa9c1e11d9bdd1cfdd544ca3a4/.

Stupp, Jason. "Living Death: Ernest Gaines's *A Lesson Before Dying* and the Execution of Willie Francis." Ryan, *Demands*, pp. 45–58.

Tarshis, Jerome. "The Other 300 Years: A Conversation with Ernest J. Gaines, Author of *The Autobiography of Miss Jane Pittman*." Lowe, *Conversations*, pp. 72–79.

"'They Tell Me Joe Turner's Come and Gone': Music, Prison, and the Convict Lease System." *Prison Culture: How the PIC Structures Our World*, 28 Nov. 2010, www .usprisonculture.com/blog/2010/11/28/they-tell-me-joe-turners-come-and-gone -music-prison-the-convict-lease-system.

Thompson, Carlyle V. "From a Hog to a Black Man: Black Male Subjectivity and Ritualistic Lynching in Ernest J. Gaines's *A Lesson Before Dying*." *CLA Journal*, vol. 45, no. 3, Mar. 2002, pp. 279–310.

Tison v. Arizona. 481 U.S. 137 (1987). *Westlaw*, 2018, Thomson Reuters, westlaw.com /Document/I6b45f49c9c2511d9bc61beebb95be672/.

Tolson, Nancy D. "'Brutal Honesty and Metaphorical Grace': The Blues Aesthetic in Black Children's Literature." *Children's Literature Association Quarterly*, vol. 25, no. 1, Spring 2000, pp. 56–60.

Toomer, Jean. *Cane*. 1923. W. W. Norton, 1988.

Tracy, Steven C. "The Blues Novel." Graham, pp. 122–38.

———. *Write Me a Few of Your Lines: A Blues Reader*. U of Massachusetts P, 1999.

Trethewey, Natasha. *Native Guard*. Mariner Books, 2007.

Truth, Sojourner. " Ain't I a Woman?" December 1851. *Internet Modern History Sourcebook*, Aug. 1997, www.fordham.edu/halsall/mod/sojtruth-woman.asp.

Turgenev, Ivan. *Fathers and Sons*. 1862. Translated by Peter Carson, Penguin Books, 2009.

Turner, Nat. *The Confessions of Nat Turner*. 1831. Bedford/St. Martin's, 2017.

Turner, Victor. *The Forest of Symbols: Aspects of Ndembu Ritual*. Cornell UP, 1967.

"Underrated Books." *Oxford American*, Fall 2009, www.oxfordamerican.org/magazine /item/233-underrated-books-a-sampling-from-the-southern-lit-issue. Accessed 21 Feb. 2014.

"Virginia Slave Laws of 1662 and 1669." Lauter, p. 14.

Vollmar, Rob. *Bluesman*. Illustrated by Pablo G. Callejo, NBM ComicsLit, 2006.

Wachlin, Marie Goughnour. "The Place of Bible Literature in Public High School English Classes." *Research in the Teaching of English*, vol. 31, no. 1, Feb. 1997, pp. 7–50.

Waller, Annette. "'Tom Moore's Farm' (1930s)." *Texas Monthly*, www.texasmonthly.com /list/the-secret-history-of-texas-music/tom-moores-farm-1930s/.

Washington, Booker T. "From *Up from Slavery*: Chapter XIV: The Atlanta Exposition Address." *The Prentice Hall Anthology of African American Literature*, edited by Rochelle Smith and Sharon L. Jones, Prentice Hall, 2000, pp. 181–88.

Werner, Craig Hansen. *Playing the Changes: From Afro-Modernism to the Jazz Impulse*. U of Illinois P, 1994.

Wertheim, Albert. "Journey to Freedom: Ernest Gaines' *The Autobiography of Miss Jane Pittman* (1971)." *The Afro-American Novel since 1960*, edited by Peter Bruck and Wolfgang Karrer, Grüner, 1982, pp. 219–35.

Wharry, Cheryl. "Amen and Hallelujah Preaching: Discourse Functions in African American Sermons." *Language in Society*, vol. 32, no. 2, Apr. 2003, pp. 203–25.

White, Deborah Gray. *Ar'n't I a Woman? Female Slaves in the Plantation South*. Rev. ed., W. W. Norton, 1999.

White, James Boyd. *Heracles' Bow: Essays on the Rhetoric and Poetics of the Law*. U of Wisconsin P, 1985.

Whitted, Qiana J. *"A God of Justice?" The Problem of Evil in Twentieth-Century Black Literature*. U of Virginia P, 2009.

Wideman, John. "*Of Love and Dust*: A Reconsideration." *Callaloo*, no. 3, May 1978, pp. 76–84.

Williams, Sherley Anne. *Dessa Rose*. Morrow, 1986.

Wilson, August. *Joe Turner's Come and Gone*. Plume, 1988.

Woodard, Komozi. *A Nation within a Nation: Amiri Baraka (LeRoi Jones) and Black Power Politics*. U of North Carolina P, 1999.

Wright, Richard. "Almos' a Man." *Harper's Bazaar*, Jan. 1940, pp. 40–53.

———. *Black Boy*. 1945. Harper Perennial, 1992.

———. Foreword. *Blues Fell This Morning: Meaning in the Blues*, by Paul Oliver, 2nd ed., Cambridge UP, 1990, pp. xiii–xviii.

———. "Long Black Song." *Uncle Tom's Children: Four Novellas*, Harper and Bros., 1938, pp. 125–56.

———. "The Man Who Was Almost a Man." *Eight Men*, Harper Perennial, 1996, pp. 3–18.

———. "Tarbaby's Dawn." Richard Wright Papers, James Weldon Johnson Collection, Beinecke Rare Book and Manuscript Library, Yale U, JWJ MSS 3.

Wyatt-Brown, Bertram. *Southern Honor: Ethics and Behavior in the Old South*. Oxford UP, 1983.

Young, Kevin. *Book of Hours*. Knopf, 2014.

———. Foreword. *Blues Poems*, Everyman's Library, 2003, pp. 11–16.

———. *Jelly Roll: A Blues*. Knopf, 2003.

Young, Reggie Scott, et al., editors. *"This Louisiana Thing That Drives Me": The Legacy of Ernest J. Gaines*. U of Louisiana at Lafayette P, 2009.

INDEX